MAXWELL

MAXWELL

The Rise and Fall of Robert Maxwell and His Empire

Roy Greenslade

A Birch Lane Press Book
Published by Carol Publishing Group

In memory of my father
1923–1992
who lived sixty-eight years without telling a lie

A Birch Lane Press Book
Published by Carol Publishing Group
Birch Lane Press is a registered trademark of Carol Communications, Inc.
Editorial Offices: 600 Madison Avenue, New York, N.Y. 10022
Sales & Distribution Offices: 120 Enterprise Avenue, Secaucus, N.J. 07094
In Canada: Canadian Manda Group, P.O. Box 920 Station U, Toronto, Ontario M8Z 5P9
Queries regarding rights and permissions should be addressed to Carol Publishing Group,
600 Madison Avenue, New York, N.Y. 10022

Carol Publishing Group books are available at special discounts for bulk purchases, for
sales promotions, fund-raising, or educational purposes. Special editions can be created
to specifications. For details contact: Special Sales Department, Carol Publishing Group,
120 Enterprise Avenue, Secaucus, N.J. 07094

Manufactured in the United States of America
10 9 8 7 6 5 4 3 2 1

Library of Congress Cataloging-in-Publication Data

Greenslade, Roy.
    Maxwell : the rise and fall of Robert Maxwell and his empire / by
Roy Greenslade.
        p.   cm.
    "A Birch Lane Press book."
    Includes index.
    ISBN 1-55972-123-5
    1. Maxwell, Robert, 1923–   .   2. Publishers and publishing—Great
Britain—History—20th century.   3. Newspaper publishing—Great
Britain—History—20th century.   4. Publishers and publishing—Great
Britain—Biography.   5. Mass media—Great Britain.   I. Title.
Z325.M394G73   1992
070.5'092—dc20
    [B]   92-23957
                                                                  CIP

Contents

	Acknowledgments	vi
1.	Welcome to Maxwellia	1
2.	The Birth of a Legend	10
3.	Unscrupulous, Unfit, But Unbowed	24
4.	The *Daily Maxwell*	48
5.	Macmillan: A Deal Too Far	77
6.	"I Treat My Editors Like Field Marshals"	93
7.	Twin Obsessions	110
8.	"Mikhail and I Like Him a Lot"	124
9.	On the Tightrope	146
10.	Juggling With Debts—and Encyclopedias	165
11.	The Scoop of the Decade	187
12.	Big Bob in the Big Apple	203
13.	Farewell to the *Mirror*	227
14.	The Pensions Scandal	253
15.	Mirrorgate: The Final Insult	267
16.	Cap'n Bob's Last Voyage	291
17.	"He Said He Would Leave Us Nothing"	314
18.	End of the Empire	336
	Epilogue	355
	Notes	360
	Index	367

Acknowledgments

I WORKED for Robert Maxwell for only fourteen months while countless others suffered under him far longer and, even after his death, they continue to suffer. I was relatively fortunate, leaving with a payoff and liberating my pension, but the story of Maxwell has been burning inside me from my earliest months as *Daily Mirror* editor. He was once said to have been unfit to run a public company; he was certainly unfit to own that fine newspaper. I opposed him not because I knew of his crimes but because of his monstrous behavior and gross editorial interference. At first that was the only story I wanted to tell the world. Now I can present the more complete truth.

This book is therefore for all those *Mirror* staff, past and present, who were fooled and fleeced by Maxwell. While none of them could ever imagine the scale of his crimes, many suspected from the moment he bought the paper that he was a crook. In a strange way they wanted him to be so, because it fitted so perfectly with his personality. But we must not forget there were thousands of people elsewhere in Maxwell's huge empire who endured a similar fate. This book is for them as well.

I have to thank so many of them—in the Mirror Group, in Maxwell Communications Corporation, and in the private companies—who have spoken to me at length or put up with my sudden calls for assistance. Their names are too numerous to mention here but many, though not all, are contained in the text. However, I must place on record my appreciation for the help of Bob Cole, who opened his private files and his heart. Few have been hurt as badly as he by Maxwell's duplicity.

I would also like to thank the various financial analysts and journalists who have taken the trouble to help me. But I want to do better; I salute them for the way they tried to publish the truth in the face of constant legal threats. Many analysts imperiled their careers in trying to do their jobs honestly. Many journalists had to fight their own editors to get their stories into print. It is a tribute to this small group that though Maxwell succeeded in muting their opposition he never managed to erase it. For the same reason, BBC's *Panorama* team, one of whom gave me special help, also deserves praise for refusing to back down.

I want to give special thanks to John Diamond, whom I knew only slightly when he joined the *Mirror* but whose friendship, not to mention sense of humor, I grew to value in those difficult months immediately after we left the paper.

Thanks are due to Lucy Broadbent and Robyn Foyster for their research work, enabling me to be able to write the book in Ireland, in County Donegal. I want to thank all my Irish friends who were kind enough to leave me alone and kinder still to ensure that I enjoyed unbeatable company whenever I desired it. A special thank you, too, to my mother, whose care of me in the final month made certain that I finished the manuscript on time.

No one deserves more praise than my wife, who plays a key role in the story, played a central role in the writing of this book, and plays the leading role in my life. Without her inspiration the book would not have been written.

I absolve all these people, of course, from any errors that may have crept in, which are my own.

I hope I do justice in what follows to everyone who came into contact with Robert Maxwell.

—County Donegal, Ireland

MAXWELL'S EMPIRE

Major holdings at the time of his death in November 1991

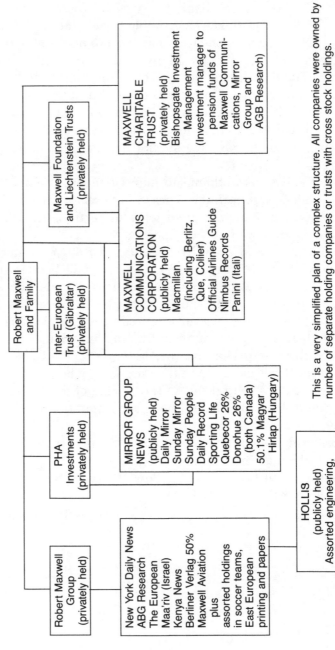

Robert Maxwell and Family

Robert Maxwell Group (privately held)

New York Daily News
ABG Research
The European
Maa'riv (Israel)
Kenya News
Berliner Verlag 50%
Maxwell Aviation
plus
assorted holdings
in soccer teams,
East European
printing and papers

HOLLIS (publicly held)
Assorted engineering,
furniture manufacturing,
office and school supplies
companies

PHA Investments (privately held)

MIRROR GROUP NEWS (publicly held)
Daily Mirror
Sunday Mirror
Sunday People
Daily Record
Sporting LIfe
Quebecor 26%
Donohue 26%
(both Canada)
50.1% Magyar
Hirlap (Hungary)

Inter-European Trust (Gibraltar) (privately held)

MAXWELL COMMUNICATIONS CORPORATION (publicly held)
Macmillan
(including Berlitz,
Que, Collier)
Official Airlines Guide
Nimbus Records
Panini (Itali)

Maxwell Foundation and Liechtenstein Trusts (privately held)

MAXWELL CHARITABLE TRUST (privately held)
Bishopsgate Investment Management
(Investment manager to
pension funds of
Maxwell Communi-
cations, Mirror
Group and
AGB Research)

This is a very simplified plan of a complex structure. All companies were owned by a number of separate holding companies or trusts with cross stock holdings.

1

Welcome to Maxwellia

I HAD enjoyed Christmas night, 1989, at home with friends, so I was not at my best when the phone rang at 7:50 on Boxing Day morning. "It's Bob Maxwell here. Could I speak to Roy Greenslade?"

I cupped the phone and whispered to my wife, "There's a guy on here saying he's Robert Maxwell."

She rolled over. "It's Paul Callan," she said unhesitatingly. Callan, former *Mirror* writer and sometime radio and television personality, was a noted mimic of Maxwell's booming baritone voice.

"Mr. Maxwell," I said. "Would you be kind enough to give me your number and I'll call you back." He took this equably enough, and my wife—a *Daily Mirror* feature writer who had become, without effort on her part, a favorite of Maxwell's—confirmed that it was the correct private-line number. However, an inebriated impressionist might just know it, too.

Collecting my thoughts, I rang back.

Mawell answered right away. "I want you and your lovely wife to come and see me."

1

"Today?" I asked. "Is it that important?"

"Yes. Are you doing something then?"

"No," I said, knowing only that we were attending a party in the early evening hosted by an editor Maxwell had recently fired. We agreed to meet at Maxwell House, in New Fetter Lane, Holborn, at 4 P.M. This left eight hours in which my wife and I could fantasize about the reason for his call. One thing we agreed on: he could not be offering me the post of editor of one of England's largest newspapers, the *Daily Mirror*, with a circulation of over 3,500,000. The job was held by Richard Stott, and his position seemed from both inside and out to be impregnable.

We were still debating the possibilities as we entered Maxwell House, to be shown by a lone secretary on the ninth floor, his office area, up to the tenth, his personal quarters. Much has been written about the decoration and furnishings of this penthouse floor. I have always regarded it as "mock potentate," an attempt at a palatial residence within a relatively small space, truly "a miniature Xanadu."[1] I did not know then just how perfectly it reflected Maxwell's personality, a mixture of styles presenting a façade of grandeur that was transparently fake. Was the designer, Jon Bannenberg, having a joke at his client's expense?

The lobby was dominated by a huge carved fireplace of baronial splendor, probably made of fiberglass to resemble wood. How incongruous, I then thought, to have a false chimney suspended ten floors up in a modern office block. But it announced the man you were to meet so well—only a well-heeled tycoon could afford it and possibly enjoy having it.

The drawing room with its stuccoed ceilings, heavy curtains, outsize sofas, ottomans, and bronze glass-topped coffers brought to mind a reception room for a sultan. On large, low, casual tables stood vases of flowers and various objets d'art, sometime gifts to Maxwell from grateful pre-glasnost Eastern European dictators. Again the ostentation was deliberate, a self-conscious attempt to dazzle the visitor with the owner's riches. I was drawn to what I supposed to be the marble columns at the doorway and ran my hand down one and followed with a gentle knock: it was hollow.

Maxwell kept us waiting for forty-five minutes. I looked at my watch and said, "We're leaving if he's not here at five P.M." A few minutes later he appeared in what I would grow to recognize as his typical casual attire: dark blue jacket, light blue shirt, dark blue trousers—but not matching the jacket—held up by a brown belt round his enormous girth. And yellow socks. His dyed jet-black hair was slicked back close to his scalp. This first appearance gave me an early sign of the paradoxes that abounded in his character. Was it not strange that a man in his late sixties should be vain enough to have his hair dyed yet care so little about the rest of his appearance, his size, and his dress?

Why were we here? Why had I come? I was happy with my job as a managing editor at *The Sunday Times*, probably happier than at any time in my career. I had been offered via two Maxwell intermediaries the job of *Sunday People* editor some weeks previously and turned it down. One of them, Ernie Burrington, the Mirror Group managing director temporarily standing in as *People* editor, made his offer in inimitable fashion, so amusingly that I took a day to think it over. "You're in a symphony orchestra at the moment," he said, "but I know you've played jazz and pop in the past. I have told the man here that I'm sure you could play jazz again. Am I right?"

The joy of Ernie's coded speech is that, being clear to the insider and opaque to the outsider, it draws you immediately into a sort of cozy conspiracy. He was referring to my having spent years as assistant editor at *The Sun* before joining *The Sunday Times*. However, I told him the *People* job was not for me. "Of course," I added, "if you had been talking about the *Daily Mirror*, and I know there's no question of that, the answer would have been different." I made a similar remark to Mike Molloy, Mirror Group editor in chief, who was the next to call.

The conversations had been informal enough, but I was sincere. Although I had switched from popular to serious journalism some three years before, the thought of editing the *Daily Mirror* was too good a chance to miss. I believed I could change it for the better and still challenge the circulation supremacy of *The Sun*. My lust for this chance, even while denying its possibility, had been on my mind all day before meeting Maxwell.

He smiled, ear to ear, almost bowing to my wife, Noreen, and asked: "Have you got a drink?" Opening the door of the little alcove that served as a bar off the main room, he began to bang bottles and glasses in a way that suggested he was unsure how to find anything. He shouted through a door about ice, and a Filipino woman appeared with a bucket. He poured clumsily into crystal goblets, and Noreen said, "I don't think you're used to serving drinks."

He seemed to appreciate the remark and began to walk up and down, asking after the family. He sat for only a minute before standing over me to make a sonorous announcement: "You are here because I have the honor of offering you the editorship of the *Daily Mirror*."

I sank farther back into the sofa cushions and looked wide-eyed at Noreen. She was speechless. I stammered, "Is it on offer?"

"What would you do with the paper?" he asked as he handed me a drink.

Still reeling, I launched into a familiar, superficial litany of my long-held views about where the paper might be wrong and might be improved: more campaigns, less vulgarity, articles to win younger readers, a more subtle stance in the market, and most important of all, content that would regain respect for a paper with a proud history. He seemed to listen to this trite list, nodding occasionally.

"Quite right," he said without much conviction. "What would you do about the staff?"

I explained that while I knew many of the journalists and suspected that over the years some dead wood had gathered, it was difficult to assess that from the outside.

He replied: "Could you bring any of *The Sun* people over?" I had already been making a mental list of those who might be useful and nodded.

"What will Mr. MacKenzie say about that?"

Maxwell, I would discover, was fascinated by *The Sun*'s editor, Kelvin MacKenzie, and in the next few weeks would chuckle whenever he felt I might be upsetting my rival. I said, "I think Kelvin will be surprised if you appoint me."

He raised his huge, bushy eyebrows and smiled indulgently.

I asked for time to think about everything, and he said he had yet to make up his mind about me, in spite of having offered me the job minutes before. "Meanwhile, absolute silence," he said, touching his lips. He then made glowing references to, and about, my wife. In less than an hour Noreen and I were clinking glasses with journalists at the home of the recently deposed *People* editor Wendy Henry, making small talk while only large talk was on our minds.

So this was the monster? He had been charming, he had concentrated, his voice had not been raised. I had made him laugh, which he seemed to do easily. I was not fooled by his being on his best behavior, which I had witnessed before in full measure on only one of the two previous occasions our paths had crossed.

Our first meeting had been back in 1985, when he invited Noreen and me to dinner to celebrate a massive article she had written to commemorate D-day, perhaps a kindly gesture or perhaps a fishing expedition to meet a senior *Sun* executive. Whatever the case, I never knew. He hosted the meal at Maxim's in Palace Gate, one of his favorite gambling haunts. I did not know until afterward that, on arrival, he had brushed china, glasses, and cutlery off the table with the back of his hand because he said he did not like the way it was laid. As plates hit the floor, he had shouted: "Get rid of this. It's not what I wanted."

The table was relaid before I arrived. Also at the table were Maxwell's personal assistant, Jean Baddeley, the then-*Mirror* editor Mike Molloy and his wife, Sandy. By any standards, it was a hilarious occasion. Molloy, clearly rattled by my presence, made an early reference to my having been a communist who had tried to wreck the Mirror Group some years before. He was also keen to ingratiate himself yet further with his boss in a period when the *Mirror* had become the *Daily Maxwell* with his picture appearing every other day, sometimes twice in an issue.

The first problem would be to remain sober. Champagne gave way to a large tub of Beluga caviar atop a mountain of ice. Maxwell demanded that we all down measures of Stolichnaya vodka, Russian-style, in shot glasses, with every helping of caviar. Thankfully he was diverted from checking on us by Molloy asking the correct way to eat caviar. I said I had been using my mouth for years and found it very successful.

But Maxwell reveled in the chance to instruct: "Take the toast so, Michael, and spread the caviar like this."

"No butter, Bob?" inquired Molloy.

"No butter, Michael." With that, Maxwell devoured fifty dollars' worth of sturgeon's eggs in one bite, and Molloy, bow tie wobbling, followed suit.

"Now fill your glass with vodka, Michael... that's right... and—" Down went a full measure of vodka, by my count Maxwell's third.

Conversation flowed easily after that though I cannot remember what we said or what we ate... until the final course. Maxwell had not once asked us for our views on what he was ordering and simply shouted at a waiter: "Strawberries. The big ones. More wine."

When the fruit was placed on Maxwell's plate he imperiously tossed the berries into the gigantic glass containing an expensive claret. Molloy quickly did the same. Maxwell said suddenly, "Oh, you do that too. I thought I was the only one who liked strawberries that way."

Molloy flushed only slightly. "Done it for years, Bob," he said, doubtless pinching his wife under the table to keep her quiet. The loyal Sandy said nothing.

Suddenly Maxwell stood: "Back to the office."

I hesitated since it was not my office. "I want you as well," he said.

So *The Sun*'s assistant editor, by now the worse for drink, found himself in the office of the *Daily Mirror* editor, offering the proprietor a critical page-by-page assessment of that night's first edition. Meanwhile, executives were being invited in for champagne cocktails personally mixed by the editor. Yet I had heard of Maxwell "cleaning up the *Mirror*." It helped to explain to me why the disciplined world of sobriety under Rupert Murdoch at News International was currently so successful. It also revealed just how much a hostage Maxwell had become to the *Mirror* style he had inherited: He boasted of having "taken on" the print unions and rationalized the Mirror Group's management. But here, on the bridge of his flagship paper, he allowed drinking and carousing at a time when the paper was losing its circulation at a suicidal rate. Was it merely inexperience or self-deception?

It was suggested to me later that this might have been an interview. I doubt it, because Maxwell seemed not to understand the points I made about the paper. It was as though I were speaking a different language. In spite of his years as a dealer, Maxwell also seemed unable to understand the fierce competition of Fleet Street. A couple of months later this kind of naïveté led to my next encounter with the man in one of his other favorite haunts, the courtroom.

Competition between the *Mirror* and *The Sun* had become so intense that each was carefully watching the other, adopting the slogan: If they have it, we'll have it too. Therefore, when we discovered that the *Mirror* was about to "exclusively" serialize a book by Peter Bogdanovich, *The Killing of the Unicorn*, about the murder of former *Playboy* model Dorothy Stratten by her jealous husband, which was hardly a new story at the time, it was easy for experienced writers to construct a similar "exclusive" from clips. Then we tweaked the *Mirror* by announcing our own series, warning readers to beware of cheap imitations. This prompted a letter from *Mirror* lawyers, warning of the direst consequences if our paper should attempt to "lift" any of the *Mirror*'s coming book serialization. In the trade this practice is known as spoiling, but Maxwell knew nothing of the business.

Bob Edwards, formerly Maxwell's deputy chairman and previously editor of three national newspapers, commented: "Unused to the wicked ways of Fleet Street...Maxwell rounded up his lawyers and called on the duty judge, Mr. Justice Hirst, by all accounts a pleasant and hospitable man, late at night at his home. The judge, as he naturally would, granted an injunction to prevent *The Sun* breaching the copyright laws..."[2] In effect this would place us in contempt of court if we lifted any words from the book.

We made every attempt to avoid duplication, but inadvertently we did publish nineteen consecutive words from the book, discovering our mistake after the first edition had gone to print. We had taken the words in innocence from yet another newspaper's clips, and once we realized their provenance we amended our story. As Edwards observed, MacKenzie, the *Sun* editor, "had not reckoned on Maxwell's motivation for vengeance."[3]

Maxwell launched contempt proceedings against MacKenzie and the managing director, Bruce Matthews. Both faced the possibility of jail sentences and what began as normal competitive newspaper activity took on a very serious tone. I had overseen the spoiling and provided a statement to our lawyers, but I was specifically told I would not be required to give evidence in the High Court. Maxwell had other ideas, insisting that both the writer and I should appear at a moment's notice. Unfortunately I was ordered to attend court after returning from a lunch where I had drunk a lot more than usual and cut a very bad figure in the witness box.

Maxwell, attending court throughout the hearing, clearly enjoyed seeing me squirm under questioning from his counsel. I could see his shoulders shake with laughter. Unprepared, unrehearsed, and unrepentant, I seemed, as MacKenzie later screamed, "to be doing your level best to get me sent to jail." In the event, the judge—while remarking on the oddness of my performance—ignored it as a sideshow and dismissed the case against *The Sun*. He decided that the nineteen-word extract did not contravene the 1956 Copyright Act and ordered Maxwell to foot the $80,000 bill for costs. Maxwell was interviewed outside the court, huffing and puffing about ethics. "I came to Fleet Street to eliminate the kind of artificial and undignified rivalry mentioned by the judge," he said. "In my opinion, today's judgment could be interpreted by *The Sun* as meaning it is lawful for *The Sun* to spoil, steal, cheat—and lie to its readers—in the interests of waging war against the *Mirror*."

I was upset the next day to see that I had been singled out for special treatment in the *Mirror* report. Unhappy at losing the case, Maxwell exploited the only criticism in the judge's verdict. He summoned writer Paul Callan to his office and told him to compose a piece about my fifteen embarrassing minutes in the dock. It was some five years later before Callan told me of Maxwell's part in this childish exercise, though by then I was not surprised.

Of course there were no references to these meetings when Maxwell was preparing to hire me, and I did not remind him of them. Both occasions should have been a warning to me, but a mixture of arrogance and innocence encouraged me to take the *Mirror* editorship. I had observed from the outside his ridiculous self-publicity campaigns. I knew he was not a man of his word. As head of news at *The Sunday Times*, I had been responsible for running several stories in which we exposed Maxwell's predilection for announcing that he was donating to this or that charity without finally parting with a penny, or flamboyantly setting up allegedly charitable funds of his own and rarely, if ever, passing on the cash.

Okay, so maybe he was given to boasting. Surely, I thought, he cannot be as bad as everyone says? If he was, I believed I possessed the right qualities to cope with him. Over the years, I had worked well under some of the fiercest and most autocratic editors in the business. With his wide-ranging business interests and my knowledge that he was abroad as often as he was in Britain, I could not imagine him being as heavy-handed as people claimed. Anyway, I was about to become editor of the *Daily Mirror*, a dream: the realization of this ambition, more than anything else, relegated good sense to second place.

2

The Birth
of a Legend

WHAT kind of man was this I was to work for? In the days before I joined him I asked as many people as I could about him. One friend who had been close to Maxwell for a year or so told me: "With Bob, what you see is what you get. Of course, you might get something different the next day, or the next minute, but it's all out there. Shouting or laughing, you'll see." I turned to go when she added, "By the way, don't believe a word he says."

I so wish I had taken that last injunction to heart, for Robert Maxwell could make a lie appear to be the truth. He rarely spoke an untruth in which he did not believe sincerely, at the time. Truth, facts, reality—Maxwell viewed these as weapons used by stuffy, boring, banal people to stifle his creativity, his genius, to prevent him from achieving, ultimately to destroy him. He had a much better world, better because he created it, where he held sway and which was peopled with those he could manipulate. There, reality could be

10

whatever he claimed it to be. This was the world of Maxwellia. For most of his life he was able to step into the real world because he was cunning enough to understand the differences between his world and theirs, but in the final years even this was to prove a trial. His excursions into the world outside his apartment, plane, helicopter, yacht, his mind, were often fraught with boredom unless he was on camera, center stage, usually boasting of some new personal triumph, sometimes belly-laughing at his own jokes, occasionally braying threats.

Inventors are rarely content with their invention, always tinkering, improving, disproving and, in the nature of their interest, taking some diversions that invariably lead to dead ends. Robert Maxwell was the ultimate inventor: he invented himself, not once, but many times over. He invented his name, his history, his voice, his persona. He invented the past and the present. If his invention led nowhere— in other words, the invention did not fit the current climate or take him where he wanted to go—then he would simply reinvent it. As we follow him through his life we will see him stand reality on its head over and over again.

But Robert Maxwell was more than an inventor: his artful fabrication provided him with the tools with which he would deceive everyone, including himself. He was arguably the greatest confidence trickster the world has known, an illusionist so clever he fooled the world's biggest banks and leading politicians and hundreds of thousands of people as well. He posed as a rich man yet had very little money. He appeared as a powerful man but it was a figment of his imagination. He boasted of being a kindly savior but was brutally unjust to those closest to him.

What makes him so fascinating is that everyone knew he was an untrustworthy character. You did not have to work next to him to know he was up to something: he was so transparently a man with a lot to hide. Hindsight has emboldened us all still further so that hardly a day passes without someone disdainfully expressing surprise that anyone ever thought Maxwell was anything other than a bamboozler. The chairmen of forty of the world's largest banks are not saying so though. For the art of the con man, whether pool hall hustler or music hall conjurer, doorstep hawker or financial swindler, is to make us believe in them just enough to think that this man, while obviously up to no good, is not like the others. He surely cannot be as bad as he seems. This time we'll take a chance.

Early on, Maxwell realized that to sustain his lies successfully, to maintain in his own eyes his invented self, he must control his environment with unquestioned authority. Money bought power, and power brought money. One of his hirelings once suggested that Maxwell understood only two human relationships, that of master-slave and customer-supplier. That is fine as far as it goes, but making it happen, winning the control to ensure the mastery, that was the real trick. This was not a conscious act—Robert Maxwell had no control over his emotions. He simply responded by reflex. There was no master plan for the conquest of the world. His lust for power was an inner compulsion worked out in a series of spontaneous, random surges of interest. He lacked what we might refer to as self-control or a sense of embarrassment because it was not within him to understand such feelings.

His image of himself was of a benevolent dictator, a kindly man forced to take harsh measures to achieve great things. Early on he would proudly say: "I am a jungle man." But he dispensed with that and his favorite phrase became: "I am only here to be of service." He regarded himself as a savior who needed power only insofar as it was necessary to orchestrate his own brand of kindness on behalf of the greatest number. The ruthlessness, the cruelty, the rudeness, the aggression, the rapaciousness saddened him. One can hear his inner voice: "If only they, the people, would understand. I am here to help them." How often did he say, hand on heart, those black, bushy eyebrows reaching for the sky: "Money and property mean nothing to me."

It was a lie, and it was his truth. His obsession for power and money meant that he could not stop buying—factories, businesses, property, people—throughout his life. His drive to buy was so great he was like a global shopaholic with an attaché case full of credit cards. In looking at Maxwell's life you will need to suspend the accepted morality, of good and bad, right and wrong, truth and falsity. Maxwell's grasp on morality and reality was forever filtered through his own distorted view of himself as the central actor in every drama on whatever scale.

Grasping for understanding, several interviewers over the years have struggled to label Maxwell. One of my favorites is the suggestion by a psychiatrist that the man was stuck at the "omnipotent baby phase" when the growing infant makes a bid to dominate his world.[1] This is supposed to occur around the age of two and, usually, parental control convinces the child that there are stronger forces after all: the world does not move to his or her whim.

This would help to explain his extreme narcissism, in which he related only to himself rather than to others, and I think it possible to build a psychological portrait based on this notion. It would incorporate, among other things, his detachment from reality, his infantile behavior as a collector of companies and people (toys), his grandiose sense of self-importance, and his consuming passion for fame.

What we know of Maxwell's background suggests this would be a profitable exercise. We know his mother doted on him and that he was the only boy child among five girls. (One brother died in infancy and another was born after Maxwell had left home). Maxwell often spoke of how he was his mother's favorite and that he missed her, too, and we know he lacked respect for his father who, we might assume, played little part in the home life of his family. I did not, however, set out with a psychological study in mind; my aim is to provide the subject matter for one.

Most of those who have looked long and hard at Maxwell's life, whether critical or fawning, have also eschewed deeper insights by preferring to see him as an eternal outsider, wrenched from his roots and his family, who arrived in Britain without an understanding of the unwritten, unspoken code of a hierarchical, class-bound society that offers no quarter to incomers. Even if this were true, and I remain extremely skeptical, it was the common lot of thousand upon thousand of immigrants over centuries. They were not Robert Maxwells. They did not strive to become tycoons living in the style of twentieth-century Roman emperors. They did not charge full tilt at Britain's establishment windmills. It is too mundane an answer, as we shall see.

Certainly Maxwell liked to present himself as a man forever struggling against the odds, though he offered few clues about how he viewed his own history. There is a hoary old tale, a legend beloved by the living but unprovable by them, that a drowning person's life flashes before his or her eyes in the moments before death. We are also led to believe that Maxwell spent as long as four hours in the water before succumbing. Even with a video on fast forward, that might not have been long enough for him to recall much of his life, whatever life it was he wished to recall.

He might not have enjoyed his obituaries the day after his body was recovered from the sea, though even cynical obituarists—and I count myself among them—were somewhat stifled by their own sense of decency, using as a yardstick that age-old adage about never speaking ill of the dead. True, there were mentions of ruthlessness, of buffoonish behavior, of hypocrisy and, inevitably, references to his sharp business practice, though these comments were always historical.

However, the muted criticism was weighed against his "un-doubted" success, his "larger than life" personality, his unconscious humor, and his "boundless" energy. What generally emerged was a picture of a lovable rogue—larded with mentions of Cap'n Bob, the Bouncing Czech, the "Max factor"—who was just conceivably a man without scruple, but one with some justification. After all, cannot one forgive the eccentricities of a man who arrived in Britain a penniless peasant orphan and rose to become a man of wealth and influence?

It is, for some, both a tribute to our political and economic system that such success was possible and a lesson to everyone that ambition and determination can succeed in spite of the odds. For others, it was merely an example of a maverick making it to the top: this was the school of you-might-love-him-or-hate-him-but-what-a-guy! And didn't he do well? With a lifetime of extraordinary activity to consider, perhaps the *Daily Mail*'s observation that he "all but defies a conventional obituary" was a fair summary of the problem.

The writers of a couple of thousand words were faced with an impossible task when they found themselves confronted by a wealth of paradoxical newspaper material in interviews and anecdotes over three decades; his authorized, hagiographic biography; one very unauthorized—and, therefore, to too many who should have known better, rather suspect—biography; and a mass of apocryphal gossip. For most journalists in those days after Maxwell's death, there was too much to comprehend and too little time in which to grasp reality.

What was true? What might be true? Who was right, and who wrong?

Relying on Maxwell's own views proved unhelpful since he was given to changing his mind about his past. Trying to be kind was a waste of time: the most farfetched story of his almost casual misuse of power was quoted as gospel by his personal biographer while apparently harmless incidents mentioned by other people had attracted writs. Hence the constant references to the mystery of Maxwell. Or, to quote Churchill—and Maxwell loved to quote, or misquote, his hero, even to the point of emulating his baritone voice and slow pace of delivery—Maxwell was "a riddle wrapped in a mystery inside an enigma." Moreover, it is obvious that if the obituarists and editorial writers knew on 6 November what they were to know a month later, there would have very different, less respectful, less circumspect, profiles on that day.

Acknowledging the advantage of hindsight, I am able to consider more carefully the man we now know and the life that led up to his posthumous accounting. It is not my intention to look back at Maxwell's sixty-eight years in great detail. However, we cannot confront the man less than two years from his death, without knowing what led up to that point. Since I believe he constantly reinvented his past to suit the present, and never stopped the process of fabrication, it is essential to grasp some factual background.

Tom Bower, without any help, has reconstructed his past convincingly and Joe Haines, with a great deal of help, could not find fault with the fundamentals. Haines once told me he found thirty-eight mistakes in Bower's first couple of chapters. If that is so, they must be very minor indeed. Both books were mined by journalists as source material for articles at the time of his death, so the straightforward tale has been told in newspapers around the world. It is important though to retell the story in terms that help our understanding of Maxwell, stressing some of the discrepancies in the two versions, especially where they cast light on Maxwell's character and on his own desire, or that of his Boswell, to gloss over his past.

It is perhaps significant that even Maxwell's birthplace has had many names, among others, Solotvino, Slatinske Doly and Aknazlatina, the result of its being ruled in this century by many countries, a territory not so much fought over as handed over, an unimportant region granted in treaties agreed upon in countries far away. Situated on the Tisza river, a tributary of the Danube, the Ruthenian town was part of Czechoslovakia at the time Maxwell was born Abraham Lajbi Hoch on 10 June 1923. Anti-Semitic Czech officials forced the family to register a Czech name, Jan Ludvik. Across the river was Romania. In this border town of a mixed population in the middle of *mittel Europa* the people needed to speak at least a smattering of several languages to get by—Czech, Polish, Ukrainian, Hungarian, and Romanian. According to Haines, young Hoch, the third of seven children, was the son of Hasidic Jews. Bower states categorically that the family was not Hasidic.

Whatever the truth, and its relevance seems slight, Maxwell was raised as an Orthodox Jew, speaking Yiddish, wearing a skullcap, and with his hair in ringlets, or sidelocks. In a poor community, his was a very poor family. When he did work, his father, Mehel, dealt in cattle or took jobs as a casual laborer. Poverty often urges people to crime, and smuggling was endemic in a border area, but Mehel was supposedly known for his honesty and integrity, and it is not without interest that the upright Mehel played little part in Maxwell's upbringing.

The greatest influences on him were his maternal grandfather, Yaacov (or Yankel) Schlomovitch, and his mother Chanca (or Hannah). The former taught him how to trade and the latter fired him with ambition and an interest, he always claimed, in politics. What Maxwell learned from Schlomovitch he never forgot and in many ways still practiced until his death. His grandfather was a dealer, a middleman, in modern parlance a man "into a bit of this and that," who took the trouble to discover what goods someone wanted and then more trouble to get hold of them. He made his profit "on the turn," talking the seller into as low a price as possible and the buyer into the highest. The boy learned the art of bartering and hustling, how a deal is never really sealed until the money is paid. Up to the moment of cash changing hands, negotiations can always be re-opened, and only then is it a bargain.

As Bower writes, by observing his grandfather "ceaselessly looking for business and haggling the two sides at both ends to increase the margin imbued Maxwell with the instinctive sense for dealing that refined businessmen in London and New York came to loathe and fear."[2] Haines does not refer to this obviously crucial development in Maxwell's life, but he does link Schlomovitch to smuggling, conceding that his house, in which Maxwell grew up, was used as a hiding place for contraband alcohol.[3] The impressionable youth cannot have failed to note that his grandfather, living on his wits, existing on the margin of the law, was making a living while his honest father toiled for little.

Maxwell once said of his youth: "The poverty, indignity and hunger have engraved themselves on my heart."[4] He never deviated in this view and, over a quarter of a century later, when asked about childhood, he said, "I remember how hungry I was, how cold I was and how much I loved my mother... my mother was a great influence on me. I was her favorite."[5]

Hoch's desire to follow in his grandfather's footsteps was interrupted by his mother's faith in her religion and in education. Combining the two, she hoped he would become a rabbi and entered him in a local yeshiva, a traditional Jewish school. It says something for the strength of her convictions that she later sent him, aged only thirteen, to Bratislava, some four hundred miles from home, to continue his rabbinical studies. There, however, free from his mother's daily influence, the lessons of his grandfather showed themselves far more significant: The rules of the school rankled, and the budding entrepreneur began to sell cheap jewelry and trinkets on the streets.

The kind of youth Hoch soon became was clear from his sister Sylvia, who remembered him returning from Bratislava as "a flashy young chap, the prewar Central European equivalent of a teddy boy." His hair was "stylish," having dispensed with his Hasidic sidelocks.[6] Maxwell told two different tales about this later. His wife told me he had told her he cut off his *payes* in front of his father. Haines reports the teenage Maxwell as being "quick to learn," with a penchant for reading and politics, but his main occupation at the age of fifteen when the German army occupied Czechoslovakia in 1939, was as a salesman. The family decided the boy should go to Budapest: Haines has him heroically walking the two hundred seventy-five miles to the Hungarian capital while Bower's assertion that he went by train is given credence by the fact that he quotes the cousin who accompanied Maxwell on the ride.

Here begins a mystery over the apparently trivial matter of what happened to Maxwell in Budapest. What is important for us, however, is that it is an example of the invention that is at the heart of understanding the man. Not content with one lie, which he always had trouble remembering anyway, he told several about this incident, a trait that can be found running throughout the rest of his life. The lies about his flight from Hungary are also typical. Each one successively magnifies his role as a hero and in the process incorporates more details that render it unbelievable.

The latest, in Haines's 1988 book, is indubitably the most fantastic—euphemistically termed "bizarre" by Haines—and begins with Maxwell being befriended by a member of a youth group who swiftly recruits him into the underground movement then helping volunteers for a free Czech army to escape to the West. Soon Maxwell began to act as a courier for the movement until the escape route was betrayed. Maxwell was arrested and accused of spying.

"For four months," writes Haines, "he was kept in a windowless cell manacled hand and foot and beaten by day or by night with rubber truncheons and bicycle chains...one blow across the face broke his nose; today he can barely breathe through his right nostril."[7]

Having refused to speak under torture, he was sentenced to death, and only the intervention of the French ambassador—then looking after Czechoslovakia's interests in Hungary—won him an appeal. If belief was not suspended some sentences ago, then it is mandatory from now on. On his way to court, the handcuffed sixteen-year-old Maxwell, after suffering continual beatings over months, found the strength to overpower his guard, fortunately a one-armed World War I veteran, and fled. His handcuffs were then removed by "a gypsy lady" before he took a train to the Yugoslavian border, got a lift by car to Belgrade, and, through the French consulate, joined up with other young Czechs.

Most people heard this slightly bowdlerized version—with the one-armed guard but *without* the gypsy—during his 1987 Desert Island Discs radio interview. In yet another variation, Maxwell explained that he hit the guard "on the head with a stick. It was fairly easy to escape."[8] Bower provided three other versions: a 1969 *Sunday Times* story; an early 1960s press release that had Maxwell, at sixteen, fighting Germans and Russians on separate fronts; and the most believable of them all, the version Maxwell told his cousin at the end of the war in 1945.

In this story there is little embellishment because Maxwell was explaining to his cousin, Alex Pearl, who would know about conditions in Budapest at the time, why he had vanished. He said he had met a group of Czech soldiers who wanted to get to France. He lied about his age and they agreed he could join them as long as he maintained total secrecy by not returning to his friends. They then traveled to Zagreb, Yugoslavia, before making their way to Palestine.

Bower points out that all the post-1945 stories have a central lie because there was no Czech resistance at the time Maxwell arrived in Budapest. Apart from that, there would have been no need for couriers leading people out of Hungary since train journeys were legitimate.

The clinching detail for me came during my time with Maxwell when he returned from a surprise trip to Zagreb where, he boasted, "I was buying all the Croatian papers." He said the city hadn't changed much "since I was there in the war." In this different context, when his mind was not on his invented saga of teenage heroism, he had forgotten that Zagreb was not supposed to have played a part in his history.

There is a little less confusion once Jan Ludwig arrived in France. He ended up joining the Czech forces who helped, unsuccessfully, to defend France from the German army, and was evacuated with the surviving soldiers from Sete, near Marseilles, in May 1940. Two weeks later the seventeen-year-old landed in Britain without a penny, without a word of English, without connections. As a Ruthenian Jew, he was even subjected to hostility from the Czechs whom he accompanied. He seemed like "a wild man from the mountains," said one of them. Another pointed out a "basic trait": he was always "trying to do anything one had just done, and to do it slightly better. If you jumped over a ditch, he would do so. He has this talent for taking what someone else has conceived and improving it slightly."[9] These were prophetic words.

Within the year Maxwell joined the Pioneer Corps, and learned to speak English, he later claimed, in six weeks from a woman who ran a tobacconist's. He was frustrated as a member of the ditch-digging, nonfighting unit, but he used this three-year period in which to become a fully-fledged Briton, gradually and consciously distancing himself from his Czech peasant background. He had some luck in being introduced to the commander of the 176th Infantry Brigade, Brig. Gary Carthew-Yorstoun, and took full advantage of the introduction to win his big break. His mentor approved his recruitment to the Sixth Battalion of the North Staffs Regiment, a peculiar privilege for a Czech national, and Jan Ludwig Hoch lifted a new name from a cigarette brand, becoming Pvt. Leslie du Maurier.

All those who served with Maxwell in the next two years as he was promoted to corporal and then sergeant, remember him as a dominating personality, a risk taker and a rule breaker. He adopted a new, more British name, Leslie Jones, before his battalion sailed to France a couple of weeks after D-day, quickly seeing action and by all accounts distinguishing himself for his reckless bravado. One of his comrades, Lance Corp. Sam Mitchell, revealed to Haines that Maxwell also indulged in some colorful and cavalier activities, relieving captured Germans of their money and handing out to his men wristwatches removed from prisoners. He even appeared on reconnaissance duty in a German officer's uniform, adopting yet another persona as Lance Corp. Leslie Smith.

In September, Maxwell arrived in Paris soon after its liberation and met up again with Carthew-Yorstoun. The brigadier recommended that the handsome soldier would find good company at the French Welcome Committee, and on his first visit he met Elisabeth Meynard, daughter of a wealthy Huguenot owner of silk factories, and a couple of years older than Maxwell. The uncultivated twenty-one-year-old peasant boy who was desperate to improve himself had found a cultured woman from the French middle class. Their romance, in the manner of many in wartime, blossomed swiftly in spite of her family's hostility.

During the course of his relationship, in January 1945, Maxwell became an officer, attaining the rank of a second lieutenant with the Queen's Royal Regiment and selecting, at last, the name by which he was to be known thereafter, Ian Robert Maxwell, though he eschewed the first name. He claimed it was a good Scottish name suggested by Carthew-Yorstoun, but it is notably close to his father's name Mehel, and closer still to one of its common written forms, Mechel.

Carthew-Yorstoun also noted in a letter to Maxwell's new commander that "for various reasons [Maxwell] will give better results when he has a certain amount of freedom of choice and movement, than in a position where he is surrounded by too many rules and restrictions."[10]

Maxwell soon joined his new unit on the German-Dutch border, then preparing for Operation Blackcock, a concerted push forward that was fiercely contested by German troops when it began. Casualties on both sides were high. In the second week of the battle along the River Roer, the Germans made a surprise counterattack that threatened the Allied thrust, crossing the river and retaking the village of Paarlo. Maxwell, according to the official report, repeatedly asked to be allowed to lead a frontal assault against the German forces. When his wish was granted he was seen to rush a window under heavy fire and kill the machine-gunner. He followed this heroic act by leading his men with such vigor the Germans were forced to retreat. The attack proved to be a turning point in the battle. Maxwell's commanding officer recommended him for the Military Cross and two months later he was awarded the medal for courage by Field Marshal Montgomery.

Many people have hinted that Maxwell's MC was a sham, especially since other deceits have been exposed. I cannot share that view for three reasons. First, the contemporaneous evidence of his comrades has never been denied by anyone. Quite the reverse, a former soldier, Verdun Besley, has recently provided a vivid account of how he nearly shot Maxwell during the action.[11] Second, the British army's own disciplines and checks would have made faking the award extraordinarily unlikely. Third, and most important, the incident is entirely in keeping with Maxwell's impetuous and reckless nature throughout his life in whatever circumstances. His next bit of impetuosity occurred four days after receiving his medal when he married Elisabeth, always known as Betty, at a Protestant church in Paris. He looked like "a young Gary Cooper," she said.

Maxwell fought with Montgomery's army in the final assault on Germany, attacking Bremen and, just before the German collapse, Hamburg. Throughout these months he wrote to Betty, who allowed

Haines to quote from the letters, one of which revealed an incident Maxwell was to refer to several times in my company in the final years of his life. On 3 April 1945, he began a letter by remarking, "I had a very amusing day yesterday" and went on to tell how he had called on the mayor of a town to persuade the German troops inside to surrender.

"One hour later," wrote Maxwell, "he came back saying that the soldiers will surrender and the white flag was put up...but as we marched off a German tank opened fire on us. Luckily he missed, so I shot the mayor."[12] When he wished to shock, Maxwell would tell a version of this tale (he could never recall the exact facts) to watch for people's reactions. Sometimes I saw him shake his head as if he had become sad at the memory. He told an interviewer that "with the benefit of hindsight," he would not have referred to the incident as amusing: "How can you be proud of shooting a human, even if he's with the enemy?"[13] I am afraid this was an act because I also witnessed him more than once relate the story with relish, with a devilish grin, to show his audience he was not a man to mess with.

A month later, as the war ended, he wrote Betty a letter that is an early example of his braggadocio spirit: "Look out for the newsreel about Hamburg, you will see me in it issuing orders..."[14]

By now Maxwell knew that his parents, his grandfather, all but two of his sisters, his brother, and various uncles and aunts had perished in the Holocaust and his hometown had become part of the Soviet Union. Long ago he had decided to settle in Britain, but he was uncertain what he would do.

Meanwhile he began to enjoy the spoils of victory in Germany, boasting to Betty—now in London—that "I am not wasting my time, I am making money...my profits...must be nearly £100 [$160]...My prospects for further profit are quite good and I am doing nothing illegal."[15]

In truth, the occupying soldiers were living high on the hog, requisitioning food, drink, cigarettes, entertainment, cars, anything they wanted. In spite of attempts at organization, this period was chaotic enough for risk takers to seize their opportunity. In these months Maxwell first worked as an intelligence interrogation officer and soon after was promoted to captain, the rank that he later exploited and later still would rue as a nickname.

His grasp of languages next won him an assignment in Berlin as head of the press section of the Public Relations and Information Services Control, known as PRISC. Maxwell made much of this when he bought the *Mirror,* constantly referring to himself as the youngest editor in history. During a discussion about his suitability to edit the *Daily Mirror* in my absence, he told me, "At twenty-one, I was in charge of a paper in Berlin selling a million. Not bad eh?"

My colleagues had to listen to this boast on numerous occasions: our only joy was in guessing by how many thousand he would inflate the circulation figure. In fact, Captain Maxwell's official task was to censor *Der Telegraph,* the first licensed paper in the British sector of Berlin, to ensure it was both democratic in tone and uncritical of the Allies.

His unofficial role, however, was the one in which he excelled: procuring the means by which the paper, "my paper," could be printed and distributed. He soon grew to admire the editor, Arno Scholtz, who used his paper to further the political aims of the Social Democratic Party, rarely vetting the content or intervening in editorial affairs. Instead he concentrated on what he did best as a Mr. Fixit—finding, filching, haggling, and hustling to supply the newspaper with newsprint, ink, and essential bits of printing machinery. He cheerfully used the black market to raise money to buy equipment. The Scholtz-Maxwell combination worked well, and *Der Telegraph* achieved a circulation of more than 250,000 six days a week, by far the biggest-selling paper of its time. Maxwell never needed to lie. The truth was impressive enough.

3

Unscrupulous, Unfit, But Unbowed

ABRAHAM Lajbi Hoch is now Captain Robert Maxwell MC, and it will be years before we learn of his background. He has been born again in a new image. But he has far from forgotten his past. Although the young hero will trade on his army rank, he will rely on those skills he learned at his grandfather's knee. We cannot look back into Maxwell's life without delving deeply into his business dealings. It is through these arrangements that we see the man of the eighties creating himself, and can distinguish the pattern of behavior that will lead to his emergence as a confidence trickster on a grand scale.

In the summer of 1946, Maxwell was demobilized from the army and quickly indulged his taste for business, especially of the import-export variety, by taking shares in and becoming a director of a firm called Low-Bell, run by a Jewish-Czech refugee, Arnos (or Arnold) Lobl. The origins of the Lobl-Maxwell relationship are obscure, but Maxwell—drawing on an army annuity and money from his wife Betty's family—soon became the majority shareholder. The amount

24

of money necessary to achieve this participation proved quite small. The firm's wholesale-retail business was perfectly suited to Maxwell's bartering talents, dealing in anything and everything, from fancy goods to caustic soda, from coal to dried peas.

Two other traits soon emerged, the public showman Maxwell astonished friends by driving around in a Cadillac, and the privately devious Maxwell added a second company to his name, the grandly titled European Periodicals, Publicity and Advertising Corporation (EPPAC). From now on, Maxwell companies would multiply and he would develop an uncanny knack for holding the strings in each enterprise.

Whenever people ask where he obtained his money "at the beginning," then EPPAC is it. Remembering a remark of Arno Scholtz's about the value of German scientific-book exports (the Germans being the world's scientific leaders), Maxwell hunted down Germany's, if not the world's, largest scientific publishers, Ferdinand Springer in Berlin. The business was then in ruins, a classic entry point for an opportunist. Internal memoranda record Maxwell's crucial role in saving the company and putting it back on the road to resuming its profitable export trade. Maxwell performed any number of tasks—negotiating allocations of electricity, coal, and paper—but none as important as his securing of an extremely favorable Deutschmark-Sterling exchange rate. Bower's speculation makes sense, that Maxwell probably convinced former army public-relations colleagues that the rate was necessary to satisfy Allied policy in the dissemination of German scientific knowledge.

Maxwell also "solved" the other major problem faced by Springer, the fact that the Allies refused to allow small packets to be dispatched from Germany, making it impossible for the company to send out journals singly. Springer needed to ship in bulk out of the country and to find someone to distribute from abroad. Step forward Captain Maxwell. He obtained from Springer exclusive world distribution rights of their journals and books for EPPAC, and to do so, of course, he had to be provided with that most precious commodity, a full and detailed list of customers.

This enterprise, good for both Springer and Maxwell, could perhaps have proceeded profitably for decades, if Maxwell had not been Maxwell, if he had been instead a bureaucratic, humdrum, cautious builder of business. It might well have lasted longer, without the rancor that quickly surfaced and grew in the following years, if only he had taken the trouble to organize properly, to manage efficiently, to keep up his end of the bargain. But Maxwell was no manager and, as a middleman, he enjoyed only the pleasure of counting money, assessing what would come from the supplier and what could be obtained from the customer, and then building upon those paper sums to seek another fortune in a fresh field. Grandfather had used his margin to buy the necessities of life. Grandson envisaged the margin as a springboard to new ventures. Once a deal was done he grew bored, and so it was with his links to Springer.

Springer soon became angry at the Maxwell company's inefficiency and incompetence, its failure to supply customers on time, and the growing number of complaints about its business methods. Records were badly kept, orders were not fulfilled quickly, accounting was sloppy. The Germans were frustrated, too, by their British partner's frequent absences from London: he had begun wandering the capitals of Europe, opening offices and subsidiary companies, rather than concentrating on running his central concern. This peripatetic activity was to become a hallmark of Maxwell's business life. Maxwell neatly sidestepped these complaints, ostensibly agreeing with Springer's analysis of the problems, and proposed that a new company should distribute the journals and books. Called Lange, Maxwell and Springer (LMS), it meant that EPPAC would remain in charge of importation while LMS dealt with distribution.

Though the Germans did not realize it, the maneuver gave Maxwell yet more control, since only he knew what was going on in each outfit. This simple split into two companies was the beginning of a deliberate method, compartmentalization, which would grow ever more complex in later years, even to the point where it occurred *within* his companies.

However, during the association with Springer, Maxwell's fertile mind began to operate in any number of directions and in 1948 he made his first influential City connection, the banker Sir Charles Hambro. The introduction was made through Major John Whitlock, the managing director of the medical and legal publishers Butterworth's, who would regret it ever after. Hambro was taken with the twenty-six-year-old Maxwell, and the friendship was to provide the budding tycoon with access not only to loans from Hambro but also from other banks. Basically it was due to Maxwell's links with Springer that he met either man, since a Springer employee was asked to help the British government in its attempts to stimulate scientific publishing. The chosen publishers for this enterprise were Butterworth's, and this led to the formation of a company called Butterworth-Springer, in which Maxwell played no formal role though LMS acted as distributor.

A thin end of a wedge was, for Maxwell, enough. When, in 1951, Butterworth's decided to end the partnership, Maxwell bought it for £13,000 ($21,000), a great deal of money in Britain at the time and much more than Maxwell owned. This was the moment that Hambro, who had been charmed by Maxwell, agreed to bankroll him. Hambro's decision was said to be an inspired hunch. Whitlock's hunch was the opposite. He later told a protégé: "I would never trust Maxwell further than I could see him. There's still too much of the Czech peasant in him."

John Whitlock's condescending justification seems to take the edge off the essential truth of his gut reaction. Such a view would have drawn from Bower an appreciative nod, because he does tend to make much of this kind of establishment class reaction to Maxwell, but I cannot see that he suffered any differently from any man on the make from outside the old-school-tie brigade. Indeed, there is a case to be made that he did better, forming, by judicious use of his army background and his blustering charm, contacts many British working-class lads in a similar position could not have made. It was his lack of social awareness, his failure to appreciate the unwritten code of behavior, that was one of the special qualities that aided his success.

I am not even sure there is any validity in the argument if one turns the problem around, suggesting that Maxwell craved acceptance, never stopped seeking it, and remained bitter that he did not achieve it. In a way he appreciated his difference, reveling in its specialness, and seeing himself, the peasant lad, as better than those who started life with an advantage.

"When I am confronted by powerful people," he was fond of explaining, "I remind myself that all men use lavatory paper."

According to the authorized story, the Hambro loan was supplemented by money from Maxwell's own relatives in America and "some help from his wife's family."[1] He now knew of the immense demand for out-of-print German scientific papers and for current German work, and he correctly forecast that there would be a growing market for British scientific books and journals. Maxwell had found a gap in the market, had secured for himself a monopolistic position within that market, and had as rosy a future as any businessman could hope for in the early 1950s. The company he would found, Pergamon Press, would become the world's second largest scientific publisher, producing thousands of books and journals in the following thirty-nine years.

Pergamon, the vehicle used by Maxwell to collect money during three decades, enabled him to set out on many other ventures, and its importance to him was shown when he briefly lost control of it and fought so furiously and tenaciously for its return. Since his death, there has been a fascinating newspaper correspondence among scientists and publishers about the ethics of one man being able to make "fat" profits from disseminating information supposedly necessary for the good of society. In passing, one wonders whether scientists now troubled by this apparent excess ever stopped to question the economic system that gave rise to it.

Now we come to the first episode in Maxwell's business dealings that should have alerted everyone in the City, London's financial district, to the nature of the man they were beginning to support. The Simpkin Marshall affair is important because it illustrates that neither Maxwell nor the City learned anything from it, an example of sharp business practice on a breathtaking scale with accounting irregularities and gross mismanagement.

In 1951 Maxwell was involved in the kind of sleight-of-hand operation that would, on a greater scale, suddenly amaze everyone in 1991. Maxwell, then only twenty-eight, must have been flattered to be asked by a group of leading publishers to "save" Simpkin Marshall, a unique organization that acted as a central distributor for the British book trade.

Simpkins was the major wholesale supplier of individual books to shops across Britain, an essential clearinghouse that cut costs for all publishers. However, the company had never recovered from its stock being destroyed in a wartime bombing raid, and Maxwell was being asked to pick up a poisoned chalice. Before taking on the task,

Maxwell should have renegotiated the company's deals with the publishers, obtaining sale or return terms and better margins. That would have taken time, it would have been logical, it just might—in Maxwell's eyes—have signaled a hint of weakness on his part.

Instead, Maxwell approached Simpkins's indebtedness with a blitz of frenetic activity and bombast, and, when that failed, he employed the kind of creative accounting he would use ever after. The Official Receiver's report makes fascinating reading, revealing how Maxwell agreed to a £160,000 ($256,000) price for Simpkins, paid an initial installment of £50,000 ($80,000) to the owners, Pitmans, and agreed to pay off the remaining £110,000 ($176,000) over nine years.

Within a year, Maxwell told Pitmans he would pay off the total debt in one go—if they agreed to take £98,000 ($157,000). They did and he gave them the money. But it was not *his* money. Maxwell simply removed the cash from Simpkins. In other words, the company he bought had paid him for buying it. The story of this maneuver echoes down the years: it was clever and, in spite of its slyness, totally legal.

In the face of a crisis, most people would concentrate on the problem in hand. Maxwell, however, approached looming crises from the opposite direction. He turned his back on the dearth of profitable activity within Simpkins, largely of his own making since he chose to move the company to unsuitable premises. His new target was the British Book Center in New York, a central distribution depot for British books throughout the United States, and it was his preparations for that purpose that required him to settle with Pitmans so quickly. Having used Simpkins funds to pay off his personal debt, in 1952 he used a further £10,000 ($16,000) of company money to buy control of the New York center, again a legally sound move since Simpkins accounts still showed them owing Maxwell money.

The purchase was also rash: the Book Center had become insolvent and would become a further drain, not on Maxwell of course, but on Simpkins. Meanwhile, Springer watched these developments in awe, while fielding complaints from old and valued customers about strange working methods used by Maxwell's distribution company, Lange, Maxwell & Springer. Even the enthusiasm of Hambro's was thin. Maxwell needed money to keep his enterprises afloat and found it from a bizarre source, a fellow barterer, a German-Jewish refugee called Dr. Kurt Wallersteiner.

Wallersteiner, a chemist who ran chemical companies, was an expert in international barter trades and not above pulling off spectacular con tricks, even to the extent of inventing a country to effect one deal. Maxwell and Waller, as Maxwell called him, were therefore soul mates. But it was Maxwell who would rook his friend. In spite of the later Maxwellian expurgated version, in which Waller was blamed for the whole fiasco at Simpkins, it is obvious from the financial records and the Official Receiver's report that Maxwell lured Waller into making bigger and bigger commitments to Simpkins. It is impossible to learn how he managed to get Waller to make the investments since the businessman-chemist was jailed for fraud and has never offered a believable explanation.

The relationship between the barter boys is also notable because it is the first major example of Maxwell using his writ ploy. As Simpkins moved toward inevitable collapse with the concerned Waller by now having invested £470,000 ($752,000), he tried to call a creditors' meeting. Maxwell's response was to seek a High Court injunction to prevent Waller from taking such a step. Maxwell swore out a lengthy affidavit that asserted that Simpkins was solvent and that any meeting called by Waller would endanger Simpkins's survival. The result was victory for Maxwell and the triumph of a barefaced lie. By swearing to a statement that was basically the opposite of the truth, he had prevented Waller from stating the facts to other creditors: Simpkins was bankrupt. This legal ploy only delayed matters. In 1955 Simpkins went into liquidation, owing £656,000 ($1,050,000).

The Official Receiver's report noted that it was "doubtful whether the company was at any time solvent." It criticized the directors for acquiring new premises, financing the British Book Center, and, knowing how bad the situation was, for not liquidating sooner. Missing from Haines's account is also the direct reference to Maxwell. The receiver urged a "close investigation" into the New York deal since "Captain Maxwell was aware of the financial difficulties of both the British Book Center Inc. and Simpkins when Simpkins was supplying the books and the debt was mounting."

Britain's publishers were outraged at the scandal, many of them having lost thousands (only nineteen pence on the pound—19 cents on the dollar—was finally paid to unsecured creditors, most of whom were publishers). However, since they approached Maxwell and gave him, according to the receiver, relatively small margins on his book purchases, they must accept part of the blame. At the time they could not know the kind of man they had invited into their trade, but the Simpkins debacle should have been a warning for the future.

At about the same time, Springer finally split from Maxwell. These reverses turned Maxwell's attentions to the scientific-journals business he had virtually neglected for years, Pergamon, and to politics. I will deal with Maxwell's short time as an MP later, but Pergamon demands attention. If the "public" is amazed by the fact that the banks bent over backward to lend Maxwell money in the years before his death, then they should be truly dumbfounded by knowing, as the City had always known, the details of the Pergamon affair that led to the famous Department of Trade report.

Until this point in the story the differences between the accounts of Haines and Bower had been, as we have seen, relatively slight. Now they diverge entirely because Maxwell's view prevailed in the authorized version: it is not that Haines avoids mentioning the criticism of Maxwell's conduct so much as he ignores the conduct itself. Haines must have known about Maxwell's behavior since it was all spelled out in the meticulous reports of the inspectors. Yet what Maxwell did is crucial to understanding his methods and the key to unraveling his later misdemeanors. Peter Thompson and Tony Delano, two former Maxwell employees whose book he prevented from being distributed, point out correctly: "In 1949 Maxwell was already acting on one of the principles that was to guide his commercial life—the more companies you have, the more they can do business with each other."[2] By the middle of the 1960s, Maxwell had honed this practice into an art.

Once Maxwell concentrated on building Pergamon into an international company selling scientific books and journals, from about 1955, everyone agrees that his combination of determination and chutzpah was outstandingly successful. Haines writes of his master's "remarkable energy" and "sheer cheek" during this period as he flew from country to country to attend scientific conferences where he would recruit authors and editorial boards for new works. He was especially clever to win exclusive rights to Soviet scientific papers and soon "cornered one of the potentially most lucrative markets in publishing."[3] Bower, who takes a great deal of interest in Maxwell's supposed KGB contacts, points out that he was treated as "a uniquely trusted westerner," but it is also true that Maxwell was fortunate in cultivating Soviet science in an era when the West was fascinated by Soviet leadership in the space race.

Maxwell, using his gifts as a showman to present Pergamon as the essential outlet for all scientific papers, overrode objections to expand at breakneck speed. He flew to Moscow to arrange the publication of the most comprehensive English-Russian dictionary; he turned up at a nuclear science conference in Switzerland to buy up rights to papers being presented by the leading speakers; he traveled across China by train, ripping out the loudspeaker in his carriage because the constant propaganda annoyed him, in a vain bid to stimulate business. He launched scores of journals in subjects as diverse as physics, insect biochemistry, optical medicine, and ocean engineering.

Then, at the age of thirty-two in 1955, he fell ill. At first he was diagnosed as having cancer of both lungs. A second, and correct, opinion revealed that he had a small tumor in his right lung. Surgeons at London's University College Hospital removed a part of the lung and discovered that the tumor was not malignant. However, Maxwell, who had smoked two packs of cigarettes a day, gave up the habit and over the years developed a pathological hatred of smoking, to the point where he banned anyone from smoking in his presence.

Soon after recovery, Maxwell resumed his globe-trotting schedule and built up Pergamon's empire of journals and books. Though the list was impressive in quantity, much of the subject matter was too esoteric to win large sales. His business depended on low-volume sales within the world's relatively small academic community. Nevertheless his success and consequent self-confidence was such that in 1959, at the age of thirty-six, he was able to write to Sir Charles Hambro: "My various businesses are flourishing. I have paid up all my debts and borrowings, including income tax, and our cash at bank since the beginning of the year has fluctuated between £70,000 and £100,000 ($112,000 and $160,000). I feel sure that you will be pleased to know that the business which you helped me start is doing so well . . . "[4]

A year later he moved into Headington Hill Hall in Oxford, his "council house" leased at a bargain rent, using it as both home and office for his Pergamon staff of two hundred; he continued to travel the world, meeting statesmen, such as Khrushchev, and acquiring yet more scientific authors for Pergamon. This success brought other rewards, a gradual, if grudging, acceptance by some London institutions. One small but distinguished merchant bank, Ansbacher's, was glowing in its praise when he took Pergamon public in 1964. Many others remained skeptical. A *Financial Times* columnist commented just before the share issue: "The City will have to make its own attempt to assess the most controversial figure in British publishing" and went on to say that Maxwell attracted "more abuse and more envy than any other publisher since the copyright acts were passed."[5]

Following the oversubscription of his share offer came a period of acquisition, of which two encyclopedia publishers, George Newnes and Caxton, were the most notable. He also failed in bids for the British Printing Corporation (BPC) and the News of the World, but both gave him an appetite. He even formed a joint company with BPC—International Learning Systems Corporation (ILSC)—in the hope of selling the fifteen-volume Chambers's Encyclopaedia, published by Newnes. He turned this into a personal mission, making a world tour to sell to book wholesalers sets of the expensive encyclopedias, and boasting of gigantic sales in faraway places. Later these lies would engender his downfall.

Even so, Maxwell did not fool, or cower, everyone. One of the Pergamon salesmen who accompanied him, Philip Okill, later told Bower that Maxwell said to him after the trip; "Okill, you don't seem to trust me. Why not?"

Okill decided to tell the truth and replied, "Because, Mr. Maxwell, you're the sincerest liar I have ever met." He laughed because, said Okill, "I genuinely think he took it as one of the nicest compliments I could have paid him."[6]

He could afford to laugh in private, but public truth was another matter. When Tom Baistow was acting editor of the *New Statesman* magazine in the late sixties, he was informed by his student daughter, then working on vacation at Pergamon, of irregularities within the company, particularly in the newly acquired encyclopedia division.

Baistow assigned a reporter to the story who "produced a damning indictment of Pergamon's con-type sales methods and the fact that it was flogging expensive, out-of-date publications to unsuspecting housewives, among other activities."[7]

Maxwell's response was to demand a right of reply and a threat to sue. Baistow had "cast-iron evidence" and, while offering Maxwell space for a short reply, refused to back down and continued with his series of articles. Maxwell did not sue but some years later he made overtures to take over the magazine, though it came to nothing.

By 1966, when Maxwell was forty-three, Pergamon employed twenty-five hundred people; producing six hundred new titles and one hundred twenty journals; winning the Queen's Award for Industry; and looking at profits of almost £1 million ($1.6 million) on an annual turnover of £5 million ($8 million). In the next three years, sales increased and profits multiplied, all recorded in wonderment by Haines. At least that is what the annual reports said. More acquisitions followed and profits for 1968 were more than £2 million ($3.2 million) with a forecast of £2.5 million ($4 million) for 1969. And then came the Leasco fiasco.

The text according to Haines has Maxwell receiving a call from Saul Steinberg, twenty-nine-year-old chairman of Leasco Data Processing Company, who had made millions leasing computers in America.[8] Bower tells us that Maxwell was searching for a partner in America and "had approached several people before telephoning Saul Steinberg."[9] Whoever lured whom on that day in January 1969, both were to regret it. By Easter they were discussing the possibility of Leasco making a bid for Pergamon, a deal based on the forecast profits of over £2 million ($3.2 million). If we believe the Haines/Maxwell view, then nothing should have been simpler: had not Pergamon been expanding its turnover for fourteen years, attaining profits in the previous year of more than £2 million ($3.2 million)?

However, the Department of Trade inspectors' clinical dissection of the Pergamon accounts—summarized and analyzed brilliantly by Bower—was to reveal a very different story. In essence, Maxwell's massaging of the profits was a straightforward piece of trickery: he set up a myriad range of private companies, nearly all controlled by trusts with unknown trustees, over whom Maxwell claimed to have no control. These companies would be used to purchase, at least on paper, books and journals from Pergamon. Therefore, Pergamon's accounts would be credited with sales, and profits, it had not made.

Even though some commentators have described this as "brilliant," since most of the fiddling was not illegal, the way Maxwell went about the deceit appeared to be clumsy. Instead of setting up the private companies to make regular orders, Maxwell simply arranged for enormous bulk orders to be made that were not credible. The 1969 Pergamon annual report contained two entries, for instance, that showed that journals worth £708,000 ($1,133,000) had been suddenly "bought." A further entry showed a £266,416 ($426,265) profit for previously worthless back issues. There were other credits, too, from private companies, including a fake claim of Spanish translation rights. The Pergamon profit was a fiction...but that was only half the story.

Part of the deal with Steinberg depended on the level of profitability of Pergamon's encyclopedia offshoot, ILSC. Maxwell originally claimed the ILSC profit would total £500,000 ($800,000) but was forced to admit eventually that it would be no more than £50,000 ($80,000), blaming his partnership with the British Printing Corporation for the shortfall. In fact, it was his own exaggerated claims of encyclopedia sales that led to the problem. It transpired that even the £50,000 forecast was false. Another huge "sale" to a Maxwell company based in America was discovered.

By the time Leasco realized, they had gone too far, spending millions buying up Pergamon shares, ending up with 38 percent of the company to Maxwell's 28 percent. Steinberg decided to pull out of the bid, and the regulatory authority, the City Takeover Panel, was asked to sort out the mess. In turn, the panel called in the Department of Trade, which appointed two inspectors to investigate. At the same time, an accountancy firm, Price Waterhouse, was hired to make a concurrent, independent audit of Pergamon's accounts, a fact incidentally that Haines fails to mention, just possibly because no amount of selective extracting from their report could conceal its tone of "remorseless censure."[10] If ILSC's genuine losses were taken into account, then Pergamon had also made a loss: there were no profits.

It is the three Department of Trade inspectors' reports that have won the most publicity though. The first, published in July 1971, was 209 pages long and contained the "notorious attack"[11] that thereafter dogged Maxwell. "We regret having to conclude," said the inspectors, "that, notwithstanding Mr. Maxwell's acknowledged abilities and energy, he is not in our opinion a person who can be relied on to exercise proper stewardship of a publicly-quoted company." The writs began to flow, and Haines's defense is larded with Maxwellian epethets—"star chamber," "contrary to natural justice," "abuses of procedure," "unfulfilled promises"—that featured in Maxwell's affidavits.

To an extent, some of Maxwell's criticisms of the procedure were absolutely correct, but that should not blind us to the substantive truth of that report. If the inspectors did make errors then these must be seen in context: Maxwell's legal delaying tactics dragged out the investigation for three years, and even when forced to answer questions he dissembled and obfuscated.

A second report appeared in April 1972 and, among its findings, noted: "The history of the Pergamon Subscription Books Division is a history of overstatement of its normal trading profits and of exaggerated claims of the sales of Chambers' Encyclopaedia... both must have played a significant part in bringing the shareholders of Pergamon to their present unenviable plight."

More writs arrived, as they did following the publication of the third and final report in November 1972. Over the years Maxwell convinced himself that the reports were overturned by the courts because one judge early on was critical of the inspectors, a judgment reversed in many subsequent hearings. In 1991, in his last major interview, Maxwell's assertion that the reports were "invalid" was accepted as fact by the interviewer.[12]

Despite the reports outlining obvious breaches of Britain's Companies Act, which regulates corporate behavior, no charges of malfeasance were brought against Maxwell. In the next couple of years, as Maxwell turned fifty, he plotted to regain control of Pergamon and to restore his public image, at least to his satisfaction. He once boasted to me: "Only I could manage it... Pergamon is nothing without me... I turned a loss into a profit..."

In fact, Steinberg found himself in trouble from the outset with his Leasco share price dropping as American investors' confidence in his abilities ebbed away. He also discovered that in buying Pergamon he had only obtained one part of the empire and that Maxwell controlled the rest, including the all-important American subsidiary, Pergamon Press Incorporated (PPI). This American company was responsible for 50 percent of all sales and for all of the American scientific journals, such as the successful *Acta Metallurgica*. Leasco's failure to remove Maxwell from control of it meant that they had to allow Maxwell a place on the board in Britain or face the possibility of a rival company emerging from within their own organization.

Meanwhile, Maxwell sought allies on the board, and since Pergamon was housed next to his Headington Hill Hall home he took every opportunity to intrude into affairs. By January 1974, at the age of fifty, he decided to bid to win back Pergamon from Leasco, who had had enough. Maxwell offered 12 pence (20 cents) a share and managed to buy back his company for about £1.5 million ($2.4 million), borrowing the money through another of his shadowy firms, Microforms International Marketing Corporation (MIMC), blandly referred to by Haines as "a newly-formed American-based company owned by a French lawyer acting for Betty Maxwell's family." Pergamon became Maxwell's private firm once again but by now "though few could have realized it, Maxwell was nearly broke."[13] From this resurrection came the nickname "the Bouncing Czech."

Throughout the years of building Pergamon and during the Leasco drama, Maxwell had pursued a parallel career as a politician. He desperately wanted to win the highest office, of British Prime Minister, and set out on the trail in 1959, when he was thirty-six. The first surprise was his choice of party. Maxwell stood for Labour, the socialist party of the workers, rather than the Conservative Party, which usually attracts the captains of industry. He always justified his socialist credentials by referring to his penniless childhood and his belief that only Labour cared enough to relieve poverty. It is much more likely that he turned to Labour because the Conservatives refused to have him at a time when the party was led by Harold Macmillan, whose family publishing firm had been badly hit by the Simpkin Marshall book distributors' crash.

In spite of Maxwell's claims of infant socialism, his entrepreneurial style and blatant publicity stunts tended to embarrass other members of his adopted party from his first election campaign in 1959, when he attempted to win the seat in Buckingham, a town some thirty miles north of London that had regularly switched its allegiance between the Labour and Conservative parties. His first error in many Labour eyes was to break convention by continuing to refer to himself by his army rank of Captain. In Britain, where convention counts, only retired career officers, not ex-conscripts, are traditionally known by their former rank. Maxwell lost.

He stood again in 1964, the year in which the Labour leader Harold Wilson ended thirteen years of Conservative rule, and won narrowly, improving his majority very slightly in 1966. But four years later, in 1970, amid the problems at Pergamon, he lost. He stood twice more, in the two 1974 elections, without success.

He proved himself in his six years in the Commons to be a nuisance, a rogue politician seeking publicity for fruitless causes such as the protectionist I'm Backing Britain campaign, a windbag in the chamber and ineffectual outside it. He was given the Commons Catering Committee to run and pulled off another creative-accounting triumph while being lampooned in the House for all manner of culinary crimes. He also attracted unpopularity within his own party for appearing as a witness on behalf of a Conservative MP who tried to prevent the publication of Hubert Selby's novel *Last Exit to Brooklyn*.

It was rare for Maxwell to undergo hostile questioning from which he could not escape, and once in the witness box this self-appointed censor exhibited a lack of knowledge and of logic. Under cross-examination he was asked about other great works of literature. What did he think of *Ulysses* and *Lady Chatterley's Lover*? He considered them works of art. And what about *The Decameron*? "De-what?" Maxwell said. He went on to declare: "I am against censorship" but added that this "brutal and filthy" book should be banned. He was aware of his parliamentary failings and many years later disingenuously admitted them: "When I went into the House of Commons, I thought I was the brightest thing on two feet, that I would be the prime minister in due course. But after six weeks, I discovered that anything I knew about, them guys knew more. I decided that was not my scene."[14]

In Buckingham, he split the Labour Party, angered a number of workers, was vindictive to one of his agents, and, just as in his business life, created controversy where none had existed and none seemed to need to exist. Politically he remained on the right of the party and was full of praise for the anti–trade-union laws introduced by Mrs. Thatcher's Tory government. It was his use of these laws at Pergamon, where he fired twenty-three workers after they had held a union meeting, that plagued him for years. No public event organized by Maxwell—such as the launch of *The European* or the announcement of his purchase of the New York *Daily News*—took place without the Pergamon strikers making a demonstration.

The month before his death I was present at Labour's 1991 Brighton conference when yet another motion condemning Maxwell was passed after being "opposed" in an equivocating and embarrassed speech by the general secretary, Larry Whitty.

Even his support for the Labour Party through the Mirror Group did not boost his standing among Labour members. Whenever asked about why he should be a socialist, he offered a moist-eyed reminiscence of his Ruthenian background. Though his biographer wrote of his having "a genuine social conscience,"[15] it is difficult to trace in any of his political activities, unless sending a card to every road-accident victim in your constituency qualifies.

As we shall see later, the point of politics for Maxwell was its benefit to business. Powerful acquaintances were useful. Looking back on his failure in Parliament, it is perhaps not without significance that Maxwell was tolerated less by politicians than by businesspeople.

By late 1974, fifty-one-year-old Maxwell knew his political career was over, but he had regained the jewel in his business crown, Pergamon. In the next two years Maxwell sought to rebuild the company out of the limelight, since it was private. Again, sales and profits increased dramatically. He also rebuilt his contacts with the Soviets, though the appetite in the West for Russian scientific works had almost vanished. After Maxwell's death it was discovered that Pergamon was listed as a "friendly firm" and that monies due to Pergamon were outstanding, which strongly suggests that the Soviet Union paid Maxwell to print its output.

Doubtless his standing in the Warsaw Pact countries was helped by the "World Leaders" series of books in which Maxwell ordered the publication of ludicrous biographies of East European dictators such as Romania's Ceausescu, Bulgaria's Zhivkov, East Germany's Honecker, and Czechoslovakia's Husak.

He later tried to evade persistent criticism by comparing himself to the Queen! Nobody complains if she meets with dictators, he argued, so why should I be attacked? Anyway the biographies were unprofitable for Pergamon but, ironically, the contacts Maxwell made in the bureaucracies later helped to smooth the path for him after the collapse of communism in those countries when he embarked on buying sprees (or "aid," as he liked to term it).

He also indulged in two other money-making enterprises that were to develop into passions: speculating in the markets and plundering pension funds. His early speculation was not wholly successful (Bower reports his losing £1.5 million ($2.4 million) in 1979, halving Pergamon's profits[16]), but he became as hooked on it as he was on gambling at roulette tables.

His pension maneuver occurred when he bought a book company, Wheatons, for £6 million ($9.6 million) and found it had an £8 million ($12.8 million) pension-fund surplus. He closed down the fund, set up a new one into which the existing members were transferred, and switched the surplus into his own coffers.

During the late seventies there were attempts to buy newspapers, more of which later, but his main interest remained Pergamon until 1980. Then fifty-seven-year-old Maxwell set his sights on getting hold of an old adversary, the British Printing Corporation (BPC), Britain's largest printing conglomerate, which had proved an unfriendly partner for Pergamon a decade before in a joint venture to sell encyclopedias. BPC was un unwieldy organization with forty-two companies trading under its umbrella, involved in all areas of printing, mainly magazines and books. Despite annual sales of £200 million ($320 million) the company incurred a £12 million ($19.2 million) loss in 1979, was continuing to lose £1 million ($1.6 million) a month and, more worryingly, owed one bank, National Westminster, £25 million ($40 million). Its future looked hopeless, with a disparate and disorganized collection of print companies using outdated machinery and management giving way too often to the labor unions.

Maxwell, aware of the beleaguered company's substantial losses and flush with profits from four good years for Pergamon, gradually built up a share-holding to just below the point at which he would need to declare himself as a bidder. Then he launched what is known in London financial circles as a "dawn raid" one morning in July 1980. In just ten minutes, he scooped up 29.5 percent of British Printing Corporation's shares for £2.9 million ($4.64 million) and immediately demanded a place on the board.

The directors of British Printing Corporation were united in their hostility to Maxwell, but their company was in dire trouble and there was little they could do to keep him out. Maxwell was supported by the National Westminster Bank, worried about its investment, and by Lord Kearton, a director of BPC's merchant bankers, Hill Samuel, who was called in by the board as adviser. Kearton, who always maintained that Maxwell was a "genius," persuaded the board to accept him. Maxwell became deputy chairman and chief executive in February 1981 and immediately embarked on a survival plan, demanding that a quarter of the staff be made redundant, restrictive practices be ended, and several printing plants be closed.

Seasoned British Printing Corporation managers smiled at Maxwell's naïveté. Nobody, they thought, could tame the print unions. In fact, Maxwell, by now fifty-eight, was ideally suited to the task. Over the following weeks he charmed, coaxed, blustered, bullied, joked, and juggled, without losing his temper. Union leader Bill Keyes can rarely have made a truer statement than to have described Maxwell as "the greatest wheeler-dealer we've ever met...a man who can charm the birds off the trees and then shoot them." Against all the odds, he won union consent to the loss of twenty-five hundred jobs, approval for his restructuring plan from the board, more money from National Westminster, and then turned to the problem of management.

He showed a less sure touch with managers, losing the good with the bad, but by the end of 1981 he had achieved such a remarkable turn-around that he felt confident enough to announce a £100 million ($160 million) investment in badly needed new machinery. He also felt confident enough to put himself in total, individual control of the company. On 26 November 1981, the British Printing Corporation board resolved "that the chairman...is hereby appointed a committee of the board and that there be delegated to the chairman as such committee all the powers of the board."

The next year he changed the company's name to the British Printing & Communication Corporation (BPCC) to signal his media ambitions, but that resolution remained in being: Robert Maxwell was not merely chairman of the board, he was the board, and could, literally, do as he wished. In 1983, he acquired the magazine printer, Odhams Press, from Reed International, took a large percentage of Central Television, got embroiled in buying Oxford football club, failed in an attempt to purchase games manufacturer John Waddington, and bought and asset-stripped Bishopsgate Trust, an investment trust company that would assume a major role years later.

When Maxwell took over BPC he also acquired Macdonald, the publishers. In many ways his attempts to turn it into a personal publishing house prefigure his Mirror Group interventions, but many managing directors found ways of subverting his ambitions. Edmund Fisher, for example, was "instructed" to publish certain works but neatly avoided doing so. A favorite maneuver was to recommend Pergamon as a substitute. Fisher's hostility to Maxwell led to his being undermined in a favorite Maxwell manner: he would deal with Fisher's staff behind his back.

One of Maxwell's unhappy secretaries was friendly with Fisher, and before resigning she leaked a specific instance to Fisher of a Macdonald sales director who had been ordered to deal directly with Maxwell and to "keep Fisher in the dark."

Fisher confronted Maxwell with the truth and thereafter Maxwell referred to him as "the best-looking man in the company," a favored way of ignoring his underhand behavior by turning the incident into a joke. "He was shrewd rather than clever," Fisher said. "But he was a disgusting man and I let him know I thought it. He did me a favor by sacking me."

Fisher's successor, Tim Hely-Hutchinson, said, "I had two jobs—running Macdonald and running a relationship with Maxwell." He also avoided publishing Maxwell's pet projects "by putting a blind eye to the telescope."

However, after Hely-Hutchinson had gone, Maxwell did force through a number of books, including, of course, his own biography. One of the most recently departed managing directors, Nick Webb, summed up his view of working for Maxwell in a sentence that encapsulates the feelings of so many employees: "What an old shit...I never felt such moral dread as the moments when I was forced to visit the Dark Tower."

If Maxwell was such a rogue, what was it like being married to him, or having such a man as a parent? Between 1946 and 1961, Betty gave birth to nine children, all at the same Parisian maternity home, so all have dual French-British nationality. The first-born, Michael, died within days of the youngest, Ghislaine, being born: he had been in a coma for six years after being injured in an auto crash. Another child, Karine, died at age three in 1957 of acute leukemia.

Glimpses of family life at Headington Hill Hall when Maxwell was in residence, provided mainly by Betty but never contradicted by the children, make chilling reading. Mealtimes appear to have been a trial with the children being grilled to ensure they were learning their lessons properly. Maxwell liked to lecture, drilling into each child the need for politeness—"Good manners cost nothing" was a favorite homily—in contrast to Maxwell's own legendary rudeness. He once caused his daughter, Ghislaine, to cry because she failed to define the word *theocracy* quickly enough in front of lunch guests.

He also had a heavy hand. "Perhaps he was too hard on them, but he was teaching them to take life seriously," Betty said.[17] She found his corporal punishment "absolutely abhorrent" but could not stop it. The children were required to prove themselves constantly, even to the point where he interfered in their private lives after adolescence because Maxwell viewed his family as a dynasty.

Though Betty once claimed "I don't think they resent that he's been hard on them,"[18] there are obvious signs of revolt. All have worked at one time or another for Maxwell, but the elder ones largely fled once they got the chance. He opposed most of their marriages and made no secret of the fact.

The four eldest, Philip and Anne, and the twins, Christine and Isabel, play no part in this story. Just one incident serves to illustrate the kind of father Maxwell was. Anne decided to become an actress after graduating and enrolled in Central, one of the leading London drama schools. One day Maxwell marched into the director's office to bellow, "Tell me frankly—is she making progress or is she wasting her time and my money."[19] When I told him once that my daughter was planning to become an actress he said his daughter had become unhappy by "failing"—though I never knew whether that was true—and I had to restrain him from ringing her to tell her not to do it.

Of the three youngsters over whom Maxwell appeared to exercise the greatest influence, two have major roles while the youngest, Ghislaine, has almost none at all, though on one occasion I witnessed an odd encounter between her and her father. She wandered in to his tenth-floor drawing room when we were midway through a discussion. "Sorry, Daddy," she said sweetly, but made no move to leave.

He was clearly irked with her, and my presence did not restrain him. "What's this I hear about you nearly drowning?"

"Oh, you don't mean that little accident. I dived off a boat and hit my head on a pole jutting into the water. That's all. It was nothing."

Maxwell was unimpressed. "Why do I have to hear from Signor Agnelli that my daughter has been fooling around and nearly died?"

Ghislaine, rattled, replied, "I wasn't fooling around. There was no danger."

"You were taking risks," he said, now raising his voice a little. "You're always taking risks, doing stupid, dangerous things."

"Oh, Daddy," she exclaimed, peeved to be questioned like this in front of me. "I've explained about the other times." He snorted as she continued: "I told you about jumping out of helicopter with my skis on... it won't happen again."

He sighed, said he was busy, and she left.

"Children." I said to placate him. I still had to get his signature on an important document and did not want him to lose his temper or his short-run concentration.

"She's like me," he said with some pride.

Ghislaine is said to have considered Kevin and Ian as the two complementary sides of her father, and at the superficial level there is some truth in this observation.

Each of the boys displayed certain of their father's characteristics, but neither showed any sign of Maxwell's grit, determination, and sheer bloody-mindedness. Both were also cool and logical, so they often suffered under his irrational, authoritarian rule. Both tried to escape him for a time, each temporarily leaving him, but they quickly returned to the fold.

Ian, born in 1955, joined his father after university and was managing director of Pergamon's French and German operations when he failed one day to meet Maxwell at Orly airport. Ian, then twenty-four, was trying to patch up a relationship with a girlfriend.

For this "gross dereliction of duty," Ian was fired. This incident was widely publicized at the time because Maxwell thought it presented him as a man of principle prepared to treat his son as he would any other employee. The event has haunted Ian ever since. Maxwell rehired his son months later and he became vice president of marketing at Pergamon in New York.

Ian later worked for a year "on loan" for the Prince of Wales's Trust before returning to France as an executive of a press agency acquired by Maxwell and an unhappy directorship of TF1, the French television service. He also spent three years as chairman of Derby County football club.

Invariably, anyone meeting Ian is struck by his good looks, good manners, a boyish sense of humor and easy charm. These qualities helped Ian deal with other executives with far more experience and knowledge in their fields, but nobody seeing Ian in the presence of his father could be in any doubt as to the shadow Maxwell cast over him. Of all the contributions made in the book of tributes presented to Maxwell on his sixty-fifth birthday, none is more illuminating than Ian's:

> I often think you unnecessarily use a howitzer to shoot a chicken, but when the smoke has cleared the chicken often discovers you were only firing blanks...I do wish, however, that you would apply your oft quoted principle of "a pat on the head being worth fifty kicks in the b——" more frequently— not just for myself as much as for the rest of the family and the many people that work with you directly every day.[20]

Kevin, almost three years younger than Ian, also went straight from Oxford's Balliol College to Pergamon, working almost four years there before suddenly leaving for a rival company. Haines refers to the reason for the split as "a domestic disagreement."[21] It is known that Maxwell objected to Kevin marrying Pandora Warnford-Davis, whom he had met and lived with while both were still at university. In her turn, the strong-minded Pandora had no time for her father-in-law and was outspoken enough to say so. Kevin, like all the children, was never drawn to make a criticism of his father during his lifetime and soon returned to the family firm. He later became a director of Maxwell Communications Corporation and showed an aptitude for financial affairs that led most people to assume he was being groomed to take over. He displayed great skill in being the man between his father and his wife, never revealing any tensions in public. He and Pandora have four children.

Whatever disquiet existed in the family, the steadfast Betty could be relied upon to assuage her husband's excesses. If Maxwell had been seeking an opposite as a partner, someone to reflect characteristics he aspired to but never managed to acquire, then he could not have done better than Betty. Though she has little time for small talk, she is unfailingly courteous. Nobody who has ever met her has said a bad word about her: she is dignified, elegant, well-mannered, polished, and charming.

These were qualities groomed in Betty's years growing up in the comfortable surroundings of her family's Parisian home. Her parents disapproved of their daughter's wartime whirlwind romance with Maxwell, whom they thought uncultivated and too fond of telling tall stories. They hoped Betty, two years older than Maxwell, would come to her senses, but they could not change her mind and apparently overcame their initial hostility before the marriage. After the wedding in 1945, celebrated at a Protestant church in Paris, Betty moved to Britain and set up house. For the first twenty years of married life, Betty concentrated on motherhood, giving birth to nine children. Maxwell wanted a large family, she explained often, to replace the one he lost in the Holocaust.

Her major contribution to Maxwell's public life in the fifties and sixties was her tireless work to get him elected as an MP for Buckingham. She is credited with much of the behind-the-scenes organization that led to his winning the seat in 1964 and 1966. However, she had to endure long periods alone as Maxwell flew off around the world. Gradually she built up her own life separate from her husband, concentrating on academic studies, which led her to obtain a degree in French literature at Oxford when she was forty-six. She then spent five years attaining a doctorate with a thesis on the art of letter-writing in postrevolutionary France.

Later she turned her attentions to fostering better relations and understanding between Jews and Christians. The Council of Christians and Jews is "my abiding interest" she tells everyone in her marked French accent, and she plans to help organize a second conference on the Holocaust to follow one she arranged in 1988.

By the time I met Maxwell, the couple's forty-six-year marriage had become a sham. They then lived apart. The worst Betty ever said about Maxwell was that he was "difficult." Her understatement concealed the fact that he often appeared to treat her as another employee, albeit a privileged one, whose attentions he found too claustrophobic.

In public both maintained the fiction of togetherness, but it was obvious from private observation that their relationship continued to exist in a form unfathomable to the outsider.

Betty and all the children have been trying to come to terms with the man they knew, husband and father, since his death. He was fond of saying that his greatest contribution to life was his family. But in 1967 he declared: "I do not plan to leave my children an inheritance."[22] It was the first of many occasions on which he made this prophetic statement.

4

The *Daily Maxwell*

POWER bestowed by the ownership of a business was all very well
for Maxwell. Political power, at least in the modified form of an MP,
carried no weight. The power of the press might be different.
Maxwell could not fail to notice that there seemed to be a disparity
between his confident self-image, his inflated view of his own worth,
and the sniping, caviling articles about him, often tinged with
snobbish undertones and facetious overtones.

In his dealings with journalists and newspapers after the Simpkin
Marshall collapse, there were many lessons he might have learned:
newspaper files last forever and can be referred to constantly; threats
of writs and the issuing of writs only engender greater hostility
among reporters and editors, and tend to confirm their suspicions
that "a story" exists; "success" in suppressing one story does not
remove the stain, it merely delays its spreading; newspaper proprietors are extremely difficult to manipulate.

There can be little doubt that Maxwell did successfully intimidate
the press, launching (and usually abandoning) more court actions
than any other individual in newspaper history. While this added to

48

the public perception of him as a malevolent business mogul, probably with something to hide, it did largely prevent the truth from emerging. There were exceptions, notably *The Sunday Times* during 1969, whose Insight team have remained the major source for his life story until that date. Even the authorized biography could not fault most of the facts uncovered by the Insight reporters. By the time those articles were written, however, Maxwell had already decided on his own inimitable way of dealing with a hostile press—buy it.

He failed so often it looked for years as though he would never become a proprietor. His earliest efforts in 1964 to buy two failing Labour Party–supporting newspapers, the *Daily Herald* and the *Sunday Citizen,* were misconceived. His first real chance came in 1968 when he offered to buy 25 percent of the shares in Britain's largest-circulation Sunday scandal sheet, the *News of the World.* The fear and hatred Maxwell had by now provoked in public life was such that the paper's owners, a family named Carr, decided to stop him from gaining control.

The Carrs invited a virtually unknown Australian newspaper owner, Rupert Murdoch, to act as a white knight on their behalf. Maxwell made a higher bid than Murdoch, but Maxwell's controversial reputation led to the shareholders deciding at a noisy meeting in January 1969 in favor of Murdoch. This was the beginning of Murdoch's British newspaper empire, itself the foundation for his future global media empire.

Five months later Murdoch beat Maxwell again. Maxwell approached the International Publishing Corporation, owners of the ailing daily newspaper *The Sun,* with an offer of £50,000 ($80,000). He promised it would remain loyal to Labour and be a non-profit-making enterprise. He made a tactical error by adding that his survival plan would depend on massive staff cuts, immediately ensuring the hostility of the print unions, especially the powerful Society of Graphical and Allied Trades, known as Sogat.

Maxwell was by now, in May 1969, embroiled in dealing with the problems of Leasco pulling out of their bid for Pergamon, and he could not take the time to negotiate properly. Murdoch stepped in to add *The Sun* to his *News of the World* acquisition. It is not without irony that Murdoch's *Sun* would eventually enter into a bitter circulation war with the *Daily Mirror,* a struggle that would weaken the *Mirror* and so cause the conditions that would lead to its takeover by Maxwell some thirteen years later.

It was 1975 before Maxwell was in a position to make another bid to become a newspaper proprietor, and this time the situation offered him a role he enjoyed: savior. He was asked by staff at the *Scottish Daily News,* based in Glasgow, to help rescue their paper, which was being run by an experimental employees' cooperative. It is possible to maintain that Maxwell's intentions at the outset were benign and similarly quite credible to hold the view that, Maxwell or not, the project would have failed anyway. It is also undeniable that Maxwell's involvement caused more trouble more quickly than any of those who invited him to help would ever have envisaged.

The story of Maxwell's months in Glasgow is one of continuous internecine strife, and a month after he pulled out—following a particularly savage *Sunday Times* article headlined HOW MAXWELL SABOTAGED THE WORKERS' DREAM [1]—the experiment ended in insolvency and closure after just six months' publication. Two commentators concluded that "the intervention of Maxwell...effectively ruined the project as a test-bed for new industrial relations in the newspaper industry," but added gallantly, "It is, of course, unfair to blame Maxwell for this...the opportunity presented itself and, in his own terms, Maxwell made the most of it..." [2]

There is one interesting aspect I must mention before continuing since it shows how Maxwell used people only when they toed his line and how, no matter the truth or the context, their names or service could be exploited when required, as in the rewriting of history.

When the first Department of Trade inspectors' report appeared criticizing Maxwell's activities at Pergamon, Maxwell was surprised to find himself being defended by Professor Richard Briston of Glasgow's University of Strathclyde, writing in *Accountancy* magazine. [3] Briston's trenchant criticisms were directed at the choice of one of the inspectors; at the problems Pergamon faced by sticking to "conservative accounting principles"; and at the Institute of Chartered Accountants for making Pergamon into a scapegoat for their own inadequacies. Briston described Maxwell as "unlucky."

Viewing this as a vindication, Maxwell asked to see Briston and hired him to analyze the second inspectors' report. However, academics cannot be relied upon to rubber-stamp and when Briston handed his analysis to Maxwell, "he started shouting, 'This isn't what I wanted'... He had expected me to defend him on every count and that wasn't possible."[4] Haines's reference to the second analysis cites it approvingly, as if Briston had agreed fully with Maxwell.[5]

The dispute with Briston did not stop Maxwell from recruiting him years later to act as financial adviser to the *Scottish Daily News* cooperative. Briston explained he did it "because I thought it was worthwhile, but not for Maxwell." In the course of events, Briston turned out early on to have "serious doubts" about Maxwell's involvement in the paper and became "the cooperative's most trusted adviser."[6]

In the end, Briston was forced by a Maxwell decision to resign. The professor blamed the government for failing to underwrite the project and thereby giving the cooperative no alternative but to accept Maxwell's money and therefore Maxwell's control. The Briston involvement in the project, at Maxwell's behest, was one of the major contributions to the *Scottish Daily News,* yet in thirteen pages of the authorized biography dedicated to the subject there is no mention of the name Briston.

Maxwell's next attempt to fulfill his press-baron ambitions came in October 1980 when the Canadian-based Thomson Organization ran out of patience with costly labor disputes at *The Times* of London and *The Sunday Times.* Maxwell made a bid but did not have the resources to make a fight. Once again, Murdoch beat him by buying both papers.

Maxwell briefly hoped to buy another London-based Sunday newspaper, *The Observer,* in April 1984 from the Lonrho organization, headed by Tiny Rowland. But it transpired that Rowland's talks with Maxwell were a ploy to scare his paper's independent directors, with whom he was in dispute. Maxwell was such a figure of hate that Rowland won his point. It looked to many as though this fifth failure in twenty years might end Maxwell's newspaper ambitions for all time. Within three months, at the age of sixty-one, he proved everyone wrong.

By the standards of Maxwell's previous negotiations to buy companies, those that led to the takeover of the Mirror Group of newspapers were short and straightforward. They were not, of course, without the controversy attendant on all matters Maxwellian. The mistake, as it was characterized from 1984 onward, of allowing Maxwell to become a newspaper proprietor had led critics to seek out many culprits.

Reed, the Mirror Group owners, were blamed for failing to honor their word that no individual would be allowed to purchase the group. The print unions were blamed for creating the conditions that led to Reed deciding they no longer wished to remain in charge. The senior journalists were blamed on two counts, for letting *The Sun* topple the *Daily Mirror* from its number-one circulation position and for enjoying expense-account lifestyles that were the envy of Fleet Street (and their own printers). The City institutions—stockbrokers, accountants, and their respective analysts—were blamed for failing to appreciate the true worth of the newspaper empire eventually hawked for a song. The capitalist system was blamed for its free market, in which the freedom to publish was available only to wealthy individuals.

It is difficult to fault any of the arguments, but there seems no point in apportioning blame because by approaching the problem from this direction a central truth is obscured. Maxwell was a myth-maker of epic proportions. My eyes glazed over as I heard him talk endlessly of his role as the *Mirror*'s redeemer. My heart sank on the night of 5 November 1991, when I saw the first edition of the *Daily Mirror* with its front-page headline: THE MAN WHO SAVED THE DAILY MIRROR. It was a lie. The Mirror Group newspapers in 1984 were far from healthy: the Group needed attention, probably urgently, but it was not on its knees. To suggest that the *Daily Mirror* required "saving" is akin to believing that a passerby has saved a swimmer ankle-deep in a wading pool by throwing him a lifeline.

Moreover, even if we were to accept that it did need saving, then nobody should live on under the illusion that only Maxwell could have performed the task. Other newspaper groups were transformed from loss makers with old technology and overmanning into profitable businesses in the late 1980s, largely by utilizing Conservative government legislation to eliminate the grip of restrictive trade-union practices. Asked in 1990 what his greatest achievement had been, Maxwell said, without a trace of a blush: "Restructuring the British printing industry and turning Mirror Group Newspapers from a dead duck into a profitable enterprise."[7]

To call into question Maxwell's part in this process is not hindsight. It is the plain, unvarnished truth that his was a contribution to it, not the pivotal role. More to the point, Maxwell's overblown claims are a quintessential example of his capability for turning himself into the sine qua non of British newspaper publishing. He had an image of himself that he projected and believed; then, assuming it as reality, he was baffled by anyone who contradicted it. At his mildest he would refer to unbelievers as fools; at worst, they would be perfidious conspirators involved in a vendetta against him. For Maxwell, the movement from one stage to the other was signaled by the fool moving from passive to active disbelief.

The truth is that Mirror Group Newspapers (MGN)—*Daily Mirror, Sunday Mirror, Sunday People, Daily Record, Sunday Mail,* and *Sporting Life*—returned a poor profit on a turnover of more than £250 million ($400 million) a year. Strangely the exact figures have been ignored by previous commentators, who accepted both Maxwell's myth and the general Fleet Street legend.

Haines claims the Mirror Group's profit was "minuscule"[8] while Bower says it was £1 million ($1.6 million).[9] Both are wrong. Reed's annual reports for the three years before the Mirror Group sale reveal profits of £2.1 million ($3.36 million) in 1982, £8.1 million ($13 million) in 1983, and £5.7 million ($9.12 million) in 1984. In thirteen years of Reed ownership the Mirror Group newspapers lost money in only one year, and this in an era of persistent industrial strife.

Clearly the Mirror Group was in a parlous state, but it cannot be said that £13.6 million ($21.8 million) profit in two years was a guarantee of catastrophe. If Reed had wished to invest time and energy into the Group (they did not even have a representative on the board) they might well have turned it around themselves. Reed's disenchantment was partly industrial and partly political: they had no stomach for the fight to deal with the constant grind of industrial action by thirteen separate unions (which cost them £2.8 million ($4.5 million) in potential profits in the year 1983–4 alone). Nor were many executives happy with the Mirror Group's support for Labour at a time when the party appeared to be standing in the way of what they regarded as necessary reform.

In Britain, where the press developed historically along partisan political lines, almost all the nationally distributed daily and Sunday newspapers support the Conservative Party. The Mirror Group is therefore unique among British newspapers in its fervent support for the Labour Party. It is therefore considered—by politicians of all parties and by the general public—that democracy is best served if the Mirror Group remains faithful to Labour. While this diversity of views may be desirable, in a free market it is difficult to ensure that an owner will maintain a partisan bias for the socialist party. Reed chairman Alex Jarratt's problem became apparent. He wanted to get rid of the Mirror Group but needed to come up with some mechanism to protect its political allegiance.

Jarratt also wanted to justify his decision to pull out. Reed executives hinted that their shareholders were aghast at discovering 60 percent of the Mirror Group's employees earned over £20,000 ($32,000), though there was no tangible evidence of shareholder revolt. In the end Jarratt decided the only way to get rid of the Group was to take it public. He pledged that the papers would not be sold to an individual and would remain loyal to the Labour Party. This was a direct attempt to forestall the man everyone knew would make a bid: Maxwell. A new chairman was installed, Clive Thornton, who had won admiration for the way he was then chairing Abbey National Building Society, and work began on a public share issue.

It did not take long before Thornton fell out with Reed and with senior Mirror Group executives. Worse still, accountants gathering information for the prospectus informed Reed that they could expect to raise only £48 million ($77 million) from the share issue, far less than Jarratt's board had expected and far less than the company's true worth. This information was leaked to Maxwell and enabled him, on 4 July 1984, to stun Reed with a dazzling bid. Reed's concern at the low return and their upset at continuing rows with Thornton were at their peak when Maxwell called Jarratt to offer £80 million ($128 million), with the probability of going to £100 million ($160 million). Maxwell finally had cash: his British Printing and Communications Corporation shares had risen from 12 pence (20 cents) since his 1980 takeover to 160 pence ($2.56). His bankers, particularly National Westminster, were well pleased with his performance in his rationalization of the business. Pergamon was also reporting supposedly record profits.

Maxwell not only obtained the money, he also took steps to ensure top-level Labour Party backing, winning support from the elder statesman Michael Foot and deputy leader Roy Hattersley[10] who encouraged his leader, Neil Kinnock, not to oppose Maxwell.

Reed was now caught in a trap because its duty to its shareholders was to take the best offer, but it had announced that it would not sell Mirror Group to an individual. Legal duty outranked a gentleman's word by about £50 million ($80 million), and Reed began to negotiate with Maxwell. Maxwell was eventually persuaded to pay £113 million ($180.8 million), though Reed returned £23 million ($36.8 million) owed to the Mirror Group. Reed's chief executive, Les Carpenter, even loaned Maxwell £6 million ($9.6 million) toward the final sum. The unions were upset and fearful, especially the journalists, who threatened to walk out.

One of the foremost critics was the *Daily Mirror* leader writer, Joe Haines, formerly press secretary to Prime Minister Harold Wilson, and one of the few people on the staff with some knowledge of Maxwell. His advice to Wilson had always been: "Don't touch that man with a bargepole."[11] Now he offered a packed and worried meeting similar advice, stating dramatically: "That man is a liar and a crook and I can prove it." One of those at the meeting described Haines as "red-faced and shaking his fist."[12] David Thompson, a political reporter who was leader of the journalists' union, echoed those feelings, joining with others in suggesting that if Maxwell walked in the front door then they would walk out the back. The journalists' protest withered within a day as they came to accept the inevitable: after years of having no proprietor they had the most extraordinary one imaginable.

Most of the Mirror Group journalists had grown up through the *Daily Mirror*'s golden era, when the paper was recognized as the nation's leading tabloid. It was not only the best-selling daily but had won a deserved reputation for authority and integrity. It was generally agreed that the impertinent and irreverent *Mirror* brilliantly articulated the attitudes and concerns of its working-class readership, trenchantly supporting its readers' favored political party, Labour. In 1964 it reached a sale of 5,000,000 copies a day and continued thereabouts for five years, a record that no British paper has come remotely close to achieving since.

The influence of the *Daily Mirror* in its heyday was incalculable. It was the bible of the British working class during the days when the

Conservative Party was limping through its thirteen-year period of "misrule," when Wilson's Labour Party seemed to offer a postive future forged in the white heat of a technological revolution and, sadly, when that bright hope was dashed. It is the only newspaper I remember reading as a child, and one I recall seeing in the homes of my friends, so I have a special affection for it.

However, sentiment does not keep a paper at the top of the circulation ladder. The history of popular newspapers in Britain shows that no paper has held that position for long, and the seventies saw the Mirror's former stablemate, *The Sun,* become a serious rival.

While the *Mirror* remained a steadfast backer of the Labour Party, Rupert Murdoch's *Sun* offered unstinting support to Margaret Thatcher's Conservatives. *The Sun* caught the political wind of change in the working class, and its circulation rose from under 800,000 copies daily in 1969 to 3,800,000 in 1978, overhauling the *Daily Mirror.* By the time Maxwell arrived in 1984, the *Mirror* was selling almost a million less than its rival.

Nevertheless, for £90 million ($144 million), Maxwell had in his pocket the second highest-selling British daily, the second and third highest-selling Sunday papers, Scotland's rock solid highest-selling daily, and its improving Sunday stablemate. He also had, though he did not fully realize it then, the best bargain of his life.

The analysts had done a poor job: the Mirror Building alone was worth almost the total he had paid; the pension-fund surplus was underestimated by millions; the Scottish property had been undervalued; shares in Reuters news agency were to become much more valuable than anticipated. In the weeks after he had moved into the Mirror Group's distinctive red-and-blue glass building at Holborn Circus, Maxwell was to discover he had bought the newspaper group for nothing. Haines wrote, "The Scottish papers and the MGN property... would have brought him in the region of £200 million altogether."[13]

From the day Maxwell arrived at the *Mirror,* the stories of his quirky regime steadily leaked out. None has been told more often than his quick decision to embrace his "enemy" Joe Haines, turning the previously antagonistic editoral writer into a trusted confidant who would become his ghostwriter, speechwriter, letter writer, and eventually writer of the authorized biography. Haines became an apologist and propagandist, eyes and ears for Maxwell on the editorial floor, his special negotiator with the journalists' union, his éminence grise.

A short, thin, sharp-featured man given to wearing wire-rimmed spectacles, Haines has a habit of looking anxious, like an interrogator facing a problem with his latest case. He is the fastest writer of fearsome prose I have ever known, the best tabloid editorial writer, and, if given the chance, he would probably shine at the same task for a broadsheet.

He was frank about his original hostility to Maxwell—"I was his most open adversary"[14]—and was prepared to leave when he was summoned to Maxwell's office two days after the takeover. Senior Mirror Group executives had urged Maxwell to keep him. One of them, Bob Edwards, praised Haines's skills and told Maxwell, "He loathes you, told the chapel you were a crook and said that if you walked in the front door he would go out of the back. But he's the one."[15]

Haines later told me he set conditions, that he would never have to write anything that he did not believe and that he could defend in public.

Maxwell told me he set conditions, that Haines must remain loyal to the Labour Party and to the royal family. Having agreed, Haines was immediately promoted to assistant editor and soon after became the Group political editor. David Thompson, the other critic, stepped into Haines's shoes to become *Daily Mirror* editorial writer. Both would become their master's voice without any discernible trace of bitterness and with a surprising enthusiasm.

In fact, Maxwell did not immediately institute a policy of firing, except at his idiosyncratic, small-time level, the odd security man or secretary, and the print unions decided to bide their time for a confrontation. He soothed the worries of reporters, subeditors, and editorial executives by announcing his first rule or Maxim One: "Journalists on top and management on tap."

Six years later he would still be using this Churchillian paraphrase to endorse the fiction of editorial supremacy in his papers, and it would be as meaningless then as it was at the beginning.

It was easily circumvented by Maxwell's Maxim Two: "I am not management. I am The Publisher." Therefore journalists, more particularly editors, found themselves subject to his whim. Never has an extrovert with an overweening sense of self-importance gotten to control a newspaper group and used it so flagrantly for self-aggrandizement. Even William Randolph Hearst, who was rather shy, never contemplated the personal publicity stunts indulged in by Maxwell in his first years as owner of the Mirror Group.

Without any sense of his public image he decided that the British people would clamor to buy the *Mirror* only if they could see a great deal of Robert Maxwell. He treated the then editor, Mike Molloy, as a sort of personal public-relations officer. His first venture was to publish a game to rival *The Sun*'s successful bingo. He appeared on the television advertisements to launch a £1 million ($1.6 million) prize game. This prompted *The Sun* to offer a similar prize and then to steal Maxwell's thunder by finding a top prizewinner first. The *Mirror* contest proved a disaster, but it merely served to convince Maxwell that "I know about games."

The next thing he did indicated he knew how to treat newspaper retailers: he reduced the cover price of the *Daily Mirror* and thereby caused an outcry by reducing storeowners' income. Sales did not increase, and he was soon forced to put the price up again.

He also knew about industrial-relations problems, so he asked senior *Mirror* writer John Pilger to set up a "secret" meeting with the miners' union leaders, Arthur Scargill and Peter Heathfield, to solve the 1984 strike. His intervention failed and Pilger later rang him to inquire about writing a story.

"You mustn't be taken in," Maxwell replied. "I'll get Haines to do a leader."

But he did authorize an article by Pilger about police violence, "an indication," commented Pilger, "of Maxwell's quixotic temperament and his assumption of the role of editor."[16] The use of the word "authorize" was to become a favored Maxwellian technique.

Within two weeks of giving an assurance of noninterference, Maxwell rewrote a column by the distinguished industrial editor Geoffrey Goodman. Next day, when Goodman went to remonstrate, Maxwell "put his arms around me and said, 'How can you ever forgive me for such a thing? I should never have done it.'" He said it would never happen again and Goodman said later: "I fooled myself that he'd keep his promise." This kind of activity led to the departure of star names such as Goodman, Terry Lancaster, the political editor, John Pilger, and Keith Waterhouse.

It was Waterhouse who dubbed him Cap'n Bob, a brilliant nickname that stuck, and a sample of the wit *Mirror* readers were deprived of when Keith left for the *Daily Mail,* where the paper's politics may not entirely suit him but where writers of his rare talent are treated properly.

Occasionally Maxwell would ring Waterhouse or bump into him at a party conference. "Why don't you come home, Keith?" he would ask. Waterhouse would smile and reach for a glass of champagne.

Disasters on whatever scale were turned into publicity coups for the caring Maxwell. He flew to Ethiopia to "help" with famine relief. There is a revealing piece of television news footage showing Maxwell descending from his chartered plane to pump the hand of the first man he meets. Ever aware that the cameras were on him, he began to make a pompous speech about the reasons for his visit. The man's perplexed face betrays his uncertainty about who this verbose giant is and why he, a minor airport official, should be the subject of a rehearsed address. Maxwell was incredulous that this "mercy mission" was the subject of derision in other papers. Yet, when fifty-three people died in the Bradford football club fire in May 1985, it was Maxwell rather than the *Daily Mirror* who launched a public appeal, publishing a picture of Maxwell visiting the hospital as if a member of the royal family.

Maxwell, expert on Eastern Europe, jetted into Poland in May 1985 to talk to General Jaruzelski, a dictator with his feet planted firmly in history's sands, and then gave an interview to Warsaw Radio. "The problem of Solidarity is solved," Maxwell declared. "I can talk for...Mirror Group Newspapers...we certainly will be devoting less space to Solidarity and more space to improving relations and trade between Great Britain and Poland because we both need, in the interests of our own and your prosperity, to do more trade..."[17]

A month later, after this interview had come to the notice of British papers, Maxwell wrote to *The Times* that he had "no intention of censoring the work of Mirror Group journalists. Events in Poland, including the activities of Solidarity, will be reported on their merits."[18]

The front page, naturally, was Maxwell's main forum. On one day there was the story on his "saving" Clive Sinclair's ailing computer company (which he did not) and on another a huge picture of Maxwell with Prince Charles and Prince William. "If I have appeared in the *Daily Mirror*," he later explained, "it is because my activities have been deemed worthy of appearing."[19]

There was more. He decided the papers should be promoted on meet-the-people train trips around Britain. "Largely empty meetings"[20] greeted executives and writers who should have been working back in London. Then there were his old-fashioned editorial ideas, such as the restoration of a long outdated cartoon strip, the celebration of the anniversary of D-day, and the hiring of veteran columnists.

All of this occurred against the background of that first press conference the day Maxwell took control and said: "Under my management editors will be free to produce their newspapers without interference with their journalistic skills and judgments."

As Bob Edwards, briefly deputy chairman of the Mirror Group, later wrote, "Editors who are sometimes summoned a dozen or more times a day must wonder what interference is, if it is not that."[21]

An insight into Maxwell's intimate involvement in the paper in his earliest period came during a February 1991 High Court libel trial. Sara Keays, a woman who had a child by Conservative Cabinet minister Cecil Parkinson during a lengthy affair, had written a book about their relationship. She told the court how Maxwell took part in telephone negotiations—which she had taped—when she was selling serialization rights of her book to the *Daily Mirror*.

There was laughter as the tape of Maxwell's voice, recorded in October 1985, boomed across the courtroom: "You are as safe with me as you would be with the Bank of England. Trust me, if you will. You know my record speaks for itself."

The conversation is remarkable on several levels: it should have been the editor's job to deal with Keays; it is a perfect example of how Maxwell projected himself as the quintessence of honesty; it illustrates his barterer's art of finding common cause with his "customer," transforming the negotiations from the realm of a financial transaction into a personalized act of "friendship"; and lastly, it reveals his continuing obsession with Rupert Murdoch.

During the phone call, made by Keays to sort out "misunderstand-ings" over the book serialization and to be reassured that the *Mirror* is not going to let her down, Maxwell is at pains to ensure the success of the deal:

> If there's anybody more powerful than I, then you must go and find them. Can I say to you that you're talking to Robert Maxwell? I'm not Rupert Murdoch. I'm not a hired hand... What else can I do other than to tell you that my record speaks for itself and that nobody on earth, or in heaven or in hell, will prevent me publishing your book... I hope you know that I have been through hell in my life, perhaps not as much as you have... I know exactly how you feel and I have total sympathy and understanding that you are, if I'm not offensive in saying so, paranoid about the worry, how this should be handled or mishandled.

He tells her he does not look on serializing her book as business. "This is a matter of major social, political, and human importance."

When talking about syndication rights, Maxwell says, "You are buying me personally as your agent. You don't have anybody like me on your team. You don't know me and I don't know you, but I have a feeling that you may be thinking that you're dealing with someone who's trying to pick, pick, pick your pocket. I am not."

Having to his mind given the proper assurances, he adds, "And if we do brilliantly well, no matter what our contract says, you will get money from us. We are that kind of man and that kind of organiza-tion." Later, on agreeing to the deal, comes the condescension: "You're quite a tough lady. Well done."[22]

It was this kind of center-stage role, getting involved in editorial affairs both in public and private, that led to *Private Eye* referring to the paper as the *Daily Maxwell* and caused a huge circulation drop across the three major titles, amounting to a total of one million copies. As *Marketing Week* observed: "It takes something close to genius to lose so much circulation so quickly."

It was also expensive. Harold Lind, a market analyst, commented in 1984: "There are four ways of tearing up £50 notes and stuffing them down the lavatory. They are: cutting the price of a popular newspaper, starting bingo, launching color magazines, and launching a London evening newspaper."[23] Maxwell was to do all four.

While Maxwell's self-promotion was going on, his appetite for enlarging his holdings continued. Having failed once to take over John Waddington, the British manufacturers of board games such as Monopoly, he launched a new bid in October 1984. He had built up a 23 percent stake through his various private companies, was promised 15 percent more, and chased a further 15 percent that was up for sale. Waddington employed what became known as the Leichtenstein defense with enormous relish (more of which in chapter 8), though it was probably Maxwell's own personality that led to the necessary 15 percent being sold elsewhere.

This activity could not cloak the fact that his British Printing and Communications Corporation profits fell in 1985. Maxwell's response to this poor performance was typical of the man, an attention-grabbing, publicity-seeking, ultimately ill-starred boast. His company's objective, said the annual report, was to become "a multifaceted worldwide information and communications enterprise with revenues of £3/5 billion by 1990 with profits to match."

He then set about more intercompany deals to boost BPCC, indulged in more market speculation, pulled off property deals, and discovered a new game, playing "white knight" to companies in the midst of hostile bids. This had two advantages—he made money and he made headlines. His interventions were rarely welcome though, since most (like Extel) considered this white knight more a dog of war.

He was certainly at war in the Mirror Group. In August 1985 Maxwell, decided, for sound cost-cutting reasons, that the *Sporting Life* should be typeset outside central London. The print unions immediately disrupted production of the *Daily Mirror* and Maxwell suspended publication for eleven days. The effect, according even to the official view, was that "hundreds of thousands of Mirror Group readers...started to drift elsewhere in search of their daily and Sunday paper."[24]

A truce was only temporary and in November another stoppage led to the unprecedented publication of thirty thousand *Daily Mirrors* by management. Inside was a Haines editorial with the resounding phrase: "The gravy train has hit the buffers."

This time Maxwell did negotiate sixteen hundred job cuts, which would have been impossible in any climate but the one existing in those months. The print unions were now in turmoil. New government legislation prevented the unions from using their favorite weapon, broadening disputes from one part of a company into other divisions, and there was concern over just what Rupert Murdoch was up to in his new London plant sited on the Thames at Wapping.

In the event, Murdoch's overnight move with his papers from their old headquarters to Wapping occurred in January 1986. A month later Maxwell obtained a 30 percent cut in staff at his Glasgow plant after locking them out and bragging that Murdoch's was "not a British way of doing things." Maxwell dressed up his redundancy agreements, which amounted to a reform, as a path-breaking revolution. Another myth was born.

More significant still was Maxwell's decision to restructure the Mirror Group in August 1986 by legally separating the papers' editorial from their printing facilities. The presses were transferred from the Mirror Group to a new company that became a subsidiary of Maxwell's British Printing and Communications Corporation.

This was not done to improve Mirror Group efficiency but was an expediency to boost his printing corporation's size and profit potential and, as such, it was successful. Its profits grew and its share price moved toward £3 ($4). One brilliant printing move for which Maxwell did deserve praise was the decision to buy German color presses. While the rest of Fleet Street scoffed at the idea, Maxwell charged on, sure that color pictures would give the Mirror Group papers the edge. His hunch proved exactly right. He led the pack and reaped the rewards—beating all the rivals into the field, picking up new advertising revenue and enhancing the editorial content for readers. Every other newspaper group was forced to follow him.

By 1986, the workaholic Maxwell, now sixty-three, was stretching his day further even than ever before on many fronts: he was running the Mirror Group papers with a heavy hand, interfering in the smallest detail of editorial or promotion matters; he was acquiring more companies through his printing corporation, asset-stripping an investment trust group to enable him to buy two American printworks, in turn dismantling one of those printers (Webb's of St. Paul, Minnesota); beginning to make overtures in France; and still indulging in publicity-seeking pranks that only brought him more odium.

His worst excess in 1986 was acting as savior—"I just want to be of service"—of the Commonwealth athletic games in Edinburgh, Scotland. He promised to raise £4 million ($6.4 million) to prevent the games from going under but never did and upset scores of creditors.

Afterward he boasted: "I saved the games." He succeeded in winning publicity for Mirror Group newspapers (though at what cost to their integrity can only be guessed at) and lots of publicity for himself, presenting a gold medal here and appearing next to the Queen there. He broke royal protocol by putting his arm around the Queen.

A couple of years later, when I was working for him, he asked me if we should "save" the Student Games in Sheffield. I said I thought it would be a bad idea, there was little interest, and then there was the memory of the Commonwealth Games.

"I shouldn't have done it," he sighed, eyebrows raised. I waited for a confession. Suddenly he stood, stretched, and said with a wink, "Still, I did save them, didn't I."

To help Maxwell deal with the multifarious strands of his life, he engaged in 1986 a White House–style "chief of staff," Britain's former ambassador to the United States, Peter Jay. In his youth Jay was once referred to as the cleverest man in Britain, winning plaudits as an economist and as a television current affairs innovator in company with his friend, John Birt, now director general designate of the BBC.

By the time he started work for Maxwell, however, Jay had suffered the humiliation of his wife—daughter of the last Labour prime minister, James Callaghan—having an affair with Watergate journalist Carl Bernstein. This relationship became famous because Bernstein's wife, Nora Ephron, took her revenge by writing a delightfully funny book about it, *Heartburn,* which later became a successful film.

Humiliation would become Jay's daily lot under Maxwell, as he dealt with a level of rudeness only those who have met Maxwell can properly grasp. On one occasion Maxwell accepted an invitation to Murdoch's Wapping plant and left Jay sitting for hours in the car. In fact, the courteous Jay was sometimes known as the parking attendant because he once wrote memos to ensure the space for Maxwell's Rolls-Royce was reserved. Jay did carry out a number of menial tasks and was subjected to being shouted at in front of guests, but many executives were thankful for his skills as a sort of senior civil servant. Behind the scenes it was recognized that in the Maxwellian chaos Jay provided some sort of order and good sense within the organization.

However, as so often with the courtiers of powerful and intimidating men, Jay could be too diligent in the service of his master. When I worked at *The Sunday Times* we published a number of stories about Maxwell's penchant for announcing that he was donating to this or that charity, only for the money never to be paid. Jay contacted one of my colleagues and, resting on his own reputation for honesty, urged us to drop our investigations. It could not be true, he said. But of course it was.

Much of the money Maxwell said he would donate for AIDS research was not given; money for Ethiopia was not distributed; his cash was not given to save the Commonwealth Games. Similarly, Jay's assiduous pursuit of the author Tom Bower surely went beyond that which was necessary in his position. Bower later wrote that Jay "became Maxwell's chief of counter-intelligence in the battle against me."[25]

The sad lesson for Jay was that no matter how often and high one jumped for Maxwell it could never match Maxwell's requirements. In late 1989, after more than three years at Maxwell's beck and call, Jay was dismissed. He soon became BBC economics editor, a role for which he is perfectly suited and carries out with distinction, but he has since remained loyal to Maxwell—"a primal force, who does not fit into conventional criteria"[26]—rationalizing his time with him by saying, "I had no complaints. Nothing happened that was outside what I expected or regarded as legitimate, once I'd agreed to take his money."[27]

Few people have been candid enough to admit money was their main motive for working with Maxwell. Jay's refusal to criticize Maxwell in public led the lonely tycoon to mistake the reasons behind it. In a telephone conversation eighteen months after his sacking, Jay offered him some advice on medicine for his cold. Maxwell "suddenly... said, 'You're the only friend I have.' And I said, 'Bob, don't be ridiculous.' Old-fashioned English schoolboy that I am, if you take someone's check, it is not civilized or respectable, the moment you're out of the door, to bad-mouth the guy. I didn't. And I suppose that explains why he called me his only friend. I was in no sense his friend."[28]

By 1987, Maxwell was uncontrollable and, to many of his senior managers, irrational. There was no strategic planning—he collected companies as some people do stamps, and for every company he bought he created two or three more private companies leading to his untraceable trusts. He had acquired in 1982 a north-of-England–based firm, Hollis Bros. & Educational Supply Association, principally a timber importer, but with a wide range of interests such as furniture manufacture, school equipment, and office supplies.

Maxwell used Hollis, a firm with a turnover in 1984 of £18.8 million ($30.08 million), as a takeover vehicle to acquire a disparate group of businesses and for intercompany dealings, particularly with his Pergamon Press group. In 1985 he acquired Oyez, one of Britain's major legal printing companies, through Hollis. In 1986, Hollis took nine printing businesses from Pergamon in a £30 million ($48 million) deal. Later the same year Hollis acquired the Grosvenor Group, an electronics-and-engineering company.

There appeared to be little link to publishing or printing in Maxwell's use of Hollis. In October 1986, Hollis bought a loss-making crane manufacturer, Stothert & Pitt, and the following month Hollis launched a £265 million ($424 million) takeover bid for the AE engineering group, best known as engine designers for leading car makers such as General Motors. There was, said one commentator, no "industrial logic" to Hollis, "a company with last reported profits of under £1 million ($1.6 million) swallowing AE, with profits twenty-five times that."[29] He found himself in a bidding war that he lost.

If there was a point to this apparently pointless activity, financial analysts could not divine it. Hollis engineering invested in a Bulgarian joint venture for unspecified "industrial projects," it failed in a bid for a Canadian computer software company, and it bought into a computer company in Oklahoma. How Hollis fitted into Maxwell's publishing dreams he never properly explained.

Maxwell was rarely forced into a position where he had to answer direct questions, but in November 1986 he had to do just that. He had sued the fortnightly satirical magazine *Private Eye* for libel for its allegation that he had given money to the office of Labour leader Neil Kinnock in the hope of getting a peerage. No evidence was produced in the High Court to prove the claim, but during the case other examples of *Private Eye*'s satirical sallies against Maxwell were aired.

There was a dramatic moment when Maxwell was being examined by his counsel over one of the magazine's regular jokes in which so-called lookalike pictures are presented above a spoof letter. For some time the letter was always signed "Ena. B. Maxwell, Headington Hill Hall." Maxwell's counsel referred him to one such letter under pictures showing the Duke of Edinburgh and Adolf Eichmann, the Nazi war criminal responsible for deporting Jews to Auschwitz concentration camp, where most of Maxwell's family had perished. Maxwell broke down into tears, stabbing his finger at the picture and shaking with emotion. He said: "My family was destroyed by Eichmann." He dabbed at his cheeks and eyes, apologizing to the judge for causing a delay. *Private Eye* lost the case and was ordered to pay £55,000 ($88,000) damages and costs of about £250,000 ($400,000).

Maxwell went on to publish, through Mirror Group journalists, *Not The Private Eye,* a heavy-handed lampoon of the lampooning magazine, and a book about the case, *Malice in Wonderland,* published, naturally, by Macdonald and coedited by Haines.[30] He always preferred the bludgeon to the rapier and, in so doing, lost some of the public sympathy he might have gained. The magazine's editor and writers had been unprepared for Maxwell's breakdown in the box. Although it was well known that his parents had died at the hands of Nazis, Maxwell's denial of Jewishness—at least his non-espousal of Jewishness—for most of his life in Britain tended to obscure to others the relevance for him of his religious background.

Bower reveals a fascinating incident in the late fifties when Maxwell visited New York and his then secretary noted that he visited the synagogue with his cousin, Irving Schlomovitch.[31] His secretary was surprised because he had no interest in Jewish affairs in London. In 1964 The *Jewish Chronicle* referred to Maxwell as a "Jewish MP," and he quickly wrote to them to announce that he had joined the Church of England. He refused to be interviewed by *The Jewish Yearbook* for the same reason. All his children were raised as Christians.

However, some twenty-two years later, Maxwell told the *Chronicle* that "I don't believe in any church, just God. I certainly do consider myself Jewish. I was born Jewish and I shall die Jewish."[32] Betty went so far as to suggest in a letter to the *Chronicle* in 1988 that her husband's so-called Christian conversion was "a prankish telephone call made as a joke to your paper twenty-five years ago."

It is hard to see the humor, and we should view it instead as an acute example of Maxwell's willingness to invent, even to the extent of this important facet of his life: He covered up his Jewishness during the war by assuming a series of gentile names, kept his religious background secret after the war, felt the need to distance himself formally from it in the sixties, and then embraced his Jewishness in the eighties.

By this time Maxwell had begun to trade in Israel and regularly attended functions involving the Jewish community in Britain, particularly through his wife, whose interest in matters Jewish bordered on the obsessional, though she remained a Christian.

The *Private Eye* case diverted Maxwell from the planning of his latest piece of vanity publishing, a new London evening paper. In September 1986 he had launched a glossy illustrated sports magazine, *Sportsweek,* which everyone in the business thought would fail. It lasted five months and wasted £2 million ($3.2 million), but that was a tiny sum compared with his *London Daily News* fiasco. It is possible that London could support a second evening paper. It may even be desirable. And it is even possible that Maxwell's paper could have succeeded. It was Maxwell who ensured that it did not.

I was asked to become the paper's deputy editor and met the editor, Magnus Linklater, for lunch. He struck me as an intelligent, honest, and very capable journalist, and friends who knew him confirmed that he was just that. But this was the period of the Daily Maxwell and I had a hunch that Magnus was not the kind of man who would cope with this rampaging tycoon, so I turned down the chance.

In the event, I think Magnus did rather well, but Maxwell set him an impossible task. The launch was delayed twice, and then Maxwell announced at a press conference—without informing his new editor—that his evening paper would instead be Britain's first twenty-four-hour newspaper. This single decision to have a round-the-clock newspaper effectively killed the paper before it was even launched.

Maxwell interrupted at every stage of planning, and he made a number of disastrous mistakes in organizing the preproduction, the printing, and the distribution. He also ignored the fact that Associated Newspapers, owners of the *Evening Standard,* would hardly take the publication of a rival in its monopoly market without a fight. On 24 February 1987, after a launch party of great vulgarity on which no expense had been spared, the *London Daily News* hit the streets. Well, some of the streets. Its distribution was so patchy that hundreds of street-sellers did not receive a copy. Lord Rothermere, owner of Associated, also pulled off a masterstroke by reviving his long-dead *Evening News* title and launching it on the same day, causing widespread confusion among potential readers about the "new" paper.

The twenty-four-hour concept, just as experienced journalists suspected, also confused readers. Should they buy the morning or evening edition? Maxwell responded to poor sales (probably no more than 100,000, if that) and distribution by dropping the price. Rothermere immediately cut the price of the *Evening News.* Meanwhile, Rothermere's *Evening Standard* sailed on successfully, picking up rather than shedding sales.

On 24 July, Maxwell closed the paper "with regret and reluctance" and with harsh words directed to the "failure" of the printers and distributors, as if they were somehow separate from him. He had chosen contract printing and selected the distribution firm. The *London Daily News* cost Maxwell £50 million ($80 million) at a time when he needed every bit of cash for his global adventures.

There was one relatively little-known purchase in this period that was rated a success of sorts. In October 1986 Maxwell visited Kenya as the official guest of President Daniel arap Moi, and it is not difficult to imagine Maxwell's joy at being "introduced... to the Kenyan masses at a huge public rally" in Nairobi.[33] Arap Moi asked Maxwell to offer advice on the *Kenya Times,* the struggling daily newspaper owned by his ruling party, the Kenyan African National Union.

"Our ideas coincided so harmoniously that His Excellency felt justified in taking us into immediate partnership," Maxwell said, who then bought 45 percent of the paper.

Maxwell also provided key staff from the Mirror Group: Ted Graham as editor in chief and Jeremy Thompson as managing director. Graham says that Maxwell was as good as his word, investing in computer technology and in new presses that turned the *Kenya Times* into Africa's first full-color national daily. Graham doubled the circulation to 35,000.

However, when Graham left at the end of 1988 he was virtually persona non grata in Kenya, having found it difficult to walk the line between running a party propaganda sheet and a populist paper digging out stories embarrassing to the government. Arap Moi needed no lessons from Maxwell in how to interfere. In fact, according to Graham, Maxwell seemed totally uninterested in the project, frequently making promises to return to Nairobi but breaking them all. Maxwell also established Kenya Television Network, Africa's first twenty-four-hour TV station. It was not bad for a rapid, once-in-a-lifetime visit, and since it brought him no financial reward we must imagine him saying this was a further example of his unheralded service to mankind.

The stretch of Maxwell's interests had by now grown alarmingly, without apparent logic. He began 1987 with intense interest in France. He bought a news-gathering agency, Agence Centrale de Presse, in France in January and installed his son Ian as chief executive. Three months later he invested 750 million francs ($134.3 million) of borrowed money to take a 12.5 percent stake in France's main television station TF1, and Ian was again made a senior executive. That month was significant, too, for his £12 million ($19.2 million) purchase of a yacht, which he named *Lady Ghislaine* after his daughter.

But his dream, and his promise, was of a company worth billions. That drew him to the United States, and on 18 May 1987, he made his most ambitious bid to date by offering $2 billion for the American educational publishers, Harcourt Brace Jovanovich. To get this deal in perspective, until that date only British Petroleum's 1987 bid for Standard Oil was a larger takeover bid by a British company for an

American business. Maxwell's British Printing and Communications Corporation's 1986 sales were £462 million ($739.2 million) yielding a pretax profit of £80.3 million ($128.48 million) while Harcourt's sales were £575 million ($920 million) with profits of £77 million ($124 million). Maxwell gave his bid a code name, Project Whale, because Harcourt, based in Orlando, Florida, had diversified into the ownership of theme parks, including the popular Sea World entertainment centers in Florida, California, and Texas. Harcourt also owned lucrative insurance companies. But its major activity was producing school and college textbooks, scientific and medical books and journals, which had made it America's third largest publishing business. Harcourt was, for Maxwell, a perfect fit with his Pergamon scientific publishing company. Harcourt was also in some trouble, having suspended its New York stock market quotation after announcing that it planned to issue 9.38 million new shares.

Maxwell said in public that he wanted Harcourt to agree to a takeover, but he knew it was an unrealistic hope and prepared for a fight. He set up battle headquarters in the presidential suite of New York's Waldorf Astoria and was advised by Robert Pirie, president and chief executive of Rothschild's merchant bank in New York. Maxwell tried unsuccessfully to contact Harcourt's chairman, William Jovanovich, by phone.[34]

He was forced instead to send a "courteous and friendly letter"[35] by fax, stating that he was offering $44 a share, a substantial premium on Harcourt's suspended quotation of $29.25. In total, the bid amounted to $1.94 billion.

If Maxwell were successful he would achieve at a single stroke British Printing's billionaire status, just as he had predicted. If he failed, he expected to benefit from the financial world's amazement that Rothschild's had been able to put together such a vast war chest on his behalf. One man who remained unimpressed was Jovanovich himself, Harcourt's sixty-seven-year-old irascible, reclusive chairman.

William Iliya Jovanovich, sometimes known as Billy Jo, was not prepared to hand over the venerable publishing house he had built up over almost four decades and which bore his name. He was to prove a fitting opponent for Maxwell, sharing a similar background and some of Maxwell's characteristics. Jovanovich, the son of a Polish mother and a Yugoslav coal-miner father, did not speak English until five even though born in Colorado. He worked his way through the universities of Colorado, Harvard, and Columbia before he joined Harcourt Brace as a salesman, age twenty-seven, in 1947. Within six years Billy Jo became the company's chief executive and set about turning Harcourt Brace into America's largest textbook publisher, eventually adding his name to the company's title.

Jovanovich's deep voice even sounded a little like Maxwell's. They also shared a passion for gambling. "I play in Las Vegas or wherever I can," Jovanovich said, and, referring to his family's earlier Middle Eastern origins, added, "It must be my Levantine blood."

Surprisingly for a man of immigrant stock, Jovanovich's first truculent response to Maxwell's bid—"a discourteous and hostile reply"[36]—was couched in xenophobic terms. In a lengthy rejection of Maxwell as a suitable suitor, Jovanovich declared: "The sudden, unsolicited and hostile offer is preposterous both as to intent and value. Mr. Maxwell's dealings since he emerged from the mists of Ruthenia after World War Two have not always favored share-holders—as Mr. Sol Steinberg can attest."

This reference to Saul Steinberg, chairman of Leasco, who had suffered during the Pergamon takeover affair, reopened old wounds for Maxwell. But there was more to come.

"My parents sent me to school to become an American," Jovanovich said. "That is a trust I have kept for forty years of publishing for American schools. I refuse to believe Mr. Maxwell can be allowed to preside over the largest education publisher in the United States."[37]

When he calmed down, Jovanovich issued another vitriolic state-ment declaring that Maxwell was "unfit to control" America's largest textbook publishers because he was not only a socialist with good connections in Eastern Europe but was also tainted by "hidden sources of income." This was a reference to Maxwell's Liechtenstein trusts being the ultimate owners of his British Printing and Com-munications Corporation.

A couple of days later, Jovanovich was even more forthright: "Mr. Maxwell has money, but not enough. He has ambition, but no standing. He ought to be sent packing to Liechtenstein."[38]

Jovanovich did not rely on words alone to attack Maxwell's integrity. He mounted a defense against Maxwell on every available front, marshaling congressmen, state education commissioners, and public officials representing states and cities where Harcourt was a leading employer. A Federal Trade Commission investigation was demanded by one congressman, an attempt to demand further information on British Printing's beneficial ownership in Liechtenstein. Others complained of "foreign" control of school textbooks.

It was Jovanovich's financial defense, however, which was most effective in locking out Maxwell and which would, in time, lead to Billy Jo's own fall from power. On 26 May, Jovanovich announced a recapitalization plan that meant shareholders would receive a bonus of forty dollars a share. In addition Harcourt would repurchase up to six million of its shares in the market and would issue $1 billion in high-yielding securities, known as junk bonds. To pay for this modified version of a leveraged buyout of its own shares—known as a "poison pill" defense—Harcourt would have to take on huge borrowings of $3 billion, tripling the company's debt to $2.9 billion. Harcourt, which had already had its credit rating revised downward, would be saddled for years with a vast burden of interest charges.

The poison pill was a high-risk ploy, but Jovanovich was taking few risks elsewhere. He hired Kroll Associates, a world-wide private investigation firm led by Jules Kroll and specializing in work for companies, which built up a thick dossier on Maxwell. He also hired the London banking and brokerage house, Kleinwort Benson, because he heard of their work defending British games manufacturer John Waddington against Maxwell by disclosing the Liechtenstein trusts.

Intelligence from these sources fed Jovanovich with more ammunition in his war of words. "What can be said about a man whose sources of income are hidden?" Jovanovich asked. "What can be said about a man who, on receiving a doctorate from Moscow State University in 1983, commented, 'I am confident that when the circumstances surrounding the shooting down of the South Korean plane have become fully known, people around the world will understand that the U.S. is deliberately using this as a pretext for stepping up anti-Soviet propaganda?'"

If Maxwell was stung by the vehemence of Jovanovich's attacks he did not say so in public, though later his biographer claimed that Jovanovich "delved deep into the dregs to fight off the English invader."[39] But some shots had hit their target, particularly those aimed at questioning the source of Maxwell's cash. Maxwell refused to say where he was obtaining the money. "The nature of the finance will depend on what the end price is going to be," he told reporters.[40]

But the poison pill made Harcourt unpalatable for Maxwell. If he pursued the bid he faced repaying the debt immediately, and so he withdrew British Printing's offer on 29 May. Maxwell said, "We pitched our price fairly and sensibly. They decided to hock the company."

Maxwell resorted to the courts to try to block Harcourt's plan to refinance its equity, choosing to make his legal announcement with typical Maxwellian flair—in a baseball cap bearing the name of his New York law firm, Skadden Arps. His first attempt on 1 June to dismantle Harcourt's defense accused the company of fraudulent conveyance and an illegal scheme of retrenchment. He also issued a subpoena against Harcourt investigators in an unsuccessful attempt to gain access to their findings.

Maxwell lost court actions in three states and tried instead with the federal court in New York. But on 24 July, federal judge John Keenan called Pergamon Holdings Foundation (the Liechtenstein trust that ultimately owned Maxwell's British Printing and Communications Corporation) a secret entity and ruled against Maxwell's injunction against the Harcourt recapitalization plan.

Maxwell was beaten, and he announced on 27 July that he would "terminate all litigation against Harcourt Brace Jovanovich." Jovanovich, supposedly the victor, would rue the name of Maxwell ever afterward. Jovanovich's poison pill turned into a suicide pill, especially when the October 1987 stock market crash occurred.

A month after Maxwell conceded defeat, Harcourt announced it was being investigated by the Securities and Exchange Commission concerned at the firm's repurchases of its securities and its recommendation that holders of its debt securities had to convert them into common stock by 8 June in order to receive the special forty-dollar dividend. The situation became so bad that Harcourt was forced to put assets up for sale and even considered seeking bankruptcy-court protection from creditors.[41]

But postcrash asset sales did not realize as much as expected. Harcourt's magazine publishing and school-supplies business was expected to raise over $400 million but fetched only $334 million in

November 1987. Critics now began to refer to Jovanovich's poison-pill defense as a scorched-earth policy. In the early months of 1988 the value of Harcourt's shares slumped from a peak of over fifty-three dollars to only six dollars, and the company reported substantial losses at every quarter.

In June 1989, under pressure from bankers and Wall Street, Harcourt decided to sell its six profitable theme parks and Sea World aquariums, finally accepting $1.1 billion for them from the Anheuser-Busch brewing empire, makers of Budweiser.

It still wasn't enough. In April 1990, with Harcourt continuing to make operating losses, it said it might have to sell some core publishing businesses. After thirty-four years at the helm, Jovanovich stepped down as Harcourt chief executive in favor of his son, Peter, and at the end of May seventy-year-old Jovanovich gave up the chairmanship as well. He was replaced by John Herrington, a former United States energy secretary.

Maxwell could not let the moment pass without a comment. He hinted that he might still be interested in buying some of Harcourt's publishing businesses, but he had no money by then, and one suspects he did it only to taunt the man who had beaten him off at such cost.

New men at the top made little difference to Harcourt's fortunes. In the year up to September 1990, Harcourt lost $80.9 million and its shares were trading at a dollar and a quarter. Inevitably the company was forced into a merger with General Cinema. Even that process dragged out over eleven months until November 1991, in turn causing General Cinema to suffer a $293.1 million loss that year.

So Maxwell's attempted bid for Harcourt Brace Jovanovich caused ripples for years without apparently giving Maxwell a moment's concern. The venture left him with an $8 million profit on the Harcourt stock he bought and sold, minus his legal and bank fees. So his war chest remained intact for another day.

But losing bids was to become a habit for Maxwell for a while yet. In June 1987 he agreed to buy the ailing daily newspaper *Today* from Tiny Rowland's Lonrho mining-hotels-newspapers conglomerate for about £10 million ($16 million) in the hope of reviving the *London Daily News*. Maxwell telephoned his rival Rupert Murdoch in California, ostensibly to ensure that Murdoch would continue with a printing contract on *Today*'s presses, but really to brag about his new acquisition. During the conversation Murdoch realized the deal had not been concluded. He quickly initiated his own offer of about £38 million ($60.8 million), and bought the paper from under Maxwell's nose. This was Murdoch's fourth victory over Maxwell after the *News of the World, The Sun,* and the Times Group. It would not be the last.

Around the corner for both Maxwell and Murdoch were problems that neither could foresee, beginning with the October 1987 stock market crash, heralding an era of high interest rates and a deep recession. In September Maxwell turned British Printing and Communications Corporation into Maxwell Communications Corporation (MCC). Implausibly, his chief of staff Peter Jay told the *Financial Times* that "people," whoever they were, had implored Maxwell "even if it is personally embarrassing... to get your name in the name of the company."

The change of name did not change that all-important 1981 board decision that delegated total power to Maxwell. He would continue to exercise complete control. In the shadows, as he moved into 1988, he was suffering from falling profits and a sliding share price.

Yet that boast for a £3 billion ($4.8 billion) empire haunted him still. Attempts to build in France were frustrated. He picked up a stake in an Israeli paper, the beginning of extensive business interests in Israel, but only America could provide him with the kind of arena guaranteed to achieve his ambition.

5

Macmillan: A Deal Too Far

MAXWELL knew time was running out. He was sixty-five years old and if he was to achieve his ambition, if the critics and detractors were to eat their words, then he must assume the role that he had promised himself and the world for so long: he must become a billionaire global publisher.

His ambition went beyond reason, given that he had no money, that his core company was generating little profit, that his share price was unsteady, that he had wasted millions on failed projects, that he had frittered away millions more on small purchases, that he consumed yet more millions on legal bills, not to mention his grandiose lifestyle.

By now, beset by troubles that might have broken most people in his position, he might have stopped, taken stock, gone off, as he said so often, to "smell the roses."

But we are not talking of an ordinary mortal dealing with the real world. His world had taken over. Therefore, if we remain rooted in

77

our own reality we will only end up repeating mundane questions: "Why? Why did he do it? Why didn't he..." Such "if onlys" lead us nowhere. Perhaps fiction offers us a glimpse of fact. In the Maxwell of 1988 we can see two Dickensian characters, Micawber and Merdle, meeting Trollope's Melmotte. Commentators and columnists have played a game to decide which fictional character Maxwell most resembled.

Micawber is straightforward enough—a great projector of bubble schemes that were sure to lead to a fortune but always ended in grief. Undaunted by failure, the optimistic Mr. Micawber felt something would "turn up" if he kept trying, if he kept scheming and dreaming. He was also fond of speechifying, a Maxwell trait, but Mr. Merdle, the financial speculator in *Little Dorrit,* comes closer still. Dickens tells us "Mr. Merdle was immensely rich; a man of prodigious enterprise; a Midas without the ears, who turned all he touched to gold. He was in everything good, from banking to building. He was in Parliament, of course. He was in the City, necessarily. He was Chairman of this, Trustee of that, President of the other." We learn that "Mr. Merdle's is a name of worldwide repute. Mr. Merdle's undertakings are immense. They bring him in such vast sums of money they are regarded as...national benefits. Mr. Merdle is the man of this time. The name of Merdle is the name of the age." If we have in mind the *Daily Maxwell,* then it is no surprise to read that "Mr. Merdle's right hand was filled with the evening paper, and the evening paper was full of Mr. Merdle. His wonderful enterprise, his wonderful wealth..."

However, the "bloated" and "horrid" figure of the financier Augustus Melmotte in *The Way We Live Now* has a similarity with the two-hundred-eighty-pound Maxwell that is hard to ignore. Melmotte, too, had "rough thick hair, with heavy eyebrows...he looked as though he were purse-proud and a bully." Moreover, Melmotte sprang from obscure origins and "declared that he was an Englishman," speaking the language "fluently, but with an accent which betrayed a long expatriation." Melmotte also shared Maxwell's delight in cultivating foreign statesmen. Like Merdle, it was his image of wealth that opened the vaults of banks. "O, what a wonderful man this Merdle, what a great man, what a master man, how blessedly and enviably endowed—in one word, what a rich man!"

Maxwell, who never read books of any kind, might not have heard of Melmotte but for a very bold report in 1987 by Henry Poole, an analyst at his then stockbrokers Alexanders, Laing and Cruickshank, entitled *Unraveling the Melmotte skein*. This purported to show that, unlike Melmotte's, Maxwell's finances were not a figment of his imagination. Twelve months later the truth was to dawn on Poole: his choice of Melmotte was more apt than he realized. Turning once more to Merdle, bankers might identify with the character who asked if, by investing with him, loss might just be possible. "Can't be done," asserts one of his fans. "Name up everywhere—immense reserves—enormous capital—great position—high connection—government influence. Can't be done!"

Both committed suicide on the eve of their frauds becoming public knowledge, unable to deal with the humiliation of being found out and the disgrace of their punishment. Merdle slit his throat in a Turkish bath while Melmotte took a dose of prussic acid. Both these fictional characters were based on real swindlers. Dickens had in mind John Sadleir, MP, briefly a junior lord of the Treasury, who fraudulently obtained vast sums from an Irish bank and the Swedish railway company in the 1850s. Mr. Sadleir poisoned himself on Hampstead Heath. Trollope's Melmotte was created in the image of Baron Grant, master of grand gestures and builder of follies, who was born Albert Gottheimer in Dublin and ennobled by Victor Emmanuel II. He became a British MP and is best remembered, if at all, for buying a large site in London, turning it into a garden, and presenting it to the city. It was called Leicester Square. Grant was eventually found to have little real money, was declared bankrupt, and died in poverty.

Perhaps in this television world it is easier to see Maxwell in terms of a tycoon in the mold of a TV soap opera character. He had all the trappings of vast wealth. He flaunted the yacht, the plane, the helicopter, the Rolls-Royces, the personal retinue of staff. He had entrée to political leaders, capitalist and communist, monarchs and presidents, anyone he cared to name, anyone he dared to fool, and he dared to fool anyone. Yet he knew, and he knew that they knew, he was still outside the billionaire bracket. He lived like one but he wanted to be one.

Only America could provide him with the size and status he required. At the end of 1987 he made a bid for the Illinois-based publisher Bell & Howell, but conceded defeat when a consortium organized a leveraged buyout for $678 million. By a little planning and a stroke or two of good fortune, 1988 would be the year his fortunes changed.

During his French adventures he had been so impressed by a managing director of the bank Credit Lyonnais, Jean-Pierre Anselmini, that he hired him as a vice president of Maxwell Communications Corporation. The eager and energetic Anselmini would be in charge of strategy. Although he hoped Anselmini would smooth his path for French acquisitions, it would transpire that Anselmini's connections would become useful for Maxwell's American ventures.

He had also built a relationship with Bob Pirie, the chief executive of Rothschild in New York, following their Harcourt Brace Jovanovich bid. In spite of the genuine financial plight of MCC, the banks had not realized what lay behind the figures in the annual reports of 1987 and 1988. Maxwell was their friend, the man who paid them back on time. He was rehabilitated. Eccentric, maybe, too full of himself, but what a track record: look at what he had done for British Printing (now MCC) and the Mirror Group. Everyone had chosen to forget the Department of Trade Inspectors' reports of some fifteen years before.

Under his new *Daily Mirror* editor, Richard Stott, he had agreed to confine his self-publicity to "page two only" and the *Daily Maxwell* jokes had subsided. What he could not face was a book about his life that would, in his view, "dredge up" his past, a past he had spent time and energy and lots of money through lawyers to cover up. Moreover, it would probably be "full of lies" from his "enemies." Whatever it said, Maxwell felt sure Tom Bower's book, *Maxwell: The Outsider,* would do him harm if he left it unchallenged, and he therefore decided to "deal with it" in the way he knew best.

In February 1988, weeks before its publication, he issued a writ, the first of twelve. When that tactic failed to stop the book that was then being serialized in *The Sunday Times* and being sold, he began to intimidate booksellers so that all but a very few of them eventually stopped ordering it from the publishers. The other unsecret weapon was his own authorized biography, *Maxwell,* by Joe Haines, which he prevailed on Stott to serialize in the *Daily Mirror.* I have touched on only a few of the distortions and omissions in that book, which effectively whitewashes his business dealings, particularly his maneuvers at Simpkins and Pergamon.

Bower, meanwhile, reacted by suing Maxwell, a bold step, but just as money and power can quickly summon the law with gagging injunctions so it can slow it down with cross-petitions and pettifogging obfuscations. The case was still awaiting trial when Maxwell died.

In the same year Maxwell also managed to prevent the publication of a second book, by the former *Sunday Mirror* editor, Peter Thompson, and another Mirror Group executive, Tony Delano. He told me that every copy of the book had been pulped. In fact, the books were stored and have since been issued. However, Thompson and Delano and their publishers suffered the usual Maxwell legal torture, paying out money to defend themselves from writs.

His reputation intact, as far as both he and the banks were concerned, Maxwell then turned to his great American bid. In clearing the decks he suddenly sold off nine of the engineering company interests he had bought through Hollis Brothers to a management team for £105.5 million ($168.8 million). He even sold one loss-making furniture manufacturer to the Hollis finance director for £1 ($1.60).

We have to view Maxwell's financial standing at this time in the context of the prerecession world of 1988. For several years entrepreneurs and corporations had indulged in a succession of huge acquisitions. Interest rates were relatively low. The banks were competing fiercely with each other to lend money, often financing the most expensive takeovers.

This period was marked by bids forcing up company prices to levels that could not be justified even by the most optimistic of earnings projections. So Maxwell found money relatively easy to come by, as long as he was prepared to take the long-term risks. Following his Harcourt Brace Jovanovich failure, he was more determined than ever to succeed, and his target this time was Macmillan, a substantial publishing company with any number of valuable subsidiaries, such as Collier's encyclopedias, Que computer publishing, Michie legal publishers, and a direct marketing group that included book clubs. Macmillan also owned 56 percent of the prestigious Berlitz language schools and was joint owner with McGraw-Hill of America's second largest textbook publisher.

Famed as the publisher of Ernest Hemingway and Scott Fitzgerald under its acquired imprint Scribners, Macmillan was founded in the last century as an offshoot of the British publishing house that bears the same name. Sold off by its parent in 1952, Macmillan of New York passed through a number of hands before it was bought in 1980 by Edward "Ned" Evans, whose background was in the steel industry. He was credited with successfully turning Macmillan around and making it into a profitable general and educational publisher. In the acquisitive late eighties, however, in an industry that had undergone a flurry of mergers and takeovers, Macmillan was viewed as the last large and attractive independent target.

In the face of persistent threats of a takeover, Macmillan chairman Evans and his president, William Reilly, prepared to erect an elaborate shareholders' rights plan to defend Macmillan against acquisitive rivals. Their first hostile bid came in May 1988 from the Bass Group, a Texas corporation controlled by oil billionaire Robert Bass. Macmillan's shares traded at fifty dollars before Bass's first offer of sixty-four dollars a share, valuing the company at $1.65 billion. Evans and Reilly responded by rejecting the bid and announcing a recapitalization plan worth $1.66 billion that involved splitting Macmillan into two separate divisions. Their defense also included raising a mortgage on the company's New York headquarters and lucrative severance payments, known as "golden parachutes," for Evans and Reilly.

Bass came back with an improved offer—of seventy-three dollars a share—before Maxwell joined the battle. He had lost his 1987 bid for Bell & Howell to Robert Bass but was determined to win Macmillan at any cost. His first bid was eighty dollars a share. It was, like much that Maxwell did, both shrewd and foolish. Shrewd because he correctly gauged that Bass would drop out, but foolish because in spite of his white-knight approach he knew his bid would be viewed as hostile, because it was his first offer and therefore he would have to improve it and because the company was not worth anything like as much as the $2.35 billion his offer totaled. Reality did not intrude.

"I will not pay a stupid price," said Maxwell, already offering at least ten dollars more a share than most analysts believed was financially sound.

Derek Terrington, analyst at Phillips & Drew stockbrokers, immediately forecast that Maxwell might have to go to ninety dollars a share and, if he did, "debt servicing costs in the first year will outstrip Maxwell's earnings by about £45 million ($72 million)."[1] In a further prophetic judgment, Terrington observed: "Maxwell's strategy looks more like a threat to his own shareholders, rather than a promise of good things to come."[2]

In public Evans treated Maxwell, as he had treated Bass, with a defiant no. In private, he and Reilly decided to improve on their Bass defense. Evans met Maxwell and offered to sell some of the company's assets, but Maxwell insisted he wanted everything and he would win because "nobody could afford" to top him in an auction due to alleged operational economies available through a merger.[3]

Evans and Reilly then sought an accommodation with Kohlberg Kravis Roberts (KKR), specialists at defending companies against hostile bids, in an attempt to arrange a deal that would effectively lock Maxwell out. Court records show that Macmillan management, led by Evans, had been so determined to beat off the original Bass bid that they misled the board on a number of occasions.[4] Once Maxwell bid and KKR were contacted it became obvious that Evans was "acting alone in his own personal interests."[5]

From 13 August, when Maxwell formally made his eighty-dollars-per-share all-cash offer, Evans encouraged KKR to outbid Maxwell in a series of raised bids. Maxwell improved his offer to eighty-four dollars a share. KKR raised it to eighty-five. Maxwell, relishing the fight but seemingly oblivious to the financial pressures he was about to impose on himself, offered $86.60. In effect, Maxwell was preparing to pay in the region of $300 million more than its perceived value for Macmillan.

Surely in this situation the banks would be rational; they would not fund a bid too far. Yet the opposite was true. Samuel Montagu, the London-based merchant bank, had put together a loan of $1 billion, and there was a further loan facility of $1.2 billion arranged by Crédit Lyonnais, the former employers of Maxwell's new deputy chairman, Jean-Pierre Anselmini. The French state-owned bank, itself keen to become a global player, was leading a mainly foreign syndicate—Crédit Agricole and Societé Generale of France, the Swiss Bank Corporation, and Japan's Long Term Credit Bank—though Barclays was also involved. Maxwell, the gambler, was being bankrolled at a time when the wider view among investors was extremely negative with MCC's share price dipping below £2 ($3.20), down from almost double a year before.

It is extremely difficult to explain the banks' enthusiasm for Maxwell. None of them have offered a coherent explanation since, and no external commentator has offered a logical reason for banks providing Maxwell with almost unlimited funding. It is true that Maxwell's track record on paying back bank loans was good and that the climate in 1988 was conducive to credit. It is also true that banks do tend to loan money to those people known to be borrowing from other banks. Indeed, banks exist to make money by lending out money. However, it remains a mystery why so many banks loaned so much to one man when there were so many skeptics in the financial world warning about both Maxwell's own credibility and his main company's internal problems.

The fact of Maxwell's borrowing power was not the only bizarre factor in the Macmillan takeover battle. On the other side, Evans was prepared to take enormous risks to keep hold of the publishing house. At a meeting between Maxwell and Evans on 8 September, Evans announced that his management would recommend to the Macmillan board a leveraged buyout by Kohlberg, Kravis Roberts and that he would not consider Maxwell's outstanding offer despite Maxwell having said he would pay "top dollar" for the company.[6]

Maxwell was undeterred by Evans's hostility, and bidding continued. Maxwell raised his offer to eighty-nine dollars a share, which KKR countered with $89.50, but since the Maxwell bid was in cash and the KKR bid involved a mixture of cash plus securities, Macmillan's financial analysts considered the offers too close to recommend either as the winner.

Then came what was to be the turning point: Evans broke the auction rules. With Reilly present, Evans telephoned a KKR representative to "tip" him about Maxwell's bid, revealing the offer price and informing him about the bids being too close to call.[7] KKR increased its bid to ninety dollars just before the close of auction and still later raised it again, to $90.05, which the Macmillan board was persuaded by Evans and Reilly to accept. The moral and legal high ground, an unusual place to find him, was now Maxwell's. He quickly offered twenty cents more than KKR and sued Macmillan for denying shareholders the better offer.

Maxwell was delighted to discover that when KKR filed documents with the Securities and Exchange Commission on 29 September, the Evans "tip" to KKR was disclosed. Maxwell lost his first court action because the judge ruled that "although KKR was consistently and deliberately favored throughout the auction process, Maxwell was not prevented from . . . submitting a higher bid."[8]

But Maxwell won his case on appeal. The court decided that Evans's and Reilly's self-interest and "deliberate concealment of material information from the Macmillan board must necessarily have been motivated by an interest adverse to Macmillan's shareholders."[9] The judge laid emphasis on the impropriety of the Evans "tip" to KKR: "Evans's and Reilly's knowing concealment of the tip at the critical board meeting of September 27th utterly destroys their credibility. Given their duty of disclosure under the circumstances, this silence is an explicit acknowledgment of their culpability."[10]

The judge specifically dismissed Evans's contention that the tip had not prevented Maxwell from making a further bid, pointing out that it had given an "unfair, tactical advantage" to KKR.[11]

So Macmillan was Maxwell's. There are many paradoxes in Maxwell's life, but it is richly ironic that someone else's act of deception was about to engender Maxwell's final phase of crookery on a colossal scale. He had brought off his billion-dollar deal and gone into debt to the tune of $2.6 billion to take over a company worth almost $1 billion less. "The market is stunned," he said afterward.

He continued to stun everyone. Five days before concluding the Macmillan deal he had paid Dun & Bradstreet $750 million for Official Airline Guides, an excellent and profitable company, but once again it had cost him far too much.

In one wild week he had taken on $3 billion of debt. Maxwell had also been buying in Britain, paying £134 million ($214 million) for AGB Research, a market research business that held the lucrative contract for Britain's television audience sampling.

And there was more. He attended the funeral of a friend of Silvio Berlusconi, the Italian media mogul, and on a handshake with a member of the Panini family agreed to buy 84 percent of the Panini football-stickers-and-albums group for £60 million ($96 million). AGB and Panini were thereafter to drain away money. In February 1989, he bought Thomas Cook Travel, America's fourth largest agent, from Dun & Bradstreet for $30 million.

How would he afford it all? His first response was to announce a change of strategy—"I am a publisher and not a printer"—and to put his printing plants up for sale. this was a typical top-of-the-head Maxwellian gesture, a headline-grabbing notion, but the financial press and the various media analysts in brokers throughout London's financial district were not fooled by it. Sales, even if buyers could be found at decent prices, would not answer the need. The central question remained: How would he fund the massive loan repayments to the banks based on the profitability of his core businesses?

We might also speculate on why the banks were not worrying about the same problem. Did any banker not ask: How will this man pay us back? Perhaps they thought, as so many had been led to believe, that Maxwell's legendary golden hoard in Liechtenstein would come into play. But why did they not stop to ask themselves that if he really did have a £1 billion ($1.6 billion) treasure he hinted at so often, then why had he not used it rather than pay interest on borrowed money? Though bankers were apparently happy, most of Britain's financial journalists were quick to warn of future problems.

Maxwell always reacted to bad publicity by erecting a smokescreen of activity that he imagined would fool his critics. The message he always wished to convey was that he was under no special pressure. With journalists and analysts raising questions about the unlikelihood of Maxwell Communications Corporation affording its new debts after the Macmillan victory, Maxwell flew off to the Soviet Union.

Many months before, he had asked my wife whom she would most like to interview. With hardly a moment's thought, Noreen said, "Raisa Gorbachev." Maxwell, palms outstretched, ever the braggart, replied, "I am the very person to make it happen."

She heard nothing until Peter Jay called one morning with a typically dramatic Maxwellian message: "The Publisher wants you to accompany him to Moscow. You will interview Mrs. Gorbachev." Noreen joined Betty Maxwell and Joe Haines on a flight to Frankfurt to meet Maxwell, who had flown there in his private jet from Spain, where he had been holding court on his yacht to tell the world about his Macmillan acquisition. As Noreen boarded the plane, a beaming Maxwell said, "Am I not a man of my word? Do I not keep my promises?"

Toward the end of the flight Maxwell rose from his bed, and after his usual lengthy toilette, gathered everyone together for an in-flight conference. Betty suddenly asked her husband: "Bob, why am I here? I don't understand what I'm supposed to be doing."

He gave her an indulgent smile. "This is what the plan is," he said. "Do I have your full and undivided attention? When we meet the Gorbachevs I will introduce you, Betty, as my wife. In turn, you can introduce Noreen to Mrs. Gorbachev as your personal assistant. Noreen will then brief you on what questions to ask and you, in turn, can relay the answers to Noreen. Meanwhile, I shall be involved with Mikhail. And Joe shall write up my interview."

So there was no arrangement. Maxwell was about to fool the president of the Soviet Union and his wife into providing the *Daily Mirror* with interviews.

Nevertheless, Maxwell clearly had a lot of pull. The Maxwell party had their passports taken and returned to them before leaving their plane, they were met by chauffeur-driven Zils and two sable-coated women arrived with flowers for Betty. As Noreen stepped into the limousine, Maxwell whispered, "Be careful what you say. They're probably KGB."

The next day, while the Maxwell party was gathered in his hotel room, three men arrived—with a message: "Mr. and Mrs. Gorbachev wish you a happy Christmas and many greetings for the new year, and hope they will be able to see you next time you're in Moscow."

It was one of those rare occasions on which Maxwell displayed embarrassment. "As you can see," he said to everyone, while studying the carpet, "I did my best." Noreen and Joe returned to Britain and Maxwell flew off to another European capital, but his courting of the Gorbachevs would continue.

Flying across Europe, Maxwell invented the fifteen-month year. Having put all his effort into the purchase of Macmillan, and taken up much of his senior staff's time and energy, he knew the accounts for Maxwell Communications at the end of December 1988 would not be ready. By "ready" he meant that they would need to be to the liking of investors and shareholders. He was alerted to the problems—the lack of genuine profits from his businesses—and knew the figures would be bad enough to make his shaky share price less stable than it already was. He therefore decided to announce that the year-end would now be delayed from December until March 1989, giving him time to pull off deals that would boost the profits and to set in motion some of the disposals necessary to ease the debt burden.

It was one of Maxwell's endearing characteristics that if he received no bad publicity in newspapers he imagined that all was well in the world, but brokers had greeted the news with growing skepticism. Even the loyal Henry Poole at his own brokers was rumored to be disillusioned by the Macmillan deal and its immediate aftermath.

From 1981 most of Maxwell's misbehavior in British Printing and then Maxwell Communications had been in massaging accounts by an endless round of intercompany deals. He had pulled strokes, cut corners, teetered on the edge of illegality. He had broken the spirit of stock-exchange rules but not the letter. People might suspect he was a crook but he had never allowed them to gather enough evidence to prove it. By issuing writs he had even prevented them from hinting it. He was, he felt, clean.

The financial world was unconvinced as analysts began to pore over figures and informed investors of the frightening indebtedness of MCC. The share price, which had reached almost four pounds ($6.40) began to fall. Maxwell bluffed: he announced lists of disposals, sometimes differentiating little between completed deals, anticipated deals, and daydream deals, and —to pretend that he was unruffled—he continued to act as if he were still rich enough to go on buying. Well, it was partly bluff and, by now, so ingrained into his character, he could not stop himself. He wheeled his shopping trolley around the world's media businesses and bid wherever he could, wasting countless thousands on brokers and lawyers' bills.

In February he dispatched John Blake, his former *People* editor, to Florida to start negotiations for the National Enquirer Group; he launched a giveaway paper in Glasgow; to the consternation and outright opposition of the staff, he tried in April to buy the *Jerusalem Post;* in the face of hostility from the Australian government he made two attempts to buy *The Age*.

The printer-turned-publisher baffled onlookers by even more suprising ventures. He increased his interests in Israel, buying 30 percent of Scitex, an electronics scanning equipment manufacturer, and "raised eyebrows" by taking an expensive stake in Teva Pharmaceuticals. He also entered into a deal with the Soviet Union to buy Finnish paper mills.

His single public concession to the "pressure of work" was his announcement that he would have to "cut back" on his charitable interests. His problem was, he explained, that he could not say no: "If I were a woman, I would always be pregnant." In March, under pressure from newspapers inquiries into his many broken public promises, he gave up his post as the chief fund-raiser of the National AIDS Trust, which he had launched some two years before.

Privately, secretly, Maxwell began to panic.With the recession biting and interest rates rising, he could find few buyers for his disposals. He needed money to pay back his bank loans and he had long been using a unique but risky way of getting new loans from banks—by pledging his Maxwell Communications Corporation shares as collateral. The best way of explaining this is by comparing it with a housing mortgage. A building society or bank loans a house-buyer money based on the value of the house. In effect, Maxwell decided to mortgage his shares, a device known witheringly in banking circles as "pig on pork."

The risk though is that shares, unlike houses, are volatile. The banks therefore attach an important clause to these kinds of loans: If the share price falls below a certain agreed level then more shares are required to be handed over as additional guarantees. Maxwell had been involved in these loans since at least 1986, when his private companies mortgaged 115 million shares in MCC. In subsequent years there were additional "pig on pork" loans. From the outside, in hindsight, it is easy to see the madness. Maxwell had taken on vast bank loans to buy Macmillan and Official Airline Guides. Now he was raising more bank loans to fulfil his requirement to pay off the earlier loans, and he was relying on his Achilles heel—his share price—as security.

He tried to make the best of the MCC figures at the end of March 1989, his fifteen-month year. The profit of £192 million ($307.2 million) on a £1.4 billion ($2.24 billion) turnover was not spectacular but a close look at the composition of the profits revealed his major underlying problem. Publishing profits, the core of the business, were down, and he had boosted the main figure by including a raft of exceptional one-time items, such as property sales and his beloved currency speculations. His other trick was to omit from the figures any reference to Macmillan. Shareholders would have to wait until the next report. It also prompted him to announce that his great boast of four years before about building a £3–5 billion business was now "meaningless" since he was big enough already.

This announcement "astounded many Maxwell watchers"[12] and the MCC share price dropped again. He hinted at taking the Mirror Group public, through he had twice made similar announcements without ever doing so, but it was his dismantling of Macmillan that caused most to wonder at Maxwell's confused operations. Why borrow to buy a wonderful, profitable company and then start selling off some of the best bits and pieces?

Maxwell had not forgotten his old intercompany experience either. On 1 June, he put on his private Mirror Group hat and offered £270.3 million ($432.48 million) for its printing presses owned by MCC. Then he put on his MCC hat and accepted it. He was misusing the profitable arm of one private company to shore up another unprofitable public company. Mirror Group might never have been forced to pay such a handsome price for the presses in a free market.

When Maxwell bought Macmillan he said he had "no intention of breaking it up,"[13] but it soon became clear that he proposed to dispense with some subsidiaries. In December 1988, Macmillan sold Michie, the legal publisher, to Mead Corporation for $226.5 million. This was quickly followed by an attempted sale of two book-club and direct-marketing divisions and a trade-magazine publisher, said to be worth $400 million, to Kohlberg, Kravis Roberts. But KKR suddenly pulled out. Then two peripheral Macmillan businesses were sold off. In May 1989, Katherine Gibbs Secretarial Schools and technical schools division went for $31.5 million, followed by Gump's, the specialty stores and mail-order firm, for $36.5 million.

In another little publicized British deal, which meant nothing to many, Maxwell paid £12 million ($19.2 million) to buy a 14.5 percent holding in Andrew Lloyd Webber's Really Useful Group, an example not of whim but of the extent the cash-strapped tycoon was willing to go to harass Tom Bower. Bower's book had been published by Aurum Press, which had been bought by Lloyd Webber. It is to the composer's great credit that he did not allow this unwelcome holding by Maxwell to deter him from continuing to support his beleaguered author.

In September 1989, Maxwell had to admit in public that the debt was beginning to hurt him, but he did so, of course, by suggesting the opposite. Maxwell Communications' annual report announced that he needed agreement for a reshuffling of loans, increasing the company's borrowing powers from £2 billion ($3.2 billion) to £2.8 billion ($4.5 billion), to allow the "prompt consolidation" of Official Airline Guides. It also forecast that by March 1990 MCC would have sold all its remaining printing and noncore businesses. Six weeks later Maxwell announced, in the *Daily Mirror,* that thirty-five of the world's biggest banks were advancing him $3 billion (£1.8 billion) "one of the biggest of its kind." Maxwell boasted: "The money will be used to repay debt and to strengthen our businesses everywhere."

There can be only one explanation for the banks lending Maxwell yet more money at this point. Their major hope of ever getting their original loans back relied on Maxwell Communications continuing to trade. There was, however, an insistence that Maxwell dispose of assets, a demand that he appeared to treat in cavalier fashion because the deeply indebted Maxwell's appetite for new ventures showed no sign of slacking.

In November 1989 he announced that he was buying 40 percent of Hungary's largest-circulation paper, *Magyar Hirlap,* for $800,000, a cheapish price tag that attracted criticism within Hungary. But the MCC share price was now below 200 pence ($3.20), and he was under so much pressure that he could not avoid selling one of the more valuable of Macmillan assets, the Berlitz language schools. He called in Goldman Sachs to organize a public share offer of 44 percent of Berlitz in New York, hoping to raise $400 million, but nothing came of the move at the time.

One bizarre footnote to the end of 1989 was a *Daily Mirror* cartoon that had, hidden in letters so tiny amidst the squiggles of the ink drawing that they could hardly be seen by the naked eye, the words *Fuck Maxwell.* Once this came to light, with *Private Eye* and rival papers gleefully publicizing it, a furious Maxwell ordered an inquiry, during which the cartoonist, Charles Griffin, denied vehemently that he had written the offending words.

Maxwell's security officer, John Pole, was still carrying out the investigation when I joined the paper as editor. After presenting me with a lengthy and detailed report from a handwriting expert, which named Griffin as the only possible culprit, I questioned Charles. He denied it and, in fairness to Pole, who would later turn out to be one of Maxwell's more devoted servants, he quietly dropped the matter.

If I had known all that I have written so far on Maxwell in December 1989 I would not have made my fateful decision to join him. But on December 27, after thinking deeply for twenty-four hours about becoming editor of the *Daily Mirror,* I called Maxwell to say I would be pleased to accept his offer. I contacted my then editor, Andrew Neil, who understood why I should take the job but wondered aloud about the problems of working for Maxwell. I later spoke to Rupert Murdoch, who joked, "We'll see you back soon." Early in the morning of the 29th, Maxwell called to say he was making a public announcement at 11 A.M. The most remarkable months of my working life were about to begin.

6

"I Treat My Editors Like Field Marshals"

W E cannot understand Maxwell unless we get much closer to him to see how he exercised power. For fourteen months—from 31 December 1989 until 4 March 1991—barely a day, sometimes hardly an hour, would pass when I was not in touch with him. Or, more properly, when he was not in touch with me. To my mind, I was editor of the *Daily Mirror*. In his mind, I was merely another employee and, as such, a servant. He was fond of saying; "I treat my editors like field marshals." As the man in a position to hire and fire field marshals he therefore saw himself as a head of state.

During my months with Maxwell I was afforded a close, almost intimate, view of the man when under the greatest financial pressure of his life. Such was the compartmentalization of his companies, indeed his mind, that it was difficult at the beginning of our relationship to catch even a glimpse of his other worlds outside the

Mirror Group. But there were times beginning in the autumn of 1990 when, seeming not to care, he would allow overlapping conversations to occur. For the quick-witted, discerning listener there were enough clues to build up an understanding of the other compartments, to grasp a pattern in his behavior and that of the people who came to see him. Indeed, friendships with people from his other worlds proved to be more fascinating in the final months of my time with him than my own job.

Daily life in Maxwell's world was chaotic. The only routine consisted of no routine. In residence he sometimes descended as early as 7:30 A.M. from the tenth floor to the ninth in Maxwell House, a building situated next to the *Mirror*'s London headquarters near Fleet Street. By that time receptionists were in place behind the glass doors, operated by special security cards, and at least one secretary was working in his outer office. Three or four more would arrive within hours, each with a grandiose title: personal secretary, diary secretary, program organizer, mail secretary, and so on. The turnover of these staff was legendary: some left because they could not stand Maxwell, many were fired at Maxwell's whim. None of them escaped his temper and his tongue.

On one of my earliest visits he shouted into the telephone for whoever answered to come in. A pale young girl, no more than nineteen, appeared with a notebook and pen. "Get Mr. Yaacov Neeman on the phone and tell him I'm coming next week. I want him to arrange a meeting with Mr. Shamir. Then tell that idiot Cole to organize this," waving at her a slip of paper bearing a couple of lines of his unintelligible scrawl.

She started to leave and I realized she did not know either that Neeman was Maxwell's Israeli lawyer nor was she sure that the Shamir Maxwell was referring to was the Israeli prime minister, Yitzhak Shamir. Instead of asking Maxwell, whom she obviously feared, she decided to ask someone in the outer office. Maxwell had other ideas. As she opened the door to leave, he said, "What's your name?"

"Kim."

"Well, Kim, what have I told you to do?"

She consulted her book and stammered: "First, I've got ring Mr. Neeman—."

Maxwell interrupted: "What's Mr. Neeman's first name?"

The girl was too flustered to admit she did not know.

"Well, what is it?" said Maxwell, whose voice was rising as he began to shout.

Kim said, "I'm not sure."

"Well," thundered Maxwell. "How can you ring him then?"

The girl said nothing. Her knees were shaking, and the other people in the room seemed distressed at this degrading scene.

None of us could look at the girl but none of us spoke up. Maxwell said: "Write this down. Y-A-A-C-O-V. Yaacov. Have you got that now?"

He repeated the performance to spell Yitzhak Shamir's name before the girl was allowed to leave. But Maxwell had not finished. He immediately hit the key on his console telephone—he rarely picked up the handset—to ask Kim another question: "What number are you ringing for Mr. Yaacov Neeman?"

"I don't know yet, Mr. Maxwell," she replied.

He winked and asked: "Where are you going to find it?"

"I don't know yet, Mr. Maxwell."

"Come in again, Kim." His voice had an edge of menace.

In came Kim, paler than before and close to tears, staring at the carpet to avoid his eyes and ours.

Maxwell said: "Have you found Mr. Neeman?"

"Not yet," she said clearly, adding, "I haven't had time—"

"But you don't have a number. How could you ring him?"

"I was going to ask somebody."

"Who?" asked Maxwell.

After a moment's thought the girl remembered the name of Maxwell's faithful aide from the public-relations office: "Bob Cole."

"Fuck Cole," Maxwell screamed, bringing his fist down on the table with a terrifying bang. "What the fuck's Cole got to do with it? He knows nothing."

The girl stared into a corner of the room.

"Why didn't you ask me for the number?"

"I-I-I didn't think—"

"You didn't think. How long have you been here?"

"Two weeks, Mr. Maxwell."

"What are we paying you?"

Kim was so frightened and befuddled she could not remember and could not speak. Maxwell turned to the four silent executives. "What do you think of her?" he asked.

We were saved by the telephone. He could never allow it to ring and soon became locked into a conversation in fractured German. Kim saw her chance to flee. Ten minutes later, just as Maxwell finished his call, Kim's shaky voice sounded on the speaker phone: "I have spoken to Mr. Neeman, Mr. Maxwell. He says he will fix a meeting with Mr. Shamir but he needs an exact date."

Maxwell smiled and, waving his hand across the console, he intoned slowly in that deep voice: "You have done well, Kim. That's more like it. You learn fast." He clicked the off button, without answering her question, and said, without a trace of irony: "That is a lesson to you all in how to train a secretary. Didn't she do well?"

I never saw Kim again. I asked one of the other office workers about her some weeks later and was told she had decided to work in her father's store.

There were two main entrances to Maxwell's ninth-floor office and a third door which linked him to his son Kevin's office. He kept it dark and wandered from one end, where there was a large rectangular desk, to the other, where he held meetings at a huge glass table. Papers were scattered everywhere and he could be relied upon to lose the most important. He often held meetings at each end of the room and sometimes left to attend a third or fourth meeting in other offices, carrying an important memo from one place to another and dropping it casually before going on elsewhere.

The telephone rang constantly and he would rarely turn away a caller, so that meetings were continually interrupted by his barking in German, French, Bulgarian, Russian, or one of four more Middle European languages. If he felt a call in English was secret he would pick up the phone, otherwise everyone heard his business. He positively reveled in having an audience for any call in which he was upbraiding someone, and most enjoyed encouraging the unknowing person on the other end of the line to be indiscreet about one of the people sitting at his table.

It would not be fair simply to stress the cruelty, however, because sometimes Maxwell's persecution of others could be very amusing. It always depended on Maxwell's mood, which was changeable, and the status or strength of character of the victim. On my first working visit to Maxwell's office we were discussing a tip that *The Sun* was about to insert a glossy color magazine in a coming issue and decided we should try to obtain a copy prior to publication.

Maxwell hit the console button for the *Mirror* news-desk, one of the favorite targets. There was an apocryphal story that when the Maxwell light showed on the news-desk phone the executive answering the call would stand to attention. What was true was that the desk usually went silent as the senior person on duty answered the phone with a smart "Mr. Maxwell."

On this day the unfortunate man was the deputy news editor, Phil Mellor. Maxwell's voice, though deep, could be indistinct because he sat some way back from the voice box and he also tended to imagine that the person he was talking to understood the context without his explaining. So when he demanded that "some of the best reporters you've got—not the usual idiots—must get me the magazine by tonight," Mellor misunderstood part of the message.

He replied: "Have you got a copy of the magazine, Mr. Maxwell, so my lads know what they're looking for?"

Maxwell looked to the sky and I felt he was about to unleash a torrent of abuse when he caught my eye. It was still the honeymoon for the new boy. He would be nice to his staff. "Mr. Philip Mellor," he said. "Am I speaking Turkish?"

The baffled Mellor, anxiously watched by his colleagues, realized something was up but was unsure quite what: "No, Mr. Maxwell."

"Am I speaking Chinese?"

"No, Mr. Maxwell."

"Well, then, let me explain. If I had a fucking copy of the fucking magazine I've asked you to get then I wouldn't be asking you get it, would I?"

Mellor replied sharply: "I understand, Mr. Maxwell. We'll get on it right away."

Maxwell shook with laughter until he coughed violently. He said "Am I speaking Turkish?" a couple of times. That was about as funny as he got because all the humor sprang from the mercurial Maxwell being aware of his authority and, on a whim, deciding he would treat it as a joke. Of course, the essence of this "joke" is that Mellor was unaware until later that he was not on the verge of being fired.

From the time Maxwell arrived in the morning there was a line of people in the hall outside the elevator that serviced his floor. Some waited for hours until meetings were canceled with a brief message delivered by a secretary; some waited without hearing a word; some brought papers with them and did a day's work in a corridor; some spent time on the phone to faraway offices. Most of the line were usually senior executives in Maxwell's own companies; some were suppliers urging him to pay; some were hopeful businessmen eager to get five minutes of his time to listen to a money-making idea. Conversation with people in the line could be enlightening, and it was surprising whom one might find—former British attorney-general, Lord Havers, who chaired Maxwell's legal publishing company, say, or the former Conservative cabinet minister, Lord Rippon, who was a Maxwell Communications director.

Secretaries could watch the throng from their office on closed-circuit television, regularly informing Maxwell of the new arrivals as he sat in his office, making and receiving scores of calls, unconcerned by the melee outside. Meetings scheduled for half an hour were lengthened by the phone calls he accepted. I passed a Mirror Group director leaving his office after a one-hour solo meeting one afternoon, a long time for anyone to be alone with Maxwell, whose attention span was too short for him to bear speaking for long to the same person. I remarked to the man that it must have been some meeting.

"Sure was," he said. "I went in to get one signature. He was just of the verge of signing when he took a call. Then there were more calls, one after the other. Finally, just as I thought he was going to sign, he told me to come back and discuss it tomorrow. We should have paid this bill weeks ago."

Since Maxwell insisted on signing for every expenditure over a certain amount—one week it was £5,000 ($8,000), another £500 ($800), one woman might have a £1,000 ($1,600) limit, another man a £5,000 ($8,000) limit—the line to see him never seemed to shorten. The business of his companies was often hampered to the point of standstill by his wish to be involved in every decision, no matter how apparently trivial. "I'm a detail man," he liked to say, and if he wanted to show off or to play teacher then he would offer a German lesson: *"Der Teufel steckt im Detail...* That's Goethe. Do you know what it means?"

"No, Bob."

"It means 'The devil resides in the detail.'"

I was never certain whether the ambiguity of this quotation ever struck Maxwell.

Given that the *Daily Mirror* was performing reasonably in the market, color having given it an advantage over its then black-and-white rivals, and that Maxwell was facing an enormous debt burden, it seemed strange to many people that he wanted to upset the profit-making Mirror Group by replacing the editor of the flagship paper. Maybe he hoped to manipulate me.

The wisest words in my first days came from Joe Haines: "The *Daily Mirror* is only a minor part of his business but a major part of his interest."

So it would prove. No matter that he was involved in complicated financial maneuvers and suffering from falling profits in the rest of his empire, Maxwell delighted in playing with the *Daily Mirror,* interfering whenever he got the chance, keeping bankers waiting for an hour as he lectured a page designer on how to do his job. There was nothing he did not claim to know better than anyone else. In the late fifties, in a film-financing venture, he had amazed and annoyed the prima ballerina Galina Ulanova by jumping on stage during the filming of *Giselle* to explain how she should move in front of the cameras. Now he said to the nervous designer, "Do you know where your eyes go?"

As so often with Maxwell he perplexed people by the strange way he framed questions and they were too nervous to say they did not understand. "Your eyes go to the right, Mr. Designer...." And the petty lecture would rumble on while important matters that should have concerned him were ignored.

On my first real day in charge Maxwell decided that every journalist from the age of fifty-five should be offered early retirement at enhanced terms "to enjoy their pensions while they're still young enough." He added, "This will allow you to hire younger people from *The Sun.*" Maxwell was obsessed with Murdoch and with *The Sun*'s editor Kelvin MacKenzie, and I was able to use this knowledge to my advantage. Maxwell bred into his executives some of his own cunning. That same evening, drinking a tumbler of champagne in Maxwell's office, I listened as he told a receptionist to get MacKenzie on the phone.

Some minutes later she rang through to say "Mr. MacKenzie will not accept your call, Mr. Maxwell."

Maxwell demanded that the girl relate the conversation in full, but she was hesitant at several points, avoiding Kelvin's exact words.

"No, no, no," screamed Maxwell. "Tell me everything he said."

The girl said she would prefer not to but Maxwell shouted, "You will not get into trouble, Patricia. But if you refuse you will be in trouble."

"Well, Mr. Maxwell, he said, 'I don't want to speak to the fat Czech bastard.' And," Patricia paused, astonished at having gone so far, "then he said, 'And tell him I never want to speak to him.'"

"Thank you, Patricia. You have done well."

Maxwell looked to me: "Why is he like that? What kind of man would do that?"

"He doesn't give a damn, Bob."

Patricia left two weeks later, in tears, escorted from the building by a security man. I never knew the reason.

The pressure applied by Maxwell to involve himself in the *Daily Mirror* was clear soon after my arrival. He wanted to write the copy announcing the new bingo contest, tried to change the headline the day Nelson Mandela was freed from jail, and tried to amend the front-page layout the day two hundred thousand protested in Moscow against the Communist Party. I was told he was "hurt" that I planned and executed a special "shock issue" on education "without my knowledge or permission" and "apoplectic" that I had planned the publication of the investigation I had inherited from the previous editor about labor leader Arthur Scargill and his odd financial arrangements for his union during the 1984 miners' strike without "discussing it in detail with me first."

His antipathy to Scargill was well known, exacerbated by the union boss's failing to let Maxwell solve the strike, but he insisted on signing the leading article on the first day of the series and appearing on television the next day, both bad tactical errors. It wrongly convinced Scargill and many miners that Maxwell was involved in a political plot against him and provided him with a useful defense against the allegations in the eyes of his members.

We must not lose sight of the other side of Maxwell, however. While he was speaking on BBC television news about Scargill misusing strike funds he was setting in motion a misuse of funds on a scale unimagined by Scargill. It was becoming obvious that he could never hope to repay his loans. On 2 March 1990, days before the publication of the Scargill story, Maxwell completed what he called the "transformation from printer to publisher" by selling Maxwell Graphics, his American printing company, for $510 million (£305 million).

It was a significant and welcome disposal, but it was not enough. Maxwell still owned any number of companies for which there were no buyers. Rising interest rates were beginning to turn the debt mountain into a mountain range. The recession was eating into publishing profits, and there was no possibility that Maxwell could find enough cash from his normal profits to repay the banks.

It is now known that from 30 March one of Maxwell's private companies bought a "call option" on ten million MCC shares. In effect he was supporting his share price, but it was apparently legal. Although directors are not allowed to buy options in the shares of their companies, other companies controlled by those same directors can do so. As we have seen throughout his career, if there was a loophole in any law then Maxwell was delighted to squeeze his bulk through it. But desperation would push him further.

This balancing act, unknown of course to me or anyone within the Mirror Group, was being organized at the time of our first major clash over the policy of the paper, and was the first time I would contemplate resigning. *The Sun* announced that it was offering a £5 million ($8 million) top prize in a game called Spot-the-Ball, a version of a well-worn contest in which the paper published a gridded picture of players in a soccer game, but without a ball. Readers were asked to decide, by studying the players' positions and other relevant factors such as the directions in which they were looking, where the ball should be. *The Sun* expected readers to buy special cards from their local retailers to play the game.

I quickly judged that this was a desperate move by *The Sun*: games were tending to have no effect on declining circulations; making people pay to play would be disastrous; the prize was too high ever to pay out, and the odds were against there being a winner; and the only reason for spending the enormous sums on organization and promotion must mean *The Sun* was beginning to suffer a slide in sales.

Here was a chance to lampoon our rivals, take a slightly snobbish attitude toward their "pathetic" game, and assert instead our growing editorial strengths. Maxwell, then in New York, appeared to agree, and when I read him some of the critical copy I had written, he laughed.

However, and this was a severe, if relatively well-hidden aspect of his character, Maxwell was prone to change his mind and, to mask the fact, would create a panic in order to shift the blame onto others.

A typical Maxwellian panic began with an out-of-the-blue phone call in which he ranted. It was followed by a burst of calls—as many as a dozen within an hour—and many calls to other executives who then began to ring each other. Having stirred everyone else into hysteria by urging several people to carry out the same order, sometimes forgetting who ran which department and demanding that advertising deal with distribution or production carry out some editorial task, he then called a meeting. "Why are you all running around like chopped worms?" he would scream. In the case of Spot the Ball, he demanded that we match *The Sun*'s game. John Jenkinson, the promotions manager, was prepared and had already set up a similar game with the *Mirror*'s bingo contractors, Europrint.

I continued to argue against the concept. Having nailed my colors to the mast by pouring scorn on *The Sun,* I could not feel happy at following them. Maxwell would have none of it and said patronizingly: "Leave this to your Publisher." His habit was to refer to himself in the third person. At meetings different people around his table would address him variously as Mr. Maxwell, RM, Bob, Chairman, and Publisher.

His decision to publish the Spot the Ball contest prevailed: "Games are commercial. You are in charge of editorial matters, and I am in charge of commercial matters. I know about these things..." I gave in, recognizing that we would, at least, have one major advantage over *The Sun* in that readers would not have to pay any more than the cover price of the paper to take part.

Next we had to decide the prize. I thought £5 million ($8 million) was out of the question but urged we offer at least £1 million ($1.6 million) as a top prize, with £10,000 ($16,000) runners-up prizes along the way. Pinning Maxwell down to spending a sum of money was always difficult, but to help make up his mind I asked our finance department to discover the cost of insuring ourselves against someone winning.

While I waited for a reply, Maxwell was making his own investigation. He asked John Jenkinson how the game would be organized in terms of judging. John explained that readers would be expected to indicate the position of the ball in a numbered square on the grid on five separate pictures published Monday through Friday and then send in their entries. The winner would be the person or persons who selected the correct position of the ball on all five days. We would therefore be in the position of judging the contest after we had the entries in our possession. Technically, therefore, it was possible for checkers to establish a sequence of squares that no competitor had chosen, and our panel of judges could then "select" that combination. There need never be a £1 million winner until, or unless, we wished to generate one.

Maxwell asked to see me. He was holding a business meeting at the round table and motioned me to the other end. "I have decided to be the chairman of judges of the first Spot the Ball thing," he said, as if imparting a state secret. "You will chair them from then on."

I nodded, holding back a smile, before he continued: "Make sure this doesn't cost me a million."

"It wouldn't be a good idea to give the top prize on the first week," I said. "Anyway, we could insure against it."

He sighed deeply. "Insurance is out," he said, putting his arm around my shoulders. "We are the insurance. I don't want to pay out one million pounds."

Back in my office I rang the finance department who, without telling me the cost, said that the insurance premium was very expensive and, yes, Maxwell had been on to them, too, and ruled it out. Forced to run the game against my will and now forced to fix it so that no reader could win, I wrote in my diary: "Tonight I spoke of resignation—the sure knowledge that I must carry out RM's Spot the Ball commands now haunts me."

I had spoken of resignation only to my wife. The next day I asked John Jenkinson to explain carefully how the fixing would occur, and I concluded that readers would quickly catch on to the fact that it was a fraud. Players would realize after a couple of games that our judges were placing the ball in squares that were nonsensical. There would be complaints and then, to allay them, we would have to generate a winner.

I felt happier: we would never fool our readers and Maxwell would be forced to give in to save his reputation and that of the paper's. I met Maxwell that morning and he told me the judging of the game must remain a secret between us. I pointed out that John Jenkinson knew and would have to know since he would provide us with a list of approved squares each week to avoid there being a winner. I also thought John's superior, the marketing director Rob Walker, would probably know.

This intelligence infuriated Maxwell because, unknown to me, he was planning to fire Walker. He dare not let Walker go now for fear of the Spot the Ball secret emerging so it stayed his hand for months, until he had forgotten about the reason for delaying his decision to fire him. I overlooked telling him that Europrint must be aware of what we were doing as well since they were receiving the entries, checking them, and providing the information that enabled us to avoid nominating a winner. Maxwell's last words on the subject were, "Make sure it doesn't cost me any money."

It transpired that my touching faith in *Mirror* readers was misplaced. In spite of the fact that I, the sole judge after Maxwell's first week, began to place the ball in the most farfetched places in order to engender complaints, there was no adverse reaction. We ended the game, having paid out some £10,000 second prizes without a squeak from readers, once *The Sun* ended theirs (they had no winner either, but had taken the straightforward step of taking out insurance).

The fixing of the Spot the Ball game was to be a highlight of the BBC television's *Panorama* exposure of Maxwell's activities more than a year later. Still, readers did not complain and no attempt was made to investigate whether there had been a breach of the Lotteries and Gaming Act. Perhaps it suggests that tabloid newspaper readers either do not care whether the games are straight or have become so cynical they expect them to be fixed anyway. Maxwell, naturally, sued the BBC over the allegation and followed it by suing *The Sun* when it repeated the story. He put immense pressure on John Jenkinson to make a false statement, which he refused to do, and without it Maxwell had no hope of ever making a case. He had by then convinced himself that he was not involved in the affair and thundered, "How could anyone think I would stoop to fiddling a game?"

The public face of Maxwell never dropped and his pace never slackened. In May 1990 he made an abortive bid to buy Gallimard, the French publisher of Jean-Paul Sartre and Albert Camus. In Sofia he signed an agreement to buy 50 percent of Bulgaria's second TV channel and then donated one thousand tons of newsprint to be shared by all the political parties fighting in the country's first free elections. He also promised to invest £10 million ($16 million) in various Bulgarian industries. He became immersed in a complicated set of deals with Alan Bond to buy stakes in Australian newspapers, all of which were blocked. Then, having failed previously to take over America's best-known supermarket tabloid, the *National Enquirer*, he announced that he had agreed to buy a rival, *The Globe*, and two stablemates.

In May 1990 came the first hint of interest in the New York *Daily News* and, in the same month, an announcement that the Mirror Group—unknown to us directors, of course—was taking a 50 percent interest in Berliner Verlag, an East German paper group.

In London Maxwell met Margaret Thatcher at a Downing Street reception and told me afterward that she now viewed him as one of her links to the Soviet leadership. Evidently she told him: "Robert, you do look tired. I do hope you are not overdoing things."

Once he had met Thatcher, his next hope was to carry "a message" from her to President Gorbachev, which reminded him to call my wife at home on her day off to explain that it would not be long before he arranged her long-promised interview with Raisa Gorbachev.

He asked what she planned to do for the rest of the day. "I'm going to Sotheby's," she replied, "to look at a collection of Scandinavian impressionist paintings."

"Are you buying?"

She said she might but the prices shown in the catalogue suggested they might be expensive.

"Buy me some," Maxwell said. She laughed: "But I don't know what you like. Taste in pictures is very personal."

"Noreen," Maxwell said, his lugubrious speech making a single word sound like a sentence. "I trust your taste. If you like them, buy them."

"How many shall I buy? How much should I spend on each?"

"I don't know. About twenty thousand pounds. Maybe twenty-five [$32–40,000]."

By the time Noreen and a Danish girlfriend arrived at the Bond Street auction house most of the paintings had been sold, but her bid for one, at £21,000 ($33,600), succeeded. Her pleasure suddenly turned to panic when she realized she had no money to pay, and then she worried whether Maxwell had been joking. She phoned his office and was told by a secretary that he was holding a meeting and could not be disturbed. Noreen said, "This is extremely urgent. I must talk to him."

It was likely therefore that Maxwell took the call in front of an audience and might account for what he said. She explained that she had bought a picture and needed the £21,000.

"You shall be sent the money," Maxwell said. "But I am surprised at how little you have spent. You are not doing very well."

Noreen's Danish friend was tugging at her sleeve to point out that three excellent paintings were among those that had not reached their reserve price. "Are you serious, Bob?"

"On you go," he intoned. "Do your best."

By the time Maxwell's valet arrived with a folder of credit cards, Noreen had agreed to spend more than £80,000 ($128,000).

Sotheby's, though delighted to hear they were dealing with Robert Maxwell, did not take plastic, and Simon, the valet, was sent to collect a check.

Maxwell was just finishing lunch with Lord King when Noreen arrived on the tenth floor of Maxwell House with four paintings. After introducing her as his art curator to the chairman of British Airways, he looked quickly at his latest acquisitions.

"Bit dull, aren't they," he said, appearing to be unimpressed. "That woman there has a big bum."

Noreen's Danish friend suppressed a smile and Maxwell added, "I'd like one with a bit of color." He was shown another painting that was still available.

"Fetch me that tomorrow," he said. "Now, they're no good on the ground. Put them up."

"Where?" asked Noreen.

"Wherever you think best."

Minutes later men in aprons with ladder and hammers appeared. Noreen took her shoes off and jumped up on Maxwell's bed to place above it one entitled *An Elegant Woman in Red*. The next day Maxwell said he was "very pleased with the boy" over his bed. He also "quite liked" the "colorful one" and had it placed in his dining room for lunch guests to appreciate.

A couple of days later the *Daily Mirror* was approached about contributing to the sponsorship of a Wembley concert tribute to Nelson Mandela. The sum was so great that I needed Maxwell's approval. In return for £125,000 ($200,000) our paper's logo would appear on signs above the stage, we could have posters displayed at key points, obtain exclusive interviews with the Mandelas, have access to the stars taking part, and our name would appear in the television credits. That was quite apart from the kudos of being associated with the event itself.

Maxwell quickly saw the possibilities for self-publicity, first offering his plane to fly the Mandelas to Britain (rejected for security reasons) and then seizing the chance to appear in grand company at Wembley. The deal was completed at the last moment, and, although the concert was a great success, the promised publicity in the form of the giant posters above the stage proved so indistinct they could not be seen on television. I was upset, but the night went off so well and the *Mirror*'s interviews with Nelson and Winnie were so good I was willing to let it pass, perhaps renegotiating the money later as compensation.

Maxwell, however, was enraged and refused to pay a penny for months. Only persistent persuasion from Dick Caborn, the Labour MP who helped organize Mandela's visit, and the paper's political editor, Alastair Campbell, convinced Maxwell to pay anything at all.

This row over money did not prevent Maxwell from attending the reception hosted by the Commonwealth secretary general, Sonny

Ramphal, at his London residence. The event was organized care-fully with three grades of guest wearing different colored identity badges. The A team, numbering about twenty and wearing red, were to meet Mandela in a private room. The B team, in green, were to meet Winnie in another room. The great majority, the yellow-badged C team, were to wait downstairs where the Mandelas were expected to mingle briefly. Naturally, this latter group included journalists.

Maxwell, who was on the A team, had other ideas, because he wanted his journalists with him, particularly his photographer, to record the occasion of Mandela meeting Maxwell. At the entrance Maxwell demanded of the man handing out the badges: "Three reds."

The official blinked in puzzlement, so Maxwell offered his name: "Maxwell—three reds." Without waiting longer for a reply he scooped the badges off the table and handed one each to Alastair Campbell and the photographer, Nigel Wright.

Once the guests had assembled, Mandela entered the room only for Maxwell to advance and greet him as if this were Maxwell's rather than Sonny Ramphal's party. He even thrust a "gift" into Mandela's hands, a specially prepared glossy proof of the *Daily Mirror* pages with the interview we had obtained with the Mandelas.

Unsurprisingly these "aquaproofs" were put down during Nelson Mandela's tour to meet the throng downstairs, and Maxwell spotted them behind a chair. "Get those things," he told Campbell as they prepared to leave. "We'll take them back. They cost a fortune."

Before Mandela returned to South Africa to begin his lengthy negotiations with President de Klerk, he and his wife were invited to the Maxwell House apartment. But the joy I felt at meeting Nelson Mandela, the heroic man who had withstood thirty years in jail, refusing to be compromised into a deal over his release, was offset by hearing Maxwell's conversational gambit. "Mr. Mandela," Maxwell said, "let me tell you how to negotiate...I have had long experience of these things. I've negotiated with every president from Kennedy to Khrushchev."

The next day another of the "honored guests" during the Mandela visit appeared for lunch on the tenth floor—Mr. Jesse Jackson, sometime Democratic Party presidential contender and all-time king of self-publicity. Here was a matching of styles. The Maxwell-

Jackson greeting was effusive: they hugged each other and kissed several times. Then the Mirror Group editors were introduced to Jesse and his retinue of bodyguards and sons.

I could tell Maxwell was bored during lunch since Jackson was the center of attention. As coffee was being served, Maxwell's valet appeared with a humidor, offered cigars from it round the table, and then left it on a sideboard. At the conclusion of lunch, as Maxwell hurried his verbose guest out of the dining room to discuss unspecified "business," my fellow editors and I were astonished to see a couple of the Jackson entourage stuff half a dozen cigars into their jacket pockets. Somehow it seemed a fitting end to Jackson's lectures on morality.

7

Twin Obsessions

DEFENDERS of Maxwell's record often refer to his entrepreneurial vision and to the dynamic energy he exerted to turn vision into substance. One example regularly cited is his "dream" weekly paper. *The European*. The idea of selling a single newspaper across the European continent in every major city, as well as in America, was truly an innovation, and when Maxwell first surprised Europe's media industry by announcing it he appeared to have grasped in detail the whole concept perfectly, from its target audience to its printing arrangements, from its editorial content to its design format. I have discovered why this was so: Maxwell had taken part in an outrageous act of industrial sabotage to steal the whole idea.

He first spoke in public of his decision to launch a pan-European paper in October 1987 when he was guest speaker at a lunch held by the Anglo-American Press Association of Paris. "It's more than time Europe told its story," said Maxwell, flanked by his son Ian and Gerry Long, a former head of Reuters, then acting as a consultant to Maxwell. He described his plan to launch a daily paper in January 1989 that would serve both Europe and the United States.

One American journalist who happened to be sitting at the same table as Maxwell was taken aback as the sketchy details emerged. For instance, the paper would have a staff of its own but would also publish translations of outstanding articles from Europe's leading dailies. As he listened to the confident Maxwell unveiling details of his idea it gradually dawned on Ronald Koven, Paris correspondent for the *Boston Globe*, that these were uncannily similar to plans he had seen elsewhere. Maxwell even referred to having carried out feasibility studies which had shown, he said, that "there's a profitable market there."

As it turned out, whole passages in Maxwell's speech had been lifted from a memorandum Koven had been shown in confidence only a couple of weeks before for a similar project being guided by the former West German chancellor Helmut Schmidt, who was publisher of the Hamburg-based paper *Die Zeit*. He could not let it pass, and while Maxwell was still standing Koven asked him, "Why do I get the impression, Mr. Maxwell, that your project is a carbon copy of Helmut Schmidt's project?"

Though Koven had expected to surprise Maxwell, he could hardly have forecast what would happen. Maxwell fell backward, scattering a serving cart of empty dishes and ending up amidst the broken crockery on the floor. Two free-lance photographers were so stunned they forgot to take pictures.

Once Maxwell got up, having waved aside offers of help, all he would say to Koven was, "Well, the difference is mine is daily and his is weekly." However, *The European* eventually became a weekly. Apart from that, Koven said there was only one other difference, in that Maxwell promised to provide four pages for news from Eastern Europe. Otherwise the plans were identical to those of Schmidt's project. In fact, the *Wall Street Journal* the next day referred to an anonymous source who had "noted striking similarities between Mr. Maxwell's plan and a proposal put forward some time ago" by Schmidt. It went on: "The source suggested that Mr. Maxwell announced his venture to forestall Mr. Schmidt's plan and based his decisions on the feasibility study conducted for Mr. Schmidt's venture."[1]

Schmidt's original idea stemmed from his concern that Europe was not explaining itself to the United States and that there would be an

American market for a paper doing just that. His plan was to launch a weekly composed largely of articles from influential dailies from Europe's major capitals. Dummies were prepared in Madrid, at *El Pais*, and in Stockholm. But the project collapsed for various reasons, especially the probable cost.

Schmidt told me he was aware of the similarity of Maxwell's plan but did not protest. However, he did not then know that some twelve days before making his announcement Maxwell had been handed the full text of Schmidt's confidential plans along with the dummies.

According to Koven, Maxwell's idea seemed to come completely out of the blue to Ian and to Gerry Long. No one in Maxwell's organization knew of any feasibility studies. Unaware of the duplicity, Long said at the time that Maxwell had been mulling over his idea for a while and that it must have been pure coincidence. Long now recalls Maxwell becoming "obsessional" about the idea, ignoring his advice that it was likely to be an unprofitable enterprise. He knew nothing of Maxwell's duplicity.

Although Maxwell set up a *European* unit within the Mirror Group soon after his announcement, the project looked as if it would wither away. Maxwell announced various deadlines to launch the paper but broke them all, concealing his reasons for the delays. He did not pursue the plan practically until January 1990, when he appointed Ian Watson, formerly deputy editor of the *Sunday Telegraph*, as editor. After three years of inactivity he then demanded that Watson launch the paper, a weekly, in May. By this time almost everyone had long forgotten the Schmidt link, if they had ever known of it at all.

Having stolen the concept, Maxwell would now do his energetic best to make the launch as dramatic as possible. Watson—an admirer of Maxwell and a convert to the European newspaper dream—began to hire staff, organize printing and publishing facilities, arrange distribution, and prepare dummies. Technical staff also required training on the advanced electronic color-scanning equipment bought from the Israeli Scitex corporation, which Maxwell owned. Whatever has been said about the paper, and Watson has been self-critical, it was a notable achievement by Watson that *The European* was launched in a professional fashion. Maxwell's next major hiring in March was the experienced managing director of the *International Herald Tribune*, Robin MacKichan, as managing director and deputy publisher.

"From day one it was a nightmare," MacKichan said. "Maxwell was irrational, suffering from violent mood swings, and he would not listen to any advice." One giant mood swing led to Maxwell ringing MacKichan one April morning at six thirty, demanding that he get into work. MacKichan arrived to find maintenance men scurrying around. Maxwell had ordered the door of MacKichan's office to be opened by a crowbar, commandeered the office, and moved his corporate headquarters to *The European* editorial floor, along with other "essential" staff such as Joseph the Portuguese butler, server of a continuous supply of soup, tea, and orange juice.

"I am taking over," Maxwell explained to a bewildered staff. "I am a hands-on publisher."

Later that day I received a solemn call from one of his battery of secretaries: "Mr. Maxwell sends you his compliments and would like you to know that from today his office is located in *The European*. He does not wish to be bothered with anything other than serious matters." A blessed relief for me; a torture for Watson, MacKichan, and their staff.

The problems that had bedeviled Maxwell's launch of the failed *London Daily News* came to the fore again. Maxwell was deeply interested in the finished product, the paper itself, but had no time for the all-important production and commercial aspects. He demanded that the paper be printed in Germany and France and that it be on sale at every newsstand in Europe, a very expensive addition to distribution costs.

As regards the paper's contents and design, Maxwell was certain about what *The European* should not be but unable to convey what he thought it should be. He wanted it to be a serious, upmarket newspaper, covering the week's main stories throughout Europe, with high-quality color pictures and graphics. Its circulation would be restricted to the well-educated since it would have to sell only to those able to read English. There were many minor changes of mind along the way, but that general brief was eventually achieved.

The memory of the *London Daily News* collapse, which led to several journalists having to sue for their contracted money, guaranteed that recruitment would be difficult. People who were persuaded to join the team by Watson demanded high wages and cast-iron contracts, while some writers hired personally by Maxwell were paid a fortune by Fleet Street standards, often as much as £100,000

($160,000). Watson and MacKichan would never know how much some people were paid. "Nothing ever was straight with Bob," Watson said. "His deals went into strange melting pots."

Maxwell reveled in the role of editor in chief, a title he awarded himself one morning, striding through the office in shirtsleeves, baffling staff by bellowing half-understood production jargon. He was bored with administration within days but never lost his appetite for seeing, and amending, the editorial content in dummies. He tried to lure outsiders, such as myself or the *Sunday Mirror* editor, into offering views. But only one opinion counted: his own.

The need for speed meant that there was no time to negotiate printing and distribution contracts properly. While Maxwell's MCC debt was continuing to grow by the day, money was being misspent at a dizzy level and *The European* was made to bear some of the intercompany costs, such as the use of Maxwell's helicopter. Mac-Kichan, unaware of MCC's problems but well aware of the soaring costs at *The European*, urged caution and finally sent a memo suggesting that the launch be delayed, but Maxwell's reputation was riding on the paper being published and his adrenaline was high.

He was also living under a misconception. He thought his rival, Rupert Murdoch, was about to beat him by publishing a special European edition of *The Times* and therefore, one more time, he would lose out to him. Under no circumstances could Maxwell let it happen: he must get *The European* out first. Watson knew that the editorial was being "thrown together" and that no research had been carried out. "We were completely on our own, making it up as we went along," he said. "There were no resources."

Ian Watson, the paper's editor, soldiered on, but the relationship between Maxwell and his managing director, Robin MacKichan, deteriorated. Maxwell had to be convinced by his advisers, particularly the public-relations consultant Brian Basham, to keep MacKichan aboard because his credibility was vital in maintaining trade confidence, especially among the small band of potential advertisers. One afternoon I visited Maxwell in his European office. "I'll get advertising," he shouted at a group of executives and called in his secretary. "Get me John King." Later, Lord King did place several pages of color advertising for British Airways.

Confronted by too few editorial staff, Maxwell said, "I'll get staff" and asked me to provide senior Mirror people. None wanted to join and Watson was not pleased to have this downmarket press gang on board. Seat-of-the-pants solutions worked as far as Maxwell was concerned, but they were not a good way to launch a dream newspaper that had been almost four years on the drawing board.

As it moved closer to launch date in May 1990 Watson and MacKichan began to worry about the promotional advertising to win the all-important initial readership. Maxwell, of course, would promote himself with various newspaper interviews (with headlines like THE EGO SPREADS HIS WINGS and THE EGO HAS LANDED, a truly brilliant parody of a day with Maxwell), most of which would lead to complaints, follow-up letters, retractions of statements, arguments, phone calls, threats of writs.

He also made a characteristically ebullient appearance on British television's most popular talk show and was hissed by the audience for overdoing his selling of *The European*.

But a newspaper launch requires more than a high-profile owner selling himself. After the paper itself, the huge expenditure for television advertising is probably the most crucial matter to decide.

I was called in for general discussions with the chosen agency, Young and Rubicam, and it became obvious that there were many ideas but none with Maxwell's all-important imprimatur. Y & R's chief, the canny John Banks, who was good at handling Maxwell, tried to pin him down. But Maxwell remained unconvinced by any advertising idea and began to ask everyone what they thought. He ordered the Mirror Group's in-house TV promotions organizer, Terry Sanders, to come up with some ideas. Then Roger Eastoe, the Mirror Group's advertising director, suggested a third party. Maxwell leapt at the opportunity: he could have three ideas to choose from. Of course, this would be very costly but, then again, Maxwell knew he wouldn't pay the bills.

Young & Rubicam were not told about the other two competitors, and on one hysterical evening the ads were shown in different rooms on the ninth floor as Maxwell moved from office to office. Then the creative people, who knew each other, had to be smuggled out of the building separately. Maxwell's response was true to form: he liked the music from one, the idea from another, and the visuals from the third. Even so, two versions were being prepared as Maxwell flew off to visit various European captials for more interviews.

On the evening of 4 May 1990, just a week before launch and two days before the advertisements were to be screened on television stations all over Europe, there was a somber gathering in Maxwell's office hosted by his son Ian. *The European*'s editor, Ian Watson, and his deputy, Peter Millar, sat at the round table with the marketing director Brian Shields, and public-relations consultant Brian Basham. Maxwell, then in Paris, had demanded that I attend—"and take your wife for the woman's view."

Y & R's Paul Wolfenden showed us their final ad, which incorporated Maxwell's musical choice, Beethoven's "Ode to Joy," and there was a general feeling among us that it was about right. "Now you must tell Bob," said his son. A surreal scene then began as Maxwell, in Paris, asked to listen to the TV ad played at full volume so that he could hear it over the phone.

There was an attempt to explain the visual images before he said: "Ian, what do you think?"

Watson said he liked it.

"What about the hippie?" This was Maxwell's affectionate nickname for Peter Millar, the deputy editor, who agreed with Watson. And so it went on with each of us stepping forward to the speaker phone to agree that it was fine.

"Okay, Mr. Wolfenden," Maxwell said. "Approved."

I was therefore astonished to see on television two nights later a different ad for *The European*. Peter Millar told me Maxwell had returned in a filthy mood from France the next day and chosen the version by the Mirror Group's own man, Terry Sanders. Same music, different visuals. It also had the virtue for Maxwell that it was an in-house version. Months later he still had not paid Y & R's bill.

The launch of *The European* a week later was celebrated at a champagne breakfast at London's New Connaught Rooms, with Pergamon strikers outside (forcing Maxwell to enter by a rear door) and a glittering array of politicians, actors, and businessmen inside. Maxwell made a speech that was sensible when he read Joe Haines's words and rambling when he wandered from the text. Peter Ustinov, who was to become one of the paper's columnists, was full of praise for Maxwell, the man of vision—and money.

Maxwell was soon saying that the first edition was a sell-out and, echoing down the years from his wild claims about sales of encyclopedias, came the declaration that one million copies had been sold. MacKichan, the managing director, became alarmed because advertisers would know it was a lie and there might be a loss of confidence in the industry. Over the following weeks MacKichan, aware of the genuine sales, tried to make inquiries into the launch costs and see whether there was money for a "second wave" advertising push in the autumn. He was surprised to be called in by Kevin Maxwell, who had played no formal role in *The European*, and told to mind his own business.

Soon after, on a morning in July, Maxwell told managing director MacKichan he was suspending him "until I decide what to do with you." There was no explanation, so a shaken MacKichan went straight to Ian Maxwell's office.

Within minutes Maxwell arrived and said to his son, "He's suspended. You will go and sit in his office."

The joint managing director of Maxwell Communications had just become chief executive of *The European*. MacKichan went home on full pay but became a worried man, concerned about being a board director of a company he knew to be losing £1 million ($1.6 million) a week. He finally accepted a "miserable" payoff.

As the months moved on, the eccentricities piled up. Maxwell's daughter, Ghislaine, joined the staff to help produce two glossy fashion magazines. Watson was unaware of the size of her salary. Maxwell told Watson he was planning to buy *The Sunday Correspondent*, a short-lived upmarket Sunday paper, to merge it with *The European*, but Watson advised him it would be like throwing good money after bad. In spite of there being no argument between them, soon thereafter Maxwell called Watson for lunch and told him that due to his "implacable opposition to the buying of *The Sunday Correspondent*," he was replacing him with the editor of that paper.

Watson and Maxwell had a mutual admiration, and eventually Watson joined Maxwell's private staff. Like MacKichan before him, he grew concerned at the costs of the paper, but Ian Maxwell calmed him: his father was wealthy, he had the money. *The European* cost

Maxwell, at a conservative estimate, £50 million ($80 million) to launch and was probably eating considerably more than £1.2 million ($1.92 million) a week for its first year.

Watson disputes these figures but concedes that he saw no budgets. Advertising and readers were difficult to find for many months, but *The European* gradually built a fairly healthy circulation. There is a lot to justify Watson's view that even though the paper was ahead of its time it did find a market. It did much better than many critics anticipated. However, its cost in time, energy, and money to Maxwell at this crucial period proved incalculable.

Maxwell's enthusiasm for *The European* was, by a wide margin, more understandable than the incidents that ran parallel to its launch. In my first five months with Maxwell it was impossible not to be struck by his personal secretary, Andrea Martin. It is difficult to avoid clichés in describing her: she was a good-looking blonde, well-dressed, cool, efficient, and apparently unflappable. As the daughter of a television comedian, she had a well-developed but understated sense of humor that probably helped her to cope with Maxwell's temper and his sudden changes of mind. As an economics graduate she was able to understand much that baffled other people in his outer office.

Andrea worked long hours, sometimes fourteen hours a day, and traveled extensively with Maxwell. For his part he was noticeably less rude to her than to others and liked her around, complaining "Where is Andrea?" if she disappeared from his side for longer than he deemed necessary. There were, naturally, malicious rumors about the nature of this relationship, though I thought them farfetched. Around the beginning of April I would discover that the rumors were right, at least as far as Maxwell was concerned.

One of Maxwell's editorial favorites was Nick Davies, the *Daily Mirror* foreign editor, who suffered the nickname "Sneaky." When I asked other staff how he had gained his sobriquet the best I could get was, "Well, he just is, isn't he?" Maxwell enjoyed the name, too, often asking: "And where is Mister Sneaky today?"

Davies was not popular in the newspaper, but, though I sometimes instituted jokes at his expense in conferences, I rather took to him. Outside of the City office, he was almost the only other *Mirror* journalist who read the *Financial Times* and kept abreast of all manner of interesting topics. He was well-informed enough about international affairs to have held his own on any foreign desk, but his advantage over the serious journalist was that he could write about complex events in a tabloid style.

Before I joined, Davies had been one of the privileged entourage who traveled with Maxwell on his foreign jaunts, and this had brought him into contact with Andrea Martin. The twice-married, twice-divorced Davies—one-time polo player, part-time business-man, and full-time raconteur—soon took a fancy to the single and petite Ms. Martin. They enjoyed late-night meals together in Paris, Berlin, and Tokyo, and she confided her problems in dealing with "RM" to Davies. Naturally they fell in love.

But both were intelligent enough to realize this was a relationship that must remain very secret for, in Maxwellia, it could prove a dangerous liaison. Maxwell's compartmentalization was threatened: What Martin knew—and she knew a great deal—Maxwell would not want the clever Davies to know. That was only part of it, though, for Maxwell's overriding concern had nothing to do with business—he was besotted by the cool blonde with whom he spent every waking hour. Vaguely aware of her friendship with Davies, he began to put pressure on Andrea to stay overnight on the tenth floor. In fact, he even suggested endlessly that she move into the spare room. It would spare her from driving home late at night!

Andrea did her best to ignore or avoid these approaches, so Maxwell—employing a breathtaking lack of subtlety—decided to sort out the "problem" by another route. "Why do they call Nick Davies 'Sneaky'?" he asked me when we were alone one evening.

"Well, Bob, I think it's because he's supposed to sneak to you about what goes on down below."

He laughed: "He does." There was a long silence. "What do you think of Davies?"

"He's a gossip," I replied. "But there are loads of those in a newspaper office. As for his work, he's the best foreign editor we've got. Great at putting tabloid words together."

"Watch him," said Maxwell. "He's not to be trusted."

A week or so later the news desk rang to say Maxwell was on the warpath because he could not find Davies. I remembered I had sent

Davies to Israel, but the desk told me he had turned up in Yugoslavia. I prepared to bawl Davies out and told the desk to put him on the phone to me, which they did, an hour later.

While waiting to speak to Davies, I had an extraordinary call from Maxwell: "Mister Greenslade, you are being taken for a ride. You must sack Nick Davies for insubordination. He has failed to report in to you. You don't even know where he is. It's an insult to you as editor and you must not stand for it. You will have Your Publisher's full backing in this matter. Byeee."

I smelled a rat, and it wasn't Davies.

When Davies came through from Belgrade I asked him why he had traveled there without any reference to me. "Bob asked me to come," he replied. "I'm sorry there was no time to let you know. I thought he would tell you. I apologize." It was so obviously the truth I decided to take Davies partially into my confidence by telling him some of the conversation with Maxwell. I was surprised by his lack of surprise and realized there was more to all this than a falling out of old allies.

An hour later Maxwell rang: "Have you sacked Sneaky Davies?"

"No, Bob. I'm baffled. He says you sent him to Belgrade."

"That's not the point," Maxwell said. "He should be sacked because he failed to inform you. You are the editor. You have been insulted by Sneaky. An apology is not good enough."

When I noted down this last sentence it did not strike me then with the force it does now. I cannot recall ever having told Maxwell during that conversation that Davies had offered me an apology. While it's possible that I did so, in retrospect it is also possible that Maxwell listened in to my phone call with Davies.

Anyway, I refused to fire Davies and I thought this was another of those dramas that would pass in the night.

Some days later, with Davies back in the country, Maxwell called again: "Have you spoken to Sneaky about lying to you?"

"No, Bob, he hasn't lied to me."

"Roy, you will never be a great editor if you are soft with your staff. You are too easy on them. Everyone says so."

In the course of the next few days there were more references to Davies, and then one evening I finally discovered the reason for this nonsense. In Maxwell's office, after discussing another matter, he suddenly said, "Now you must make up your mind who will be your new foreign editor. I want to be involved in the interviews."

I protested again about Davies having my full confidence and added: "Surely you can't want him sacked, Bob, he's one of your great supporters on the floor."

He rambled on about the danger of untrustworthy people and fixed me with narrowed eyes: "By the way, this has nothing whatsoever to do with Andrea."

This was the first time I had ever had the slightest indication that Andrea had anything to do with anything, let alone Davies. It was like one of those escapades in a Billy Bunter book where the guilty schoolboy was always owning up to his misdemeanors by denying them. I was too surprised to reply, and on my way back to my office I began to realize part of the scenario. I called in Davies for a heart-to-heart talk and told him there must be something between him and Maxwell that they must talk about together.

At that moment Maxwell called and I took his call on the speaker phone so that Davies could overhear. The script was much the same as before, and Davies reddened with anger, mouthing "not true" at various points. Afterward I told Davies about the mention of Andrea; he refused to be drawn into this first conversation but later told me of Maxwell's obsession with her. As Davies observed later, "It was like John Fowles's *The Collector*. That was how [Maxwell] wanted her. He wanted her totally, to live her life for her."[2]

In the following weeks Davies complained to me that Maxwell was bugging his phone and he was possibly being followed, as was Andrea. It was only then I understood just how close Davies and Andrea had become. I asked John Pole, the head of security, to investigate. To placate Davies he said he would check but privately told me, "Bugging a single phone in this building is just not possible." I accepted Pole's advice; Davies did not.

It transpired that Davies was probably right. A couple of weeks later, in May, Andrea Martin left her highly paid job after almost three years as Maxwell's senior secretary and rejected all his pleas for her to return. Out of guilt, possibly, or embarrassment, Maxwell gave Davies a grand new title as Group foreign editor and a massive pay raise, making him a confidante once more but never a traveling companion. All this would come to mind over a year later when Davies himself would become headline news.

Perhaps Maxwell should have been concentrating more on problems at Maxwell Communications. The company's shares began to slide downwards from 196 pence ($3) in June 1990 after the company reported lower-than-expected profits and higher-than-expected debt. The price would slip away throughout the summer months to 145 pence ($2.30) as investors realized the problems Maxwell faced.

Within the *Daily Mirror*, it was difficult to deduce the sense of panic that his debts were causing, though his bouts of temper increased in frequency and severity as the months passed. "The banks won't let him" became a refrain whispered by all who knew and many who did not. It was the excuse for cost-cutting, failure to pay bills, failure to close deals, changes of direction, and eccentric behavior.

One day a worried director rang to ask me if I could help obtain a Metropolitan Police press pass for Maxwell.

"Why?" I asked. "What's it for?"

There was no explanation, but coincidentally I later overheard Maxwell booming down the phone at the man to explain why he had not provided it. "Idiot," screamed Maxwell. "Just tell them I'm the crime correspondent of *The European*."

I successfully prevented Maxwell from some bizarre late-night interventions in the paper by talking of production problems. For all his proud boasting about his printing expertise, it was easy to pull the wool over his eyes. Unlike Murdoch, he knew nothing about newspaper production.

But late one evening in May, after I had left for home, Maxwell suddenly made one of his rare appearances on the editorial floor and demanded that the night editor publish a story and picture about him. We are back again in the surreal world of Maxwellia. He had ordered a photographer to take a picture of himself talking to a satellite screen while receiving an honorary doctorate from Washington University in St. Louis, Missouri. He had then insisted on "helping" to write the article. If this nonevent merited any space at all it should have been five lines. Maxwell demanded a biggish picture, a big headline, and more than ten inches of copy.

The story, on reflection, is full of wonderful irony. Maxwell's degree was for "using the power of communications in the service of knowledge and the world community." He wrote the story like a child's essay, lavishly praising the university, "rated as one of the top ten in the U.S.," and ending with a very truthful statement indeed: "This is one story that the lying *Sun* could not steal or fake..."

Maxwell, unaware of edition deadlines, had no idea that the hour he spent writing this article and the maneuvers of the night editor, Mike Ryder, meant that it appeared in only a couple of thousand papers. Ryder, pleased at his subterfuge, gleefully rang to tell me what he had done. The next day Maxwell, pointing to his headline MIRROR PUBLISHER RECEIVES HONORARY DEGREE BY SATELLITE over his picture with his story, had no idea he was one of the few people able to read it.

Typically he told me: "Mister, you'd better get new journalists down there. They're no good. I had to write my own story last night. Not bad, eh."

8

"Mikhail and I Like Him a Lot"

IN my first months with Maxwell various members of staff would visit my office to offer advice on how to "deal with" Maxwell. All, it appeared, had found the key. In essence they said that he most appreciated people who "stood up to him," "took no nonsense," and "didn't let him get away with anything." I was therefore surprised when one of the most militant of these advisers—"I won't stand for him shouting at me like he does the others"—took a full-frontal, and undeserved, verbal assault from Maxwell in my presence. He later explained that, privately, he had returned to Maxwell and complained about his dressing down. Maxwell had apologized.

It was true that Maxwell alone was slightly more pliable and a little less of a bully, but there can be no doubt that there was much rewriting of scripts among those directors and executives who had to deal personally with him. I smiled every time I heard someone begin a sentence with: "So I told Maxwell..." Maxwell was never told anything.

124

As far as Maxwell was concerned, there were staff who did what he said and stayed—at least, until he tired of them—and those who would not do what he said and went, of their or his accord. It was simply a matter of time.

However, there were executives who were confident enough or clever enough, or both, who pretended to do as he said, who found ways of evading his commands, who played politics with the devil. There was no question of winning a straightforward argument with him, especially in front of witnesses, no matter how logical and sensible your point of view. *Logic* and *sense* were not in Maxwell's lexicon.

Editors, by having a public position of sorts and some regard from Maxwell, had a slightly better deal. First, we were able to step past the ninth-floor queue whenever we wished to see him. Second, we could reach him by phone at any time of the day. Third, he usually avoided criticizing us in public, though he could not avoid making an occasional remark at the regular Tuesday lunch. Fourth, our jobs placed us in a position that engendered arguments.

There are no written rules or demarcation lines between an editor and proprietor (Maxwell called himself publisher for legal reasons, but he was the proprietor). Maxwell was hardly the first cantankerous old despot with delusions of grandeur and the gift of infallibility: Hearst, Pulitzer, Northcliffe, and Beaverbrook spring quickly to mind. Inevitably the relationship between owner and editor demanded compromise.

The former Mirror Group chairman and one of Britain's most lauded editors, Hugh Cudlipp, observed: "It is a nonsense to expect any proprietor to say to his editor, 'Here it is. I will take all the financial risks in this precarious industry, but you can say what the hell you want to say in my newspaper any time you like.'"[1]

Some kind of accommodation had to be reached. However, to do so required an understanding of just why the owner owned: money, power, esteem, as a social service, political influence. In Maxwell's case, it was supposedly all of these, but narcissism ruled. I had agreed to two main goals: to increase the paper's circulation while making it more authoritative. To achieve the second, I needed to keep Maxwell out of the paper and, although he agreed "there should be less of me," he could not stop himself from breaking his word. If that alone had been the center stage of confrontation, then the job might just have been possible. But Maxwell's interference was never confined to one area.

I left the office for a holiday weekend in Ireland at the end of May 1990 feeling rather pleased with myself. The *Daily Mirror* circulation had begun to rise slightly while *The Sun* was declining. One or two media commentators were saying the things I wanted to hear about the paper being "better." The soccer World Cup was coming: we had a big competition planned and the circulation director had arranged a special distribution and sales initiative in Italy. I kept in touch with the office over the three days and there were no problems... until my deputy, Bill Hagerty, phoned on my way back from the airport. "I've been Captained," he said, his elliptical phrase for Maxwellian mayhem.

It appeared that Maxwell had suspended a sports desk executive, Mike Bowen, personally ordering the man home, without any reference to me or to my deputy. Bowen's crime had been to upset the senior football writer, Harry Harris, who was with the England soccer squad in Sardinia as they prepared for their World Cup games. He had argued heatedly with Bowen, on the desk in London, about an incorrect agency report that had appeared the day before under his name.

These kinds of disagreements, which are hardly uncommon, are extremely unlikely in the normal course of events ever to reach the ear of an editor, let alone a proprietor. But Harris was among that select bunch of journalists known as "Maxwell's favorites" and took the extraordinary step of ringing Maxwell to complain. So Maxwell, without speaking to the sports editor or the deputy editor, or instituting an inquiry to discover what had happened, suspended Bowen.

I realized that Maxwell had overstepped the mark and reassured Bowen that it would be fine for him to come back to work in the morning. If he was fired I said I was ready to go with him. Having reinstated Bowen, I then phoned Harris, who would not take my call until I got a message to him saying that if he did not call I would suspend him and order him back to Britain. I harangued Harris until he apologized to me and agreed to do the same to Bowen. "I didn't mean to get him into trouble," he said unconvincingly.

The next call was to Maxwell. Why had he usurped my role or that of my deputy? Maxwell, on the defensive for once, replied, as unconvincingly as Harris, "When you are away from the office I assume the editor's role. Just as, when I'm away, you are the publisher."

I told him that if Bowen's job was on the line then so was mine, and he surprised me by agreeing to apologize to Bowen. It might have ended there, but the incident was too juicy to escape publicity and was the lead story in the trade magazine, the *UK Press Gazette*. Since Maxwell emerged as a buffoon I was not surprised to hear that he was displeased. Hard luck, I thought. But Maxwell could not stomach public reverses of this kind and had other ways of taking his revenge.

At the end of that week we had our worst row to date over his unwarranted intervention in the paper's World Cup promotion. Of course, in the land of Maxwellia where truth was constantly deprived of oxygen, he would forever claim that he "saved" the promotion, which consisted of two simple, straightforward games based on the time goals were scored in World Cup matches and the number of the scorer's shirt. The games, Golden Goals and Lucky Shirts, had been carefully worked out in discussions with the promotions department. They had the virtue of being topical, being linked to television, and of utilizing our color advantage. They were also perfectly understandable. Their vice, in Maxwell's eyes, is that he had not been "consulted" about them—and he was extremely angry with the editor for making a public fool of him.

Behind my back, a position he grew to enjoy more and more, he intimidated the marketing and promotions department into changing the rules of the game. He said that men should be "banned" from playing Lucky Shirts and later came up with the slogan: "One for the ladies." For weeks afterward he would smile while intoning "One for the ladies...clever, eh." He linked this to one of the costliest and most disastrous decisions conceivable. He demanded that every *Mirror* reader who took part should receive a free T-shirt.

"It will be the biggest contest of all time," he said. "If only you'd come to me at first, I'd have saved you all."

One executive, doing mental arithmetic on the likely cost, stumbled from the room.

Maxwell said to those remaining, "I don't want him hanging around like a fart on a curtain rail." No one even smiled.

The annual promotions budget was about to be eaten up in one contest. We stood to give away, for nothing, one million T-shirts. In the end, it was a few thousand fewer, but the cost was enormous and the litany of complaints was counterproductive, attracting more hostility than the goodwill he hoped to foster.

Maxwell had put Jean Baddeley, his former personal assistant and his most loyal employee, in charge of offers, and she was therefore responsible for the manufacture of the T-shirts. Her report on costs alarmed him so much he ordered the shirts to be made as cheaply as possible. The quality of some was so poor they fell apart before readers had a chance to put them on. This was a common Maxwell maneuver, engineering an entirely unnecessary crisis to satisfy his hidden agenda of manipulation. An editor might resign over a member of his staff being fired, but surely not over Lucky Shirts.

Just a day or so later—a week in the life of Maxwell was nothing if not relentless—Maxwell launched the English-language version of *Moscow News*, a pro-Gorbachev paper he published in Russia. He then flew to America in a bid to steal some of the limelight in the aftermath of the U.S.-Soviet summit. The Gorbachevs were to visit Minneapolis and St. Paul, to see how Middle America was enjoying life under capitalism. Maxwell spotted an opportunity for publicity, to underline his "friendship" with Gorbachev, and announced that he was to become the benefactor of an environmental research institution in Minneapolis called the Gorbachev-Maxwell Institute. According to Maxwell, the Minnesota governor, Rudy Perpich, had "campaigned for years to bring the institute to Minneapolis."

It was a Maxwell lie, a ruse to gain Gorbachev's ear and be pictured with Gorbachev, since the institute was a fabrication and Maxwell had no intention of donating $50 million, supposedly to match a further $50 million raised by the state of Minnesota. No money arrived from either source and nothing came of the enterprise, apart from a brass plaque on a wall, and the entrée Maxwell desired. I published a picture of a beaming Maxwell and a bemused Gorbachev toasting each other with a "quote" from Raisa: "Your publisher Robert Maxwell is doing many good things in my country. Mikhail and I like him a lot."

Maxwell's *Moscow News* link did not survive for long. For all his claims about knowing the Soviet Union and acting as a go-between for presidents and prime ministers, his political understanding was slight. He did not grasp the groundswell of discontent among those elements who had swept Gorbachev to power and who had become disillusioned with their champion. So when *Moscow News* began to reflect this growing criticism, he tried to bully them into a slavish pro-Gorbachev line, without success. He had always viewed his printing-and-publishing contract simply as a way of cozying up to Gorbachev. When it did not, he dropped it. Gorbachev, for Maxwell, was his passport to becoming an international power broker and, in turn, assuming the kind of political influence that could open the doors to banks in many countries.

"Reading" Maxwell was impossible. I had reached the end of the road with one journalist, but we could not agree on her severance terms. I made the mistake of allowing her to appeal to Maxwell. He was delighted: "Let me deal with this for you. You shouldn't be troubled. That is what Your Publisher is for."

I warned the woman that she could not expect as good an offer as mine from Maxwell. I imagine her smiling at the memory—he gave her substantially more, plus her company car for £1 ($1.60). "She seemed so upset," Maxwell explained.

If his private condescension was unbearable, his public displays could be gruesome. He stood next to me while I was making a farewell speech to the retiring city editor, Robert Head, which I started by saying how sorry we were to see Bob go.

"Which one?" shouted a wit amid much laughter.

Maxwell chuckled and, as he patted me on the head, said, "He's not been here long but he's doing well, isn't he." There was a loud groan of sympathy.

If the staff had listened in to my phone every day—as, it transpired, Maxwell did—there would have been more sympathy, and a great deal of laughter. "Have you got a splash?" he asked one day on the phone from Israel, using the newspaper jargon for the main front-page story. "I have an exclusive for you."

My heart sank at such moments because they were usually the start of a row: he had no idea about the content of the *Daily Mirror* and tended to refer to my guidance in these matters as defiance. "What is it, Bob," I said.

He noted my lack of enthusiasm: "I'll only give it to you if you splash it."

I desperately wanted to say, "In that case, don't tell me," but I was polite enough to inquire what it was all about.

"I have just bought both of Jerusalem's soccer teams," he said.

I was so glad he could not see my face as I replied with some sincerity, "Wow, Bob, that's amazing."

"Right," Maxwell said. "So it's the splash."

"I don't think so, Bob. It isn't, in fairness, the greatest story in Britain."

"Fuck you," he shouted. "Why are you always arguing with me? I'll go and give this exclusive to one of your rivals."

He slammed down the phone. Maxwell, the man strapped for cash, the man who had taken little interest in any of his British soccer clubs for many seasons past, had just paid $4 million to buy up the Israeli equivalent of the Yankees and the Mets—except that HaPoel and Betar fans take their rivalry much more seriously—and hinted that he might merge them. It was as absurd as his joke to an Israeli journalist amazed at his deep pockets: "I do not yet have a license from George Bush to print dollars." He didn't need Bush while the banks were handing him cash.

Maxwell's spend-spend travels and his clever accounting did not fool everyone. In June, when he presented MCC's annual report of the year up to 31 March 1990, one young financial analyst started to question what was going on. Brian Sturgess, an unconventional but extremely bright man in his mid-thirties, realized that the company was heading for trouble.

The £172 million ($275.2 million) profits had included £41 million

($65.6 million) from property sales and were further flattered by a £19 million ($30.4 million) "exceptional item" involving the sale of a lease to the Mirror Group. Sturgess, from Barclays Bank's stockbroking subsidiary Barclays de Zoete Wedd, said tactfully that "this made the figures difficult to analyze effectively." But it meant that during the coming months he would be watching the situation at MCC very carefully indeed.

He was not alone in his concern that operating profits were contributing so little to the company's final profit figure. Derek Terrington, then at stockbrokers' UBS Phillips & Drew, called it disappointing, and a third analyst, voicing everyone's private view, said, "I am worried about the debt." This person remained anonymous, aware that Maxwell made life difficult for anyone brave enough to put his name to a negative view. Both Sturgess and Terrington would suffer Maxwell's wrath in the coming months.

But it was the presentation itself that astonished commentators. Maxwell announced that he had decided on a further "refocusing of the group's strategy." Maxwell, the printer who had less than three months before talked of transforming himself into a publisher, now said he was planning to take the company out of publishing businesses that were dependent on advertising revenue. He would concentrate instead on professional publishing and information. This refinement, which seemed to indicate he might dispose of his business and consumer divisions, was further complicated by his determination to hold on to his minority printing stakes in British Printing, and the Canadian holdings, Quebecor and Donohue. It did not mean, of course, letting go of the Mirror Group, which was dependent on advertising revenue.

Analysts and journalists shook their heads at the confused messages from Maxwell. One quipped, "I think it's called the no-strategy strategy." Shareholders began to walk away. None of them was interested in the smokescreen Maxwell threw up about the possibility of his buying Australian entrepreneur Alan Bond's stake in British Satellite Broadcasting. The Maxwell Communications share price slipped that day and went on slipping. He also mentioned a long list of assets he would sell, which he suggested would easily cover his pressing loan repayments. What he was really saying, however, was that these businesses "are to be sold." He assured everyone his bankers were sleeping peacefully. It is doubtful that he was.

If Maxwell was under suspicion in London's financial district, he could always find someone to believe in him, someone somewhere to fawn over him, to accord him the status he considered a right. So the emergent democracies of Eastern Europe became a fertile ground, where the spreading of a little now and the promise of spending countless millions in the future brought red carpets, headlines, and influence. In Poland, he bid for half of the country's press without success. Throughout June and July 1990, Maxwell turned Bulgaria into Maxwellia. It was a terrific scam. Having pledged a £10 million ($16 million) investment back in April he raised it to £30 million ($48 million). He could name a sum and double it. There was no chance that the Bulgarians would see the cash.

He sent Joe Haines and Helen Liddell, a former Scottish Labor Party organizer and Mirror Group director, to advise the Bulgarians on how to run elections in a democracy. Maxwell, who had received in 1983 the Order of Stara Planina (first class), the highest honor awarded by the Bulgarian Communist Party, for his services to President Todor Zhivkov, was now "helping" the people who had toppled the hated dictator. Once Maxwell had called Zhivkov the builder of "a prosperous and happy nation." With Zhivkov in jail, it fell to Maxwell to bring prosperity and happiness.

The election produced an impasse, with no party strong enough to form a government and none willing to form a coalition. A rash of strikes crippled the country and there were outbreaks of violence against ethnic Turks. In stepped Maxwell to "knock heads together" as one Western diplomat put it. He announced that he would withdraw his £30 million ($48 million) investment in Bulgaria unless the bickering politicians got together and set up a working government. "Time is running out for Bulgaria," he said, sounding like Churchill. He convinced party leaders that his threat would lead to withdrawal by other unspecified Western business interests.

He also demanded a very strange editorial in the *Mirror* on 19 June, extolling the Bulgarian Socialists (formerly Zhivkov's Communist Party) as "genuine" in their promise to create democracy and urging them to "create a coalition." A childhood prejudice emerged, too, in the final sentence: "The last thing the Bulgarians want is to be compared to Romanians."

The result was the formation of a coalition, a renewal of Maxwell's fanciful promises, and off went Maxwell to Turkey. There he met President Turgut Ozal and announced that he was "negotiating" to buy 49 percent of the mass circulation newspaper *Hurriyet*. "What do you think of that?" Maxwell asked me on the phone from Ankara. "A Jew is about to buy a paper in a Muslim country."

At the time I was trying to tell him of my own modest success. I had dispensed with several old-fashioned items in the paper, including a cartoon strip and a column by a former TV talk-show host, Michael Parkinson, which was supposed to be funny. I had hired a new columnist, John Diamond, whom we shall hear much more of in the future. Aside from the Scargill labor union investigation, which I had inherited, I concentrated on vigorous campaigns against Margaret Thatcher's unpopular housing tax, and her government's health and education measures, without losing the essential diet of trivia. I also made a number of subtle design changes. What I hoped to achieve was an evolutionary change in the balance of the paper.

If circulation is any guide to success then I could point to the fact that five months after taking up the job the combined sales of the *Daily Mirror* and our Scottish sister paper, the *Daily Record*, overtook those of *The Sun* for the first time since 1985. We were selling 3,903,000 copies every day. The difference was only twenty-one thousand but the trend was clearly moving our way, confirmed by the June figures, which showed a sixty-thousand lead. A month later, it had stretched to ninety-two thousand.

Maxwell's response to this success proved enlightening if depressing: "You see, my Lucky Shirts game was a winner for you. Mister Greenslade, you must consult Your Publisher more often." The use of "mister" before a surname was a sign of tetchiness; the use of "mister" alone signified anger.

One person on the staff who had shown no enthusiasm for my arrival and had never warmed to me was Maxwell's confidant, Joe Haines. After several mentions of taking early retirement, he finally wrote to Maxwell to explain why he was leaving. His typed letter was, naturally, private and confidential, for Maxwell's eyes only. Just as naturally, Maxwell tossed it across the desk one evening and urged me to read it. It was no surprise to learn of Haines's views about myself, nor that he felt that the *Daily Mirror* was no longer "what it used to be." Maxwell studied me carefully as I scanned the lines. "Much as I would have expected," I said.

"It's a pity," said Maxwell. "I told you right at the beginning to make friends with Joe."

There was an edge of menace in Maxwell's voice and I would hear that sentence several times. At the farewell party in the executive canteen, Maxwell presented Haines with some Bulgarian silver coins. His main gifts were given in private: Haines would remain a director, continue his weekly *Mirror* column (after a lengthy layoff), retain his car (even though he could not drive), and maintain a handsome salary. If everyone retired like this, there would be no one in full employment. Haines would also keep his place as Maxwell's adviser and scriptwriter.

To celebrate his semiretirement, Haines hosted a party one Saturday afternoon in late July 1990 at his home in Kent to which Maxwell dropped in, literally, by helicopter. He looked out of place in this suburban setting, but he did his best to circulate for a while. At one point, sheltering from the summer heat he took refuge inside and sat on a sofa. A small, angelic-looking child was brought forward with her parents to be introduced to the famous publisher.

Niceties were exchanged until Maxwell peered closer at the apprehensive little girl and said gruffly, "Why don't your parents do something about your teeth?"

The girl's flustered mother answered, "We have been meaning to take her to the dentist's, Mr. Maxwell."

Maxwell had such presence that this commonly happened. I was told by one executive that during the *Mirror*'s promotion tour at the beginning of Maxwell's reign they arrived in Cardiff and visited a shopping mall. Store owners and their staff gathered round Maxwell, who surprised them and his own staff by immediately suggesting how the area would benefit from certain environmental improvements. By chance there was a local councillor present who began to note down the suggestions that he reportedly attempted to implement.

Maxwell seemed to have forgotten he was there to promote his newspaper group.

Haines believed that Maxwell had the attention span of a gnat, which I can confirm, yet he had the wit to keep his compartments quite separate. There were we Mirror Group Newspapers' staff quartered in the Mirror Building. There were Maxwell Communications Corporation staff, largely located on the eighth floor of neighboring Maxwell House, notable for its distinctive light blue carpet patterned with the MCC logo—a purple *M* embossed on a globe girded by a red band. And there was "the private side," a constellation of disparate interests including soccer clubs, Macdonald's publishers, AGB market research, Panini, the soccer-stickers manufacturer, cable television, helicopters, magazines, comics, and the various foreign newspapers. There were also unspecified investment and holding companies with offices in the nearby financial district.

This private side of the private side resided partially in Maxwell's head and, of course, in Liechtenstein. It was the compartment that counted, the equivalent of the illusionist's black cloak: you could see it but could not see past it.

There were two entirely opposing theories about Maxwell's Liechtenstein trusts. Until the last couple of years it was assumed that there was a great deal of money salted away there, a personal fortune approaching £1 billion, collected under the heading of the Maxwell Foundation, and available for all sorts of charitable purposes after the death of its philanthropic founder. Maxwell's biography was explicit: it had an annual income of £25 million ($40 million) and the foundation "will be the richest of its kind in the world."[2] Maxwell's mystery was no mystery after all.

The second story, circulating among journalists and analysts from the middle of 1989, was that there was not even a cent in Liechtenstein. The black cloak was hiding the biggest Maxwell secret of all: there was nothing there. Even in August 1990, Maxwell was telling the *Financial Times* that there was "big, big money" in his foundation and in the same breath mentioned Rockefeller and Ford.[3] Commentators wondered why, if Maxwell was in such desperate straits with debts, he did not dip into his £1 billion pot. Of course, Maxwell might have argued that he did not control the trusts and could not touch the money once it had reached them. Even in 1989 that would have stretched credulity too far.

Liechtenstein is a tiny European principality that has built an economy based on the business world's fetish for avoiding tax and avoiding prying eyes. Its laws enshrining financial secrecy were designed for Maxwell's game of bluff. Anyone setting up a *stiftung*, a tax-free trust, or an *anstalt*, part company, part foundation, is guaranteed anonymity. The funds (or the lack of them) are hidden away, and those responsible for managing the trusts—the lawyers and accountants—are required by Liechtenstein law to maintain secrecy. No questions need to be answered. Here was the place where a poor man with big ambitions could provide himself with credentials that made him appear to be a very rich man indeed. Better still, a rich man with a conscience.

Maxwell discovered this haven in the early 1950s, claiming that a lawyer recommended it to his sister, Brana. For over thirty years, until 1984, Maxwell operated trusts in Liechtenstein without any apparent controversy. Then the satirical magazine *Private Eye* and the brokers acting for games manufacturer John Waddington in their defense against Maxwell's hostile takeover bid brought the link into the open. The lawyer who had always acted for Maxwell in Liechtenstein was revealed as Dr. Walter Keicher who, confronted by reporters, served with the required discretion and cited the confidentiality laws as his reason for refusing to answer questions.

Maxwell, however, was forced to explain the existence of his trusts and offer some reasons for them, to counter bad publicity suggesting he was avoiding tax, which of course he was. His foundation even enjoyed local tax-free status by the simple expedient of a donation to the Liechtenstein Institute. This was the moment in which the world heard of his charitable intentions and the funds building up for good works in the next millennium. The Maxwell Foundation was dressed up in such a light as to suggest that all other bequests to the world would be small by comparison.

In subsequent years a number of journalists, convinced that there was more to Liechtenstein than Maxwell had revealed, vainly tried to break through the secrecy. They ended up outside a four-story building in Vaduz, the capital, talking through push-button entry-phones to secretaries in the office of corporate lawyer Dr. Keicher, who resigned in 1985 in favor of his son, Werner. (Walter died at age seventy-four in 1989.) Maxwell's biography revealed just a little more, suggesting that the Maxwell Foundation had developed, via the Pergamon Foundation and the Pergamon Holding Foundation, from the Swico Foundation, itself established in 1970 by Dr. Ludwig Gutstein, "a leading Swiss lawyer and old friend of the Maxwells."[4]

Incidentally, in Maxwellese, everyone connected to him is "leading," "the top," "the respected," "the famous," and so on. According to the official story, Gutstein was so worried about the Maxwells in the Leasco era that he "set up and funded" the foundation. In 1987, Gutstein replaced himself with another Swiss lawyer, his friend, Dr. Werner Rechsteiner. The "director" from inception was Dr. Walter Keicher until his son took over.

All of this is fascinating for its deception by omission. We shall hear more later of Dr. Rechsteiner, but here we should be aware that Maxwell was attempting to suggest that in Liechtenstein there was a single entity called the Maxwell Foundation. That was not so. There were a collection of *anstalts* and *stiftungs* linked to Maxwell with exotic names such as Allandra, AKIM, Baccano, Corry, Hesto, Jungo, and Kiara. The Swico (standing for Swiss Company) *anstalt* existed separately in spite of Maxwell implying that it was a step on the road to his foundation.

Ultimately every holding in Maxwell's companies, whether public or private, led to Liechtenstein. Once it came to light, Liechtenstein became a nuisance but, for Maxwell, the virtues of his trusts outweighed their vices and there was no question of dismantling them. He was hamstrung by John Waddington's argument that there was no genuine proof of the ultimate ownership of Maxwell's companies, a successful defense to his takeover bid that became known as the "Liechtenstein card."

Other hostile takeover targets played it, too. In 1987, Extel and Harcourt Brace Jovanovich both employed the defense. This enraged Maxwell, who complained of xenophobia and amusingly accused Waddington of erecting a "smokescreen," but there was little he could do. He could not afford to be flushed into the open. His secret had to be protected at all costs. So sensitive was he about Liechtenstein that

I never heard him even mention the word in the months I was with him. His only references occurred when he was interviewed and all he would say was: "I've explained all that. There's nothing to it."

Maxwell's desire to compartmentalize was about control. As his former personal assistant, Jean Baddeley, said. "He operated on a 'need to know' basis. He had a lot in his head."[5] Only he could call the shots.

In my first weeks with him he asked me to help one of the directors, Vic Horwood, draw up a new management plan. "How does Rupert do it?" he asked. "Tell Vic how it's done over there."

Horwood, who was a survivor from the Reed era and ran the Scottish newspapers, was a pleasant and sensible man who knew he was wasting his time. I explained the hierarchical structure of Murdoch's *News International* and he noted it all down. "That's what we need here," he said. "But—" Maxwell would never contemplate it, claiming that departments would "lack accountability." What they would lack would be his long periods of apathy, stifling any initiative, and unpredictable cataclysmic interventions. Since nothing could happen without him, nothing did.

However, when he did turn his attention to a department he inevitably made bad, if not disastrous decisions. His internal compartmentalization within the Mirror Group led to bizarre accounting procedures. For instance, the preproduction departments could "charge" the editorial department for a page change. Yet the editorial budgets had no provision for such charges, quite apart from the cavalier decision making that led to the charge in the first place. This internal market was, however, protected. Even if services could be obtained cheaper outside the company, and this was frequently the case, the compartments were forced to trade with each other.

The worst example came in my second month. Executives were invited to a subbasement of the Mirror Building, one of those dingy caverns where printers had formerly set up electrical bargain shops or watched blue movies, for the grand opening of the Mirror Colour Institute poster-printing machine. The incongruity of vols-au-vents and canapés served in this sweatshop setting was magnified by Maxwell stepping on top of the machine to make a speech about this being one of the greatest and most significant moments in the history of the Mirror Group: "Now the editors here have something none of their rivals have. You will sell more papers because only we can print high-quality, full-color posters."

"Off his tree," whispered one executive near me. "Quite," answered his companion. In the following months I discovered that the institute charged more to print posters than an outside outfit, so I stopped ordering them. I then received a memo demanding that I order posters even though the circulation department reported that their budget was insufficient.

A day or so later came a call from Maxwell. "I have somebody here for you to meet. I think you'll like her."

In the tenth-floor drawing room, where Maxwell entertained his favorite or important guests, I was introduced to Melissa Richardson, "the daughter of one of my oldest friends." He turned to her: "How is your father? It's ages since I've seen him." Without waiting to hear her reply, he added: "Melissa has a great idea for you, which has my full support. Of course, you are the editor and it is for you to decide."

I smiled at the woman who seemed a little wary of Maxwell.

Before she could speak, he said: "I've known her since she was a little girl, haven't I? I must speak to your father." A phone rang for Maxwell, and Melissa explained that she ran a model agency and was always looking for new talent. She had an idea about how to find them: could the *Daily Mirror* run a contest to find girls who wanted to be models? This was not a new idea, but it was not a bad one. A "face of the 90s" competition was born, and some months later we published the contest with some success. This was one of Maxwell's entirely uncontroversial suggestions, but his reason may not have been. Melissa's father was Sir Michael Richardson, chairman of Smith New Court, the stockbrokers, and vice chairman of NM Rothschild's, the merchant bank, and one of Maxwell's closest advisers. It seemed strange they had not talked "for ages."

Maxwell's calls were unpredictable and could prove unhelpful and hilarious in equal measure. The *Daily Mirror* launched a weekly supplement largely to attract regional advertising. I suggested to Maxwell in front of other people that it be called "Extra," but I should have made the suggestion in private. The result was that he decided the name would be "Plus," and a couple of weeks before

launch we were sued by a magazine entitled *Plus*. He had to back
down and I pressed again for "Extra."

"I have decided it will be *Xtra*," said Maxwell. "Leaving off the *E*
will win us terrific publicity. You'll sell many more." For weeks after
he would niggle about what he called "the *Xtra* logo." I took that to
mean the front-page title, known in the business as a masthead, but
ignored him until the Call: "I want you to come up with your
designer. I don't like the logo for *Xtra*, and I have the answer."

Unfortunately the senior designer responsible was away, so I
arrived with his deputy, Tony Keenan, a quiet and somewhat timid
man, carrying a copy of *Xtra*.

Maxwell said truculently, "Why have you brought that?"

"Isn't this what is troubling you?"

"No. I don't know how many times I have to say it. It's the logo."

Keenan looked helplessly at me. I realized this was one of
Maxwell's frequent misunderstandings about jargon. He loved to use
it but invariably without knowing what he was talking about. After
some minutes we grasped that Maxwell was referring to the "blurb,"
a front-page advertisement for the *Xtra* supplement. There was none
to be found in his pile of papers. Panic. Maxwell called his
secretaries, the news desk, and his butler, demanding that a copy be
brought to him that minute. I was called to the phone to deal with a
news story, and Maxwell took this opportunity to question the
tremulous Keenan. "How long have you been with us?... How much
are we paying you?... Did you know that I'm an expert on layout
myself?"

Thankfully, before Keenan could get in deeper, the butler turned
up a copy. "See that," Maxwell shouted triumphantly. "It's tilted."

This was altogether too trivial to waste time in argument and I
said, "Let's straighten it."

At that moment two secretaries and a news desk reporter arrived
with papers containing the offending blurb. He testily waved them
out along with Keenan to speak to me alone: "Roy, please remember,
in matters of design, always consult Your Publisher." A victory of
whatever kind reinforced Maxwell's power.

My Publisher also liked to play reporter, though his tips always
proved false. Toward the end of July, two British girls were arrested

in Thailand on charges of drug smuggling. A fortnight later Maxwell phoned to tell me he had it "on the highest authority" that a deal had been made between the British and Thai governments to deport the girls within weeks.

I thought this unlikely. Surely a British initiative to free the girls before trial would send the wrong signals to other British nationals contemplating similar activity? Why should Thailand comply? I agreed to check it and asked for a clue to his source—Foreign Office, MP, someone else?

"I cannot say," he said conspiratorially.

I believed it even less. Minutes later he rang back to ask who was doing the job, and I lied by giving him the name of a senior reporter.

"That's no fucking good," he shouted. "You must ring that man handling the Guinness case, what's his name, he'll know."

He eventually revealed that he was talking about Michael Sherrard, Queen's Counsel, acting for the businessman Gerald Ronson, who was accused of being involved in an illegal share support operation. Ronson had been paid to buy shares by Guinness, the brewery conglomerate, when it was fighting to take over a Scottish distillery. I rang Sherrard, whose initial reaction was to laugh and, on thinking about it longer, to laugh some more. He thought it "highly improbable" but promised to make a call, though I was none the wiser why this eminent barrister in the middle of one of the longest and most complex trials in history should know anything at all or care enough to take any trouble. He rang back later to "confirm" that he was correct. I forgot all about it for a couple of weeks until Maxwell mentioned it at the regular Tuesday lunch for directors and editors. Unmoved by my denial of the story, he touched his nose and said, "I am right." At this time of writing, some twenty-four months on, the girls, having been convicted, remain in a Thai jail.

The Tuesday lunchtimes in the dining room on the tenth floor were often uncomfortable. Around the magnificent sixteen-foot three-pillar Regency table usually sat five editors and half a dozen of the most senior Mirror Group executives plus Joe Haines, before his retirement. Maxwell chose the topic for conversation—the worrying level of expenses claims, the problem of edition times, the Soviet economy, or the weather in Spain—and set the mood. He also had a console phone placed next to the table to interrupt the flow with conversations in German or Hungarian.

As if that wasn't bad enough, the food was bland and meager. Perhaps to maintain the facade of dieting he often swept his own food away. He drank wine from his own bottle while we were given inferior plonk, and he scattered crumbs from his personal basket of matzos like a child.

Maxwell's unpredictability meant that lunches were often canceled or started very late. After a succession of delayed starts over a number of weeks, I turned up to find Maxwell had arrived on time and ordered lunch to start. The voice boomed: "Why are you late, Mister Greenslade?"

"Sorry, Bob, but I was sorting out an exclusive story."

"That is not a good enough reason for being late for me."

Two minutes later the advertising director, Roger Eastoe, arrived to a similar growled inquiry.

"I was sealing a deal for a million quid's worth of business," he said brightly, expecting a word of praise.

"That's not a reason for being late, Roger the Dodger," Maxwell said. "Don't do it again."

Some five minutes later still, the then *Sunday Mirror* editor, Eve Pollard, turned up and was also called to account.

"I was talking to my daughter," she said.

"That is family," Maxwell said. "Family is the only reason I will accept for lateness at my lunches."

The following week Maxwell kept us waiting for more than an hour before arriving for lunch, drank a mouthful of soup from his huge bowl-size cup marked I'M A VERY IMPORTANT PERSON, and suddenly left.

At lunch one got some idea of the gigantic costs of Maxwell's lifestyle. In the restaurant-size kitchen the food was cooked by Martin the chef. It was served by Simon, the valet, and Joseph, the butler. Washing up was Juliette, the cleaner. She was the full-time organizer of several part-time Filipino women who scurried around the apartment. Downstairs, waiting for their master's whim, were John, the chauffeur of the red Rolls-Royce, and Dick, the pilot of the Aerospatiale Twin Star helicopter (with a second pilot always on call as well). At Farnborough airport there was Karen the stewardess, and the two-man flight crew of the Gulfstream 4 jet, bought in summer 1990. His "old" 1976 Gulfstream 2 (plus a second crew) remained as backup. In Spain Maxwell kept on hand the thirteen-strong crew of his yacht, the *Lady Ghislaine*.

At Headington Hill Hall Maxwell supported Betty's own permanent staff of three, not to mention gardeners, lodgekeepers, and security men. In addition, of course, there were Maxwell's personal battery of secretaries and personal public-relations staff. He also "borrowed" people from the Mirror Group, such as drivers, caterers, waiters, and lawyers, especially lawyers. One firm of solicitors, David Maislish, maintained a permanent office in Maxwell House.

Maxwell lived like a latter-day emperor and questions about his being in debt were hard to reconcile with the display of wealth. This was just as Maxwell desired: it was both gratifying to partake of the luxury and necessary as part of the façade so essential to fooling outsiders. Business and pleasure wrapped in one.

Maxwell reveled in his celebrity. He was notorious for squeezing himself onto tabletops at functions where he was not expected, and for failing to turn up at functions where he was the honored guest. Everyone had to accommodate his appalling manners. At a Press Club luncheon where the *Daily Mirror* was to receive a major award, Maxwell became bored while waiting for the ceremony and decided to leave early. His giant camel hair coat was buried under scores of others on the coat stand. He scowled at the commissionaire, lifted armfuls of coats off and tossed them on the floor until he found his own, pulled on a baseball cap, and nodded a farewell.

Once traveling between London and Oxford by car, he decided he wanted fish and chips and ordered his chauffeur to pull up next to an old woman. She began to explain the way to the shop but Maxwell told her to get in and take them. At the shop Maxwell strode to the front of a long queue and made his order.

Far from protesting, several members of the queue asked him to sign his autograph on scraps of newspaper wrapping. He gave the old woman a ten-pound note to get a taxi home and drove off in his Rolls-Royce tucking into cod and chips. He was, according to all those who traveled abroad with him, recognized in the strangest of places; in

Turkey, for instance, children would shout his name if they saw him passing in the street.

In August 1989, he attended the party to celebrate a genuine millionaire's seventieth birthday. How could Maxwell upstage the host, Malcolm Forbes, and ensure that his own picture would appear in newspapers across the world? The answer was to be the only guest to appear in costume. Sightseers thronging the approach road to the party in Tangiers, Morocco, thought Maxwell so imposing as a beturbaned maharajah that they threw petals in his path.

One of his yacht crew, Nigel Hodson, who accompanied the Maxwells, said, "He lapped it up. He loved being the center of attention." Hodson, a good-looking young man in his naval uniform, managed to wangle his way into the party as well. "Maxwell enjoyed that, too," Hodson said. "He told me, 'Not even Signor Agnelli could get his skipper in.' It was one-up for him."

Reflecting on the fussing attention he received at a function in Brussels in contrast to Prince Philip—once described as "a close friend of ours" by Betty[6]—he told an interviewer: "Wasn't it embarrassing... The same thing happened to me once in Moscow with the prime minister of Belgium. Everyone was lined up ready to greet him. Then I arrived, and he was left standing. And I don't even have tits like Elizabeth Taylor."[7]

These little episodes must not conceal from us the serious problems he was facing. At the end of July 1990, the MCC annual report made fascinating reading. Critics were quick to note that exceptional items and property deals accounted for most of the profits; that interest payments, amounting to £108 million ($172.8 million), were growing faster than operating profits. There was scarcely enough profit anyway to cover the dividend payment. Maxwell was enraged by media accounts of this report, and it became known in the Maxwell office, following a 9 pence (14 cents) drop in the share price, as "the July crisis."[8]

True to form, Maxwell actually boasted that having spent $600 million on acquiring new businesses during the year proved his debt was not a headache. This fooled only a few in the financial world, though most remained silent. One who did not was Quintin Price at James Capel who argued that the sole reason for anyone owning

MCC shares was the yield; in the absence of a dividend the shares would collapse. Essentially, Price was suggesting that MCC was on the verge of going bust. Separately, the *Financial Times*'s influential columnist Lex reached a similar conclusion, arguing that the group's net worth was a negative £1.2 billion ($1.92 billion).

Maxwell felt he could not let these criticisms pass. He discovered an error in Price's penetrating analysis, which had estimated MCC's cash flow at £68.7 million ($109.92 million), and called Capel's chief executive. In the end Price was encouraged to revise the figure to £141.1 million ($225.76 million), but he and his company refused to change their forecast. So, while Maxwell trumpeted about the "mistake" in public, the private note to salesmen—which was what really counted—still urged them to sell. "It was typical Maxwell," Price said. "I got ninety-nine things right and one minor point wrong and he seized on it. When my chief executive and I went to see him he backed off. I thought he was bananas."

Meanwhile, Maxwell harried the *Financial Times*'s Lex by arguing that it was "irresponsible and impermissible" for him to have excluded intangibles from the net worth of a publishing company such as MCC. Maxwell loved dealing in "goodwill" and "intangibles" in his accounts, which have their rightful place in accountancy, but the very looseness of the terms was fertile ground for Maxwell's imaginary forecasting. In the end Maxwell settled for a letter in the *Financial Times* and an "explanatory" feature, which might have pleased Maxwell but was deftly written in order not to mislead the City. These "scribblers," as Maxwell referred to analysts and journalists, were now beginning to agree that MCC was heading in only one direction.

9

On the Tightrope

MAXWELL spoke nine languages, fathered nine children, and lived nine lives. The date 14 August 1990 marked the birth of the ninth, the beginning of the end. From this point on, the scale of the debt and the impossibility of servicing it transformed Maxwell the ingenious illusionist and adept juggler into an ungainly tightrope walker. Maxwell had done his best to cover most of his tracks, alternately swaggering and suing as he blurred the distinction between immorality and illegality, and he was transformed into a panic-stricken con man unable and unwilling to recognize the inevitability of failure.

The arcane world of high finance is not always easy to understand and even less so in the City of London, where the rules and regulations tend to be subject to custom and practice and underwritten by that most charming of old-fashioned concepts: A gentleman's word is his bond. There has been a tightening of the rules in recent years, but New York's Wall Street is policed more firmly. It is not so much that millions change hands by word of mouth within minutes, as they do, it is the continuously fluid definition of what is fair play and what is not. This means that while many people in the City understand the laxity of the rules, they discern the reason for them and are content to obey both letter and spirit.

Maxwell enjoyed nothing better than to pour scorn on investment bankers and brokers, fulminating against some alleged failure to observe their own codes. However, throughout his life, he ignored the notion of there being any difference between letter and spirit. As we have seen, he always operated on the margins and—depending on one's view of him—was therefore either a breath of fresh air in the fusty world of the City, or a chiseler out to make a buck at any cost. If the latter is the case, then it is also true that he gathered many financiers around him in his dubious dealings. It is not easy for people outside the world of business (like myself) to grasp easily some of the strokes pulled by Maxwell, since they also stretched the credulity of experienced insiders, but I have simplified them as much as possible to make them understandable to all. I will try not to let City jargon defeat us either.

The first major date on Maxwell's calendar was 23 October 1990, when he was due to repay $415 million to the banks. Selling off businesses was proving difficult, so he was intent on raising loans by mortgaging shares. This was fine, as long as the share price went up or remained constant. If it went down too far then the banks would demand more shares as collateral for their loans. Yet he was confronted in early summer by a steadily falling share price. His initial response in July was to try to shore up the price by buying his own shares in the market. He spent more than £75 million ($120 million), and the total of shares traded that month far exceeded any other month in the year. Even so, the price continued to fall.

This continued loss in value not only alarmed Maxwell, it also troubled Goldman Sachs, the American-based merchant bank that held millions of MCC shares as loan collateral.

In order to allay their fears, Maxwell took his first hesitant step on the tightrope by entering into an extraordinary agreement. He sold, through his private companies, a "put option" to Goldman Sachs for 15.65 million MCC shares. In layman's language, Maxwell was acting as a kind of safety net to the bank, agreeing to buy back his own shares at a certain price (185 pence [$2.96]) on a certain future date (30 November 1990) so as to ensure the bank did not lose out. All manner of myth has grown up around this deal, which is without doubt a controversial one, mainly because of the cloak of secrecy drawn around it and partly because analysts, and consequently investors, failed to spot its significance at the time.

That was hardly surprising. The first communication to the stock exchange was made on 23 August and merely stated that Maxwell's private company, Bishopsgate Investment Trust, had "acquired an interest" in 15.65 million MCC shares. If that disclosure had stated honestly that it was a "put option" then the alarm bells would have sounded among analysts, and it is not too farfetched to imagine that it would have led to a run on the shares. If one were charitable it might be considered an oversight by Maxwell, but that stretches credulity too far since it was so much in his interest to conceal the truth. It was obviously a ploy.

Six days later the same Bishopsgate company disclosed that it had bought a further ten million MCC shares. Then, in a carefully worded statement written on 5 September and delivered by hand to the stock exchange the next day, Maxwell hinted at the true nature of his 14 August transaction. The previous announcements had "omitted to include the price per share," it said, and cleverly linked the two purchases even though they were very different: the first was a "put option" and the second was a straightforward acquisition. There was no clear mention of the "put," though experienced analysts would have been under no illusion if they had noticed it. How then did they miss it?

There were probably overlapping reasons. Analysts provide information to potential share buyers, and by this time there was almost no interest in MCC stock from their major clients, the institutions, so there was no reason for paying too much attention to Maxwell's deals. Most of the holdings in MCC, except for Maxwell's own, were in computer-linked institutional funds that invested in the top one hundred quoted shares. Maxwell Communications' membership of the prestigious top hundred was, in fact, under review.

Most analysts were genuinely diverted by more pressing matters. Some were, frankly, so fed up with the problems of dealing with a domineering Maxwell they had virtually given up on MCC. He was just too much trouble for analysts, denouncing them to their bosses and putting them under intolerable pressure through his well-connected City allies. When the "put" did eventually come to light, there was a suggestion that the stock exchange had not announced it on their screens, but this was not so. It just escaped everyone's attention—to Maxwell's benefit.

The other importance of the "put" was the 30 November date on which Maxwell chose to buy back the shares from Goldman. This meant that the option spanned the special "closed period" that exists in the two months before the declaration of interim results when it is against stock-exchange rules to purchase one's own shares. The rule is unequivocal and there was no question of Maxwell breaching it. It has therefore been generally assumed that Maxwell's "put" agreement with Goldman was a neat dodge to circumvent the closed-period ban. Unable to buy his own shares, he simply encouraged someone else to do so on his behalf, a maneuver not unlike being banned from a casino but bankrolling a friend to play the tables for you.

Indeed, the friend, Goldman, was being given a good incentive to enter the market since MCC shares were then being quoted at about 170 pence ($2.72) and Maxwell was guaranteeing to buy them back at 185 pence ($2.96). Goldman, alarmed by criticism of its part in the transaction, has pointed out that this was not true, since the "put" agreement occurred some six weeks before the start of the closed period, at a time when the company already held a substantial number of MCC shares. This tends to suggest that Goldman could have exercised its option without buying up more shares.

While I am inclined to regard this as a disingenuous defense, even if we allow it, we should turn from Goldman to consider instead Maxwell's intentions and the effect of his "put." One of Maxwell's major worries was that a failure to support his share price would lead to the then gradual decline accelerating into a downward spiral. If Goldman used its option to buy shares then the share price was being supported, and Maxwell's secondary aim—to stimulate a false demand for his shares—would also have been achieved. There is evidence that some private shareholders were materially affected by not knowing about the "put." At least two of them began to make inquiries that would be passed on to the authorities, the consequences of which we will consider later (see Epilogue).

Maxwell's share buying caused another headache for him. By buying up more and more of MCC, his so-called public company was in danger of reverting to his private ownership. At the end of March the accounts showed Maxwell and his related interests owned 55.5 percent of the company and by August it had leapt to 64 percent. Under stock-exchange rules there is a 75 percent limit, but questions would be asked at 70 percent. In this atmosphere only Maxwell could dare to announce that MCC was about to raise a fund of $250–500 million (£134–269 million) to invest in the emerging democracies of Eastern Europe. He announced that he was putting $52 million into the fund and that the American banking-and-brokerage firm Merrill Lynch, which was to raise and operate the fund, was to invest $5 million.

In mid-1990 Maxwell also changed his stockbrokers. Alexanders Laing & Cruickshank, who had been responsible for the July 1987 British Printing rights issue, gave way to Smith New Court under its new chairman, Sir Michael Richardson, father of Melissa, whose model agency the *Mirror* had helped, and the man Maxwell had not spoken to in ages. Smith had developed as one of the City's biggest stock dealers and was considered to have formidable market-placing power. This was important for Maxwell as he sought to dispose of businesses and, possibly, take the Mirror Group public.

Fiddling with millions did not stop Maxwell from interfering in the *Daily Mirror,* especially if his wider interests were threatened in some way. On the evening of 1 August, the news desk heard on the grapevine that the rival *Daily Mail* had "a big one." In the incestuous world of Fleet Street it is impossible for a newspaper to keep an exclusive story entirely secret, and these kinds of tips are common, but nobody had a clue about the subject. "All I know is that it's bloody big and will run and run," said the news editor, Steve Lynas.

It was enough for me to stay at work until the *Mail* first edition arrived close to midnight. The story was indeed remarkable. The Hungarian ambassador to Britain, Dr. Jozsef Gyorke, had been recalled to Budapest after police had begun investigating the fact that his unmarried daughter had given birth to a child in London and disposed of its body in a refuse bin. Scotland Yard wanted Dr. Gyorke to forgo his diplomatic immunity in order to launch a full inquiry, but the Hungarian authorities refused and recalled their man. The *Mail* and its reporter had done a superb job on the story, which was fully authenticated with long interviews, and it had all the elements of a terrific tabloid tale: sex, death, drama, and international intrigue.

Competition demands that on occasions such as this rival papers do all in their power in the limited time available to cover the story in their final editions. There are two normal approaches: if the story can be proved true it must be matched; if the story can be proved wrong, it is knocked down. At the *Mirror* I had the best source of all because I knew Dr. Gyorke was closely associated with Robert Maxwell. I rang Maxwell but before I had gotten one sentence into explaining the story he said, "Don't touch it. It's all lies."

I thought he had not understood and tried to go on.

"That's an order."

I protested and he put the phone down. I allowed the news desk and night desk to continue to catch up until the night news editor walked in to say Maxwell had been on the phone and shouted at him for "disobeying orders."

I rang Maxwell back and told him, not for the first time, that news was news and the *Daily Mirror* could not be seen to miss a big story.

He said softly, "Roy. I promise you there's no truth in it."

I butted in: "No truth in what?"

Maxwell kept his temper: "I know about this. It isn't true. You will get an exclusive on this—the full interview. Only you will get it. This will cost the *Daily Mail* millions. We must print nothing."

I began to explain that Gyorke had spoken to the *Mail* and confirmed the story. It was not a case of there being room for error. The story was correct. He hung up on me and called the news desk again, ordering them not to publish anything to do with Gyorke. Naturally they came to me for advice. Did they obey the owner or the editor?

I told them to continue to work on the story. Maxwell phoned again, speaking softly: "Roy, there are things you cannot know. I want you to accept my word on this. I have never asked you to do this before..."

I smiled as he continued in a conspiratorial tone: "I am requesting you not to publish this story or anything about it. However, if you refuse my request then I'm afraid I will have to issue a direct command to you as Your Publisher. I have the right to do this, as you know."

No such "right" existed, of course. Maxwell made up these rules as he went along to suit himself. I said, "It will have to be an order."

"So be it," he replied. "Good night."

The reactions of the news desk and night desk executives said it all. Their editor had failed. I did not attempt to fool anyone by suggesting it was my decision, and from then on I decided to make it as clear as possible to staff when unfair pressures were being exerted by Maxwell. As chance would have it, in spite of every paper but the *Mirror* following the *Daily Mail*'s story, it did not run after that single day because Saddam Hussein ordered his troops to invade Kuwait on 2 August. Fleet Street was diverted by a much bigger story.

I next heard of Dr. Gyorke many months later when he arranged an interview with the Hungarian president Arpad Gonz for *The European* and I bumped into him on the ninth floor of Maxwell House. He had left the diplomatic service by then and was MCC's director of International Relations.

The Gyorke intervention was unwelcome, but the outbreak of war ensured that it did not become public knowledge. The next intrusion was of an altogether different order with far more sinister connotations. I was returning from my summer holiday when my deputy, Bill Hagerty, phoned to say he had been given a bizarre order by Maxwell. That day the Guinness trial, in which three men were charged with orchestrating an illegal share-support operation during a 1986 takeover battle for Distillers, a whiskey manufacturers, had ended. The rival bidders were Guinness, the famous brewery firm, and Argyll, a chain store. The three men in the victorious Guinness camp—Ernest Saunders, Anthony Parnes, and Gerald Ronson—were charged variously with fraud, false accounting, theft, and conspiracy. All were found guilty and sentenced to jail terms.

Hagerty told me that Maxwell had "requested" that Ronson's name be excluded from the *Mirror*'s report. Hagerty scoffed at the idea: it would make the paper a laughingstock and there was no question of deleting one man's name. In typical fashion, Maxwell made several phone calls trying to harass Bill, but he stood his ground. Thwarted by the direct approach, Maxwell ordered a "soft" equivocating editorial to be written, the opposite of what the *Daily Mirror* should have been saying about bad behavior in big business.

Of course, Bill and I were unaware at the time that Maxwell had himself been involved in the takeover. There were whispers, and I recalled Maxwell's sudden demand in July that I call Ronson's defense counsel about the British girls arrested in Thailand—but no hard facts. During the course of the trial Maxwell spoke to me twice about the defendants. Once he observed that "it was stupid of them to get involved" and the other time he suggested that "Ronson and the others" should not have been charged. In public statements he strenuously denied any involvement and threatened writs against journalists who suggested he was linked.

It was not until the *Mail* on Sunday of 6 October 1991, one month before Maxwell's death, that the truth emerged. Maxwell had, through Pergamon Holdings, one of his Liechtenstein-owned trusts, bought one hundred thousand shares in the closing stages of the bid. The purchase, though small, might well have helped to sustain the Guinness share price at its most crucial stage. He bought the shares through Parnes, the stockbroker convicted of organizing Ronson's part in the illegal share-support operation. A few months later Maxwell did admit to having "an interest" in 4.5 million Guinness shares and spoke out on behalf of Saunders.

But the story does not end there, because Maxwell always called in his favors. Some months after the Distillers takeover, Morgan Grenfell, the merchant bank, approached Guinness and asked it to help underwrite Maxwell shares (in British Printing) that were being issued in connection with Maxwell's bid for an obscure investment trust. Guinness agreed to do so, as long as it was indemnified against any loss, which it was. Someone who was very close to Maxwell and who would like to remain anonymous explained to me when I queried the Ronson request: "Guinness made him sweat. He knew he came close." In other words, he might have faced charges—and jail—with the other three men.

In the month of August 1990, at the same time that he was juggling millions and should have been doing everything he could to calm investors' fears, the man who could not say no said yes to another strange deal. Off at another tangent, he became embroiled in a bid to take over one of Britain's leading soccer teams, the London-based Tottenham Hotspur team. Maxwell already owned two other clubs and had stakes in two more. Over the next couple of months he wasted time on a failed attempt to buy the team. Soccer supporters mounted a publicity campaign against Maxwell, illustrating the depth of public distaste for him. He tried to counter this hostility by courting journalists on newspapers outside the Mirror Group.

Maxwell enjoyed dealing direct with journalists; many often got through to him surprisingly easily. But he still wanted a public-relations person to handle the scores of requests and inquiries that flooded into his office. There was no rush for the post since Maxwell's track record with personal publicity was abysmal.

He began to pester me to give him someone from the *Mirror* staff. I refused, but Joe Haines suggested a news-desk assistant who, amazingly, agreed to step in for a period. He lasted for a couple of months until he pleaded to return.

I suggested to Maxwell he hire a professional from outside, and a week or so later, at a Tuesday lunch, we were introduced to Bob Beaver, an eager American. He was a fresh and open young man who smiled a lot and talked even more. Everything about him suggested to me that he would get on Maxwell's nerves.

I asked Joe Haines: "How long do you think he'll last?" Haines did not have time to reply before Maxwell, clearly in a black mood, arrived to eat. His manner set the tone and nobody attempted to speak. Suddenly he launched into a tirade against the production director about problems in the Mirror Group printing works that were wasting newsprint, and he concluded: "You can't fool me. I'm a detail man."

Young Beaver, bright eyes shining and keen to ingratiate himself with his new boss, spoke up: "I'm sure finding that out, Mr. Maxwell."

"What," said Maxwell, turning the single word into a roar.

Haines whispered in my ear: "Less than a week."

The young publicity man did not appear at another lunch, but before he vanished from the company he had a walk-on role in a magazine article about Maxwell. Asked about Maxwell's schedule for the day, he unknowingly summed up his own fate: "I'm as loose as a goose on that one."[1]

Maxwell then began to harass me. "If you had any regard at all for Your Publisher you would provide him with a PR," he would say, his face downcast. Haines came to the rescue again, recommending one of the political staff, Andy McSmith, to stand in during the Parliamentary recess. He had previously been a Labour Party publicist and, as a bonus, spoke Russian. He proved so capable at the task that when he asked to return to his proper job Maxwell demanded that he stay. "Politics won't be interesting in the next seven or eight months," Maxwell said two months before Thatcher's resignation. Wisely, Andy went back to reporting.

When a certain job needed to be done Maxwell was oblivious to people's positions and to their routine. Kevin and Ian appeared in my office one evening in September: "Bob would like you to go to East Berlin tomorrow." They both had found good reasons not to go, and I was intrigued by the opportunity. So off I went by helicopter and private jet with production director Bob Lindsay and an interpreter. Our task was to accept the handover of Berliner Verlag, the largest publishing firm in East Germany, from the previous owners, the Communist Party. Maxwell had joined a fifty-fifty joint venture with Gruner & Jahr, a subsidiary of the giant Bertelsmann group in West Germany, paying £67 million ($107.2 million) for his half share. The source of Maxwell's money for this venture was a mystery. It was bought through one of his private trusts.

On the plane I was amused to read in the notes for my speech that I was to assure the senior staff of the group's flagship paper *Berliner Zeitung* that "Mr. Maxwell has no intention of interfering in the editorial content" and that I was also to tell them that tomorrow (until then unknown to me) a leading article signed by Robert Maxwell welcoming the unification of Germany would appear in the *Daily Mirror*.

It soon became obvious that Gruner & Jahr were not happy that Maxwell had sent a substitute, because they had to deal with all the detailed questions during a tense meeting at the paper. The editorial staff exhibited great suspicion about the West German firm and little or no interest in a Maxwell emissary. All their questions were about money—"When will we get Western wages?"—and job security.

At the printers I realized the shock they had coming: it was overstaffed almost five-fold. In my diary I noted: "Those poor Germans on the other side of the Wall don't know what's about to hit them. The 'freedom' they seek is not the freedom they will get."

For Maxwell it was just a diversion, and he eventually left it to Bob Lindsay, a tough and capable production executive, to run Berliner Verlag.

The real reason Maxwell had avoided going emerged later. Some senior staff had voiced concerns about his previous involvement with East Germany's deposed leader Erich Honecker. Maxwell declared after his 1989 trip to see Honecker that he had been "a reformer all his life." A week later Honecker was arrested on charges of stealing his country's national treasures. Maxwell explained to *Guardian* journalist Hugo Young: "What you don't know is that I went for that meeting on a major and important mission for the West, to deal with refugees."

"Who asked you to perform this mission?" Young asked.

"Just leave it at that. The highest level."[2]

Variations of the deliberately obscure phrase "there are things you cannot know" kept most persistent interrogators at bay.

Maxwell's claim to have met Honecker on behalf of the Bonn Government to arrange the release of East German political refugees might have carried a little more weight if any official or politician at any level or, better still, any refugee had been willing to authenticate it.

He enjoyed mystery because it lent glamour to the truth. It was also a necessary way of life. If we at Mirror Group had had an inkling about his true financial state we might have understood better what lay behind his mysterious decision to hold a "strategy conference" at the end of September. It was held at the Selsdon Park Hotel, Croydon—famous in modern British political history as the place where Conservative leader Edward Heath and his team met early in 1970 to finalize plans that would result in their winning that year's election.

The Mirror Group conference was supposed to be about planning the Group's next three years, but there would be no victory to crown our work. Of the seven tasks outlined for detailed discussion the last, issue of stock to the public, public flotation, was dismissed by virtually every one of the two dozen people present. "He's told us twice a year for every year since he bought us that flotation is about to happen. It never will," one director said. Instead, as would be expected of all good managers, we concentrated on the drive for improved market share in sales and advertising revenues.

I was particularly concerned because the sales success of early summer had gone into reverse, and I attributed this drop directly to the comparative amount of time and money spent on television advertising by us and *The Sun*. They had responded to our improved figures with a sustained TV ad campaign, spending £2.85 million ($4.56 million) in August and September. We had spent just £1.1 million ($1.76 million) in an uncoordinated response, with Maxwell refusing to allow the marketing department the right to spend its agreed budget.

This had led to my losing my temper in an early-morning row with Maxwell; I argued that his restrictive hold on budgets interfered with my ability to edit. It became so heated I screamed at him, swearing at him for the first and only occasion: "Fuck you and fuck your job." I then walked out of his office to find a group of nervous but appreciative secretaries, which was handy because one was kind enough to go into the office to retrieve the briefcase I had left behind.

The unpredictable Maxwell took this encounter with commendable calm, asking an intermediary—the ever-tactful and shrewd Ernie Burrington, the managing director—to persuade me to join him for a drink that evening in his apartment. "Roy," he said, "How did it come to this? People tell me you're good, but all you do is defy me and shout at me. I have told you before, the relationship between a Publisher and an Editor has to be closer than that between a husband and wife. We're not close enough. You don't consult me. And when I do make suggestions you always say no and start arguing with me. You wouldn't do that to your wife. You mustn't do it to me."

He added with a touch of menace: "We cannot go on like this. You must change your ways or it will have to end." Then, slyly, he asked, "Do you want it to end?"

"No, but I—."

"There you go, arguing with me... Roy, I want to make you a millionaire. I'm going to make you a millionaire very soon. Please don't defy me all the time."

I had this row in mind as I listened to the various heads of department make their presentations at the Selsdon conference. As forecasts of future revenue were debated and amended, the finance director and his assistant crunched and recrunched numbers. Then, on the afternoon of the second day, Maxwell's helicopter landed. Within a couple of minutes it was clear that he was totally uninterested in any three-year strategy, only in a single stratagem.

What would happen if the cover price of the *Daily Mirror* went up? No editor is happy about a price rise because sales are often badly hurt, but rises are inevitable and I guessed one was coming. With television promotion of bright editorial content and promotion material, the affect can be minimized. Traditionally, though formal agreement between rival newspaper groups would be against competition policy, there has been a close shadowing of rises; usually, within a week of one paper increasing its price, its closest rival or rivals follow suit. I knew I must plan for one before Christmas.

Maxwell seemed to be in an affable mood at the conference, though I now realize he was preoccupied. He was under great financial pressure but acted as if all were well. As the conference broke up on the Saturday evening, with Maxwell flying back to Holborn, I was unaware of his true desperation. As normal on a Saturday night, I collected the first editions of the Sunday newspapers and read them before going to bed. On my way into work next morning the car telephone rang and a woman said: "Mr. Maxwell for you."

"Good morning, Roy." In three words I detected the slightly apologetic tone, always a worrying sign. "I tried to reach you at home last night. I have decided that the *Daily Mirror*'s price should increase by three pence on Wednesday."

The paper was currently selling for twenty-two pence (about thirty-five cents) so the hike to twenty-five pence (about forty cents) represented a 13.5 percent rise.

"Which Wednesday?" I asked in some alarm.

"This Wednesday."

"That's madness," I shouted. "We aren't ready. There's been no television, no planning...three pence is huge. Our circulation will dive—"

"Be quiet," he said. "Come and see me as soon as you get in."

If anything, I grew more angry during the ten-minute drive, I believed it was commercial suicide but, at the personal level, I considered it a snub, a blow to my pride, to take such a step without informing me first. I thought I would persuade him to delay it. It was only when I arrived at the office that I found that he had made a public announcement of the price rise in the later editions of the *Sunday Mirror* and *Sunday People*.

In his office I raged at him for the second time in two weeks, even employing his own favorite tactic by banging his desk before he had the chance to. But temper does not always generate the best argument. Only later did I realize I should have quoted to him his line about a publisher and editor being closer than a husband and wife. What editor ever had his price rise announced behind his back in another newspaper, without consultation, with only three days' notice, without coherent planning?

Though he was surprised by my anger, Maxwell played his twin cards: feigned sorrow at my plight and the familiar ruse of this being a bigger matter than I could possibly know about. "Don't worry," he said. "You're going to be all right."

There was worse news to come as the other shocked heads of department arrived in a variety of sweaters from their Sunday mornings at home. Maxwell had decided to reap still more of the price-rise harvest by reducing the margin paid to the newspaper retailers. In Britain, papers are traditionally sold through specialized shops known as newsagents. Many individual retailers have formed themselves into powerful trade associations to defend their interests. All of us realized a cut in newsagents' margins would cause a storm of protest from them since it amounted to a cut in their wages.

The whole episode would rankle ever after, and though I now understand the reasons for his move, it proved to be one of the most disastrous decisions he made. Murdoch, equally strapped for cash, followed suit a week later with a similar price rise for *The Sun* (though his editor had time to plan for it) and, craftily, blamed his decision to reduce newsagents' margins on Maxwell, suggesting he had been "forced" to do so "reluctantly" to remain competitive. However, the net effect of the two tabloids raising their price by one of the largest amounts in history added to both the long-term downward circulation trend and the decline caused by the recession. From October 1990, sales of the *Daily Mirror* and *The Sun* have fallen relentlessly. As I write, both papers are hovering at daily sales of 3,500,000, a decline of 400,000 each since October 1990.

Although Maxwell did not want to issue stock in the Mirror Group because of the internal financial problems it would cause in unraveling his intertwined companies, it is probable that at this point he had decided it was inevitable. He therefore needed to begin boasting of the *Mirror*'s profitable status. Unfortunately he chose to publish the fact that the group had made "a record" £84 million ($134.4 million) profit on the same day the *Mirror*'s price rose and the newsagents took a pay cut.

It was a public-relations blunder of the first order. A vociferous minority of newsagents began to whip up anti-Maxwell propaganda, and the angriest took the only route open to them short of confronting Maxwell in person; just a few removed the *Daily Mirror* from sale altogether (though probably only for a day or two) while many others indulged in a variety of tactics unhelpful to the paper, such as placing copies in a poor position on the counter or refusing to order extras after running out. It is doubtful if this revolt lasted for long and it was difficult to assess its effects, but it certainly hurt us at a sensitive time.

On the day of the price rise I had little time to think about its consequences. We were due at the Labour Party's annual conference in Blackpool for the traditional Mirror Group reception, and a lunch for the party leader and his wife, hosted by Maxwell. It was one of the handful of occasions on which I was able to study Maxwell and Betty together. On his Gulfstream jet up to Blackpool he lay down on his bed in the curtained-off front section of the plane and Betty fussed around him, gently chiding him for working so hard, which, she said, was making him ill. For some time he had suffered from a cold and could not seem to shake it off. He barked at her to leave him alone, but she took this display of temper in her stride, eventually joining us in the seating area, apparently unconcerned at his mood.

"He works too hard," she said to no one in particular, and settled down to read what appeared to be a Jewish religious text. Minutes before touchdown, Maxwell, having changed his shirt, which he did at least three times a day, appeared in the cabin and smiled lovingly at Betty. Her delight at this slight show of affection was obvious.

Maxwell's reputation as a maverick within the Labour Party while an MP was reinforced from 1984 when he bought the Mirror Group.

He was variously thought by outsiders to be the Party's paymaster, a puller of strings, a figure of peculiar prestige. Yet he was none of these. In spite of his penchant for launching legal actions he never sought to sue anyone who made false allegations about his supposed power within the Labour Party, nor did he even issue a public statement of denial.

Indeed, the only action involving Labour he did fight—the one against *Private Eye* for falsely suggesting he had offered Labour leader Neil Kinnock a favor in order to receive a peerage—illustrates how keen he was to preserve his public image as a man who would not need to stoop to such levels to attain his wishes. This was the main reason he allowed misunderstandings to flourish, because he enjoyed being thought of as a man of influence. Nothing could have been further from the truth. He had few friendships with MPs, most of his contemporaries having left Parliament by 1987, and none with Kinnock's senior team.

Neil Kinnock's relationship with him was almost nonexistent, amounting to no more than a polite cordiality in public. Kinnock's wife, Glenys, found even this demeanor hard to maintain and disliked intensely the few occasions on which she needed to be in his company. There were very few private meetings, perhaps stemming from the embarrassing night when the Kinnocks invited the Maxwells out to dinner at their favorite local Indian restaurant. Bob and Betty, dressed as if they were attending a banquet at the Ritz, arrived separately, chauffeur-driven, in His and Hers Rolls-Royces.

The uneasy relations were not helped by Maxwell relying on Joe Haines as his major political adviser and party go-between since Haines, as Harold Wilson's former press officer, was viewed in Party circles as one of yesterday's men. To complicate matters, Kinnock viewed the *Mirror* political editor, Alastair Campbell, as his link to the paper. Haines was certainly not well disposed to the new leadership, and his constant refrain to Maxwell was: "They want your money, Bob, but they don't want you." For all that, Maxwell never deviated in his general support for Labour and consciously endorsed the Mirror Group papers' faithful adherence to the Party.

Since Maxwell flaunted riches it was natural that the Party, particularly those elements worried about raising funds to fight elections, should look to Britain's foremost "millionaire socialist" to provide more than just the backing of his newspapers. This was brought home to me during a meeting in Maxwell's suite at Blackpool's Pembroke Hotel which reminded me of a scene from the film *The Godfather*. The people asking a favor were Jack Cunningham, the MP charged with running Labour's election campaign, and Larry Whitty, the Party's general secretary. After mumbled introductions Maxwell, playing Brando playing Don Corleone, said, "You have my full support. Now what can I do to help?"

There was a general clearing of throats, a mention of communications, maybe fax machines. Oh, and transport, perhaps. Suddenly Cunningham said, "What about your helicopter?"

It was a clumsy request. You must not ask for the helicopter; you must be given the helicopter. Requesting the gift removes from the giver the pleasure of giving. Maxwell coughed and the meeting broke up. Every hand I shook was clammy. Lunch with Maxwell was awful, too, especially for the reluctant Glenys. "He's a monster," she confided.

The evening reception was notable for being thinly attended, due partly to the Party's antipathy to Maxwell and partly to the Pergamon strikers' boisterous picket. Earlier in the year the firing of the strikers had led to a call for Maxwell's expulsion as a member of Oxford East constituency party for his dismissal of local workers, and a motion to discipline him was down for debate by conference. Some union leaders ignored the picket line, including the former white-collar union chief Clive Jenkins, who spoke to Maxwell for a good while. After an hour, to the relief of the squad of Mirror Group journalists whose presence gave a semblance of there being a crowd, Maxwell decided to leave. Limousines delivered us to the steps of his plane at Squires Gate airport. As he grumbled, Betty fussed, and less than an hour later we landed at Farnborough, an airport located fifty miles southwest of London.

There were two stories about the reason he had recently moved his plane from London's main airport, Heathrow. One suggested he was being pressed for unpaid bills, and the other stated he had angered Heathrow authorities by failing to stick to his agreed takeoff and departure times. Either or both could have been true. The helicopter took us only to the London heliport rather than Maxwell's Holborn headquarters because private helicopter flights over the capital were banned after dark. Waiting at the heliport were two cars, one to take Betty to Oxford and another to take Maxwell to Holborn. A day of public togetherness was over.

If Maxwell had little influence in party politics, he did try to compensate by interfering in the labor unions. He met Roy Lynk, president of the Union of Democratic Mineworkers, and immediately agreed to back the union's £1 billion bid to buy PowerGen, the electricity-generating company. This was one of those Maxwellian promises made with his tongue firmly in his cheek, costing nothing and winning him yet another headline.

His involvement with the *Daily Mirror*'s journalists' union leader, Steve Turner, was more sinister. A godfather's style is to grant wishes today and call in the favor at some future date, and Maxwell mistakenly thought he would do so with Turner. The waspishly wise Turner served as union leader at the paper for years, winning respect from his membership and the management. Everyone agreed that he was a skilled negotiator and the last man to indulge in secret deals. Turner was not without power; in spite of Maxwell's highly publicized "breaking" of the print unions, the Mirror Group's journalists' union remained virtually untouched, with an almost 100 percent membership and, unlike at virtually every other Fleet Street paper, the union still functioned successfully.

But Turner had ambitions to transform the whole union and successfully stood for the post of National Union of Journalists general secretary, a job with a salary substantially less than his *Mirror* wage. Some weeks before Turner left, Maxwell offered him £20,000 ($32,000) as an ex gratia payment in recognition of his long service with the company. Maxwell phoned to tell me of this while Turner was with him, so in the week of his leaving, the money still not having been paid, Turner asked me if I could sort it out.

I tried the straightforward method first, preparing through the editorial manager a special payment slip for Maxwell's signature. I then put it in front of him and he exploded, tearing it into pieces and screaming, "Fuck! No one must know about this. Not even your wife. This is secret. It has to be paid another way."

After cooling down he said, "Why are we paying this anyway?"

"It was your decision," I said.

"Then I will deal with it."

A month or so after Turner had started his new job he rang to complain that he had not received his money. Could I help just once more?

Remembering the secrecy, I waited until I was alone with Maxwell. Had he overlooked Turner's money? No, he had just not had time to get round to it. "Would you be good enough to ring Mr. Turner for me," Maxwell said. "I would like him to persuade his executive council to accept Clive Jenkins as arbitrator in the Pergamon dispute."

I knew this was unacceptable to the union and to Steve Turner because Jenkins was viewed as being a friend of Maxwell's and therefore could not be construed as an independent judge of the case for the twenty-three Pergamon strikers to win back their jobs.

I said I would speak to Steve, and Maxwell said he would "authorize" the £20,000 payoff. As I turned to leave, Maxwell said straight-faced, no wink, no nod, no smile: "There is, of course, no linkage."

I relayed the whole conversation to Steve, who was already beset by internal union troubles that would lead to his being controversially fired by the executive committee. He dismissed any idea of supporting Jenkins as arbitrator and reluctantly acknowledged that Maxwell was about to break his word on the money. Members of the executive council who were so critical of Steve should know that, even though he was facing financial peril, not for a moment did he contemplate accepting what amounted to a bribe. Having failed to pressure Steve, Maxwell eventually paid him £10,000 ($16,000) months later. "Even getting fifty percent of a Maxwell promise was better than expected," Steve commented.

10

Juggling With Debts—and Encyclopedias

LUNCH on Tuesday 18 September 1990 was unusual. It began on time and Maxwell appeared to be in a good mood. He asked the production director Jack Ferguson: "When will the new towers be ready at Watford?"

Ferguson explained that the towers, additions to three of the twenty-one lines of presses used to print the *Daily Mirror* and various other publications at Watford some twenty miles north of London, were in place. The paper, which could print only a maximum of forty-eight pages a night, was also published simultaneously in Oldham, in the north of England, and on the south bank of London's Thames.

"Now, Mister Greenslade," Maxwell said. "You'll be able to publish sixty-four-page *Mirrors*."

"Well, Bob," I said warily, "that won't work on just three presses. We can't have sixty-four-page *Mirrors* and forty-eight-page *Mirrors* on the same day."

"Of course we can. I want to see dummies next week."

In the nature of these things, even the collective shaking of heads was performed discreetly. Nothing, of course, came of it. By those standards his next statement seemed relatively straightforward. "I am pleased to announce that Mirror Group has just bought the Canadian print and paper works of Quebecor and Donohue," he said with a contented smile.

"Great," said someone at the end of the table.

"What can we say?" exclaimed another.

There was always safety in this sort of irony because Maxwell mistook it for acclamation. Almost every Mirror Group Newspapers board member was present (with the notable exception of the finance director) and since there had never been an MGN board meeting in the time I was there I suppose he imagined this substituted for it. There was no discussion. How could there be since hardly anyone at the table had the slightest knowledge of the business transacted on our behalf? We had no idea about the worth of the stakes in these companies and no inkling about how they were supposed to fit into the Group. It was a fait accompli.

By Maxwell fiat, the Mirror Group had just agreed to pay £58.3 million ($93.28 million) to Maxwell Communications Corporation for 25 percent of Quebecor, Canada's largest, and North America's second largest, commercial printer, and £71 million ($113.6 million) to MCC to acquire 26 percent of Donohue, a paper manufacturer and one of the Mirror Group's minor suppliers of newsprint. There was no clue about how he would fund these sales. The deal was, once again, a switch between a public and a private company.

The Quebecor and Donohue holdings had been acquired by MCC the previous February, and the sums paid by MGN were similar to those originally paid by MCC, but the significance of the transfer did not escape the City. One analyst commented: "It's a bit incestuous when it looks like MGN is acting as the buyer of last resort." It was a typical Maxwell transaction, in that Peter had paid Paul.

Given that directors, even of private companies, have certain duties, Maxwell's cavalier treatment of his boards was perilous for members. Marje Proops, the *Daily Mirror*'s most famous journalist noted for her "Dear Marje" agony aunt column, was a member of the Mirror Group board when a Maxwell aide suddenly turned up during a Mediterranean holiday to "request" that she sign a document. It was a formality she was told, but she had no idea what she had signed and worried about the incident so much she gave up her place on the board.

To the world outside, with the exception of a now suspicious City and an increasingly skeptical Fleet Street, Maxwell was at the zenith. He was the epitome of a tycoon, seemingly impervious to the financial disasters happening around him and inured from any passing phenomenon such as the recession. He continued to boast, employing the third person: "If anything happens in the media world—east, west, north, south—who do you call on? Maxwell is undoubtedly one of the people you select."

He believed his notoriety resulted through his encouragement of journalists that they should mention his name on any suitable occasion. So we were led to believe he was involved in takeover bids for Hollywood's MGM studios, satellite broadcasting, and countless papers in any East European country anyone cared to name. Rumors of his imminent involvement in the New York *Daily News* began to circulate, though he refused to confirm them. It was part of the game.

He cultivated certain journalists, leaking to them "exclusives" about potential deals, and dropping them if they failed to toe his line. "My most pleasant memory," said Andy McSmith, his temporary publicity man, "was a hot afternoon on the roof as Maxwell was interviewed by John Jay of the *Sunday Telegraph*. He was relaxed, calling him John the Jay all the time. We were served with drinks by a beautiful girl. Kevin joined us. It was like a party."

The gullible Jay remained an enthusiast, but Jeff Randall of *The Sunday Times*, who refused continual job offers from Maxwell, eventually realized his phone was not ringing after he had written about Maxwell's put-option maneuver. Maxwell enjoyed his games with journalists, seeking to give them "stories" to divert them from discovering the truth about his gloomy situation. It was a doomed exercise in the long run; for every journalist that was fooled there was another skeptic, and this growing band knew that by the beginning of October 1990 he was deeply in trouble.

His first skirmish was with the *Independent on Sunday*, which, on 30 September—the day of our disagreement over the sudden *Daily Mirror* price rise—argued that his program of selling assets would prove far from easy and that the Maxwell Communications share price was likely to continue falling in the coming week. Maxwell's fury was understandable: only he knew of the put-option agreement and only he knew of the trigger clauses in his share mortgaging that would force him to provide banks with yet more collateral for his loans. Maxwell feared that if he left the article unchallenged it would lead to yet more downward pressure on MCC's share price as other papers followed suit. He was particularly upset that the *Independent on Sunday* carried the story because he owned some 6 percent of the company. He sent a letter to Andreas Whittam-Smith, editor of the *Independent*, describing the report as "untrue, unchecked, and therefore unforgivable." It was a good phrase, redolent of Haines, but it did not answer the substantive issues. Rather than deal with the detail, Maxwell, echoing Mrs. Thatcher at the time, broadened his argument into a general attack on those who were talking Britain into recession.

In a further attempt to quell the rumbling, Maxwell leaked to media reporter Ray Snoddy at the *Financial Times* that he was about to "unveil" a string of asset sales to raise $450 million, though he misled Snoddy on the Donohue sale, claiming he was selling his stake to a British bank. He told *The Times* that, because of the "wildly inaccurate" *Independent on Sunday* article, he was bringing forward an announcement on asset disposals totaling $600 million. Truth was a moving target for all Maxwell-watchers. The next day he issued two statements, one from Maxwell Communications and another from the Mirror Group, which listed agreed sales, probable sales, possible sales, and improbable sales. He claimed these would net him $769 million, but it was obvious now that he was in trouble. The only agreed sales in the MCC statement were Quebecor and Donohue to his own company.

Incidentally, it is amusing to note that these sales were subject to approval by the shareholders of MCC but not by the board of the Mirror Group, which was paying for an unsalable burden. He said that MCC's 22 percent stake in De La Rue, the world's foremost banknote printer, would be auctioned; that negotiations to sell

Collier, Macmillan's encyclopedia business, were at "an advanced stage," along with three consumer publishing businesses and "surplus properties" worth about $100 million.

The Mirror Group statement boasted less about potential sales of properties, concentrating instead on the company's profitability and pledging expansion in America. Stakes in papers in East Germany, Hungary, Bulgaria, and the Soviet Union were presented as an example of the company "taking advantage of the new opportunities in Eastern Europe," followed by a single paragraph that listed several valuable disposable assets. MGN would sell 20 percent of Central TV, the 12.5 percent of France's TFI channel, and the 51 percent of the satellite rock music station, MTV. All interests in cable television were also to go. It was difficult not to notice the nonsense of this merry-go-round with the public company selling to the private company and the private company then selling off assets. Brokers pointed out the dangers, but the banks appeared to remain unmoved.

These statements together showed Maxwell in total retreat. Gone was any pretense to becoming the world's dominant media mogul. His decision to sell the TV interests surprised those who recalled Maxwell's July boast that all the major shareholders of British Satellite Broadcasting were courting him to take the crucial 20 percent stake owned by Australia's troubled tycoon Alan Bond. Anyone with any knowledge of TV also realized that the Central stake was likely to soar in value (as indeed it did, since the company secured a lucrative regional franchise). The audience for MTV was growing daily and the company had a bright future. As for the stake in banknote printer De La Rue, he was about to sell it at a £50 million ($80 million) loss.

Unsurprisingly, most independent commentators concluded, not out of prejudice as Maxwell maintained, but merely by looking at the available facts and figures, that the sale of peripheral companies would not generate sufficient cash to meet his debts. He would need to sell off parts of his core businesses.

The significance of such a move struck Brian Sturgess, the media analyst at Barclays Bank's stockbroking offshoot, Barclays de Zoete Wedd (BZW), who had been studying MCC's accounts closely since June, as illogical. He had come to the conclusion during the summer that the company was in a more perilous position than he, or the rest of the City, had originally realized. He grasped that the conjunction of a number of factors was allowing Maxwell to present a false picture of MCC, not the least of which were Britain's broad accountancy rules and the pressure the chairman was exerting on consultants or auditors in applying those rules.

While much of his analysis was technical and therefore difficult for the layman to grasp, the thrust of it was straightforward enough: accounting definitions were blurred and therefore misleading; assets were overvalued, especially by the bloated claims about supposed values of intangibles; one-time profits, such as foreign-exchange transactions, contributed greatly to the overall profit; the assets sold were merely a juggling act.

That would have been bad enough, but Sturgess also noted that MCC's strategy was "totally off course"; the projected sale of core assets would make the company worse off in future because it would reduce its earnings capability. This devastating report, entitled "Debt at The Captain's Table," which not surprisingly concluded by urging investors to sell MCC holdings, was sent to BZW's clients, including major institutions, on 4 October 1990.

In Sturgess's own words "Maxwell went mad" the next morning, and his first call went not to the analyst, as might be expected, but to Sir John Quinton, chairman of Barclays Bank, demanding a comprehensive retraction. Later Maxwell barked at Sturgess for what he called an inaccurate and irresponsible report. "Young man," Maxwell said, "I want a written apology to newspapers."

Sturgess replied: "I can't retract it without reasons."

"You're implying I'm selling off my assets to pay my debts," Maxwell said. "Not one penny of that money is being used to settle debt."

Several times in what Sturgess called "a real ding-dong," Maxwell repeated the phrase "not one penny," among the liberal references to him as "young man," but the analyst was unconvinced. He said he was unwilling to change his recommendation to salesmen.

Sturgess may have been skilled at reading balance sheets, but reading Robert Maxwell was an entirely different matter. The point at which you thought you had stood your ground and convincingly won an argument with him was the point at which Maxwell was at his most devious and determined. He launched a three-pronged counterattack.

First, he brought so much pressure to bear on Sturgess's firm that BZW researchers were ordered to take another look at MCC to ensure their analyst had it right. Second, Maxwell's own team pored over the Sturgess analysis to seek out any possible errors, of whatever magnitude. Third, and this was a Maxwell move par excellence, was the creation of an intimate dialogue with Sturgess himself. Maxwell—once described as having "twenty different personalities"[1]—was able to play angry tycoon, hurt child, father confessor, or jovial giant at a moment's notice. He was the nasty policeman or the nice policeman as the occasion demanded.

During their last conversation that first day, Maxwell chose his indulgent father role, treating the whole affair as a minor indiscretion by a son who should know better. The result of the BZW research was a vaguely worded retraction that Sturgess read to Maxwell over the phone that evening. Picking up on Sturgess's description of his Maxwell Communications sales to the Mirror Group, the apparently mollified Maxwell told him: "I forgive you for the juggling."

Sturgess went to sleep thinking that, at least, it had been only a minor retraction and he had not, after all, had to take back the recommendation in his notice. Maxwell, ingrained with the experience of barter trade where haggling is an endless activity, was far from finished. One little victory was to be a stepping-stone to others. Next day Sturgess was amazed to find that Maxwell's friendly, almost offhand approach of the previous evening had been replaced by a barely suppressed fury. His new objective was to remove from Sturgess's report the claim that MCC's earnings prospects were "weakened." This fresh assault came at a difficult time for Sturgess since his own position within BZW was far from stable.

"The political wind at the firm was against me," said Sturgess. Therefore he did not receive the kind of support most analysts might expect, and the result was that Barclays de Zoete Wedd backed down again, concluding in a second retraction that, on sober reflection, the sale of assets would sort out MCC's debt problem. We cannot know if Maxwell was aware of Sturgess's internal problems, though I doubt it because he might have been tempted to force a bigger retraction.

His next victory came when his in-house analysts spotted a genuine mistake, the transposition of a pound sign and a dollar sign, and BZW was forced to issue a third retraction. According to Sturgess, this is a common error, and he was happy to correct it. But these kinds of retreats—descrbed by Maxwell as "three major errors"—were all he required to damn the whole report, undermining its substantive truth by referring to it as "flawed" and pointing out, incorrectly, but with typical Maxwellian gusto, that "it's all been retracted."

By 11 October, Sturgess was contemplating "one of the grimmest weeks of my life." Two months later he was contemplating life outside BZW; he was made redundant. He realizes that Maxwell played only a part in the loss of his job but could not help wondering just how much of a role was played by Barclays Bank. Later he was to discover that the bank had made substantial loans to Maxwell, and his advice would surely have upset them. He believes there must have been a clash of interests between what the bank would have wished to happen to MCC's share price and what might have happened to it if the bank's brokers, BZW, had stuck with the informed, impartial advice he had given to clients. So much for the Chinese walls, thought Sturgess.

What cannot be denied on hindsight is that Sturgess's report, in essence, was right. It is a perfect example of how Maxwell prevented the tide of truth from overwhelming him as early as autumn 1990. It also suggests that if banks were nervous about Maxwell's ability to pay back their loans they needed to keep his company trading.

This damage limitation is a tribute to Maxwell's powers at manipulation for, while fighting off the analysts and journalists on one front, he was continuing to juggle dangerously elsewhere. With the share price in decline and the 28 September "closed period" deadline approaching, Maxwell decided to buy up vast quantities of MCC shares. He hoped doing so would arrest the decline and provide him with the collateral for more bank loans. He followed a 24 August purchase of 15.38 million shares with 1 million more on 18 September, using his Liechtenstein-based Maxwell Foundation to purchase half of the shares and Bishopsgate for the other half. He had acquired the shares at prices ranging from 153 pence ($2.44) to 185 pence ($2.96). The interim results were due to be announced on 28 November, so this was the last possible date on which Maxwell could officially buy his own shares before the closed period in which he was banned from buying his own stock.

Unofficially and illegally, it is now obvious that in the same period he also used his Liechtenstein trusts to go on what amounted to an MCC share-buying spree. The bank account statements of one Maxwell family *stiftung*, or trust, with the odd name of Corry, show substantial movements of money in and out from various Maxwell companies and attorneys toward the end of October 1990. Varying sums of money from the Corry account in the Private Trust Bank of Vaduz were used to purchase shares during the closed period.

There are also other mysterious entries that suggest he was switching money to America, though the reasons for doing so are unclear. For example, about £4.5 million ($7.2 million) was paid in through Maxwell's London solicitors on 17 October and £4 million ($6.4 million) went out the same day to a private Maxwell company, identified as Pergamon Holdings (U.S.) Inc., registered in Delaware with an address in Elmsford, New York.[2] There is no clue where the money came from in the first place and even less is known about the source of the millions he spent on the share-support operation at this time, anywhere between £85 and £150 million ($136–240 million). The same question sprang to mind on 23 October when Maxwell confounded his critics by meeting the deadline to repay his short-term debt of $415 million. How had he managed to find such sums?

One clue came in a very short *Daily Mail* article by Max Hotopf on 24 October, but nobody was then in a position to make the link. One of the reporter's neighbors was Tony Boram, formerly editorial director at the Mirror Group, and one of the founders of the Association of Mirror Pensioners, an organization formed specifically because of concern at Maxwell's handling of pensions from his first year of ownership. By the beginning of 1990, Boram and his association had "amassed considerable evidence of a wide range of pension problems in the Mirror Group."[3] Pensioners were most upset because since 1985 they had received an annual increase in their pensions of only 3 percent, the legal minimum, in spite of Maxwell having promised to "preserve and protect all pension rights."

After a series of complaints about lack of information, in early May Boram finally saw the pension scheme's report and accounts covering the year up to 5 April 1990. He was appalled on several fronts. First, millions of pounds of fund money had been removed from the previously conventional investments in big British companies and placed in unquoted or foreign firms. Second, £20 million ($32 million) was invested with Maxwell Communications. Third, there was a £149 million ($238.4 million) surplus, yet pensioners were being restricted to the minimum payout. Fourth, in spite of Maxwell not having made a company contribution since 1985—taking advantage of his legal entitlement to a pension "holiday" because of the surplus—he was charging the fund £1.9 million ($3.04 million) a year for professional fees to administer it.

Boram's fears mounted in midsummer when he realized that the funds were heavily invested in Maxwell-related companies. Why, for instance, was £13.3 million ($21.28 million) invested in Teva Pharmaceuticals, the Israeli drug firm in which Maxwell had a large stake? What was IBI Holdings, a Luxembourg-registered bank, where £7.9 million ($12.64 million) was invested? Should £3.5 million ($5.6 million) be invested in Maxwell's private company AGB Research? Why had funds once invested in blue-chip British shares such as Shell, ICI, and Glaxo been removed?

Boram and his association colleagues—Don Wood and Ken Hudgell—were further alarmed when a letter seeking information from a trustee received no reply. It was time, thought Boram, for "young Hotopf"—the reporter whom he had befriended—to investigate. Hotopf's 24 October report in the *Daily Mail* amounted to barely 150 words and was carried at the bottom of the financial page. But it can now be seen as a genuine exclusive, justifying for once the word *sensational*. It began: "Large amounts of Mirror Group pension fund money have been invested in companies in which Robert Maxwell is interested. This may breach the National Association of Pension Funds' voluntary code of practice."

Hotopf's final paragraph was, if anything, even more revealing. "Bishopsgate Investment Management, associated with Maxwell, is shown as managing 51 pc of the funds. The NAPF says funds should not invest in companies where directors have interests."

This was the first time the link between the pension funds and Maxwell's own Bishopsgate company had been mentioned in public, and it stung Maxwell. He reacted in his usual style: belligerently phoning Boram and threatening the *Mail* with writs. In a bid to throw everyone off the scent, Maxwell decided to increase the 3 percent annual increase in pensions to 5 percent.

Of course, Maxwell should not have been able to make this sudden announcement since the pension-fund trustees were supposedly an independent group, but over his six years of ownership he had gradually replaced almost all the original trustees. Meetings were called at short notice to prevent "unhelpful" trustees from attending. Maxwell eventually persuaded the *Mail* to carry a letter setting out his new deal for pensioners. But the following Sunday a short *Observer* article repeated the *Mail*'s allegations, stating that "Mirror Group pension funds have been large investors in companies linked to Maxwell, possibly in breach of the National Association of Pension Funds' voluntary code of practice."

It is remarkable that these allegations did not ring alarm bells with the authorities and prompt them to take a look at Maxwell's pension-fund management.

Maxwell's anger at the *Mirror* pensioners' campaign seemed to me to be out of all proportion to their supposed crime. It was also evident that the pensioners had been treated very unfairly by receiving such low annual increases. I did not know Boram but I remembered meeting him once or twice when I worked at the Mirror Group back in the seventies; we were on opposite sides of a tense management-union battle. We may have been opponents, but I recognized that he was straight. By now I was convinced that Maxwell was not. Like everyone else, I had no idea what he was really up to, but I knew from my dealings with him that he was a habitual liar. I therefore decided he could not be trusted with my money and began the tedious preparations and paperwork that would lead to my removing my money from the pension fund. For the moment, though, we will leave the pensions trail where it ended in 1990—in mystery.

From October my relationship with Maxwell became very strained. It was as if he relieved the tension of his apparently insoluble financial worries by flexing his muscles in an arena he believed he controlled. Unknown to me, before the *Daily Mirror* reporter Bill Akass and photographer Ken Lennox had left for Saudi

Arabia after the Kuwait invasion, Maxwell had summoned them to his office "for a briefing." He began by asking Akass where he was going.

"To Dhahran," Akass said.

"I want you in Riyadh," Maxwell said. "I will get your ticket changed."

Akass decided to ignore this command but wisely pointed out they were having trouble getting money to take with them. Maxwell shouted at someone on the phone and thousands of dollars appeared.

Akass and Lennox managed to suppress smiles at the next injunction: "Don't get Delhi belly." He evidently repeated this several times.

"I know people in Saudi," Maxwell said grandly, and gave them the name of his "representative," a Mr. Adjani. He also said, "I want you to talk to the oil minister."

Once Akass arrived in Dhahran he was phoned by a man called Mohammed Zaghloul, who described himself as Adjani's assistant, offering to help in any way necessary. Akass met him but there was little he needed, except a four-wheel-drive jeep with a phone, which was evidently unobtainable. He could not discover what business Adjani and Zaghloul were involved in though there was talk of a publishing company, and he almost forgot about them as he went about his job filing copy for the paper.

Then he received a call from Adjani, and suddenly the tables were turned. "I understand you will give me all assistance," Adjani said, and he requested personal introductions to American and British military chiefs, the trade consul, and other people. Akass, realizing this request was made for commercial reasons, offered numbers but said he did not think he could make introductions.

After a tiring trip into the desert in October, Akass rang the news desk to tell them he had just phoned in a story about large-scale Iraqi troop movements. The news editor said excitedly, "Maxwell wants you. Evidently you've been rude to someone."

Akass, showing commendable calm, decided to tape record the conversation with Maxwell, who accused him of failing to help Adjani and finally revealed the secret agenda: he was expecting Akass to make introductions so that Adjani could sell sets of encyclopedias to the troops.

"I'm here as a journalist," Akass told him. "It will make me a laughingstock to do this."

Maxwell shouted, "Don't be silly...I'll have to replace you." The line went dead.

Maxwell next rang Steve Lynas, the news editor, to complain that Akass had hung up on him and must therefore be recalled from the Gulf. At last I was informed about the drama: "Sorry, Roy, I know you won't believe it, but Maxwell has told Bill he'll be sacked unless he sells encyclopedias to the troops."

I told Lynas to assure Akass he had our full backing. In the meantime I rang Maxwell, who seemed convinced that American soldiers would like nothing better than to relieve their boredom in the trenches by reading volumes of his unsalable books.

"Don't worry about this," he said to me.

"Bob, we cannot have a reporter covering a war selling encyclopedias to troops. He's right to say no."

"Is he right to slam the phone down on his Publisher?"

"He says he didn't."

"Is he calling me a liar," Maxwell asked, quickly adding, "or are you calling me a liar and encouraging him to disobey?"

"No, I—"

The phone hit the receiver, as it had with Akass. I suspected he had an audience and so could not bear to lose an argument. I then spoke to Akass and decided to defuse matters. I knew if Maxwell carried out his threat to recall Akass, the *Daily Mirror* would lose an all-important visa and a place on the media team.

"Don't worry," I told Akass. "Just play him along, placate him. Don't commit yourself to anything, but keep him happy." I know now that Akass was not pleased with this advice, preferring to have had an unequivocal statement of support and a straightforward rejection of Maxwell's demand. But I thought Maxwell would forget the matter as quickly as he had raised it. It took several phone calls before Maxwell was mollified. In one telling conversation, Lynas told Maxwell: "There's been a misunderstanding, Bill didn't put the phone down." Maxwell replied: "Do you think I'd put the phone down on my staff?"

I smiled when told what Maxwell had said. Some months before, in his early evening instruction mood, he had explained his method of "phone terrorism." He said: "When you make a call you say what you want to say. Then cut them off."

As if this wasn't sufficient explanation he added, "Never forget. Phone down quickly It always works."

Quite what was meant to work I never really knew. However, after seeing him perform this trick with tedious regularity, I noted that whatever the outcome he preened himself at the result.

If a person rang back he would beam: "I knew he would."

If the person did not, he would say: "See, I frightened him. Just as I expected."

The other striking fact about the Akass affair was the way Maxwell forgot the substantive issue. We heard no more of encyclopedias in Saudi Arabia, nothing of Adjani. It was a spontaneous eruption by Maxwell which, once he knew he was in a losing situation, became a matter of no consequence.

On 14 October Maxwell demanded the publication of a pro-Israeli editorial that sought to justify the continued building of settlements in the occupied territories. It was so depressingly partisan I told the editorial writer, David Thompson, it was outrageous but, sadly, I made only the feeblest of protests to Maxwell. I had taken the view that his almost total control of the editorials was a small price to pay to keep him out of the rest of the paper and consoled myself by thinking that in tabloids editorials were relatively unimportant.

Maxwell took the opposite view, using the column as a sort of personal bulletin board with which he imagined himself addressing the world's statesmen who were noting each nuance. Every day the editorial writer was required to ring Maxwell wherever he was in the world to agree to the topic and take down a briefing on what the Publisher required. Then the editorial was faxed to him for his final comments and amendments.

Thompson's annual holidays provided me with the chance to write the editorials myself. I ignored the convention of agreeing to the subject in advance and often faxed the editorial to him so late he could do little about changing it before the first edition. Not that I was seeking to preach revolution or take the paper in a fresh direction; for two weeks only I was merely refusing to surrender to his control.

There were still times when I almost felt I was an editor. Maxwell's vanity stretched to the belief that he was a writer of distinction so I often heard him speak of "my editorial" or refer to a piece "I once wrote." Haines often had to nudge him to remind him of the real author but, after a grudging acknowledgment, he would continue to make the same false claims. The insertion of one word, even the deletion of one word, transformed the article in Maxwell's mind into being "mine."

The editorial on Israel was, however, undoubtedly Maxwell's and the reason for it, I discovered the next day, was that Maxwell was off to visit "my friend Yitzhak." From Jerusalem he would fly to Moscow to visit "my friend Gorbachev." The Minnesota institute had paid off and he was about to get his audience at last. Although the Israelis have never defined what Maxwell's role was, he hinted to me that he was acting as a go-between for them and the Soviet Union. His major aims, he said, were to help reestablish diplomatic links between the countries and so provide better conditions for Jews to obtain exit visas. I cannot explain why I should believe this when much else was false. Anyway, I believed him then and I have not changed my mind since. After all, Shamir would have had few emissaries to state his case to Gorbachev. I got a glimpse of the mission's importance because Maxwell, ever forgetful, arrived in Moscow without the memorandum he was supposed to deliver to Gorbachev on behalf of Shamir. It had been drawn up at Shamir's request by Yaacov Neeman, Maxwell's lawyer, but Maxwell left it beside his bed on the tenth floor. When I called in to the news desk that evening from my car I was on my way to Lincolnshire to take part in a charity walk, so my mind was not on Maxwell's travels.

The desk could talk of only one subject because for the only time any of them could recall Maxwell had been courteous to them. One man told me: "There's been an incredible flap, Roy. He left some important papers behind. We got that Filipino up to sort it out."

It transpired that Juliette had been roused to find the memo and hand it to the desk. Although Maxwell had told the man in charge,

Eugene Duffy, that it was "dynamite," he was forced to allow its "highly confidential" content to be dictated over the phone to his secretary in Moscow for retyping.

One of the reporters who had taken his first call told me later: "You would not have believed it was him. He was so nice."

Maxwell did meet Gorbachev the next day. "I was alone in the Kremlin with Gorby," he told me the following week. "What do you think of that, mister? Alone with the president of the Soviet Union. For an hour... an hour."

If only TASS had not issued a communiqué, published in the *Sunday Mirror*, giving the names of V.I. Boldin and V.A. Kriuchkov as having attended, I would have believed him. Nevertheless, months later, diplomatic links were restored between Israel and the USSR, and Jews were allowed to fly out of Russia.

Trips like this blinded many people to reality, but not in the financial world, where MCC's troubles were an open secret. The presentation in November 1990 of the interim accounts for the six months up to the end of September could not be ignored; the company's operating profits were falling so badly that even the inclusion of Macmillan and Official Airline Guides in the figures for the first time made little impact. While operating profits had fallen from £134 million to £130 million ($214.4–208 million), and the real-estate profits had slumped from £32 million to £15 million ($51.2–24 million), there was also a cut of £8.3 million ($13.28 million) in American profits due to the decline in the dollar. Only the extraordinary gains of £45.7 million ($73.12 million) foreign-exchange transactions rescued Maxwell.

Again, analysts were "scratching their heads in bewilderment" at the figures,[4] and gave up trying to assess what might be going on. All they could see was debt, and all they heard about was cash raised by speculation. No wonder one commentator noted: "MCC moves so fast nothing is ever strictly comparable or sensibly forecastable. The only thing that can be said for certain is that Mr. Maxwell will make some major moves before the next six months are up."[5]

Rarely was a truer financial forecast made about Maxwell. A day or so later *The Independent*'s Jason Nisse, in a short article that later appeared not to have been spotted by many other journalists, wrote of Maxwell's put-option deal with Goldman Sachs. He also pointed out that if Goldman had bought during the closed period it would have had the effect of supporting the MCC share price. Of course he was unaware then that Goldman already had the shares prior to the closed period, but Nisse smelled something fishy at Maxwell House and would remain a close observer.

When at war in one area Maxwell would often explode with anger in another so that any day there could be an eruption in the Mirror Group without warning. My secretary, who visibly shook if Maxwell came on the line, asked me one morning: "Have you heard about Iain Herbertson's secretary? She's crying outside the building. She's been sacked."

The subtext of this announcement was self-preservation: you won't let this happen to me, will you? Herbertson, the circulation director, did not let it happen either. It appeared that Maxwell had rung to speak to him and his secretary, mistakenly assuming she was dealing with a mortal and not a monster, informed Maxwell that her boss was on the telephone. Maxwell transformed this into an act of insubordination, claiming the woman had treated The Publisher improperly by not immediately interrupting Herbertson's call. He ordered his "police" from security to escort her from the building without delay. In Maxwellia, as in certain South American countries, people did have a habit of disappearing overnight.

An outraged Herbertson went off to plead his secretary's case and was prepared to resign if necessary. Maxwell was struck by his director's loyalty and agreed to the woman being reinstated—but she had to agree to the deduction of a day's pay. How Herbertson and his staff made this up I do not know, but I understand the woman was not out of pocket. I was reminded that some weeks previously I had been facing a potentially difficult union problem that, unfortunately, came to Maxwell's attention. He rang to offer help, which I sidestepped, and concluded by saying, "Remember, if you want instant injustice, call me!"

Every so often during the summer, Maxwell would raise the subject of the satirical columnist John Diamond. In his first sallies he began by saying: "I don't like what he writes." I asked for examples but none was forthcoming. I argued that I was happy with him and he let the matter go, only to return to it at intervals.

"I didn't think much of Mr. Diamond's column this week," he said one day in September.

I defended it and took a risk: was not the item on firemen very amusing? Even the staff had laughed at it.

"That was just about all right," he replied, "but the rest was awful. It's just not funny."

I had caught Maxwell in a lie. There had been no item on firemen and, as I suspected, he was not reading the column at all.

"He should never have been hired," said Maxwell on another occasion. "We should only have big names like that TV woman [Maxwell even forgot the big names; he was referring to the Mirror's columnist Anne Robinson, who has a weekly comment slot on BBC television] and Joe [Haines]."

I suddenly thought of a way to divert him and suggested I carry out market research, through his own company AGB, to test the relative success of all *Mirror* columnists in terms of readership and readability.

I would never argue the merits of market research as a basis for what an editor places in a newspaper, but I viewed the exercise, carried out at the end of October, as a political move to end Maxwell's nagging about Diamond. I thought the results unsurprising, with Marje Proops, the advice columnist, way out in front, followed by Anne Robinson and the investigative, campaigning columnist Paul Foot.

There was little difference in the scores of the long-established Joe Haines and ingenue John Diamond, and I was particularly pleased with the phrase used by the disinterested market researcher who had written the summary: "John Diamond's column has already established a wide readership." I eventually sent the results to all the columnists and to Maxwell on 6 December. I was not to hear from him about it for three weeks.

By presenting the occasional run-in with Maxwell, I am failing to describe adequately the stultifying nature of his daily hold on the paper, the negative influence he exerted, which made editorship such a trial. An editor must have some room to maneuver in terms of editorial and promotion budgets or the job becomes a nightmare. One day a memo appeared stating that if staff were to travel out of

Britain the relevant forms would need his signature. I pointed out to him that with him out of the country so often and the need for swift response in news situations, obtaining his signature would prove impossible.

"Quite right," he said. "As you know, when I'm not here, you are in charge. You are a field marshal. Your signature will carry my full authority."

Fine words. In practice, staff in the department responsible for allocating funds and arranging travel were so cowed by the fear of Maxwellian retribution should they disobey him that they relied only on his signature. I told him the staff wanted a written note of my supposed plenipotentiary powers. "Your word as editor should be enough," he said.

"It isn't, Bob. You have got them so scared of you they think they'll get the sack if they disobey you."

He laughed: "Quite right. Byeee."

I rang back. "Bob, I must have written authority from you to secure foreign travel."

"You have it," he said. How could one argue with this man? I decided on a different ploy. I woke him in San Francisco at 4 A.M. to sign a faxed form allowing a photographer to travel to Ireland, taking the opportunity to point out how absurd it was to do this.

"Tell the idiots you are the Publisher in my absence," he said with gusto. I told the idiots and we all laughed together.

Television advertising was another fraught area between me and Maxwell. For months I planned the launch of a new weekly supplement entitled "Mirror Woman," and I had managed to keep his hands off it entirely. I did not show him dummies, explain budgets worked out without his knowledge, or consult him at all, knowing this was treason but reasoning that the capital crime was worth the risk since even the slightest involvement by him was likely to ruin the enterprise. I also agreed on television ads for the launch and authorized their transmission without reference to him.

Unfortunately, he often spent a large part of his evenings alone, bored, in front of the television, switching from station to station by remote control, and he came across one of the commercials I had authorized. He immediately called to say it was the worst ad he had ever seen and demanded that future bookings be withdrawn, a childish and self-defeating act that stopped a fairly successful launch from achieving its full impact. He lost money, amounting to many thousands, because the time had been booked but consoled himself by refusing to pay the agency's fee. He harmed the *Mirror* sales just a month after the price-rise drama.

On another occasion, the Mirror Group's deputy managing director, Roger Eastoe, and I lined up a circulation-boosting promotion for cheap vacations. In other newspapers I had worked on, this would have been so uncontroversial that owners might not have cared to know about it. In Maxwellia it was different, so Eastoe and I researched it, costed it, and planned it down to the last detail before presenting Maxwell with our great offer. We needed his blessing so that he would release budgeted funds for promotion.

As we started to tell him he flew into a rage. "You have gone behind my back. I should have been consulted. I will not authorize it. It's all chopped worms. This holiday company is taking you for a ride. How much are they worth?"

He pushed a console button and thundered at his secretary: "Get me Richard Branson [owner of the Virgin empire] on the phone."

Eastoe and I were baffled and then amazed as Maxwell proceeded to reveal details of this confidential promotion offer to a potential rival (it is to Branson's credit that he made no commercial use of the information). Maxwell did all he could in the next half hour to find a loose thread in the fabric of our arguments in favor of the promotion. In the end though, power does not need to win an argument; it merely has to exert itself. We were stunned—a straightforward, honest promotion with the likelihood of winning sales for the *Mirror* was being discarded for no other reason than Maxwell's pique.

"Never go behind my back again. I must be consulted at every stage."

I protested. Eastoe protested.

Maxwell bellowed, "This is a commercial matter. I am in charge of commercial matters."

Leaving his office, I recalled the time some months before when the Spot the Ball saga had occurred and he had exploded over the promotion department's failure to organize in advance. His cry then was: "Does nobody do any work if I'm not here?"

1 Cuckoo in the nest. Outside the *Scottish Daily News* in 1975: 'The intervention of Maxwell... effectively ruined the project.'
(Glasgow Herald)

2 Checking on the Commons catering in 1968. As an MP he was outshone by others, such as Ted Heath: 'That was not my scene.' (Press Association)

3 Royal charmer: Maxwell – motto, 'I'm only here to serve' – with his daughter Ghislaine, meets the Queen at a 1983 gala. (Associated Press Ltd)

4 Getting a kick out of football. Maxwell at Oxford in 1986:
'Remember, I own the stadium, you are only the manager.'
(Press Association)

5 Merciful Maxwell flies into Ethiopia in 1985 on a mission which fed his appetite for publicity but few of the starving millions. (Syndication International Ltd)

6 With wife, Betty, at Malcolm Forbes' lavish 1989 birthday party in Morocco: Why isn't anyone else in fancy dress? (Associated Press Ltd)

7 With Erich Honnecker, East Germany's soon-to-be-deposed dictator, in 1989: 'No one complains when the Queen meets these leaders.' (Associated Press Ltd)

8 Building bridges and contacts in Israel: Robert Maxwell with Premier Yitzhak Shamir (left) and his Labour Party rival Shimon Peres. (Reuters/Bettmann)

9 A meeting of world leaders at the Kremlin in 1990: 'Gorbachev,'
said Maxwell, 'wouldn't do anything without ringing me first.'
(Syndication International Ltd)

10 Cap'n Bob in front of the Lady Ghislaine, one of his many tycoon
toys: 'I'm not interested in money or property.' (Associated Press Ltd)

11 Holding aloft the *Daily News* after delighting New York by saving
their paper: 'I'm not just a hero, I'm a cult figure.' (Associated
Press Ltd)

12 'Mister Greenslade' and the Publisher keep their own counsel
during a farewell party for the retiring City editor Bob Head.
(Syndication International Ltd)

13 The boys most likely to succeed.... But Ian (left) and Kevin were to inherit only debts, stress, and the disgraced name of Maxwell. (Syndication International Ltd)

14 'I was born a Jew and I shall die a Jew.' Maxwell's family at the funeral in Jerusalem of the man born Abraham Lajbi Hoch. (Associated Press Ltd)

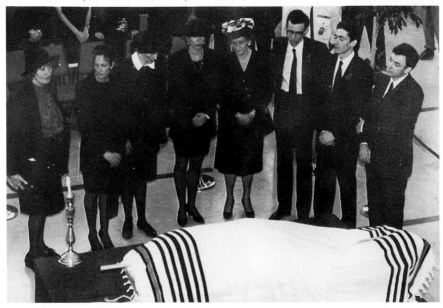

The trouble was that if you let Maxwell know too early about a project of any kind—news story, promotion, game, staff hiring—he invariably found a way of screwing it up, as in the Lucky Shirts debacle.

"I am firm but fair," he would often say, though he was neither.

The reverse also happened regularly; the *Mirror* was forced to publish promotions by Maxwell that were plainly not working. One regular "favorite" was an offer for children's soccer cards, made by Maxwell's Italian company Panini, which was successful only during the soccer World Cup. With that one exception, there was no circulation increase and relatively little interest in the stickers. Panini had proved to be a disaster for Maxwell ever since he had bought it in November 1988. The man who knew so much about everything had made one of the worst deals of his life with the Panini family who, with 16 percent of the company and being on the spot, in Modena, northern Italy, continued to run it. Carelessly, Maxwell even forgot to enforce the normal noncompetition clause in the purchase agreement and allowed one of the Panini family to set up a rival firm.

Panini rarely turned in a profit, and Maxwell found it impossible to sell, though it did not stop him from announcing a sale. In Maxwell's office in December 1990 I came across a former Disney executive, Keith Bales, who had been hired to sort out Panini for Maxwell. Bales was full of enthusiasm, but it proved a fruitless task at this stage of Maxwell's life. Bales soon recognized that the problem was one of gross managerial negligence and, in an attempt to solve it, decided to fire several managers. Maxwell, for reasons that are still not clear, refused to back him, and Bales left.

By coincidence, Bales was around when I was invited to lunch by a senior executive at Disney and offered the chance to launch a color comic of Disney favorites inside the *Mirror*. Knowing that we were planning to introduce a weekly television guide in early March to take advantage of the deregulation of program listings, I soon saw the potential of picking up an additional audience of younger people with the best brand name in children's cartoon characters. In spite of our holiday promotion experience, Eastoe and I decided it would be foolish to mention the project to Maxwell until we had done our homework. We carried out research and costings in the expectation that this innovation, linking the *Daily Mirror* brand with the Disney brand, would strike Maxwell as brilliant, especially with the Euro Disney venture opening in France in April 1992, the following year. If we had recorded our previous holiday promotion meeting we could have saved our voices and his.

"Why was I not told about this. I know the Disney man. Your agreement stinks. You are going behind my back without authority."

I threw my hands up. "How could I ask for authority to go to lunch with a Disney vice president when I didn't know what she was going to offer me?"

"You had no authority," he said to the midair.

Eastoe patiently explained the scenario and Maxwell did agree to consider it, because even he was not about to slam the door on Disney. What should have been a triumph became a lengthy nightmare as we played pig-in-the-middle between Disney, pressing for a signed agreement, and Maxwell, refusing to discuss the matter. His only practical contribution in the end was to commit the paper to a longer-term deal than we had thought wise, wishing to restrict the contract to one year initially to test readers' reaction.

But the man who knew about these things demanded a three-year agreement and decided he must meet the Disney president in person. Dennis Hightower, the Paris-based head of the European arm of the organization, duly turned up for Maxwell's benefit. Maxwell, misjudging the quality of the man with whom he was dealing, appeared condescending.

"Mr. Hightower," Maxwell said, "I always say confidence is like virginity—it can only be lost once." He sat back with a self-satisfied smile after delivering this cherished bon mot.

Hightower smiled back and replied, "I've got one like that myself, Bob. But it's a bit more to the point. You only screw me once."

Maxwell was not amused at the laughter that followed.

11

The Scoop
of the Decade

THE Conservative Party leadership contest in November 1990 should have been a great time to edit the Labour-supporting *Daily Mirror*. Margaret Thatcher, for eleven years prime minister of Britain and fifteen years leader of her party, had been forced by a rebellion within her own ranks to stand for election. The only people who could vote for the party leader were the 350 Conservative Members of Parliament (MPs) but the days leading up to the first ballot between her and her rival, Michael Heseltine, stimulated a huge public debate.

The issue was difficult for the newspapers that backed the Conservatives. After years of remaining faithful to Mrs. Thatcher, they suddenly had to decide whether to desert her. While they agonized over their loyalty, mostly tending to support Thatcher in spite of the obvious public clamor for change, the *Daily Mirror* could have a ball at the Tories' expense. For the first time in more than a decade, the splits within the Conservative ranks were out in the open and presented the *Mirror* with a rare opportunity to show readers the reality of the ruling party's disunity. By exploiting the differences of opinion we might have turned the battle for succession to electoral advantage for the Labour Party. Maxwell had other ideas. On the day Heseltine announced his candidacy Maxwell demanded the most ridiculous editorial.

"It'll be just a few words in big type," he said. "We must stay above it."

"Surely this is a big chance to have fun at the government's expense," I replied.

"Mister Roy Greenslade, you know nothing about politics. Joe and I will sort this out."

"With respect, Bob, that's an insult. Write whatever you like, and I'll cover it my way."

"I have noted your defiance," he said. "Byeee."

His editorial stated in four short paragraphs that it was not for us to involve ourselves in the internal affairs of the Conservative Party. It was a bizarre attitude for an opposition paper to adopt. Staying aloof in the manner of a latter-day Pontius Pilate might suit a serious broadsheet but not a sensational tabloid. Of course we should be involved.

Over the tense and exciting days leading up to the ballot between Thatcher and Heseltine, the *Mirror* performed creditably enough without intervention from Maxwell. I ignored his strictures, and the *Mirror* took as much advantage as possible by shining the spotlight on the splits in policy and personality without reporting unfounded rumors, of which there were many. We did not need to invent or mislead; the truth was riveting enough.

The ballot produced the best result of all for Labour, and therefore for the *Mirror*. Neither Thatcher nor Heseltine obtained enough votes to secure the leadership outright. There would have to be a second ballot. Thatcher vowed to fight on, but the divisions within her party—over the controversial housing tax, over the pace of European Community integration, and, more pertinently, over Thatcher's style of leadership—were too deep to allow her to remain as the party leader.

On the evening the ballot result was announced, the *Mirror*'s political editor, Alastair Campbell, produced a story suggesting that senior Conservatives were urging Thatcher to step down, which I headlined TIME TO GO. His piece reflected the mood of the party prior to the anticipated meetings Thatcher would hold to sound out opinion within her cabinet and the party. Elsewhere, Conservatives who did not support either Thatcher or Heseltine were meeting in secret to press John Major, then the chancellor, to stand as a leadership candidate.

After designing the front page, I took a call from Maxwell, who was in his apartment. He sounded agitated and pugnacious. My deputy, Bill Hagerty, was superb at divining from a short telephone conversation just when Maxwell had been drinking.

"The Captain had obviously had a stiff one or two last night," he would tell me the morning after, and this emboldened him in his own conspicuous acts of "defiance," since he correctly guessed that Maxwell would never remember his orders the next day.

I was less sure, but on this occasion I thought from the first words that Maxwell had definitely been at the bottle.

"Clear the front page," he said. "I have a world exclusive."

I tried to ensure my single-word reply covered all eventualities: "Really?"

"Six cabinet ministers will resign in the morning. Only you know about it. We'll be ahead of the field. Six! She's had it."

At last, I thought, Maxwell had come up with a great story, Thatcher facing mutiny from within her own cabinet.

Maxwell continued, "Not bad, eh? She'll have to go when they tell her."

"How do we get into this?" I said, meaning that I needed a source, possibly the names of at least two of the six, some kind of lead to pass on to Campbell and his political team.

Maxwell exploded: "I've given you the fucking scoop of the decade."

"I realize that, Bob, but we can't just print it. We must have a source and we need more facts."

Maxwell hung up and I phoned Campbell in the Commons to give him the outline of Maxwell's tip.

"Nonsense," he said. "Who says so?"

"At the moment, only Maxwell."

A news-desk reporter put her head round my office door: "Maxwell's on the phone out here telling us he has a new splash [front-page lead story]."

It was, I could tell, going to be one of those nights. In spite of his oft-quoted attention to detail, Maxwell remained unaware of the various functions of each department and therefore did not realize that the news desk did not produce pages. I called Maxwell to explain that the first-edition front page had already gone, and meanwhile Campbell was checking out the story.

"He can't check it," Maxwell said. "Who with?"

"I think he's going to speak to Tim Renton [a senior party figure]."

"He won't know. This is much higher." Maxwell's deep voice was so loud I had to turn down the volume control on the speaker phone. I could imagine his red face as he bellowed, "You'll give the scoop away to everyone else. You don't know how to handle it."

I kept as cool as I could. "Bob, I must attribute the story to someone. We cannot say six ministers will resign unless I have a source. We'll be a laughingstock. It will be bad for the *Mirror*."

"Just print it," Maxwell shouted. "I am Your Publisher. That should be good enough for you. I am your source. Do you think I would tell you lies?"

Minutes later he phoned Campbell, who had already effectively been told the story was untrue. Renton had informed him that the minister in charge of education, Kenneth Clarke, would probably resign if Mrs. Thatcher remained in office, and that two other senior figures, the environment minister Chris Patten and the Scottish secretary Malcolm Rifkind, might possibly go, too. But there was no suggestion this would happen the next day, if at all. There was no question of six ministers resigning.

The barrage of calls—to me, to the news desk, to Campbell—went on for more than an hour. I was reminded of a remark by Phil Mellor, the deputy news editor, on a similar occasion: "We had fourteen calls from Maxwell today when one would have been too many."

Campbell arrived in my office and we decided it was possible to write a paragraph into our story saying that sources within the cabinet were suggesting that some ministers might threaten to resign unless Thatcher stood down. Maxwell was not placated by this tiny amendment tucked away so far down it appeared on the turn in page 3.

In his final conversation with me past midnight Maxwell said, "You have just thrown away the scoop of the decade. You would have been the news. You have made a bad error."

Throughout the next day I made several calls to Campbell to ask if there were any hints of six ministers resigning. There were not, and nobody did go in advance of Mrs. Thatcher's own resignation a day later.

The intriguing question for me was how Maxwell had come to be involved. Though convinced of Maxwell's tenuous hold on reality, I still could not imagine his having made it all up.

Campbell got a glimpse the following Sunday when Maxwell rang him to say: "I am very disappointed with you for having missed the scoop of the decade. You showed bad judgment and defective political antennae. It was the biggest mistake of your career and I am considering your future. I'm not having the political editor of the *Daily Mirror* treat me like somebody offering a story off the street. This was high-grade information."

Maxwell added darkly, "You have sided with the editor and ignored Your Publisher."

Campbell replied, not unreasonably, that as scoops go it was hard to spot on hindsight that he had missed one since six cabinet ministers had not resigned. With his job on the line, Campbell asked if he could see Maxwell, who suggested he join him in his apartment to watch the afternoon television interviews of the three contestants for the leadership—Heseltine, Douglas Hurd, and John Major. Once they were together, Maxwell told Campbell it was bad enough that he had given him the scoop of the decade on a plate "but for you not to see you have missed it is even worse."

Campbell said, "History proved us right. It came out exactly as I told you on Tuesday. The only resignation was hers [Margaret Thatcher's]. No other minister resigned."

Maxwell countered, "They probably would have done if we had run the story."

It is doubtful if Maxwell had read much Lewis Carroll, but conversations between the March Hare and Alice spring to mind. Next came the familiar Maxwell oil. "I value you," he told Campbell. "I've always supported you and given you what you want, and this is how you treat me."

Campbell gamely continued to argue his case: "If only you had given me a hint of your source."

Suddenly Maxwell said: "Let's phone Norman Lamont." Lamont—a junior minister known to have favored Major—was soon found. Campbell heard the short conversation because Maxwell used his speaker phone. Lamont was cagey in answering Maxwell's questions and gave nothing away, but after the call Maxwell said to Campbell: "I have very good sources, too, you know," obviously implying that Lamont was his source for the resignations story. It would certainly have been in the interests of Major's supporters for suggestions of cabinet disarray to have emerged.

Days later Campbell met Lamont, by that time elevated by the new party leader, Major, to chancellor. Campbell asked him how many times he had spoken that week to Maxwell. "Twice," Lamont replied. "Once to ask for a cartoon and again on Sunday."

Weeks later, when Campbell spoke to Maxwell and had to listen once more to having missed the scoop of the decade, he asked Maxwell if Lamont had been his source. Maxwell said he had. "Why didn't you tell me?" Campbell inquired.

Maxwell replied, "If it had got out Lamont might not have become chancellor of the exchequer."

On the day Margaret Thatcher resigned, *Daily Mirror* photographer Ken Lennox took a picture of her, tearstained in the backseat of a car, leaving Downing Street. This picture, which has been reproduced scores of times in papers and magazines across the world as the perfect representation of the occasion, made the *Mirror*'s front page very special indeed. I mentioned this exclusive to Maxwell, hoping to evince some word of praise for the photographer or even a reward. He said, "I gave you the world scoop of the decade, but you refused to use it."

I replied, "But Bob, no cabinet minister did resign. It's lucky we didn't go with it."

"Of course they resigned," he said. "And you would have had it first."

I knew our relationship was at an end, and it was only a matter of time before we made the divorce official. Yet it was difficult for him because although the *Mirror*'s circulation was undoubtedly falling, a perfect excuse for a proprietor in normal circumstances to ax an editor, *The Sun*'s was decreasing at a faster rate and the *Mirror-Record* combination was once more outselling the rival. To revert to the argot of the advertising world, in a declining market we were outperforming the brand leader and increasing our market share.

Sales figures and my future were not in the forefront of my mind, however, at the beginning of December 1990. While John Diamond, the columnist, was on holiday I had agreed to let a former *Observer* journalist, Ian Walker, take his place. A couple of days after writing his first satirical column he died in a tragic accident. Ian's death at the age of thirty-four was to have a profound effect on me and on subsequent events. In the dozen or so times I had met Ian over perhaps a year I recognized him as one of the most challenging of men, humorous, provoking, intelligent, uncompromising, undogmatic, and unorthodox. The recognition that these rare qualities had been lost so early, too early, contributed to my deep sadness at his funeral on the morning of 15 December. I have never been able to reconcile going to this ceremony with the fact that, in the evening, I attended Robert Maxwell's grand Christmas party at Headington Hill Hall.

What made this still more implausible was that Robert Maxwell did not attend. Betty and the boys did their best to pass off this lapse by suggesting Maxwell had a cold; he always had a cold, but this had not stopped him from taking recent trips to Israel, Hungary, or Yugoslavia. Betty, whom I sat next to at dinner, told me the doctor had given him permission to travel, but by then it had grown dark and he was not allowed to take off in his helicopter from Maxwell House. By this time it was not thought strange that Maxwell and his wife lived apart; it had become accepted as a matter of fact. She, however, continued to cover up and made a speech in which she referred to his being "very upset" at missing the party. The two hundred guests did their best to conceal their disappointment.

Betty told me she was planning to take a trip to San Francisco after Christmas to attend the wedding of her daughter, Isabel. She had taken the precaution of arranging her own flight, she said, because she suspected Bob would break his pledge to turn up. With father missing, Kevin and Ian looked more relaxed as well.

Kevin, sporting a multicoloured waistcoat, was unusually loquacious. Ian was twinkling with happiness, introducing us to his wife-to-be, Laura Plumb, from Chicago. As she chatted to my wife, Ian told me she was "in cable TV." I said she looked beautiful. "That's not all," Ian said, pretending to mop his brow and assuming a self-satisfied smile. "The best thing of all is that Bob approves."

Three days later, at the regular Tuesday lunch, Bob made it clear he did not approve of me. After a ritual pulling of crackers and the donning of party hats, the overdone turkey was served and Maxwell spoke: "I have decided to institute a new tradition," he said. "I want to go round the table and ask everyone what their best and worst moments were this year." After a pause he said, "I'll start."

I cannot recall what his best moment was because of what followed: "... and my worst moment came when I gave the editor of the *Daily Mirror* the scoop of the decade about the Thatcher resignation, which he saw fit not to print."

There were several gasps of surprise at this astonishing announcement. Unusually, I was sitting at the opposite end of the table, and I realized all eyes were on me.

My tongue stuck to the roof of my mouth as I stuttered, "It wasn't a true story, Bob."

Almost everyone around the table had no idea what we were talking about.

Maxwell turned to Charles Wilson, the former London *Times* editor who was attending his first lunch after being appointed editor in chief of the racing-form newspaper the *Sporting Life,* to win support for his argument: "Charlie, I gave Mister Greenslade the scoop of a lifetime. Two nights before she resigned I told him that six cabinet ministers were about to resign unless she went. What do you think of that? What would you have done about a story like that on *The Times*?"

Wilson, proving in a sentence that he was not about to curry favor at any price with his new boss, replied firmly, "I would have said it sounded like a flier to me, Bob."

"What?" Maxwell said. "A flier, eh. It was a scoop. The scoop of a decade."

Maxwell was a little uncertain about the meaning of *flier*—a slang journalistic term for a risky story that is lacking in facts, a short way of saying "Let's run it up the flagpole to see if it flies"—but he realized it was not support for his view.

I wish I had taken a note of what everyone else's highs and lows were, but I concentrated on how outspoken I would be when my turn arrived. "My best moment," I said, "was refusing to publish your Thatcher story and therefore standing out against pressure from the publisher."

I then said my worst moment was having him raise the price of the paper behind my back. I added that the really worst moment was the death of Ian Walker. Maxwell nodded through all this and simply said, "Next."

At the conclusion of this pantomime, Eve Pollard, editor of the *Sunday Mirror,* who was sitting at Maxwell's right hand, was appalled to observe Maxwell remove his paper hat and noisily blow his nose into it.

On that same day, before lunch, I had sat in my office with Jean Morgan, chief reporter on the newspaper industry's leading trade weekly magazine, the *UK Press Gazette,* while she interviewed me about my first year as editor. I knew what was required on these occasions—an upbeat, positive report on the paper's general well-being, a massaging of the sales figures to show how well we were doing, and a prediction about how much better we were going to do. I loathe those self-serving interviews at the best of times and my recent months had not been the best of times.

In an atmosphere of siege with the man on the tenth floor I eschewed any hint of immodest boasting in favor of a mea culpa for not having performed better and decided to take a hard, rational look at the tabloid marketplace. I also sent a coded message of disgust to Maxwell. Morgan, noted for an excellent shorthand notetaking, could hardly believer her good fortune as her pen sped across her pad. She was used to thick-skinned editors justifying the most gigantic falls in circulation as temporary aberrations. She had often listened to convoluted arguments that suggested that if you took into account comparative advertising expenditures, an ongoing minor internal printing dispute, unforeseen fog in the Midlands on succeeding Saturdays, the loss of regional editions during a period of midweek soccer, and the changing habits of dog-walking casual buyers in an area of high unemployment, then, considered against that perspective, the plummeting sales figures should be seen as a triumph.

I am no angel; I have taken that route, too—but not on this occasion. I chose instead a time of relative success for the *Mirror* to predict that we must expect things to get a lot worse. I had taken into account long- and short-term factors and, to be honest, it was partly a hunch based on the fact that television advertising was having so little impact on sales.

Ms. Morgan is not the kind of person to rush off and publish willy-nilly, however, and after a discussion in her office with her editor she called to ask if I was happy for her to write what I had said. Would I like to withdraw anything? I did not take back a word, and she informed me that the interview would be published during the first week of January 1991. As she told me later, she knew it was "pretty good stuff" but not as sensational as it turned out, nor did I realize how unfortunate would be its timing. On the other hand, to put the interview in perspective, it was hardly a full-frontal assault on my employer. Within the newspaper industry I hoped it would open a debate about declining circulations but, cynically, I expected it to cause hardly a ripple.

Meanwhile, the insanity of life in Maxwellia went on.

"Which genius was responsible for this?" Maxwell was holding aloft the proof of a promotion poster entitled "Millions switch to the *Mirror*" which we were encouraging retailers to display in their shop windows. The sarcasm and the tone were calculated to instill fear.

"Me," I replied bluntly, beads of sweat breaking out on my forehead as I contemplated yet another battle.

"I thought I had done it," Maxwell said, tossing the proof on the floor. Once again, I was discovering how difficult it was to second guess him, but just as I thought I was about to avoid a row he added, "It's got to change."

I had been tipped off by the circulation department that some retailers were refusing to display the promotion because it contained anti–Conservative Party propaganda. I explained that I knew of the complaints and, on balance, since it was of more use to us than them, I was happy to rewrite it.

"Why did you do this alone?" he asked. "I should have been involved as Publisher. It is not a pure editorial matter."

I let this pass. There was a knock at the door and in came the marketing director, Rob Walker, with members of the *Daily Mirror*'s advertising agency, Gold Greenlees Trott (GGT), for a presentation of ideas for a television commercial campaign.

Maxwell loved an audience. "Who are these heroes?" he said, and Walker began to introduce the team when the phone rang. "Mister Sheinberg," Maxwell said and plucked the phone from its hook, an increasingly common occurrence if this particular gentleman, managing director of Goldman Sachs, called.

After the call Walker restarted the introductions, but Maxwell, his body quivering with some kind of inner volcanic rage, shouted him down. "Forget it, mister, I know who they are. Let's see what the heroes have to say."

GGT's account director did not get far before another call interrupted his flow; then a secretary arrived with a letter demanding Maxwell's urgent attention, which he started to read aloud. Diverted by this, he began to upbraid the woman for an error. "Get Kevin to deal with it," he said. She was about to leave when he asked, "Is the ambassador here yet?" (Maxwell was expecting the Greek ambassador to Britain for tea.)

"No, Mr. Maxwell. When he arrives I'll put him in the study upstairs."

"Has Herr Genscher called?" (Maxwell was referring to the West German foreign minister, Hans-Dietrich Genscher, with whom he claimed a friendship.)

"No, Mr. Maxwell, not yet."

He sighed as if to suggest there was so much to do, so little time to do it, and he was surrounded by incompetents unable to carry out his commands. The account director coughed, smiled, and was about to restart his prepared address.

"I don't like it," Maxwell said, not yet having a clue what it was he was supposed not to like. Turning to Walker, he said, "How are the bingo plans?"

"Fine, Bob."

"They aren't fine, mister. They are chopped worms." I cannot say where he picked up this phrase, but it was in vogue for a couple of months.

"Everything is in hand," Walker said, as another call came in.

Five of us stared at each other and the ceiling, wondering when this charade would end, while the white-faced marketing director, Rob Walker, looked ready to strike Maxwell. At the end of the call, Maxwell said to Walker, "What is Murphy's Law, mister?"

"I think it's the one about if anything can go wrong it will."

"Precisely," said Maxwell. "But do you know Maxwell's Law?"

Most of us had heard this piece of tea-towel philosophy from him before and looked away in collective embarrassment as Maxwell intoned, "Maxwell's Law states that Murphy was an optimist."

Thin smiles and a wince or two greeted this remark as Maxwell stood up. "The ambassador is waiting," he said and left the room.

One of the GGT team said: "I wouldn't have missed that for anything, but I wouldn't like to do it again."

Walker and I reflected that we did not have a choice. A couple of days before, I had sat through a similarly bad-tempered meeting with Maxwell in which he had decided that in future all television commercials for the *Daily Mirror* should be only ten seconds long.

"That will teach Rupert," he said cryptically. I think he meant that the ads would cost less and therefore illustrate to Rupert Murdoch, his rival, that he, Maxwell, was clever enough to save money on TV. Of course, viewers—and potential readers—might see it differently, failing to notice the blink-of-an-eye *Mirror* ad and therefore not buying the paper.

I ventured to suggest that there were many occasions when ten seconds would be too restrictive; it would be impossible to get our message across. It was a physical impossibility for anyone to speak the voice-over fast enough.

"Then I should speak in the commercials," Maxwell said. I nodded. When in Maxwellia act like the Maxwellians. This was also the occasion on which he issued another rule, lifting a *Mirror* from the desk and stabbing a finger at a page: "There are dotted lines. Where are the scissors?"

I quickly scanned his desk for a pair before grasping his meaning. "Whenever we put dotted lines around a coupon in the paper there must be scissors."

"Good idea, Bob. It helps readers to know how to cut out the coupon." His look of disgust told me that, for once, he had detected the irony.

Maxwell told me "in private" that he expected a general election very soon, and we set up an election committee—attended by, among others, Labour's campaign organizer Jack Cunningham, MP, and the short-lived party publicity director John Underwood—to prepare for the eventuality.

"This is of utmost importance. Joe [Haines] must be involved. You will understand now why I requested you not to speak in public on Calcutt."

This was a reference to a committee set up by the government, and chaired by David Calcutt, an eminent Queen's Counsel and master of a Cambridge University college. The Calcutt Committee's brief was to consider whether intrusion into people's private lives by the press had reached the point where a law on privacy was required or whether the newspapers might police themselves effectively enough to prevent abuses of privacy. Calcutt's committee eventually produced a report in which they decided that the press should be allowed one "last chance" to regulate its own activities; otherwise a legal curb would be introduced.

Maxwell's claim that he had "requested" silence during the public discussions on the Calcutt Report was interesting since he had in fact issued "an order" to all his editors not only not to make any public statement but not even to take part in any private discussions on the action to be taken following the report's publication in June 1990.

I was struck by the paradox of editors fighting for freedom being gagged by their own proprietor, and though I honored the public obligation I enthusiastically ignored the private one, working on the Newspaper Publishers' Association's committee that drew up a code of practice for the industry.

Maxwell's "evidence" to the Calcutt committee was a superb piece of window dressing and hypocrisy, calling for the reform of the libel law (main user: R. Maxwell) and excoriating the misuses of injunctions against investigative journalists (main abuser: R. Maxwell) while disingenuously railing against the possible introduction of any privacy law.

"There is a real risk that unscrupulous individuals... may use a new right to privacy to hinder legitimate newspaper activity by seeking last-minute injunctions," Maxwell wrote in his submission.

"Pinocchio-wise, it's a wonder his nose didn't grow out as far as his stomach," commented a colleague on the committee.

Maxwell told me that, on the return of a Labour government, "our role" in terms of the press's relationship with Parliament would become "crucial." He confided, "We will be in charge. They [presumably other proprietors and editors] will look to us."

He imagined, without having raised the subject with Labour's leadership, that he would play a key role in the event of the party assuming power.

We set off in different directions to spend Christmas 1990, he to his boat in the Caribbean and I to Ireland, and I innocently thought that he could not shock me this Christmas as he had the last, when he offered me the editorship. On the morning of 27 December, a secretary in London rang to say an "important and urgent fax from the Publisher" was on its way to me. I quote it here in full:

Thank you for your note of 18th December 1990 concerning research into columnists.

1. I note that you carried out this research to test the reaction to John Diamond's column. You should not have appointed him without my consent.

2. We are not in the business of appointing unheard-of people, to columns on a major, national tabloid.

3. I want him terminated. By copy of this memo to Personnel I am giving them authority so to do, as from the 1st January 1991.

4. You can use this space liberated by this move for better purposes unless you can get back the columnist whom we lost to the Mail.

Regards, Bob.

This was about as direct a challenge to my authority and my courage as I had ever faced. I tried to act rationally, ensuring with my office for instance that I did have a copy of the memo approving Diamond's appointment with Maxwell's signature on it. But all I could feel was extreme anger at Maxwell's demand, the terms in which he couched it ("terminate," for God's sake), the timing, the lies, and the underlying threat. (The man from the *Mail,* incidentally, was Keith Waterhouse, the star columnist who had left the *Mirror* soon after Maxwell's takeover.)

Had he really needed to send this kind of message at Christmas? My family looked concerned as I began to write a lengthy and detailed document setting down the grossest examples of his interference and irrational behavior over the course of my year with him. It ran to a dozen closely typed pages, and, as I joked later to a colleague, I decided that it was much too long for the normal suicide note. I decided instead to fax a shorter one:

Your memo about John Diamond is breathtaking. Its implications also suggest that you have a short memory.

1. John Diamond was not appointed without your consent. I have a copy of your signed approval to his being hired in February 1990.

2. You knew I was carrying out the research and you asked for the results. Presumably, you do not like the results!

3. He was not unheard-of in February 1990 (he was then a columnist on *The Sunday Times*) and he is not unheard-of now (as his postbag would testify—confirmed by the research).

4. I refuse to terminate him. He is a National Union of Journalists member, he has a contract of employment, he has my full backing.

Regards, Roy.

I was uncertain what I expected from this tendentious reply, though it must be one of the few occasions on which an editor has threatened an employer with union action, albeit implicitly. Maxwell again called on Ernie Burrington, MGN's deputy chairman and managing director, to act as a go-between. After several phone calls it was agreed that Maxwell would not order Diamond's dismissal and, in return, I would "apologize" for my memo so that we could return to the status quo. It was interesting to note how quickly Maxwell pulled back from the brink, though there was no illusion on my side that this was anything other than a temporary truce.

I did not know until a couple of days later that Maxwell's yacht had run aground in the Virgin Islands, breaking the propeller and causing damage of around £60,000 ($96,000). Many of us imagined Maxwell's towering rage as he dismissed the captain. I now know that the skipper offered to resign, Maxwell rejected it, but the man went anyway. Such was Maxwell's own mythology that he suggested to me he had fired the captain when he had not. A couple of weeks later he told me, "You wouldn't believe how difficult it is to sack a captain. It has to go through Trinity House. Impossible."

Betty had correctly forecast that her husband would miss their daughter Isabel's wedding. He said "business and the boat" kept him, but I overheard him say to someone on the telephone, "Well, it was her second marriage."

If business had kept Maxwell occupied it would not have been surprising, since there was a great deal for him to worry about. He had fought off the "scribblers" for the moment, but he knew their analyses were broadly correct and he could not hope to solve his debt crisis by selling off parts of Macmillan or other of his American businesses. There was, however, one genuinely worthwhile firm in his empire that would fetch him millions—Pergamon. He had not yet decided definitely to let it go, but early in January he allowed a suggestion that it might be up for sale to be leaked to a newspaper and, having baited the hook, waited to see who might bite and how quickly.[1] Valuable as Pergamon was, it would still not be enough.

12

Big Bob in the
Big Apple

IF Maxwell was upset at my end-of-year interview in the *UK Press Gazette,* his first reference to it was far from critical. "What a densely argued point of view," he said on his return from the Caribbean yacht drama. "Very interesting." Kevin came into the office at that moment and Maxwell extolled its supposed virtues to him. I thought he must have overlooked the sly digs at him, but the next time we met it was obvious he had changed his mind. Someone had convinced him that this was a full-frontal attack on tabloid newspapers with a bit of back-stabbing thrown in. He said, "Whatever made you give that interview to the *Gazette*? It was so pessimistic. You didn't ask for my permission. You just went off and did it."

"Surely I don't need permission to speak," I replied. "It's what I believe, and so do others."

I did not dare mention that in June 1990, in an interview with the *Financial Times,* Rupert Murdoch had expressed similar concern about the "long-term downward trend in newspaper sales." I said that my view of a sales decline due to the growth of television and to falling educational standards should be seen as a contribution to the debate.

He replied, "It is for me as Publisher to debate matters like this. If you are going to give interviews about important debates then you should have cleared it with me."

After that conversation there was barely a day without an argument between us. When Gulf peace talks broke down, he tried unsuccessfully to browbeat my deputy, Bill Hagerty, into changing a perfectly acceptable front-page headline NO WAY OUT into IT MUST BE WAR. Maxwell made incessant demands on the news desk, treating it like a personal switchboard and messenger service, especially at night; he was obstructive about authorizing foreign-travel documents, even jeopardizing for a while the use of Hagerty's hard-won Gulf visas; and he maintained a guerrilla campaign against the Disney comic proposals.

It was that subject that led me to his office on 11 January and to the accidental discovery that he was indeed planning to make an issue of his privately held Mirror Group stock to the public. He made this momentous announcement through one of his favorite channels, a newspaper leak, without bothering to inform the Group's senior executives or editors. There was no board meeting at any time, so there was no question of consultation with directors.

I was sitting in his office when Ian McIntosh, head of corporate finance at London's Samuel Montagu merchant bank, called Maxwell to complain that he had just been contacted by a journalist seeking information about the proposed Mirror Group stock sale. Maxwell had hired Montagu to begin making tentative arrangements, in secrecy, for the sale, so this conversation was news to me. Maxwell took the call on his speaker phone and made no attempt to pick it up, and I heard every word.

The reason for McIntosh's alarm soon became clear. He had received a phone call from George Parker-Jervis, a business reporter on a Sunday newspaper, the *Observer*, who made it clear he knew all about the secret of the stock sale. McIntosh was worried on two counts: Maxwell might think he, or someone in his bank, had breached the secrecy agreement and, like so many in London's financial world, he disliked any publicity, especially at such an early stage. McIntosh, his exasperation clear in his voice, said "Bob, [Parker-Jervis] says you told him about it."

"I did," Maxwell said, beaming at the phone on his desk and then winking at me.

"But I thought we agreed nobody should know about—"

Maxwell cut in: "Mr. McIntosh, let me speak. This journalist asked me a straightforward question and I gave him a straightforward answer. I do not believe in lying to journalists. I do not believe in dissembling. When I am asked an honest question I give an honest answer. He deserves his exclusive. He is obviously a very clever man with good contacts."

In other words, Maxwell had leaked the information himself to Parker-Jervis and suggested he call McIntosh to confirm the story. Maxwell, unlike almost everyone else in the London business world, thrived on publicity.

"He's asking for numbers," McIntosh said.

"No numbers," Maxwell replied. It was clear that the proposed stock sale was in its very earliest stages. Maxwell and McIntosh had not even agreed which components of the private company would be included in the sale, let alone the company's probable value.

"I'll have to give him something now or there'll be speculation," McIntosh said, concerned that the journalist might publish a low value.

"Say six hundred million to one billion pounds ($960 million–$1.6 billion)," Maxwell said, apparently off the top of his head. There was some discussion about the merits of these figures before McIntosh agreed. Then Maxwell told his banker that he had given the story to Parker-Jervis on the understanding that it was unattributable; he would not be directly quoted as the source in the article.

"I think you should do the same," Maxwell said, and after putting down the phone he turned to me: "What do you think of that?"

"Astonishing," I said, and meant it. It was my first genuine intimation that Maxwell had decided to issue stock to the public. It seemed an odd way to announce such a major move and I was struck also by the sincerity with which he had said he would not lie to a journalist.

After a pause he said, "Now you can see why your interview in the *Gazette* was so wrong. You should not have done it."

I protested, "Perhaps if I'd known, if you'd told me, I might not—"

"You did know. I made up my mind on the flotation [stock issue] months ago and I told you. You would need to be a blind Turk with one leg not to have known."

It was, in fact, unlikely that a prescient editor with two legs and a long memory would have guessed that this was to be the historic moment, given that Maxwell had made at least five separate announcements about the imminence of issuing stock since his original pledge of a public sale of shares in January 1985. In January 1987 he said the stock issue would be "sometime this year"; in June 1987 he forecast it would occur in autumn 1988; he announced in December 1988 that stock-issue plans were shelved; in April 1989 he said the stock issue was back on the agenda, "probably by the end of the year"; in July 1990 he thought it likely at the end of that year; and in October 1990 said it was now likely in "the second half of 1991." What was the point of regaling him with a litany of broken promises from the past?

It was fruitless to continue with a your-word-against-mine argument. To divert him, I said, "I'm surprised you are leaving it to the *Observer*. Why not *The Sunday Times*? It's got a far bigger circulation and its City pages are well respected."

"No, that would be wrong," Maxwell said in a tone of mild rebuke. "An exclusive is an exclusive."

He returned to the subject of "your unauthorized *Gazette* interview" pulling out a new complaint from his hat. "You revealed that the *Daily Mirror* circulation has dipped below the three-million mark without informing the advertising director."

This was baffling. I could hardly credit that an editor needed to inform anyone before talking about his circulation figure.

He went on: "You also spoke of the *Mirror* figure without mentioning the *Daily Record* figure. This is not allowed." Faced with my silence he asked, "Why did you give away our private figure?"

Echoing his statement to McIntosh, I replied, "When I'm asked a direct question by a journalist, I don't like to lie."

He waved me out.

After leaving his office and walking to the elevator, I remembered I had left a file with his secretary. I ran back to his outer office to collect it in time to hear her say on the phone link to Maxwell: "Your call to Mr. Andrew Neil, Mr. Maxwell."

Neil, editor of *The Sunday Times,* later confirmed that this was Maxwell's tip-off about the Mirror Group stock issue so that, on Sunday, 13 January 1991, the *Observer*'s supposed "exclusive" also appeared in the rival *Sunday Times.*

I was heartened to see that the story in the former paper referred to the stock issue as "long-heralded" and the latter spoke of "several false starts."

The stock sale, set to be one of the largest issues of the year, was obviously fraught, a sign of Maxwell's acute financial worries. As one banker remarked the next day: "Frankly, you couldn't float a duck in this market."

Another commentator put her finger on the central problem: "Mr. Maxwell faces tough negotiations with the Stock Exchange over the issues which are likely to focus on ensuring a clear separation between Mirror Group and Maxwell Communications."[1] Maxwell's history of intercompany deals meant skeptics did not believe he could, or would, unravel the links between his private companies, the publicly quoted Maxwell Communications and the Mirror Group. For example, the *Mirror* was printed by a subsidiary of Maxwell Communications, the building was owned by a private Maxwell company, and several bureaucratic services were performed on behalf of the Mirror Group by either Maxwell Communications or one of Maxwell's private firms. More important, the accounting procedures dealing with revenue flowing in to the Mirror Group—and newspapers generate a lot of money on a daily basis—would need to be kept separate from Maxwell's private interests.

Some financial analysts thought Maxwell would not go through with the stock issue. One analyst, Colin Tennant of Hoare Govett, thought Maxwell was merely testing the market and considered it no more likely to occur than in any of the previous years it had been suggested. Without the New York *Daily News* success later in March, he may well have been correct.

After being told I would need to be interviewed at length by various accountants and banks, I commented to two Mirror Group directors that this proved Maxwell must be serious. "You're joking," said one. "We've all been through the same exercise in the past."

In fact, the interviews were conducted in such a way that I was refreshingly surprised by the positive and helpful attitude of the teams I met. They asked for figures, of course, but they also seemed genuine in their desire to know how the paper worked, about plans for the future and the gradual repositioning in the market. As one of the Dewe Rogerson marketing team observed: "Editors hold so much power on a paper they are the key to success or failure."

Maxwell did not see it like that and set out to prove his own preeminence in a startling series of confrontations. On 13 January, Gorbachev sent Soviet tanks into Vilnius, capital of Lithuania, in a bid to quell the growing movement for independence. Several people had been killed, and pictures showed troops acting with undue severity against protesters and the press. With Maxwell on his way to New York the editorial writer, David Thompson, and I were in a position to assess the situation ourselves. His excellent editorial pointed out that the Soviet president was either a liar, having promised not to take military action, or had lost control of the army. When Maxwell arrived at his hotel to read the faxed editorial, he exploded.

Thompson got the first call, describing his piece as "immature" and "politically naïve." He demanded that it be rewritten to point out that the Lithuanians had brought all this on themselves by refusing to let their young men be conscripted into the army. Regrettable though the deaths were, it was their own fault for making a "direct threat to Soviet authority." Inconsequentially, it ended by suggesting that if the Lithuanians wanted independence they should negotiate it with Gorbachev.

A reluctant Thompson was forced to comply unless I could change Maxwell's mind, and we both doubted that were possible.

"Why have I received this disgraceful leader?" he shouted.

"Bob, the pictures of violence are horrific. What appears to be happening is a virtual invasion of the country."

Before I could continue he shouted again, "We must not abandon Gorbachev. I will decide."

As so often in the past, I tried to explain that news was news. The journalists on the *Mirror,* and the independent agencies, were reporting what was happening.

He interrupted and his tone was at its most menacing: "Look, mister, (the code-word for extreme anger) you are talking nonsense. Don't you realize that Gorbachev wouldn't do anything without ringing me first?"

He was suggesting that Mikhail Gorbachev, facing strife in every quarter of his crumbling empire with rampant nationalism, ethnic disturbances, food shortages, and internal rebellion, was going to worry about the contents of a two-hundred-word editorial in Britain's *Daily Mirror.* I quickly decided what I would do regardless of his views; he could have his partisan editorial, but my news coverage would reflect the true state of affairs. I published a huge page-one picture of a stick-wielding Soviet paratrooper lashing out at a cameraman under a headline: BACK TO THE BAD OLD DAYS with a subhead: "Gorby soldiers massacre 13 in night of blood."

This point of view was enthusiastically endorsed by Nick Davies, the foreign editor so many wrongly believed was in Maxwell's pocket. I also briefed Charles Griffin to draw a cartoon of Stalin looking over Gorbachev's shoulder saying: "Now that's how to do it, Mikhail." He improved it by showing Gorbachev tucking away his Nobel peace prize into a drawer.

The next day I spoke to Maxwell about other matters and went off to deliver a speech at the British Press Photographers Association annual dinner, an occasion of mirth. After midnight I spoke to the office and was told that they had been "Captained." Maxwell had rung my deputy to complain that the *Mirror* had not included a story about Gorbachev having appointed a new prime minister, Valentin Pavlov. At most, this might warrant a paragraph; he had demanded a picture of himself with Pavlov, which was published as small as possible on page 2.

Maxwell then asked for the published story and picture to be faxed to him—and hell had broken out. In the story of barely seventy-five words the rewrite man had included a description of Pavlov as "an old-style Communist bureaucrat unlikely to push for rapid reforms." The rewrite man had obtained this information from Reuter's. The night editor was instructed by Maxwell to delete this "scandalous and untrue" reference.

"It was quite hot here for an hour," I was told. Another of those occasions of a dozen calls too many.

Maxwell decided to make an issue of this allegedly mistaken description of Pavlov, and the following day he ordered me to hold "a full investigation." He was particularly keen to know the name of the rewrite man, which I refused to provide.

"How could anyone think I would be associated with a Stalinist?" he thundered, overlooking his hobnobbing with Honecker, Ceaucescu, et al. "The man responsible for this must be sacked."

I told him that was out of the question and that it was too unimportant to hold an inquiry.

"Is that what you think of your Publisher?" he asked. "How do you think Gorbachev will react when he sees this? You have disappointed me. Why do you defy me?"

He would raise the Pavlov episode throughout the next month, but the sweet postscript came many months later when Pavlov joined the conspirators who attempted to overthrow Maxwell's "friend" Gorbachev in a failed coup.

I had to wait only one night more before the outbreak of a real war, in the Gulf, and, at last, I was pleased to take up one of Maxwell's few good suggestions. A week before he had told me he had an ex–field marshal on his staff.

"What's his name, that general I have?" Maxwell asked one of his staff. Eventually I was put in touch with Lord Bramall, former chief of staff in the Falklands conflict, who was a director of the Maxwell-owned Brassey's Defence Publications. He agreed to be interviewed throughout the period of the fighting to provide an expert commentary in a column we called "Bramall's Briefing."

I foolishly thought the Gulf War might lead to a truce with Maxwell. Whenever he was abroad he would demand that the news-desk staff read every paper that arrived during the night to seek out references to him, his companies, or the media in general. These stories were then cut, photocopied, and faxed to him in an East European hotel—where phone links were notoriously unreliable—or to his boat.

He often turned this exercise into an excuse for a row. One night he complained that he could not read the fax copies, though his yacht captain told the desk he found them perfectly legible. With Scuds flying at night, the news desk was stretched and found the task of sending Maxwell news reports too onerous, postponing doing so until after the final edition. Maxwell immediately complained, through his delightfully patient young secretary, Charlotte Thornton. Bill Hagerty and I came up with the same answer: "Doesn't he know there's a war on!"

One night, with Israel fearing an Iraqi strike and the Saudi bases under attack by Saddam Hussein's missiles, Maxwell rang the news desk to ask why he had not had his faxes. The exasperated executive replied, "It's the war, Mr. Maxwell. Two Scuds have landed. Everyone here is working flat out and —"

"Fuck the war," Maxwell said. "I want my faxes." The desk looked to me and I rang to tell him it was out of the question.

He thundered, "There will be an inquiry into this when I get back. You are encouraging your staff to defy me."

On my way to the office on 21 January, having arrived home from wartime work at 2 A.M., I was phoned and asked to pick up "a package" personally from Kevin Maxwell. This was a two-page letter from Maxwell that began with the most outrageous piece of Maxwellian doublespeak: "As Publisher...I am exercising my duty to advise you." Building on my "pessimistic and mistaken" analysis in the *UK Press Gazette,* he rehearsed a number of trivial complaints and a threat or two ("We must put a date on John Diamond's departure") before a flourishing conclusion: "It is my responsibility as Publisher to advise, warn and, when necessary, to command."

Perhaps Saddam Hussein would have been an easier boss, I thought, as I fired back a short memo with a coded threat about having kept a note of his activities: "I can list any number of examples from my diary of the extraordinary pressures you bring to bear on me and on the newspaper's staff every day...it seems to me that we need to reach an accommodation before the flotation [public stock issue]."

We were obviously at the end of our relationship, and I saw no reason to placate him. He replied with another note on 25 January demanding a detailed reply to his first memo, and I responded with an eight-page defense of my role as editor and attack on him as proprietor. I was not expecting to stay and began to clear my office. Maxwell chose to consult Ernie Burrington, the managing director, about the wisdom of firing me. He was advised that if there was a public row about my going it might harm the Mirror Group stock issue and added that I was the sort of person who might be unlikely to go quietly. This probably stayed Maxwell's hand longer than he wished.

A couple of days later Maxwell asked to see me. He told me I was "too quick-tempered...always firing from the hip." In spite of his memo, he agreed that he liked the paper, then asked to meet John Diamond. I suggested the following day. Maxwell held so many strings it was impossible to move without him, and the next day Roger Eastoe, the deputy managing director, and I spent two hair-raising hours with him trying to discuss the launch of a television listings section, the Disney comic, and two other promotions.

Eastoe fought valiantly to concentrate Maxwell's mind on these important matters, which could not proceed without his release of budget money. Maxwell disappeared for ten minutes to talk to a Russian visitor and wasted half an hour by ringing people about a top-of-the-head idea to promote the launch of the TV listings section by organizing an exhibition for Japanese high-definition televisions. "I know who'll know about this," he said suddenly. "That man at the *Financial Times*. Lord What's-his-name." He paused. "Blakenham."

He told his secretary to call the *Financial Times* and a minute later was put through to Viscount Blakenham's secretary, who suggested that he wait a moment. Maxwell took the opportunity to cover the phone and ask us: "What's his first name?"

We had no idea and hardly cared, since this diversion was so annoying, but I spotted a copy of *Who's Who* on the shelf behind him. I took it down and leafed through the pages. "Blackburn... Blair... Blake... ah, here it is, Blakenham, Michael.

At that moment Maxwell was put through. "Michael," he said without hesitation. "How are you?"

I had to smile at the rogue and in spite of my annoyance and the tension between us, he then made me laugh. After looking at the proof of a bingo card he declared, "Even Winston Churchill couldn't understand that with the aid of a shepherd guide dog and a Chinese dictionary."

Meanwhile, John Diamond had been waiting two hours elsewhere on the tenth floor for his meeting. Maxwell began by showing off by bawling out two distribution managers. After they had slunk out, he greeted Diamond disarmingly: "I won't bullshit you, John. I wanted to sack you, but Roy tells me you're a good writer."

Diamond also realized, as we suspected, that Maxwell had not read any of his columns. After a couple of minutes he asked John where his grandfather had come from. Stamford Hill, he was told.

"A good Jewish area," Maxwell replied. "Another good reason for keeping you on. We'll talk again in three months."

He referred to Diamond as a *mensch* (a good person) and as he showed him out he put his arm around him and said, *"Gei gezint"* (Yiddish for "Go in good health").

Maxwell rang me later: "I met your Mr. Diamond. He's all right." I should have gotten them together much sooner, I thought.

A couple of days earlier Maxwell had called the news desk to "suggest" they cover a "story" about a group of Jewish businessmen who were gathering at N.M. Rothschild's London offices, at the invitation of Sir Evelyn de Rothschild, to discuss how they might help Israel financially during the Gulf War. "I'm on my way there now," he said from his car phone. Before setting out, a reporter called Rothschild's for information and was told there was no meeting and, even if there was, it was private. Maxwell could never keep anything quiet; he would not have made a good spy.

Soon after, Maxwell became sick, complaining about a cold he could not shake off, a bad back—requiring massage sessions—and a bad temper, which he did not try to cure. One evening he tried to fire a night news-desk assistant because his first edition of the *Daily Mirror* had arrived late. I took the opportunity of a lull in the war to spend a weekend in Ireland and arrived to an "urgent" message to ring Maxwell. When I got through he could not remember why he had called.

He was well known for memory lapses that were one degree better than his habit of falling asleep while talking on the phone. Andy McSmith, his temporary publicity aide, told me he was briefing Maxwell one evening and looked up to find the tycoon had nodded off. He waited several minutes, saw his eyes open, and continued where he had left off. Maxwell appeared not to have been aware of his own nap.

What Maxwell had conveniently forgotten to tell me was that he had decided to appoint an editor to head a new section of the *Daily Mirror,* and he knew I regarded this as unnecessary. We were about to launch, at great expense, a TV listings supplement. Until March 1991, British newspapers and magazines were prevented from publishing weekly television guides because TV companies jealously guarded the copyright to their program information. The only weekly guides available to the public were two magazines produced under license by the two major TV networks. Papers were allowed to publish daily program guides but no more. The deregulation of TV listings was therefore a historic moment for British newspapers, allowing them to compete with the magazines, and each other, by publishing seven-day guides. Producing them, however, was expected to be costly.

Maxwell therefore came up with a revolutionary idea to save money. He approached Rupert Murdoch with a plan to share costs by going into partnership. Maxwell thought Britain's two most bitter rival newspapers, the *Daily Mirror* and *The Sun* should publish the *same* TV listings guide. Naturally, Maxwell told me the opposite.

"Murdoch is in such trouble with his debts he can't afford to produce a TV listings section," Maxwell said to me days after I had discovered senior executives from News International and the Mirror Group had met in a London hotel to discuss the proposal. Maxwell continued, "What do you think of that?"

"Will I edit it or will Kelvin [Mackenzie, *The Sun* editor]?"

"Neither of you. We will appoint an independent editor."

"It won't work," I said.

"I knew you would object. You object to all my ideas. Why do you always turn down every idea I give you?"

It was a coincidence that I was sitting so close to Maxwell the evening Murdoch rang him. Although he picked up his phone I could hear almost every word of the conversation. Murdoch had obviously had no intention of any joint venture with Maxwell and had strung Maxwell along for weeks while allowing *The Sun* to prepare its own section. On reflection, he was saying, he had decided against the idea. "Another time, perhaps."

The debt-laden Maxwell would, after all, have to fund the *Mirror*'s guide. It was therefore strange that he should go to the extra expense of hiring an outsider to edit the section. I told him my features staff could handle it easily, as proved by the succession of dummies we had prepared. I soon discovered the identity of Maxwell's man but waited to see how and when he would tell me. Instead I walked into his office one evening to find the man, Peter Jackson, former *TV Times* and *Sunday Times* magazine editor, seated at Maxwell's table.

While I had no reason for animosity toward Jackson, he happened to be caught in the crossfire in the final battle between me and Maxwell. The poor man was therefore subjected to some rough behavior from me and my staff in the next couple of weeks as I sought to prove Maxwell's decision wrong. I soon realized that the kind of magazine envisaged by Jackson was too upmarket for the *Daily Mirror* and, with help from the production departments, attempted to undermine it by producing our own edition. Unknown to Maxwell we even published hundreds of copies of a separate section, which I later showed him to illustrate what I considered we should have been distributing.

Some people later believed that he had hired Jackson merely to force my resignation, but if that was so he jeopardized the *Daily Mirror* and its prospects in the process, since we lost that window of opportunity in the early weeks of TV listings deregulation to build a new audience.

All the time his mind was on ensuring the successful stock issue. On 20 February he revealed that he would be recruiting "a number of independent-minded non-executive directors" for the new Mirror Group Newspapers board "to avoid the perception that he would exert too much influence on the company."[2]

This announcement was little more than a ploy meant to divert attention from the unpleasant news that Maxwell Communications, his public company (which now included Macmillan, Official Airlines Guide, and small printing interests in Britain) had been downgraded by a New York–based credit-rating agency. Maxwell was also alarmed by the possibility of bad publicity because MCC's deputy managing director, Richard Baker, had taken early retirement the day before, the third of the company's directors to resign within a couple of months.

It was also the month in which Maxwell exercised a second "put option" through Goldman Sachs for thirty million Maxwell Communications Corporation shares, which would prove to be the beginning of a sensational rise in the MCC share price. It took the Maxwell family interest in MCC close to 68 percent.

In spite of his pressing financial troubles, Maxwell was diverted once again in late February 1991 by thoughts of yet another purchase. He had not commented when the *Wall Street Journal* first revealed his renewed interest in the New York *Daily News*. There had been rumors running on both sides of the Atlantic that Maxwell was stalking the *News*. He was never quoted himself, of course, and after much speculation I asked him if it were true.

"They haven't asked me," he replied. In fact, they—the unions— had indeed asked him, after being prompted by an unknown intermediary many months before. I knew well enough that he wanted the paper because it symbolized for him another step on the path he still believed would eventually lead him beyond his rival of almost a quarter of a century, Rupert Murdoch, one-time owner of the city's other tabloid, the *New York Post*. Reluctantly, Murdoch had sold the *Post* after launching his Fox TV network because he was not allowed under American law to own a paper and television station in the same city. Inexplicably Maxwell considered Murdoch's sale of the *Post* as a "failure," and would often shake his head in mock sadness: "Poor Rupert. He cannot pay his debts."

In late February, as we were parting, Maxwell said; "If only things had been different. I would like to have consulted you about New York." He added, with a broad grin, "Rupert will be mad, won't he? I'm going to succeed where he has failed. Not bad for a pensioner eh?" This was his latest catch phrase.

Maxwell finally confirmed on 28 February that he had "accepted an invitation" to begin talks to acquire the New York *Daily News* from its long-suffering, strike-hit owners, The Tribune Company of Chicago. Talks had recently collapsed with another prospective buyer, Mort Zuckerman, the real-estate tycoon and proprietor of *US News and World Report*. It was suggested that the Tribune Company had then called on Maxwell, though it appears that the print unions were the prime movers in the original approach. Neither company nor unions would have thought of Maxwell if he had not leaked to them his intense interest.

The situation was tailor-made for Maxwell: the company was desperate to sell; nine of the paper's intransigent unions had been on strike for five months; a paper of sorts—with a poor circulation— was being produced by management and journalists bought in from other Tribune papers. In short, there was chaos.

As tabloids go, the New York *Daily News* has a proud heritage. Founded in 1919 as the *Illustrated Daily News* by the socialist Joseph Patterson and his cousin Robert McCormick, its role model was Britain's *Daily Mirror.* The first issue's front page would not have been out of place in the *Mirror,* featuring a huge picture of the prince of Wales, in army officer's uniform mounted on a horse. The reason was his planned visit that summer to the millionaires' playground of Newport, Rhode Island. Then, as now, on both sides of the Atlantic, the poor and aspiring were urged to peep at the rich and decadent.

The *Daily News* developed into a part of New York City's legend; Damon Runyan wrote about it and Frank Sinatra sang about it in *Guys and Dolls;* it won enduring frame as the *Daily Planet,* the paper where Clark Kent, Superman's alter ego, worked as a reporter. There are similarities, too, with the script of Ben Hecht's brilliant *Front Page* in one of the lurid stories told by the former *News* city editor, Sam Roberts. In 1928 a *News* photographer hid a camera on his ankle and snapped a convict, Ruth Snyder, being executed in the electric chair in Sing Sing.

"In the newspaper's executive dining room, meals were served on plates engraved with famous front-page stories," Roberts recalled. "Guests rearranging their vegetables often lost interest in lunch after uncovering the picture of Miss Snyder under the headline 'Dead.'"[3]

For over seventy-two years the paper chronicled life in the city. By 1924 it became America's largest-selling paper. In 1947, its circulation highpoint, it sold 2,400,000 copies every weekday and 4,700,000 on Sundays.

The *News* won a reputation, which it seemed to relish, for its enthusiastic coverage of crime and for its brash, irreverent reflection of the views of its readers, the authentic voice of New York's working class. As one of its columnists, Jimmy Breslin, put it, the *News* "became part of this city by telling stories with the rhythm of a person walking down the sidewalk."

This meant snappy headlines and punchy news stories with the juiciest and choicest of all reserved for the eye-catching front page. One pithy headline in 1976 when President Gerald Ford refused federal aid to bail out the city's finances—FORD TO CITY: DROP DEAD—has become something of a legend because later that year Ford lost very narrowly to Jimmy Carter in the presidential election.

Millions of New York's working people were reared on the *News*, which once adopted the class-based slogan: "Tell it to Sweeney. The Stuyvesants will take care of themselves." Sweeney represented the *New*'s target reader—a prototypical white Catholic workingman— while the Stuyvesants, the old money, patrician offspring of the early Dutch settlers, were not the sort who read tabloids.

For a time, the paper became right wing, a bastion of McCarthyism, lambasting liberals and condemning Communists throughout the fifties and sixties, but by the beginning of the eighties there was a gradual moderating of this tone, a recognition that the former buyers, the old Irish, the Sweeneys, had largely departed from the inner city to the suburbs and developed a taste for the opposing *Newsday* or even the heavyweight *New York Times*.

In a period of declining sales, the *News* found itself in stiff competition with its main rival, the *Post* (renowned for headlines such as HEADLESS BODY FOUND IN TOPLESS BAR), as both fought for the same readers in a period of declining sales. Fewer of the newer immigrants have chosen the papers as their guides to the city or the English language.

By 1990 circulation on the *News* was down to 1,200,000 a day, a 50 percent decrease from its heyday, and falling steadily. In spite of vast advertising and sales revenues, it is thought the paper lost $100 million during the eighties. As profits evaporated, the Tribune Company, echoing the British experience, decided to take on the print unions. The Tribune Company knew it must cut overstaffing and decided to renegotiate contracts, such as the one stipulating that fifteen men must man each press requiring only five. The company demanded of its ten unions that they accept the management's right to set new manning levels and refused to renew contracts until all agreed. This threat to the unions was not a bluff since the company's chief executive, Charles T. Brumback, had planned meticulously with his publisher, Jim Hoge, for all eventualities. They had trained executives secretly in Britain to operate presses; they had set up a standby newsroom in New Jersey surrounded by security guards; they had prepared for teams of replacement workers in various key areas.

The stage was set for a union-busting war, and Tribune imagined they had all the weapons. The unions, aware there had been preparation, tried to avoid any conflict, but in October 1990 the management, clearly frustrated at the delay, found a pretense by firing a driver. His colleagues walked out, and within twenty minutes a bus arrived with substitute drivers. The first battle of what would become a bloody industrial war happened straightaway as two hundred *News* employees attacked the bus. George McDonald, the experienced president of the Allied Printing Trades Council, announced: "We're pulling the plug" and struck.

McDonald followed up by demanding a boycott by loyal *News* readers. Logic would suggest that this tactic would quickly fail, but soon New York's citizens were assailed by a war of words on placards and billboards and in radio advertisements with slogans such as "The *Daily News* is Bad News." Hundreds of replacement workers and executives, and the journalists, most of whom—except for big-name columnists—did not strike, managed to publish a paper every day.

But from the first edition, circulation began to fall. As the dispute progressed so the strikers' tactics got more desperate and nastier. Mobs threw Molotov cocktails into printing plants, burning dozens of trucks; gangs of men roamed the streets wielding baseball bats and iron bars to attack delivery vans (which eventually had to be accompanied by armed guards); vendors who persisted in selling the *News* were liable to indiscriminate assaults.

Unlike the British equivalent, at Wapping, where unions won little if any public sympathy, the *News* strikers attracted wide support, some of which was heaven-sent, with Cardinal John O'Connor denouncing the Tribune Company's replacement policy. Both the mayor, David Dinkins, and the governor, Mario Cuomo, lined up with the unions, as did Jesse Jackson. The rival papers rarely reported the vicious acts of violence that would lead to eighty people needing hospital treatment. The police, again unlike at Wapping, did little to help management.

News readers deserted over the weeks as they showed their "loyalty" to their institution by refusing to buy it. This boycott led to the circulation falling to well below 600,000. To try to boost flagging sales, the Tribune Company was reduced to hiring the homeless to sell the *News* on street corners and in the subway, not one of the brightest marketing initiatives since many New Yorkers turned their backs on beggars advancing toward them. Then the advertisers, especially the key department stores, pulled out, sometimes for hardheaded business reasons but occasionally adding to the chorus of voices supporting the strikers.

Tribune's Brumback and Hoge, faced with losses some claimed were as high as $700,000 a day, decided to give up and close down the *Daily News* forever from 20 March... unless someone was willing to take it off their hands.

Maxwell, in touch with the unions and therefore on what was considered to be the side of the angels, sent over a negotiating team on 1 March headed by the former London *Times* editor Charles Wilson, now Maxwell's general aide, to meet Hoge and then representatives of the nine striking unions, led by McDonald. From the first moment there was no question of Maxwell resisting the deal. He would not have to buy the *News* in the normal sense of the word because the Tribune Company was offering him $60 million to take it as long as he assumed responsibility for its pensions and redundancy liabilities.

Although there was little time, both sides having signed up to a 15 March deadline, the general agreement about the number of jobs that would need to go was reached early on. Maxwell wanted 850 off the payroll, just under a third of the total, and expected to reduce a number of overheads with the introduction of new technology. He also pledged to give the paper color.

During the early, detailed talks, Wilson proved to be a canny and tough negotiator, making a lot of headway by winning concessions from McDonald's team, who recognized this was their last chance of saving the *News* and salvaging jobs. When Maxwell arrived on 8 March, however, Wilson was surprised to hear his boss deny him many of the fruitful victories he had patiently engineered.

"Let them have it," he would say nonchalantly to an exasperated Wilson, who frankly admitted, "Bob gave away more than he needed to."

Maxwell had arrived with Ian Watson, former *European* editor, who said: "Bob was desperate to get it at any price. The union guys' faces were always beaming after their meetings with him."

Watson's job was to handle the press, to generate interest in Maxwell, because he was virtually unknown in the city in spite of owning Macmillan. Buying the *News* and Maxwell's own extravagant gifts as a showman would change all that. He had ordered his yacht the *Lady Ghislaine* to sail into Manhattan and tie up beside the fashionable Water Club restaurant not far from the UN complex. This yacht would become his headquarters during the talks. This was the kind of flamboyance New Yorkers appreciated. On Tuesday 12 March, Maxwell won the unions' handshake agreement to redundancies, and the next day New York woke up to find they had a new tycoon to replace the fallen Donald Trump.

MAXWELL'S PLUM, said the *News* headline, a reference to the city's celebrated sixties nightclub, and the rival *Post* chose the same two words. Another rival, *Newsday,* must have pleased Maxwell still more by proclaiming: BRIT SAVES DAILY NEWS. He won the kind of instant celebrity status that had always eluded him in Britain, and a love affair broke out inside a day. Everyone seemed to adore the big man beaming in a succession of baseball caps with slogans like I LOVE NY and UNION YES."

Journalists' union negotiator Peter McLaughlin said, "He's got charisma. He acts like an English lord." George McDonald's joy showed in the pictures of him shaking hands with the new owner.

Jack Kennedy, leader of the pressman's union, shouted to his new proprietor at a rally, "We're gonna build it up for you, Mr. Maxwell, we're betting on you!"

Even rival *Post* proprietor Peter Kalikow had words of praise: "I like his background. His kind of rags-to-riches story happens in America a lot, but not in England."

The *New York Times* commented: "He brought a dash of British pomp and even a twist of Broadway showmanship to the 11th hour negotiations."

USA Today remarked on his "New York-sized ego" while *Time* magazine said he was a "buccaneer billionaire and a professed socialist, renowned for a blend of macho charm and armored-tank aggressiveness."

Everyone in Maxwell's contingent who had known him for some time spoke of his delight at the way New York greeted him. After one outing he boasted, "We were mobbed like Madonna...I haven't seen a reaction like this in my life." Confident that he was by now a household name, he must have enjoyed announcing: "I have no desire to be a household name in this town."

Maxwell must have reflected that this enthusiastic embrace had not occurred in Britain in 1984 when he took over the *Mirror.* Then he was traduced; now he was being feted. "Miracle Max," as his own paper dubbed him, was a conquering hero who became so famous so quickly that people began to stop him in the street to shake his hand, and taxi drivers would shout "Good for you, Max" from passing cabs. A woman handed him her baby for a kiss.

Bob Pirie, the president of Rothschild's in New York, took Maxwell to Fu's, one of the city's best Chinese restaurants. He said: "As we drove up First Avenue, people would recognize him, and open their car doors and come out and shake his hand. At Fu's, the entire restaurant got up on its feet and started clapping. He was overwhelmed. He told me, 'In my whole life in London, no one's ever acted like this.'"[4]

After the days of celebrity came a dose of reality. As Murdoch remarked privately: "Bob doesn't know what he's taken on. He hasn't a clue what's going to hit him." Half of the Tribune Company's $60 million "gift" went on redundancy payments of up to $40,000 for more than eight hundred ex-staffers, and it became clear once the dust had settled that Tribune had not sold the valuable real estate, having kept its 40 percent share of the building. True, Maxwell did promise to make the paper his pet project and pledged to spend six months in New York as a hands-on publisher, though claiming he would not interfere in editorial. Hoge was persuaded to stay on initially, as was the editor James Willse, but there was a need to win back, or keep, columnists who were followed avidly by readers. Breslin had gone to *Newsday* and was determined not to return, even though Maxwell announced to Dick Oliver on the "Good Day New York" show that "money is no object" to win back Breslin.

Liz Smith, the most widely read gossip columnist, friend of the famous, and retailer of tabloid exclusives (such as the Trump divorce), met Maxwell on his yacht the day after the *News* deal had been settled. She said, "Maxwell showed me pictures of his children and told me that he had been happily married to the same woman for forty-six years. He and Hoge were arguing over who would be called publisher. Hoge made an effort to convince me to stay, when he knew *he* couldn't stick it out, because Maxwell was a real piece of work. Maxwell offered me a $15,000 annual raise—this after I'd been there for fifteen years and killed myself for the *News*—it just wasn't enough."[5] Smith, who joined *Newsday,* was a sad loss, but Maxwell ignored the setback, saying: *"C'est la vie."*

Maxwell came up with a "new" slogan for the *News,* "Forward with New York"—a blatant copy of the one he had reimposed on the *Mirror*—"Forward with Britain." His editorial said: "This city will overcome its troubles and so will the *Daily News.* I love them both. Your slogan, our slogan, my slogan, has got to be 'Forward with New York.'"

He also won publicity for his usual quirky behavior, reading out a poem written by a striking worker and declaring that she would become the paper's poetry editor, or firing security guards. He called in Grover Howell, supervisor of the paper's 130 security personnel, and told him he would be the first person to be laid off along with his entire staff. He enjoyed doing this because he carried out the dismissal in front of a *Vanity Fair* journalist and knew it would be the kind of anecdote that would add to his reputation for ruthlessness, though the target—given that security staff had largely been there to protect staff from strikers—was a soft one.

In front of a British journalist, he summoned executives in charge of the telephones because, he claimed, of poor service: "Do you value your jobs, sirs? If so, how do you demonstrate that? I still have no service...I pay your salary and you just sit on your backsides doing nothing. What on earth are you guys doing?"[6]

He was playing to the gallery, but here was a new audience to entertain. He fired two secretaries in eight days, saying of one: "She is not a secretary, she is an experiment." This deluded Maxwell into thinking he was running the paper that went on around him. Hoge quickly recognized his new owner's shortcomings: "I was amazed at his willingness to accept things without much background knowledge. He had no interest in operations and no respect for professionalism."[7]

Instead, Maxwell entertained advertisers in the stateroom of his yacht, itself a lure for sightseers, chuckling to himself because he demanded they take off their expensive shoes before stepping on deck. "The reception I got from them was almost as amazing as the honeymoon we appear to be having with the media," he said. That was no bluff because twenty of the thirty major New York retail outlets did begin to advertise again in the *News* within the next two months, though rates were cut to between 60 to 80 percent of prestrike levels and Maxwell's promise to give them a cash rebate if the circulation did not reach 800,000 probably prompted their enthusiasm.

He also introduced his executives to his imperious and impulsive management style, in a rerun of my experience, by deciding to raise the paper's cover price from thirty-five to forty-five cents. A master of mistiming, he did this two hours before the presses were running without informing or consulting any other senior executive.

As a Jew he was soon made an honorary grand marshal at the Salute to Israel parade down Fifth Avenue, introducing his new-found assistant Carolyn Hinsey, a well-built six-footer he nicknamed Tiny, to Mayor Dinkins as "my blonde." He attended a lunch at which President Bush was present, clung to his side, and secured a seat next to him during the meal. He had a new audience to amuse and amaze with his old routines, older jokes, and his name-dropping. One lawyer was amazed when he interrupted a business meeting to show everyone a picture of himself shaking hands with Gorbachev.

He was in his element. He loved New York and New York loved him. At one point he was moved to exclaim that he should be seen as "not just a hero, [but] a cult figure." While this kind of immodesty was to be expected, he was so taken aback by the adulation after a couple of weeks that he told a journalist: "This will not last long. No doubt some banana skins are being readied for me now, and if not, I'll find them."[8]

He was right to question the strength and depth of the adulation. The public enthusiasm was tempered from the start by private skepticism among professional media watchers on Wall Street, and when Maxwell audaciously declared that the *News* was "in danger of making a profit this year" (a phrase he regularly used about *The European*), they began to question whether there was any substance to the hype. Soberly they spoke of the poststrike *News* facing an uphill struggle for survival, that it would not reach its old circulation, that it was even unlikely to reach a million, that advertising would not return quickly, especially the profitable classifieds, that more staff cuts would be necessary along with more investment, and, most important and serious of all, the paper was still incurring a hefty daily loss.

Journalists, paid cynics, started to wonder if there was more, or less, to Maxwell than the initial razzmatazz. McDonald, head of the printers' union, confided to *Time* that his union brothers in Britain had warned him: "Maxwell is a rogue. Watch out for him."

Now papers began to ask difficult questions of the man who, according to the *New York Times,* spoke with a "booming, upper-class English baritone" but, according to *Time* writer Martha Smilgis, proved on closer attention to be "very crude... his polish was not very deep."

On 21 March, his second day in full command, there was an ugly row when he was reminded of his past during an interview on "The MacNeil-Lehrer Report." The interviewer annoyed him right away by quoting a union man called "Juan" who had said that anyone dealing with Maxwell ought to get things in writing.

"What's the betting he never said that?" Maxwell declared, and ordered the editor to find the man. Having dodged that ball, since "Juan" proved impossible to trace, he ran straight into a more lethal delivery. Charlene Hunter-Gault, the interviewer, quoted a piece in the *Financial Times* that referred to the 1971 Department of Trade inspectors' criticisms of his business dealings. Maxwell barked, "I will not participate if there are libels... I'm not going to answer shit."

He refused to appear on a program that might "besmirch my reputation" and phoned the *Financial Times*'s Washington correspondent to upbraid him, accusing him of quoting from Tom Bower's book. In Maxwellia, Bower's book equated with malicious lies. He went back to the TV crew and demanded they "scrub" the questions or "I'm not appearing."

The rival papers were also quick to declare war. The *Post*'s star columnist, Mike McAlary, launched a volley of disgraceful xenophobia about the "foreigner." He did make one telling point though, by saying Maxwell "has put the words 'Forward with New York' on the paper's masthead and announced a series of backward intentions that would run the paper into the ground." *Newsday* chose the personal attack, telling tales of discontent among the *Lady Ghislaine*'s crew.

The *New York Times* loftily referred to the "bare-knuckled" feud among the city's three tabloids but was not so far above the fray, headlining one front-page review article AN IMPERIOUS MASTER and detailing alleged anxiety among Maxwell's staff.

None of this was as worrying to Maxwell as *Business Week*'s cool appraisal of his tangled empire and its conclusions about the size of the debt and the method he was using to raise loans. The magazine claimed to have documents "proving" that Maxwell's private companies owed $1.5 billion in addition to the $3 billion MCC debt, and pointed out that Maxwell's private businesses "have borrowed heavily against much of their assets" and that these "private investment vehicles borrow extensively and use their shares in Maxwell Communications as security." This reference to "pig on pork" spurred the *Wall Street Journal* to take an interest in Maxwell as well, and a team began research into his dealings.

Behind the smiling image of the global media tycoon in the Big Apple this was the canker worm that would gnaw away in the coming months. His first lie was soon exposed. The man who promised to spend six months in New York was there very little and sometimes not even in touch. Editor Jim Willse said in early June, "I will go for days without speaking to Mr. Maxwell—but I can always get him if and when I need him: Bulgaria, Britain, Brooklyn."

It goes without saying that Maxwell meant to stick to his word about his New York commitment, but problems were too pressing elsewhere. He amused visitors on both sides of the Atlantic by wearing a watch with two faces, displaying the time in London and New York, a double reminder that time was running out. However, his New York reception and New Yorkers' perception of him was to prove crucial in the next major enterprise—the issue of Mirror Group stock to the public.

13

Farewell to the Mirror

THE day before Norman Schwarzkopf launched the final assault on the Iraqi forces occupying Kuwait, Robert Maxwell launched his final assault on my editorship, though Desert Storm was probably carried out with more subtlety than Maxwell's offensive. Charles Wilson, editor in chief of the *Sporting Life* and treated by Maxwell as his general factotum, rang to say he had been asked to tell me that the *Daily Mirror* must carry a promotion offer for bottles of vitamin pills.

I had already been sent details of this offer and quickly decided not to run it. I was being asked to promote a multivitamin pill, marketed under the name Vitachieve, on the understanding that by taking it regularly children could expect to improve their IQ. The whole exercise stank, and I could see nothing but long-term problems for the *Mirror* if we lent our name to the project. That was quite apart from the fact that I was not being asked to check out the offer in the normal way but was being ordered to publish it without any verification. I was expected to encourage children between the ages of seven and seventeen to take "IQ pills," as they soon became known, on the basis of results from two trials that had yet to be published.

Charlie was candid: "If you want my opinion," he said, "I wouldn't touch it." In such circumstances the messenger can afford a conscience.

I was sent the research material, published in a special issue of *Personality and Individual Difference* and immediately understood Maxwell's interest. The publisher was Pergamon Press. The briefest of glances suggested that the trial results, while apparently encouraging, were inconclusive. There was no incontrovertible proof that by taking vitamin pills the children tested in California had improved their IQ. I was told I would have to wait to hear the results of the equivalent British trial, carried out in Barrow-in-Furness, Cumbria, until the screening of a BBC documentary, "QED," the following week. Maxwell expected me to use the program as the peg to launch the offer.

After I told Charlie I would not run it, Maxwell rang to ask why.

"I'm not keen on it, Bob. I don't think it's good for the *Mirror* to be seen peddling pills to youngsters."

"Nonsense. These aren't drugs. They're perfectly safe. It will blow *The Sun* out of the water. It will be the circulation winner of the year."

"I realize they aren't drugs. But if we create a belief among young people that a bottle of pills is the answer to all their problems then we might set them on the wrong course."

"Mister Greenslade," he said, so slowly and deeply it seemed like a roll of thunder, "you know nothing about science. I have had years of dealing with scientists and I have read the official scientific journal. It is perfectly safe. It is backed by the top men in their fields, top scientists, top dieticians. You will publish the offer."

"I'll look at it again," I said. "But I'm not keen."

This inflamed him to one of his favorite analogies: "Remember, I own the stadium, you are just the manager."

I was subsequently contacted by the investigative journalist Duncan Campbell, who was writing about the BBC's part in the "IQ pill" saga for the *Independent on Sunday*. He revealed that Maxwell had a second major link to Vitachieve pills, having been one of the three backers of the trials, which had cost £500,000 ($800,000). I was beginning to understand more clearly why Maxwell was so keen to market the pills through the *Mirror*, and I was determined to resist, recalling a statement Maxwell had made during an interview a year before: "You will not find my papers championing anything I'm in business for."[1]

I could imagine the outcry from readers for months, maybe years, to come about the pills having "failed." Little Jimmy was still a halfwit in spite of having taken a pill every day before going to school. Worse, of course, would be the mother who might suggest that taking a harmless vitamin pill had led her son to experiment with other, more dangerous, pills.

A director rang me to urge me to comply, saying, "Do you want to go down the tubes for a few pills that won't do anybody any harm?" That is how compromises are born, and I had had enough of them.

The next time I heard from Maxwell, from his yacht, he said nothing about the pills. With the land battles in the Gulf raging, he wanted to air his views about the course of the war and to offer "help" to his flagship newspaper. The week before he had told me, "We have a man in Schwarzkopf's team. Why are we not getting inside information from him?" It was Maxwell's style to start conversations with you as though you knew instantly what he was talking about. "Why do you ignore Your Publisher? If you want to know about the war, about what's really going on, you should contact me. Why do you ignore me?"

When the smoke cleared I discovered that he believed that a former U.S. colonel now writing for one of his American magazines, the *Armed Forces Journal*, was acting as an adviser to Schwarzkopf and would therefore leak information to the *Daily Mirror*. I found that this was factually inaccurate and told him so; he grunted.

Afterward he phoned to ask: "How's the war going?" I began to give him the latest news when he interrupted: "Listen, mister, watch out for the Jews, Turks, and the Kurds. They will be tomorrow's news, and I'm giving it to you today." I never did discover what he meant by that.

This day's intemperate "advice" was of a similar nature. "If you want to know what's really going on in this war call *Maa'riv* [Israel's second largest daily paper]," he boomed. "They have the inside track.

Your reporters are being censored. They're hopeless. Tell *Maa'riv* to send you their stories down the wire every day. You'll be out in front. If you'd asked me earlier I'd have done this for you."

I rang an executive at *Maa'riv*, a newspaper in which Maxwell had a large stake, and the man sighed. "Did Mr. Maxwell say this? Surely he knows we suffer worse censorship here than you do. We have to rely on America and Britain to know what's happening in our own country, let alone the Arab nations. You tell me what's going on." After a short chat he concluded, "By the way, who would have translated our copy from the Hebrew at your end?"

Originally Maxwell had taken me into his confidence to assure me there would be no war. He soon changed his mind and his close links with Israel ensured a hawkish attitude to the point of ordering an editorial attacking Neil Kinnock for proposing that sanctions should be given more time to work. I thought this a misguided view for the *Daily Mirror* to adopt, since the essence of the paper should be to provide a sensible alternative view as often as possible, and when questioned about it by *The Sunday Times*'s Brian MacArthur I told him the truth. In his column that week he said the prowar leader suggested to some rival editors that the *Daily Mirror*'s "editorial policy is being dictated by Robert Maxwell, its publisher."[2]

Most of his involvement was negative: I called him to inquire why he had refused to sign a travel form for one of our reporters to go to Germany where she was to interview the wives of front-line soldiers. "It's a waste of time," he said. "Let the other papers go. They won't get anything. There won't be any casualties. The war will end tomorrow." He hinted that he had information from "the highest sources," and I gave up.

It was fortunate that I was staying at the office until 2 A.M. because he rang the news desk well after midnight with "a new splash (exclusive)." The night news editor told me Maxwell had demanded a new front-page headline: WAR TO END IN 24 HOURS. I told him to ignore it.

Half an hour later Maxwell began one of his telephone terrorist campaigns against the news desk for sending him unreadable faxes.

"Is it just me," said a news-desk man who had dealt with Maxwell for many years, "or is he getting crazier lately?"

The next morning, 26 February, fourteen months after I had joined the *Mirror*, Maxwell returned from the boat and rang to ask if I was coming to lunch. Since it was a Tuesday, the ritual lunch, I confirmed that I was. "See you then," he said brightly, and I thought nothing of it until I arrived on the tenth floor and found, in the drawing room, a small table set for two. He had arranged for the other editors and executives to be entertained by Ernie Burrington in the Mirror Building. During my fifteen-minute wait I wrote in a notebook: "Is this to be the final act?"

Maxwell began with a splendid understatement: "You and I are not getting on... our relationship isn't working. That may be fifty percent your fault, it may be fifty percent mine." Then came that familiar list of differences once more—the *UKPG* interview, the rejection of his Thatcher story, opposition to all his ideas, assorted acts of defiance—before he referred to my always "shooting from the hip" which he sometimes called "shooting from the lip."

I was not going to fight, simply saying: "You want to be editor."

"There you go," he replied. "The trouble with you, mister, is that you have a short fuse."

At a divorce it is not usual to discuss the next wedding but then Maxwell was not predictable. He said, "Who should take your job?"

We spent ten minutes or so running over the candidates before he asked, "What is it about me, about coming here, that you didn't expect?"

"Interference," I said without a pause. "You interfered more than I thought possible, and not just with me, but by ringing so many staff, dealing with so many people. Murdoch doesn't do that, and it took me by surprise."

He beamed: "That's me, a man of detail. I must be involved. Anything else?"

I had been mulling over a way of explaining to him in a more graphic way why I had accepted the challenge. "It's a bit like the lion tamer, Bob. He has to find some way to fool the lion into acting unnaturally, to ensure it won't bite off his head when he sticks it in the animal's jaws. I thought I'd find a way to tame you, but you just kept biting my head off anyway." He liked that, of course, and laughed.

"I know you don't have a contract," he said. "But I'll look after you. Meanwhile not a word to anyone. This must be a secret between us for the moment, and I hope, on this matter, I can count on you."

I told only my wife and continued to work. There was a war on after all. Maxwell rang several times over the next two days with odd questions, one of which was, "When would you like to go?"

I said I would leave once the war was over. Then came one I had been expecting: "In view of your decision to leave [*my* decision!] I take it there will be no opposition any longer to the vitamin pills offer."

I said I would get my deputy to handle it, though Hagerty and I managed to play it down. It must have been the first newspaper offer in history where the headline was so skeptical it invited readers to disbelieve the claims: "Can you REALLY make your kids brighter?" Maxwell also contributed to its lack of success by offering such a small reduction, only 50 pence (80 cents) off a £5.99 ($9.99) bottle, that there were few takers.

Bush announced the ceasefire the following morning, 27 February 1991, and Maxwell agreed to pay me a year's salary. "In return I will want you to sign a confidentiality document," he said. "I won't keep you waiting long for a leaving date. Meanwhile, remember, it's still a secret."

Two days later, when I was at home on a Saturday, he called to say he had had "a good idea" about the public statement. He said he wanted to say I was going because I objected to the appointment of an outside editor for the TV listings guide. "We can both talk about that subject till the cows come home because it's roughly the truth," he said, foolishly adding, "It will also be good publicity for the guide."

I agreed, since I thought I would emerge better than he in public from such a statement.

The next day, five days after that final lunch, I announced my departure to a group of colleagues at conference and, by arrangement, a statement was issued saying I was leaving "by mutual agreement" after the decision to launch an independently edited television magazine.

There was a bizarre twist the following day when I discovered that Maxwell had already informed the features staff to prepare themselves to take over the TV magazine, having decided—after taking widespread advice—that our "pirate" edition was superior. I mentioned this when I visited him in his study to sign the leaving document. "If only our relationship had been better it wouldn't have happened," Maxwell said. He put in front of me what he called a termination contract, and I noted immediately that he was trying to prevent me from working for any Murdoch publication for a year; after an objection he amended the restriction period to six months.

I read the document carefully and noted it was tight on confidentiality, as expected, but failed to spot the implication of a clause restricting my right to say anything *forever* that might damage Maxwell's reputation. I signed and collected my severance pay. I was under no illusion that refusal to sign would have led to anything but a lengthy court case in order to ensure any compensation payment. There were many examples of senior executives who had spent years trying to make Maxwell pay up their agreed severance terms.

"Do you want John Diamond's head as well?" I asked. He nodded. I had agreed with John that I would negotiate his severance for him rather than leave it to an unknown and possibly less sympathetic successor. Maxwell agreed to give him a year's salary, too.

I learned that Charles Wilson would step in as acting editor, though he was then in New York negotiating to buy the *Daily News*. Media correspondents saw through the thin veil of the TV magazine excuse, and though I refused to say anything, there were plenty of staff on the *Mirror* eager to talk. I was immediately heartened by a journalists' union meeting at which staff voted 139–0 for a resolution recording their "regret and anger" at my going and noting "with dismay" that I had left because of "proprietorial interference." They had not been fooled, so why should the rest of Fleet Street?

One of the most lucid reports appeared in *The Sunday Times* where Brian MacArthur analyzed the reasons for my departure and, at last, pointed out the underlying message of my *UK Press Gazette* interview. I had been telling Maxwell to get his tanks off my lawn. Every report referred to Maxwell's high-handed and intrusive style, mentioning examples of his interference during my editorship culled from staff. This obviously rattled him, and on my second morning at home he called: "Your friends are not doing you any favors... you need to control your friends."

"I can't help having so many friends, Bob."

He did not even say goodbye after what I regarded as a threatening call, making it obvious that he was intending to use the termination contract as a gag to prevent me from saying anything at all.

Ernie Burrington consoled me by mentioning that I had impressed the financial team preparing for the stock issue. "I told him this wouldn't help the float," he said grimly. This aspect of my going was noted on the business pages and it should have worried Maxwell a great deal more than the anecdotes elsewhere. *The Times* City diary noted: "If the senior executive of a prospective public company were to be shown the door within six weeks of a flotation on the stock market with the possibility of union unrest thrown in for good measure, most merchant bank advisers would be urging at least a temporary delay in the proceedings."[3]

Ian McIntosh, head of corporate finance at Samuel Montagu, told the reporter, "This is obviously something we have been aware of but it is not going to upset our plans."

Ivan Fallon in *The Sunday Times* enlarged the point: "Six weeks from its £600 million ($960 million) stock-market flotation, Mirror Group Newspapers is without a chief executive, a finance director, and an editor for the *Daily Mirror*.

"When he was challenged, Robert Maxwell replied, 'Oh yes it has—I am all three.'"[4] That, indeed, was the problem.

Soon after, Maxwell reappointed my predecessor Richard Stott as *Mirror* editor.

Even though I had agreed to go, the loss of the editorship was a far worse psychological blow than I had expected. I felt I had let myself and my staff down, and it seemed so unfair that the awful truth of his gross misbehavior, which had forced my hand, would remain a secret. True, I had taken what amounted to hush money, but half of it was because I could not work for six months and the other half was compensation for loss of a unique job. Friends quickly advised me to try to forget Robert Maxwell. He is not worth worrying over any longer, they said. Tony Delano, one of the biographers who had suffered Maxwell's wrath, wrote from Australia to say I must sit back, enjoy the show, and laugh. My wife and children were even more forceful, urging me to stop talking and thinking about him. I rejected any number of requests by newspapers, radio, and television to talk or write about him since I did not think I could do so truthfully without breaching my contract. Nevertheless, his phone-call threat often came to mind, and I seethed over some of the lies he was telling about the impending Mirror Group stock issue.

Knowing some of the truth, it was hard not to avoid giving help to those people who contacted me wanting concrete information, especially when I received so much gossip from inside the Mirror Group. I was told of one piece of sleight-of-hand: the Mirror Group's valuable building was to be omitted from the company in which stock would be issued. Yet in one major interview, Maxwell had encouraged the writer to refer specifically to the "Holborn Circus properties" which "according to Montagu . . . are valued at more than £100 million ($160 million)."[5] By coincidence I received a phone call from Andrew Davidson of *The Sunday Times* business staff, who was to interview Maxwell about the stock issue: "Could you offer any advice?"

I told him that I thought the building was to be excluded, yet this was worth at least a fifth of the proposed market capitalization. If it wasn't to be in the new company then what was, and how much was MGN worth? Indeed, what was MGN? Davidson's approach took Maxwell by surprise and prompted him into making a mistake. Davidson probed and then sprang the trap, as his *Sunday Times* article explained in a bit of question-and-answer repartee with Maxwell:

> But what does the investor get, apart from the titles, the management and the staff?
> "You also get the printing subsidiary and the Holborn building which MGN occupies." [said Maxwell]
> All the building, all £100m worth?
> "Yes, all of it."

After talking to Maxwell, Davidson then phoned Tony Carlisle, chief executive of Dewe Rogerson, marketing advisers to the stock issue, who was stunned by Maxwell's statement: "Did he really say that? There's been a misunderstanding. I'll get back to you."[6]

This was four days before the publication of the issue prospectus and cannot have engendered much confidence in the City, where talk of "the Max factor" had become commonplace.

It is now plain Maxwell had lost control of events within his own empire. He was unable to cope with the burden of debt and, from the beginning of March, he was no longer the master of his own fate. There was no question of "coming clean," of confessing to anyone or any institution the dreadful truth that Robert Maxwell was broke. He would not give the outside world the opportunity to gloat; he had pulled through crises before, and he would do so again. All he needed was time and a change in the economic climate and it would all come right in the end.

Meanwhile, he must keep up that ebullient public front—in this case, it was some front, since he was embroiled in bargaining for the New York *Daily News*—because he could not afford to allow any light to penetrate Maxwellia. He had always been suspicious; now he would exhibit signs of acute paranoia. He would not be able to trust even those closest to him. Guilt would feed fear, and fear would eat the soul. If he had been willful and irrational in the past, from now he would be gripped by a frightening dementia. He had always been liable to violent mood swings, and these would become more frequent and more pronounced as he contemplated day after day his inevitable but unacceptable fall into the chasm of ruination and ridicule.

For Maxwell watchers, 28 March 1991 became the turning point, the day on which there was the most obvious sign of his impending downfall. He announced the sale of Pergamon Press to Elsevier, the Dutch scientific publishers and major Pergamon competitors, for £440 million ($704 million). If Maxwell had done nothing but create and build up Pergamon, he would be remembered as a wise and wonderful entrepreneur. In the classic capitalist way he had spotted a need and fulfilled it, making profits for himself while apparently pleasing the majority of his suppliers—the scientists—and customers, the scientific and academic community. By the time of the sale the company, still based in Oxford at his Headington Hill Hall mansion, was publishing more than four hundred scientific journals. There had been a single hint in one paper back in January that he might sell, but Bob Pirie, chief executive of Rothschild's in New York, revealed Maxwell's reluctance to let it go. "He always said he would never sell Pergamon. But over coffee one Saturday evening I suggested it and he said yes."[7]

His need for cash had made the sale crucial. "I knew something was up when Pergamon went," said Brian Moss, for thirty-one years a loyal Maxwell employee who had risen to executive rank in Pergamon and latterly ran the group's transport division. "It must have been heartbreaking for him, like selling the family jewels." He was not referring to sentiment alone. "There was £60 million ($96 million) taken in advance orders every year for years," said Moss. "Checks for millions arrived."

Pergamon made pretax profits of £27 million ($43.2 million) in the year up to March 1990. Maxwell was forced to deny himself this guaranteed yearly profit out of his desperation for a single, larger sum. It was perhaps unsurprising that he would lie about this sale being the answer to all his problems.

Playfully he boasted to an American interviewer: "Before you write this article you will find I have done exactly what I have predicted: repay a lot of what I have to repay in October '92."[8]

He was referring of course to the long-term public debt and *not* the secret, enormous private debt. His lie to the British media took a different form. Having failed to buy Elsevier or America's Harcourt Brace Jovanovich, he said: "I could never be king of the scientific journals so it was wise to sell."[9]

In a circular to shareholders recommending the sale six weeks later, he forgot those two lies and admitted he was selling Pergamon because he could not find buyers for anything else and, anyway, it was still not enough to solve his debt problems. "I and my family have a strong emotional attachment to it," he wrote, and this was probably not a lie.[10]

The surprise of 28 March did not end there. It was announced that Maxwell was to resign as chairman of MCC in favor of the former Conservative Party cabinet minister, Peter Walker. His son, Kevin, was to become chief executive. When this news broke I rang a friend in Maxwell's private office to ask, "Is he seriously giving up?"

"He's got to," I was told. "He has to...the banks."

Walker, then fifty-nine, was regarded as a shrewd politician with a successful business track record before entering Parliament. Whatever had lured him to front this company with such a controversial figurehead? Knowing that he had already decided to quit as a member of Parliament, it appears he had been approached by Kevin, who made him an offer that, for most people, would have been difficult to refuse. There was to be a £100,000 ($160,000)-a-year salary with normal perks, big car, and expense account, plus a share-option deal worth more than £1 million ($1.6 million) over three years.

The former secretary of state for Wales later insisted that the money was irrelevant: "I was wealthy at a young age and I have remained wealthy. I had no need for the money. The attraction was the challenge."[11] He has since said that he laid down conditions before accepting the offer.

After meeting Kevin, "I had a word with his father and said I would do it on condition that it was my board, and that I could appoint and decide who should sit on it," Walker said. "I also said I would wish to run the business on a conventional basis with monthly board meetings and financial accounts and that Mr. Maxwell was not to sit on the board or on any of its subsidiaries."[12]

Astonishingly the man who ran his public company as a one-man band agreed to this proposal, and Walker accepted a nonexecutive directorship prior to becoming chairman on 1 July. On the day of his appointment he spoke of the company's "tremendous potential for organic growth" and added, "I think the company is going to enter a new phase and be a high-quality publishing house on both sides of the Atlantic." One experienced Maxwell observer noted that, without Maxwell, MCC "is a bit like the Vatican without the Pope" and quoted a banker who commented: "Robert Maxwell as a passive investor is a contradiction in terms."[13]

A week or so later Maxwell spoke of reducing his family's 68 percent holding in MCC to 49 percent once Walker and Kevin had been "at the wheel" for six months, another of Walker's stipulations. The chairman-designate was given an office in Maxwell House and set about discovering the details of his new domain. It was to prove a strange adventure.

The initial City response to Maxwell's announcement was, on the face of it, wild enthusiasm. The MCC share price took off like a rocket from the end of March throughout the first three weeks of April, gaining almost 90 pence ($1.44)—a rise of 60 percent—and making it one of the top market performers of the period. This could not be explained solely by investors' antipathy toward Maxwell and regard for Peter Walker. It was a reaction out of all proportion to the announcement. The truth was far more straightforward, yet, by its nature, totally secret. Maxwell had organized a huge share-buying operation to support MCC's share price, arranging for several separate purchases of MCC shares through his Liechtenstein trusts and similar trusts in Switzerland, Panama, and the Virgin Islands. He simply removed sums of money from MCC in the form of unsecured loans to private companies such as Robert Maxwell Group or Bishopsgate Investment Trust, which were then passed on to the offshore trusts. These trusts either bought MCC shares on the market themselves or transferred money to other companies to do so.

For example, two secretive Swiss companies, Servex and Yakosa, bought twenty-five million MCC shares worth about £50 million ($80 million) in the last week of April 1991. Yakosa's administrative president was none other than Dr. Werner Rechsteiner, the Zurich-based lawyer mentioned earlier as a leading light in the Maxwell Foundation. In the same period two directors of Maxwell's Liechtenstein trust, Swico *anstalt*, Ellis Freedman and Geoffre de la Pradelle, bought 10.1 million shares for about £22 million ($35.2 million). This holding was registered on the day that the share price rose by 22 pence (35 cents) to 241 pence ($3.85) its highest point.[14] In all, it is thought he spent £150 million ($240 million) in this period and may have used as many as twenty-one separate offshore companies.

These shares were largely purchased through a partner at Goldman Sachs, Eric Sheinberg, a longtime business associate of Maxwell's who spoke frequently to Maxwell throughout my time with him. I noted that this was one caller to whom he was always civil and one who was accorded the rare privilege of being spoken to without the rest of the room listening in. Goldman Sachs has since made it clear they had been assured that though clients such as Yakosa had been introduced to them by Maxwell they had no formal connection with him.[15] However, before dealing, it appears that Goldman obtained only verbal confirmation that buyers were not connected to Maxwell. Written confirmation arrived later. This was not a breach in the rules, but, given the risk of accepting such large purchases, it was unusual.

This was only the beginning for Maxwell; it would get worse as he became more desperate. But we need to stop and contemplate just what kind of deplorable mess Maxwell was now in and consider the virtual impossibility of his breaking out of the vicious circle. To pay off bank debts owed by his private companies (and to bankroll many of his loss-making projects which included, among others, *The European* and Berliner Verlag) he had raised more bank loans by using his MCC shares as collateral. More than £300 million ($480 million) of borrowings by his private companies were secured on MCC shares, and it was essential that his share price did not fall below 145 percent of the value of those loans—or the banks would require more security in the form of more shares.

However, MCC's share price was notoriously unstable since institutions were largely ignoring the stock and there was little trading. To reverse this decline, Maxwell conceived the not unique idea of supporting his price by buying his own shares, thus creating a false market. Apart from the guile necessary to carry out this illicit operation, he also needed a great deal of money. Where could he find it? By offering more banks more MCC shares as collateral. And how could he obtain those shares? By using the bank loans to buy up more MCC shares, in effect robbing Peter to pay Paul. At some stage there would be no shares to pledge as collateral, the debts would fall due, the trading losses would mount up, the share price would crumble. In City slang, "meltdown"—the complete collapse of the company—was inevitable. It was just a matter of time.

The Mirror Group stock issue offered Maxwell some respite, providing immediate cash and the potential of yet more shares to pledge. So on 17 April, against the background of a strengthening MCC share price, the appointment of Walker, and the successful sale of Pergamon, the introductory document for the Mirror stock issue was published. It was not yet clear quite how many shares would be for sale, but MGN's total market value was expected to reach £500 million ($800 million).

The "scribblers" had a field day. The *Financial Times* columnist Lex commented: "Past experience might suggest that no investor in his sober senses would bother," but since MGN was more transparent, "it is perhaps less likely to be the chosen vehicle for Maxwellian escapades." He could not, however, see institutions lining up to invest "at any price."[16]

In spite of claims that MGN would be protected from Maxwell, *The Times*'s Neil Barrett pointed out that it would "remain inextricably woven in Mr. Maxwell's web of public and private interests" and proceeded to detail the strange examples of how the "hand-in-glove relationship" among MGN, MCC, and Pergamon Holdings related to the *Mirror*'s building.

The Mirror Group was paying £7 million ($11.2 million) a year to rent its Holborn Circus headquarters from MCC, which was, in turn, leasing the building from Pergamon Holdings. MGN was also paying MCC a further "license fee" of £342,000 ($547,000) a year for seventy-six car parking spaces. Given that Maxwell had obtained the building in 1984, not to mention the parking lot, it was odd that it was not part of the stock issue.

Equally it seems reasonable to ask: Where was the ring fence on this part of the deal? The real reasons for its omission were, first, that Maxwell could raise bank loans by using the building as collateral, and second, he had obtained planning permission to demolish the building and, in the future, might hope to make a killing in the property market for such a valuable site in London's financial district.

However, this does not explain his mistake in the conversation with *The Sunday Times*'s Davidson, which remains a mystery, unless one imagines that Maxwell had allowed the building matter to be handled by another person in his organization and therefore was unaware of the details. On the other hand, in his state of panic, he might have forgotten or changed his mind.

Although his high-powered City advisers had done their best to tie up loose ends, they found themselves dealing with a capricious man.

During the preparations for the stock issue, Maxwell was asked whether he would include the New York *Daily News*. "No," he said warily, suddenly adding brightly, "but MGN can have the option to buy it for £1 ($1.60) before the end of the year." Nothing came of this seat-of-the-pants decision, but it was symptomatic of the confusion. The Holborn buildings would have been a far more sensible inclusion in the new company than the two Canadian stakes in Quebecor and Donohue, as another scribbler pointed out: "They have little to do with the core activities of MGN."[17]

Smith New Court, Maxwell's brokers, and Samuel Montagu, the merchant bank, made such of their "ring fence," their phrase for the arms-length terms on which MGN would deal with other Maxwell companies. They assured everyone that MGN assets could not be used by Maxwell's private companies. Part of that fence was supposed to rest on the strength of the independent directors, only three of whom—Sir Robert Clarke, the former chairman of a merchant bank; Alan Clements, ex-finance director of Britain's biggest conglomerate, ICI; and Lord Williams, former chief executive of merchant bank Henry Ansbacher—were genuinely independent. Excluding Maxwell, the chairman, and his son Ian, deputy chairman, the other nine were all dependent on Maxwell for their income. "When all is said and done," commented another scribbler, "the mercurial Mr. Maxwell will retain control."[18]

All of this, while fascinating for the light it throws in hindsight on the press's genuine skepticism about the Maxwell empire, did not deal with the major underlying reason for the stock issue. One commentator was under no illusion. "It might fairly be asked why Mr. Maxwell wants to return to the public arena at all," he wrote. "Part of the answer...can be summed up in one word: debt."[19] He went on to show how the switch of the Canadian newsprint companies Quebecor and Donohue from Maxwell's private hands to MGN in October had landed the company with £210 million ($336 million) of short-term debt, which would be paid off by the proceeds of stock issue. What nobody realized was that the MGN shares themselves would become a valuable source of more loans for Maxwell in the next few months. When asked to explain his major motive for the stock issue, Maxwell avoided the real reason, replying:

"The cash is useful but people prefer to work for public companies, especially in the media. It makes you much more accountable."[20]

None of this, however, was as important to me that day as what occurred during the press conference at which he presented the prospectus. In the early afternoon I was telephoned by the news agency reporter who told me Maxwell had "revealed for the first time" the real reason I had been "dismissed" as editor. I moved from disbelief through surprise to anger in two minutes as he explained what had happened. The *Financial Times*'s media correspondent Ray Snoddy asked Maxwell if it had not been careless to lose an editor of Roy Greenslade's caliber just before the stock issue. Maxwell could have sidestepped the question with ease but in spite of his love for calling press conferences I was often surprised to note how poor he was at thinking on his feet and dealing with journalists.

Upset by the opening question—a hostile reference to the Department of Trade inquiry's criticism of twenty years earlier—Maxwell's charm and humor deserted him, and it was in this charged atmosphere that Snoddy asked his question about my departure being "careless." A now thoroughly grumpy Maxwell retorted, "It was rather careless of that editor to give an interview to the *Gazette* in which he expressed a large amount of pessimism about tabloid newspapers." Pressed on whether I had been dismissed because of this pessimism, Maxwell said, "That pessimism, publicly expressed, and publishing information about the company without clearing it with the company directors."

In a sense, this was what I had feared over the weeks since I had left, a rewriting of history by the man who had been revising it down through the years, a breach of agreement by a man who broke his word as a matter of course. I imagined this would be for internal MGN consumption though, not a public denigration.

I issued a statement that said: "I'm astonished that the publisher has broken an agreement we made of silence over my reasons for leaving the *Mirror* and introduced a new argument into the affair. I am totally innocent of the charge of giving away confidential information." I added that I thought his breach freed me to reveal the true reason I left and I would do so in a national newspaper article, having agreed with the *Guardian*'s media correspondent, Georgina Henry, that I would do so.

The next morning Maxwell, at his most menacing, phoned to say: "Don't declare war on me."

I told him I must be allowed to defend myself. He repeated his warning and hung up the phone. I also received a note from a Maxwell aide, whom I respected, warning me against any rash step: "Prior to the completion of the flotation he is at his most volatile, and irrational...he loves a fight, and he's got a much bigger arsenal and less to lose."

Lawyers were adamant; any attack on Maxwell would contravene the contract. I was effectively gagged while he could say what he liked.

John Diamond had signed no such contract and the *Guardian*'s Georgina Henry kindly offered him the space. He detailed under the headline WHY GREENSLADE'S MIRROR CRACKED some of the more bizarre Maxwellian intrusions I had relayed to him over the months. I was pleased that the record was being put straight in public. As a bonus, the editor of *UK Press Gazette* wrote a stinging editorial saying that if I had been dismissed for what I had said to the magazine "then it will have been the first time in our memory that an editor has been sacked for being too honest... If an editor cannot, honestly, discuss the problems and challenges facing him without fear of dismissal then it's a sad day for all editors." This Maxwell smokescreen did not obscure the truth from him: "Frankly, however, we doubt that this was the full reason for his departure."[21]

There was no response from Maxwell, and I imagined that, with far more important matters to concern him, the subject of a departed editor would blow over.

There was the stock issue for a start, and Maxwell took off on an international roadshow to sell the shares. In the first week he also made his only known visit to Liechtenstein, where he was treated as a VIP, being invited to a private audience with the head of state, Prince Hans Adam II. He also met the prime minister, and he was pictured with the president of the Bank of Liechtenstein, Egmond Frommelt. It is known that Maxwell often sent couriers to the principality; his aide, Bob Cole, went in the summer of 1990. "There was nothing unusual in that," Cole said. "People were always carrying packages personally to various places around the world."

There was nowhere Maxwell would not go in his effort to ensure the stock issue did not falter, addressing institutions in Scotland one day and New York the next, flying to France and back across to Canada. He finally agreed to sell 49 percent of the Mirror Group. He set the price at 125 pence ($2.00) and the deadline for applications for 9 May, saying that "even a one-eyed Albanian" could expect to see a premium from his shares on the first day of trading.

Many, many people turned a blind eye. Several large British institutions shunned the offer and most were reluctant to participate; *Mirror* readers largely kept their hands in their pockets; European institutions ignored it.

I must declare an interest here: I bought the minimum allocation to become a Mirror shareholder. There was said to be oversubscription in the United States, where Maxwell's New York *Daily News* magic had rubbed off on the institutions. On the first day of trading there was relatively little turnover and the price moved up just 0.5 pence (.8 cents). One City analyst blamed the lack of Albanians.

Nevertheless Maxwell had managed to sell the 49 percent of MGN and his brokers, Smith New Court, deserved praise for their work. One of Maxwell's closest advisers told me it had been a close-run thing in the final days and there were many relieved faces at the party he hosted at Headington Hill Hall to celebrate the event, not least his own. Now he had more shares to use as collateral in raising loans, and he managed it all with a public ring fence he knew he could penetrate in private whenever he desired. One of his first decisions was to try to pare down Mirror Group costs.

At the end of May 1991, I received two telephone calls, one from a *UK Press Gazette* journalist, the other from a concerned union official on the *Mirror*. Both informed me that the *Mirror* management had demanded seventeen compulsory redundancies among the journalistic staff and that management had suggested this was a consequence of my having hired too many people. I scoffed until I was told that this outrageous claim was being published in the *Press Gazette*. As an editor without a job, I was naturally protective of my reputation since it might affect my future employment. Now I was being accused, in effect, of mismanaging, and I could not let that stain remain on the record. I issued a statement to the union, supporting them in their fight to retain jobs and denying that I was the cause of their problems. To their great credit, and possible surprise, the union—in a show of solidarity reminiscent of a past Fleet Street era—speedily forced Maxwell to back down, and he shelved the plans, asking instead for volunteers.

The union was lucky; the last thing Maxwell could have faced at that moment was a costly industrial battle. I then made a similar statement to the *Press Gazette* that concluded with the words: "I warn Robert Maxwell, and not for the first time, that if he continues to encourage his hirelings to tell lies about me, I shall break my silence and tell the truth about him."[22]

It was a hollow threat that still echoes as I write it, but I was unaware that if I had been seeking a phrase calculated to send a tremor of fear through Maxwell I could not have selected a more apposite one. What I therefore hoped would serve as a shot across his bows, to remind him that he must not continue to muddy my name, he read as a threat to his very stability. Maxwell was terrified of what I might know and what I might say. What truth? What did he mean?

After reading my threat to speak out, Maxwell called me at home, the third time since my departure, to ask me if I had made statements to the union and to the *Press Gazette*. I told him I had because I had had to protect my reputation. "Byeee," he said.

I was baffled by this phone call until the next day when a bailiff served me with a writ for alleged breach of confidentiality. Maxwell had made the call on his speaker phone so that his attorney, David Maislish, could overhear me admit having issued the statements. He thought, for some reason, that this would significantly improve his case against me in court.

It was weeks before this case was heard, weeks in which Maxwell seemed powerless for the first time in his life to prevent the flow of bad publicity about his activities. One of his first targets was an analyst, Derek Terrington, at brokers UBS Phillips & Drew, who entitled a critical statement about the MGN stock issue "Can't Recommend A Purchase." The acronym, once brought to Maxwell's attention, incensed him and he complained to UBS chairman Rudi Mueller that it was "totally unprofessional and...extremely rude."

Maxwell later claimed the statement had been withdrawn, but UBS made only a number of minor corrections and amended the offensive title. Terrington soon after joined another brokerage, but Maxwell pursued him by complaining to the Securities and Futures Authority. Nothing came of it.

At last the outside world glimpsed more and more of the real Maxwell. One of the worst-kept secrets within Maxwell House and the Mirror Group was that Maxwell did not believe in paying any bill until the last moment, if at all. He would do everything he could to find an excuse to reduce the cost of an invoice by trying to renegotiate it months, sometimes years, after it was due. He seemed to encourage small companies, often individuals, to make their expensive way through the courts to get satisfaction. Since the costs of his legal bills were spread between two public companies and myriad private ones, it was impossible to discover just how much litigation cost him, but over the years the cost must have been enormous.

However, this expense was probably offset somewhat by the evasion of many bills since some firms inevitably wrote off their bad debts rather than take the time and trouble to institute court action. His was the classic example of the powerful, large company squeezing the weaker, smaller ones—bad form for a supposedly socialist businessman. A *Mail on Sunday* journalist, Lawrence Lever, realized Maxwell's penchant for this bully-boy activity, and over the course of the spring months he brought to public attention a host of examples.[23]

I knew slightly about one case against two former *Mirror* employees whose tiny company, Complete Publicity Services, often worked on the paper's promotions. When he ended their contract, which was his right, he refused to settle their outstanding debts of £150,000 ($240,000) with the Mirror Group, which was inexcusable. This relatively minor case bears all the hallmarks of Maxwell's approach to the "problem" of such creditors. Once the two women sued him he paid £23,000 ($36,800). When it became obvious they were pursuing their case he offered them £60,000 ($96,000) more "in full and final settlement."

They turned the offer down and on the morning of their appointed High Court hearing Maxwell's attorney, David Maislish, called them. Maxwell was prepared to pay all but £5,000 ($8,000) of their demand plus 15 percent interest, a total of $173,000 ($276,800), and their legal costs of an extra £9,000 ($14,400). That £5,000, incidentally, was a typical Maxwell move, a piece of internal window dressing; for ever after I can imagine him referring to his "victory."

Many less determined people than those two women might have given up, but Maxwell always gambled on wearing the opposition down before the case reached court. Inevitably, if it did, he lost. Among Lever's instances of Maxwell's failure to pay suppliers were multimillion-pound claims from, among others, Vanguard Engineering, Harland Simon, Plant Construction Ltd., and Taylor Woodrow. All were settled in the companies' favor and Maxwell was forced to foot heavy legal costs. Yet when the *Mail on Sunday* reported the outcome of the Harland Simon court case, in which the Mirror Group was ordered to pay £1.3 million ($2 million), Maxwell had the nerve to announce in the *Sunday Mirror* that it was part of a "continuing vendetta" against him and he would be issuing four writs for malicious libel.

The following week was not a good one for Maxwell. On 14 June he unveiled MCC's accounts for the financial year up to 31 March 1991, and he announced a fall in profits of 5 percent. He had warned in April in a statement to shareholders that profits would be less than the previous year's £172 million ($275.2 million), blaming the difficulty on the sale of assets in "exceptionally difficult market conditions." (The Pergamon sale was too late to be included in these figures.) Pretax profits were £145.5 million ($232.8 million), but it was hard not to notice that 87 percent of these earnings came from one-time items, such as property sales, and included an eye-opening £80.7 million ($129.12 million) from foreign-exchange transactions (known in City slang as forex). To achieve such a forex success, analysts believe Maxwell would have needed to have wagered up to £1 billion ($1.6 billion), opening up the terrifying scenario of what might have happened if his gamble had failed.

John Kenny, analyst at Barclays de Zoete Wedd, said, "Most analysts recognized at the time that if you can win £81 million ($130 million) on treasury functions, you can lose that much and more."[24] One or two analysts were even more suspicious, wondering whether this unprecedented good fortune could really be true. Were the forex profits genuine?

Whatever the case, this dependence on one-time profits and the consequential lack of operating profits alarmed almost every analyst. Smith New Court, Maxwell's brokers, did its best in public to boost MCC, arguing that while MCC's one-time items could not "conventionally be claimed to represent high-quality earnings...theoretically the accounting practices that have generated disquiet should fade once the debt burden lessens." Smith added: "It is a measure of the market's skepticism [that the company appears to be in trouble] which is manifestly not the case." While recognizing uncertainties, Smith recommended "buy."

Privately, Smith's media analyst, Terry Connor, was singing a very different tune, questioning MCC's ability to pay debts or dividends.[25] He produced a confidential memo expressing worries about the size of the debt and stating that disposals would be inevitable at fire-sale prices. Connor predicted that the company might have to "break itself up in order to pay its debts, and there ends the great adventure." There was an alternative "to reschedule the debt because of cash constraints... but that just defers the repayments and leaves the company carrying an interest charge that can only be terminal as far as dividend and profit growth is concerned. Either way... there seems little way out of the mess."

His memo was given to salesmen who were instructed to contact certain clients with MCC holdings and persuade them to sell. In passing, Connor also referred to "the curious support of Goldman Sachs." Considering the special position Smith New Court was in as Maxwell's adviser, with Maxwell's friend Sir Michael Richardson as Smith chairman and the MCC chairman-designate Peter Walker a Smith director, the decision to issue this secret statement was extraordinary, symbolic of both the stockbrokers' real worries about MCC and their real fears about alienating Maxwell.

If Smith had had an inkling of what was going on inside Maxwell House, the directors would have been more worried but perhaps less fearful about exposing him. According to firsthand accounts, life at Maxwell Communications in 1990–91 bordered on the farcical. Maxwell appeared to treat the company like some kind of giant automatic teller, inserting his bank card every day to withdraw as much money as possible. Mornings began with Albert Fuller, head of treasury, trying to gauge from his staff how much cash could be expected that day and then exhorting them to pass it on to him. "We were under the lash to provide funds every minute of the day," said one insider. "The only word that properly describes the method of daily cash management is 'bizarre.'"

The eagerness to collect was not matched in paying bills, however. For Maxwell, by the early summer of 1991, revenue was all that mattered, and Fuller, along with all the other executives, was kept in the dark about what happened to the money once he had collected it. Since Maxwell could do as he pleased without board approval, having arrogated full powers to himself some ten years before, there was no need to inform or consult. In normal circumstances this would have disquieted senior staff; in abnormal circumstances, where many suspected wrongdoing but could never prove it, they were unsettled enough to feel uncomfortable in continuing to work for Maxwell.

Some maintain that they had no suspicions at all and point to the fact that the directors were uninvolved in any activities outside Maxwell Communications—owner of Macmillan and Official Airline Guide. In a sense, they say, they were "independent" of Maxwell. They observed no wrongdoing inside MCC and assert that their professionalism ensured that the company ran as any other. The accounts, even if they attracted criticism for their impenetrability and for what they revealed about the company, were properly presented within normal accountancy rules.

Reg Mogg, who spent eight years with the company and was the finance director when he left in July 1990 to join a larger organization, said that as far as he was concerned, there was nothing alarming. "Everything was done in an orderly fashion." His theory is that too many similarly strong-minded directors—such as John Holloran, Brian Gilbert, and Richard Baker—left without being replaced. This caused a dilution of the experienced team and allowed Maxwell to exercise his formidable powers without any brake.

Holloran, who led the buyout of British Printing from MCC in January 1989, was acknowledged by Maxwell for his toughness. "Maxwell knew I would never take any shit from him," he said.[26] Certainly Richard Baker, the managing director who retired early in February 1991, is remembered by staff as a man who would refuse to do Maxwell's bidding if he felt it wrong to do so, though Baker conceded that Maxwell's special "committee of one" authority was problematic. All MCC decisions were made in advance of board meetings.

"The board did not rubber-stamp decisions," Baker said. "They would be discussed at the board and comments would be made, but the money had already been committed."[27] He added, "To the best of my knowledge the system was not abused."

Losing these directors from a public company was a publicity blow for Maxwell, and it is clear that there was a considerable delay in notifying the Stock Exchange about Mogg's and Baker's resignations. But if these were noted as bad losses for MCC in the wider financial community then the rapid loss of another senior figure would have been catastrophic. Jean-Pierre Anselmini, the man Maxwell had brought in from Crédit Lyonnais to be deputy chairman, objected strongly to the first put option—the device Maxwell used to shore up his MCC share price—in the autumn. He was angered further by the second put option in February and won an agreement from Maxwell that the practice would stop.

Then Maxwell broke his word over another matter; having agreed not to take a cash dividend for the year up to March 1991, Maxwell changed his mind and took the money even though Anselmini felt MCC could not afford it. There were other objections from the Frenchman too, such as to the salaries he discovered were being paid to directors in Maxwell's private companies. Anselmini resigned in June, but a worried Maxwell averted the crisis by persuading him to stay. Both knew it was a short-term agreement only, and Maxwell would rely even more on MCC's chief executive, his son Kevin, who was also a director of many of Maxwell's private companies in company with his brother, Ian.

The man who took over in November 1990 as MCC finance director was thirty-two-year-old Basil Brookes, who had also been a director of various private Maxwell companies. He was to face constant pressure from Maxwell throughout 1991 to ensure cash was flowing in as quickly as possible from every outlying part of the empire, especially during the crucial period between April and July.

To sum up, Maxwell was engaged in a wholesale plunder of MCC by any means possible and any means necessary to shore up his debt-ridden empire. Although senior executives in the company would be aware individually of certain operations to speed money into MCC's coffers they could not be aware of the scale. Nor, of course, would they be aware that the money was flowing out of the company at an equal rate into Maxwell's private companies. Compartmentalization remained a key to Maxwell's methods. In all, between 29 April and 22 July, £339 million ($542.4 million) was removed from the publicly held MCC, plunging the company into an overdraft of £105 million ($168 million).

The documents authorizing transfers of money out of MCC reveal that over the eighty-five-day period Maxwell himself signed for various sums amounting in total to £241 million ($385.6 million). The other signatories would not, of course, have known the purposes of the transfers. Kevin was responsible for £52 million ($83 million). Albert Fuller signed for £33 million ($52.8 million), a large total, but he could not have suspected what would happen to the money and would have viewed the transfers as part of the regular activity of his job. Lesser sums were authorized by Ian, Anselmini, and Brookes.

Even Maxwell, all-powerful, willful, careless of rules, frantically juggling vast sums around the world's banks through a variety of secret trusts, desperate to evade prying eyes, was not so foolish as to imagine that his daylight robbery from a public company could go undetected forever. He therefore set in motion a different sort of grand larceny.

14

The Pensions Scandal

W HEN Robert Maxwell bought the Mirror Group in 1984 he could not have known the value of its pension fund. The employees did, and they were jealous, if somewhat casual, guardians of the monies that they were saving for future retirement. One of the sad truths of life, however, is that while pensioners worry about pensions, and those about to retire worry about pensions, the majority of younger, high-earning employees who contribute a lot of cash to funds they know little or nothing about tend to let nature take its course. They will cross that far-off bridge when they reach it.

Fortunately, a minority of concerned individuals do take an interest, and they were alarmed at Maxwell's early decision to take a "pensions holiday." This meant that the company suspended its payments into the fund of 14.5 percent of each member's salary; employees, of course, continued to pay in 6 percent of their wages. Maxwell's holiday decision, just six months after buying the Group, saved the company millions every year, money that was credited as

253

profit. In 1990, for instance, this accounted for £8.5 million ($13.6 million) of MGN's profits.

Though controversial, the pension holiday was not illegal and was presented as a sign of the pension fund's health since there was, according to actuaries, such a good surplus. It was perhaps a sign of the contempt Maxwell would have for the fund's beneficiaries that he extended the holiday indefinitely, even forecasting in the Mirror Group's public-issue-of-stock document that it would be eleven years before the company would ever need to make any contributions again.

The minority of staff interested in pensions asked Maxwell to explain what he was up to at a meeting in 1985, and he faced some tough questioning. As more and more people voiced their skepticism he spluttered; "Do you honestly believe I would put my hand in the pension fund and steal it?"

"Yes!" came a shout from the back.

A red-faced Maxwell shrugged and left. It was his last open pensions meeting.

Thereafter he adopted a twin policy. First, pensioners would receive only the legally required minimum increases in their pensions each year, amounting to 3 percent. Second, he would gradually oust all "hostile" trustees—union officials, workers' representatives, unhelpful individuals—from their positions. He would reduce the number of trustees, thereby reducing the size of the quorum, and he would ensure, wherever possible, that newly appointed trustees were people he believed might be more sympathetic. When he arrived, there were six trustees from management and six from the unions. As the union representatives left, he replaced them with management, if at all. As far back as 1986 Maxwell was holding trustee meetings of two people, authorizing the use of assets to support his private businesses. Many trustees were not invited to meetings; in June 1991 he held a meeting of the MCC staff fund, the Maxwell Communications Works Pension Scheme, which some trustees only learned had taken place when minutes were discovered in January 1992.

As I have tried to make clear, Maxwell had no strategic plan in any area, yet in regard to pension-fund trustees he did set out to undermine their independence over a number of years. That does not necessarily mean that he always had it in mind to plunder the fund;

rather, it should be seen that his gradual removal of obstacles meant that he would provide himself with the opportunity should the need arise. He knew a sudden coup would fail and, pragmatically, he realized that the only way he could ever take command of the pension fund was to slowly take it over. However, it is essential to keep in mind that none of these maneuvers broke British law. The recurring phrase throughout this saga is "unusual but legally acceptable."

There had been some concern voiced over the years at the laws covering private corporate pension schemes. But there has been little pressure to change the arrangements because no employer had been known to have abused the schemes. British governments welcomed the growth of private-company schemes because their introduction largely removed the nagging pressure to improve the state pension payouts. There was therefore a reluctance to saddle the private pensions industry with restrictions.

As we have seen, Maxwell enjoyed taking advantage of loopholes in the law. He was perfectly entitled to decree who should be a member of the board of trustees governing the fund, treating the Mirror Group Pensions Trust (MGPT), of which he was the chairman, just like one of his ordinary private companies. One trustee told me he did not know he had been placed on the board of trustees until he received a memo asking him to attend a meeting.

It was also quite legal for MGPT to engage another Maxwell-owned private trust, Bishopsgate Investment Management (BIM), as manager of more than half the assets of the pension fund. Furthermore, this company's decision to invest pension funds heavily in other companies linked to Maxwell, while unusual and possibly in breach of voluntary guidelines, was not illegal. Many companies running pension schemes take the view that investing in their own company is not only acceptable but good business sense.

Maxwell took advantage of lax rules wherever he found them, caring little in his interpretation of them for the morality of his actions. If questioned about this kind of activity, Maxwell would roll his eyes in surprise and declare that everyone knew Robert Maxwell was a man of his word. How could anyone think he would do anything underhand? He felt this thundering assertion was good enough to satisfy all doubters. I was often struck by Maxwell's strange belief that the world saw him as a benign philanthropist while, without a great deal of factual, public proof, the world instinctively viewed him as an incorrigible rogue.

The Association of Mirror Pensioners, led by former MGN editorial director Tony Boram, became very concerned before the public stock issue. They wrote of their worries about investment policy to Samuel Montagu, the merchant bank advisers to the share issue, and were surprised to receive a reply from Maxwell saying lawyers had advised him that their claims were unsubstantiated.

The stock-issue document revealed that the Mirror Group pension-fund surplus had risen from £85 million ($136 million) in April 1988 to £149.3 million ($238.9 million) in December 1990. But an interim report by the pension scheme's actuaries, Bacon & Woodrow, stated that they could not give a full picture of the fund's assets as complete accounts were not available.

The pensioners' campaign for fair treatment and for information began to win sympathy among the working *Daily Mirror* journalists, and in May the union decided to take the extraordinary step of contributing £5,000 ($8,000) from its union funds to the Association for them to hire legal advice. The minutes of the chapel listed ten separate concerns, among them the placing of investments, the low payouts to pensioners, and the lack of union representation on the board of trustees. Union leaders were harangued by Mirror Group executives for making this decision, one that was said to have outraged Maxwell.

"They are calling into question my word," he told directors. "There is nothing for them to be worried about. They're wasting their money." As only Maxwell knew, that final sentence proved correct.

The Mirror pensioners were to hire Giles Orton, a lawyer with a reputation for securing improved pensions rights for staff in large companies. But Maxwell was on the verge of wholesale robbery. In late June, with Maxwell Communications' treasury all but run dry, Maxwell ordered Larry Trachtenberg, managing director of London & Bishopsgate International Investment Management (LBIIM), to gather £100 million ($1.6 million) worth of MGN pension-fund share certificates and place them in his personal safe. Trachtenberg took the shares from the safe at the LBIIM office in Shoe Lane, off Fleet Street, and delivered them round the corner to Maxwell House, where Maxwell deposited them in his safe on the ninth floor.

These certificates—the official proof of ownership—gave Maxwell exclusive, total control of a vast portion of the pension funds' investment portfolio, which he then passed through two of his own small investment firms, before selling or mortgaging them, sometimes more than once. Until then, there had been a well-established procedure in which records of pension-fund investments would be checked every two weeks. After the removal there was only a cursory glance into Maxwell's safe. This exercise was soon discovered by Coopers & Lybrand Deloitte, the auditors, in their initial investigation after his death.[2]

Trachtenberg cannot be accused of any wrongdoing himself because he was simply following orders from his boss. What he did was not illegal and he could not have known what Maxwell would do with the share certificates. However, the date is significant since Trachtenberg had been suspended by his fellow directors in March for his involvement in a stock-lending operation. Lord Donoughue, then head of LBIIM, has confirmed that the suspension occurred after "strong pressure" from himself "and another senior Maxwell employee."[3]

Donoughue went on to explain that the stock-lending conflict with Trachtenberg was linked not to the pension funds but to First Tokyo Trust, an investment trust Maxwell had taken control of in January 1989. It leads us straight to the desperate deal that was to haunt Maxwell right up to his death and that was to be the first major public indication of his wrongdoing.

We have seen how his frantic need for cash led him to plunder MCC from April onward. In early summer he began to pillage his companies' pension funds, siphoning shares through a company called Bishopsgate Investment Management (BIM) which was totally separate from, but very easy to confuse with, the similarly named London & Bishopsgate International Investment Management (LBIIM). BIM, which Maxwell chaired, was supposed to act as a professional fund manager for various pension schemes attached to his companies. Following the Mirror Group stock issue, transfers from the Mirror pension scheme merely required the signatures of two of the six directors of BIM, thereby sidestepping the trustees.

Huge sums were involved. In this period BIM managed total assets of about £700 million ($1.12 billion), and its common investment fund included 56 percent of the Mirror fund and 72 percent of the

£200 million ($320 million) assets of the Maxwell Communications Works Pension Scheme. Maxwell loaned most of the portfolio to two other private Maxwell companies: the Robert Maxwell Group and Headington Investments. The easiest way of picturing this is to imagine Maxwell moving wads of paper from pocket to pocket in his outsize suits. To cover this movement Maxwell referred to it as a stock-lending. This has been described as "an innocuous trading technique ... commonly used by stockbrokers to balance their books."[4]

In effect this means that when a stockbroker buys shares for a client there are occasions when, for a variety of reasons, the shares are not on hand when due for delivery to a client. So the broker borrows the required shares from a big institution, for a fee, and hands them to the client. Once he receives the shares bought in the market, he hands them to the institution. The process usually takes no more than a day and it is viewed as perfectly legitimate for pension funds to lend stock in this way. It is obvious that the system is based on trust. The broker must hand back the right shares and there must be as little time lag as possible.

Maxwell's version of stock-lending abused that trust. He siphoned off shares held by pension funds for months at a time. BIM lent stock to his private companies, those companies then gave the stock to banks as collateral for loans, but the banks were unaware that they were holding pension-fund stock that did not belong to the private companies. Even that did not satisfy Maxwell. He soon realized that he could borrow more than one sum of money on one set of shares by offering notes guaranteeing the same stock to different banks, thereby doubling his loans. To pay back loans he simply pledged more and more of the pension fund's portfolio.

It is not clear how the Bishopsgate Investment Management portfolio found its way into London & Bishopsgate International Investment Management's safe, but it is now obvious that the reason Maxwell took hold of the certificates was to sell the assets. The money raised by these sales should have gone back to the funds, but Maxwell used the cash either to buy up more MCC stock through his offshore trusts or doled it out to his various loss-making pet projects, such as the New York *Daily News, The European,* and AGB research group.

Some light was cast on activities at BIM, Maxwell's fund manager for various pension schemes, by Robert Bunn, the finance director to Maxwell's private empire, who spoke of Maxwell's "bullying tactics" to avoid scrutiny by other directors. "Robert Maxwell isolated us in boxes and we did not know the extent of what was happening," he said. "All investment decisions were made by Robert Maxwell—he used to buy and sell shares without talking to other people and we would just get the contract note."[5]

Bunn resigned from BIM in September 1990 but was appointed to the board of London & Bishopsgate International Investment Management in May 1991. According to Bunn, that month, May, heralded the turning point. "It started to go wrong in terms of business after the Mirror flotation (stock issue) when it was clear that the remaining businesses on the private side were primarily loss-making. Consequently the private side of the group was dependent on dividends and a large disposal program."[6]

Bunn was sure that prior to that month there were no irregularities at BIM. Over at LBIIM, Lord Donoughue has said that the stock-lending program he knew about in March and April "was legal and conducted on proper procedures."[7]

There was nothing proper about Maxwell's next bit of recklessness, though. On 3 July, Maxwell asked to borrow £60 million ($96 million) from one of Switzerland's biggest banks, the Swiss Bank Corporation (SBC), through a new company with the strange name of Adviser (188), which he had set up with the single aim of making a takeover bid for First Tokyo Index Trust. Trachtenberg had convinced Maxwell he would improve his and Maxwell's fortunes by taking over the fund management of First Tokyo and changing its investment strategy. Trachtenberg had written a computer program that was supposed to track a broad Japanese market index known as Topix. It flopped because the Japanese market fell throughout 1990, with the Topix plunging 45 percent to reduce First Tokyo's asset value from £80.4 million ($128.64 million) to £46.3 million ($74.08 million). To offset these losses the First Tokyo board agreed to allow London & Bishopsgate, its fund manager, to lend out some of its stock.

Once again, this stock lending was not of the normal variety, and in the early spring the board was astonished to discover that 80 percent of its portfolio had been lent to other private Maxwell companies. First Tokyo's 1990 annual report had been critical of such activity, but by April 1991 they discovered a £38 million ($60.8 million) portfolio had been loaned to Maxwell-related companies and that Maxwell was then using it as collateral for more loans. The scale of the lending threatened the tax privileges that First Tokyo could claim as an investment bank. First Tokyo's board reacted with understandable anger, and two members who were most embarrassed were Maxwell's own board representatives.

In a bid to quell what looked like the beginning of an embarrassing public row, Maxwell delivered another shock to First Tokyo. To settle the affair "amicably" he offered to make a takeover bid, on very generous terms, for the 72.4 percent of the company he did not already own. He also agreed to pay £500,000 ($800,000) toward the trust's legal and professional costs. He was eager to avoid any bad publicity and was lucky that the City was then diverted by the BCCI banking scandal. It was going to cost Maxwell somewhere in the region of £60 million ($96 million). Hence the loan from the Swiss bank for his shell company, Adviser (188). The bank entered into a complex agreement with Maxwell over security for its loan, accepting £52.9 million ($84.64 million) in Japanese shares owned by First Tokyo as collateral.

As it turned out Maxwell could not deliver these shares right away because it would take several weeks for First Tokyo to be transformed into a private company, and it was a breach of Britain's Companies Act, which regulates financial dealings, for the Swiss bank to control the shares prior to that transformation. To cover itself, and ensure it did get its security eventually, the bank therefore required Adviser (188) to sign a special clause of their loan agreement not to sell the First Tokyo portfolio or to pledge its shares as collateral elsewhere. In effect, the bank should not have been able to lose. So, on 6 August, Adviser (188), under Kevin Maxwell's signature, drew down £55.8 million ($89.28 million) from the Swiss Bank Corporation and paid First Tokyo's shareholders.[8]

When Adviser (188) took the loan, Maxwell had already defaulted on the special agreement. At the end of July he had given instructions that part of First Tokyo's portfolio of shares should be liquidated, and the first sale, netting £16.4 million ($26.24 million), occurred on 1 August. Maxwell had moved too fast, forgetting that the original First Tokyo board were still in place. They had demanded that the portfolio be frozen and so Maxwell's fund manager, London & Bishopsgate, was forced to repurchase an identical portfolio of shares on 5 August to cover the misdeed.

Ten days later, having replaced the First Tokyo board, Maxwell sold the portfolio again. Another block of shares, worth £29.1 million ($46.56 million), was sent as collateral to one of SBC's Swiss bank rivals, Crédit Suisse, and a further amount, worth £4.6 million ($7.36 million), was forwarded as collateral to the American bank of Lehman Brothers. Neither of these banks realized what Maxwell was up to. It meant, of course, that Maxwell had broken the agreement with SBC and was unable to deliver to them the promised portfolio as security against his £60 million ($96 million) loan. It was an unprecedented piece of villainy in which he had, in succession, cheated First Tokyo, SBC, Crédit Suisse, and Lehman Brothers, not to mention having compromised the board of his private company LBIIM.

Lord Donoughue had resigned as Maxwell's representative to First Tokyo. He decided in July that the situation had gone far enough. He later said he had "strongly protested" to Maxwell about the unauthorized stock-lending ventures, including the use of pension funds, as early as January. Certainly such activities must have been on his mind that month, for on 31 January he rose in the House of Lords to address his peers: "Most of the recent highly publicized corporate scandals could have been avoided or exposed at an earlier stage by alert and truly independent directors. Unfortunately such animals are still too rare in Britain." Donoughue said that too often companies most in need of alert directors "sometimes try to avoid them, or choose tame ones."[9] After his protests "the stocks were returned with a promise that such stock lending would cease."[10]

When he discovered it had not, Lord Donoughue asked Maxwell for the matter to be placed on the agenda of the next meeting of the pension-fund trustees, a move that Maxwell sidestepped by postponing the trustees' meeting. Following what Donoughue called "vigorous exchanges," he was treated, as I had been so often, to one of Maxwell's familiar rank-pulling "instructions."

Donoughue said, "He accused me of betraying him, because I sided with those who complained about his stock lending. I said, 'The stock lending must stop.' He said, 'It's none of your fucking business.

I'm chairman and I'm responsible.' I said, 'I have an obligation, too.' We also had a row about our trying to tell pension-fund trustees what he was doing. And he said, again, 'It's none of your fucking business to tell the trustees. *I'm* the chairman of the trustees.'"[11]

Maxwell informed Lord Donoughue that all such affairs were a matter for Maxwell in his capacity as chairman of Bishopsgate Investment Management, chairman of the pension trustees, chairman of London & Bishopsgate International Investment Management, and chairman of London & Bishopsgate Holdings (LBH). Donoughue, who also clashed with Kevin over the same matters, resigned from LBIIM and LBH. However, his resignations were not recorded at Companies House until 17 October 1991.[12]

In a life of confrontation and conflict, with a history of dismissals and resignations behind him, it was nothing new for Maxwell to lose high-profile staff. He managed to keep Donoughue's departure quiet for some time. July also turned out to be the month that Peter Walker, the former Conservative Party minister, would not after all become chairman of MCC. At first, it appeared as though Walker had decided to reject the chairmanship after his three-month look at the company. This about-face was revealed in the *Independent,* which said it would be "a massive blow to MCC and to Mr. Maxwell personally."[13] The report went on to suggest that Walker had carried out an internal review of MCC and had come to the conclusion that "after stripping out nonrecurring items, the group made a loss of £8 million ($12.8 million)" in the year to March 1991. It even suggested that Smith New Court had also "expressed severe reservations about the financial state of the company," as, indeed, we know they had since they had circulated their secret analysis to clients.

Maxwell's cover story to try to limit the damage was that he and Walker had reached the conclusion that they needed to restructure by splitting off the group's North American interests. In other words, the bulk of MCC, which was now Macmillan and Offical Airlines Guide, should be listed in the New York stock market. Walker, before becoming "unavailable for comment" for weeks, appeared to support this view: "I came to the conclusion that with 90 percent of the company's profits coming from the U.S. and with 70 percent of the assets based there it would be crazy to try to manage it from London."[14]

Despite a rising market and the secret support operation, MCC's share price slipped 6 pence (9.6 cents) to 190 pence ($3.04). Maxwell was forced again into a manic share-support operation, reaching new heights of buying in late July 1991 to prevent his price from falling through the floor. The press, meanwhile, had another field day.

"Coming apart," said *The Economist*. "Doubts grow over Maxwell," said *The Sunday Times*. The *Financial Times*'s main columnist, Lex, was severe: "It is one of the depressing features of the Maxwell empire that every time its rickety finances seem finally to have been patched together it gives another lurch."[15] Just as predictably, Maxwell issued writs against the *Independent* for libel and threatened to sue anyone suggesting there was any truth in these reports.

Maxwell always denied the existence of any report on MCC by Walker. But Walker has since revealed that he did write one following a close look at the business in London and New York.[16] After presenting his critical report to the Maxwells, they told him his services were no longer required and agreed to a compensation package. He said later: "The main part of the business was very sound and good. The important point was to de-Maxwellise [the businesses]."[17] Later Walker added: "In retrospect, I suppose it was probably convenient to get me out of the way. I would have discovered everything. One had no idea Mr. Maxwell was propping up the shares."[18]

The end result was a welter of bad publicity on both sides of the Atlantic that Maxwell could ill afford. It marked the end of his American honeymoon; those New York institutions who had bought the Mirror Group shares were upset to see the price falling. Where was that promised premium on shares priced at 125 pence ($2) which had floated gently down to 95 pence ($1.52)? And the suggestion of a fresh U.S. stock issue for MCC was viewed universally as a nonstarter. Even a success, such as Maxwell's huge profit on his August 1991 sale for $234 million of his privately owned stake in the Israeli computer-imaging firm, Scitex, for which he had paid only $39 million two years before, brought little relief.

The heat was on now in the MCC boardroom where nonmanagement directors were beginning to ask awkward questions. After discovering at the 4 July board meeting that £126 million ($201.6 million) was missing due to unauthorized lending, they decided to get independent legal advice.[19] Weeks later they found more than £300 million ($480 million) was missing.

Peter Laister and his fellow nonmanagement directors retained a prestigious law firm. "We were particularly concerned to make sure there were no breaches of the Financial Services Act," Laister said.[20] But he stressed their priority was to get the money back, and after a series of what he called "confrontational" meetings with Maxwell, it was decided the best approach would be to unwind the intercompany debt. Laister said: "We took the view that it would be extremely damaging to shareholders and the company to have gone public on the position then."[21]

They were not alone in their worry. Basil Brookes, the MCC finance director, had become alarmed at the size of the debt, which he had been monitoring "for a few weeks," and the intercompany deals. Shareholders normally need to be informed if a company carries out transactions with one of its own directors. Instead the directors obtained a scrawled, handwritten note that said: "I confirm that the borrowings by Headington Investments from Maxwell Communication Corporation have not been used in any way which would mean that MCC breached the Companies Act." It was signed by Maxwell and his son, Kevin.[22] The Companies Act was the main law regulating the behavior of the boards of public companies. Over the next two months all but £73 million ($116.8 million) of the money taken from MCC had been repaid, which was a victory for the directors, but Laister has also observed that this pressure to repay MCC may well have forced Maxwell to begin his pension-fund plunder.

Laister is probably correct, but it is difficult not to feel sympathetic to his plight. He could not know of Maxwell's intentions nor Maxwell's private-company debt crisis. His duty was to shareholders, and they might not have thanked the board for going public, causing the company to crash with huge debts. While Maxwell was facing this hostility at MCC, he was assuring the pensioners all was well. When Mirror Group pensioners complained about fund investments in July, attorneys for the funds wrote back to say there was no cause for concern. After a meeting with trustees at the time, one of them, the bluntly spoken no-nonsense editor of the *Sporting Life*, Mike Gallemore, said Maxwell was in a very buoyant mood. In fact,

Maxwell was already involved in looting the retirement money of his employees.

Wary of all those outside who asked questions, Maxwell grew unaccountably worried by the persistence of a team from BBC television's *Panorama*. They had told him openly of the "profile" they were putting together, asking him to take part, a request he turned down. From April onward he knew they were stalking him. It was significant that in his affidavit to the court when he sued me in June, he claimed I might appear on *Panorama* and my well-chosen words— "I shall break my silence and tell the truth about him"—terrified him more than I would realize until six months later. Neither *Panorama*'s producers and reporters nor I had an inkling about his pension-fund plunder, stock lending, or his mortgaging of his shares to raise loans. Once he launched his court action against me I knew I could not appear on *Panorama,* but I was determined to help them.

First, I had to face up to a High Court hearing in which Maxwell sought an injunction against me. What struck me, picking up the nuances at an adjourned appearance and in the subsequent hearing on 12 July, was that though Maxwell was one of the most frequent litigants any legal historian could remember, and, as such, a great contributor to legal coffers, his reputation within the legal community was low. His rambling affidavit—brimful with half-truths, non sequiturs, and insinuations, laced with prejudice and paranoia—did little to help his cause. But I was informed from the beginning of proceedings by my attorneys and by counsel that judges are usually disposed to granting injunctions prior to the full trial. On this occasion, however, the judge was not moved by Maxwell's action and on 31 July issued a judgment in which he rejected the application and ordered the Mirror Group to foot the bill for my costs.

I felt I had beaten Maxwell in his favorite arena, but if he was upset there was no clue. By now he was beset with a host of problems, all of his own creation. The New York *Daily News* was proving far costlier than he imagined and his promise of investment to buy color presses remained unfulfilled. Having convinced himself that he had "saved" the loss-making Mirror Group, when he did not, he had taken on more than he could handle, especially in view of his need to spend so much time in London to keep the lid on his stock-lending and bank-loan activities. *The European* continued to lose money he did not have. His German venture was eating more cash than anticipated. Many other private businesses—AGB Research, Panini, the soccer clubs—generated no profits.

The recession had even hit the *Mirror.* Figures for the first half of 1991, announced at the end of July, showed a modest rise of 1.4 percent in pretax profits to £42 million ($67.2 million), described as "genuinely impressive" by the *Financial Times,* but their publication only tended to turn the spotlight on the share-price weakness, which hovered around the 100 pence ($1.60) mark. According to Maxwell, the weakness of the shares was due to "a conspiracy." It was a bluff to divert attention.

Within days of announcing the figures it was discovered that Maxwell was trying to raise a £90 million ($144 million) loan through yet another new company, Robert Maxwell Estates, by mortgaging the property at Holborn—the Mirror and MCC buildings—and AGB Research's West London building. This could have explained why he did not include the building in the Mirror Group stock issue. It certainly raised eyebrows among "conspirators," though they were in the dark once more because, in spite of the signs of doom, it remained impossible for outsiders to gauge the level of debt without being able to penetrate Maxwell's complicated web of companies.

One analyst said: "It is now impossible for any analyst to give you an accurate impression of the financial standing of Robert Maxwell's empire because no one knows what the private side is geared at."

If only they had known.

15

Mirrorgate:
The Final Insult

T HE City, as London's financial district is known, is a small world
dealing in big money. With hundreds of millions of pounds changing
hands daily by word of mouth or on computer screens, there must be
rules and regulations to ensure there is no foul play. One of the City's
most important currencies is information, every scrap of which is
analyzed for its importance, especially for the signals it provides
about a company's state of health. Therefore there are strict rules
about certain information that must be declared openly (details, for
instance, about the buying and selling of shares). The publication of
such information allows the City's community to understand what is
going on inside the companies quoted on the stock exchange. Every
nuance has significance for those paid to watch the screens and assess
the data.

Maxwell did his best to frustrate this City practice, for example, by
concealing the resignations of directors or his "oversight" in failing to

make clear the autumn 1990 put option. But the City is used to buccaneers trying to buck the system.

There was great surprise in August 1991, however, when Goldman Sachs, the American investment bank, was suddenly forced to admit that it had breached the City's rules by not disclosing sooner that it was holding a 7.5 percent stake in Maxwell Communications and a 10.48 percent stake in Mirror Group Newspapers. This was four months after it should have declared an interest, and Goldman claimed its "regrettable technical error" had occurred because it had "overlooked" the fact that only banks, insurance companies, and stock-exchange members can avoid disclosing such holdings. Goldman does not hold bank status in Britain.

Two days earlier Goldman had disclosed that it held forty million shares in the Mirror Group as security against a private loan of £60 million ($96 million). A great deal of MCC and MGN stock, amounting to £106 million ($169.6 million), was also held as collateral against loans. Goldman had long been Maxwell's major ally, mainly through the special relationship between Maxwell and the managing director of the London office, Eric Sheinberg. For months up to August 1991, other dealers were aware that Goldman was by far the keenest buyer of one of the market's least popular stocks.

Maxwell and his companies also used Goldman to negotiate huge foreign-exchange transactions, known as forex. His main dealer was one of the bank's vice presidents, John Lopatin, whom he got to know in the mid-1980s. Lopatin was then based in Goldman's London office but once he returned to New York in 1989 Maxwell began his heavy forex trading.[1]

The August disclosure by Goldman marked an end of a close friendship as the bank became nervous about the loans Maxwell had failed to repay on time, the amount of collateral it was holding, the bad health of MCC's and MGN's share prices, and the level of foreign-exchange losses. Sheinberg's support for Maxwell was being undermined by the powerful American-based partners. Goldman gradually withdrew its support in the market, leaving the MCC and MGN share prices to drift down a penny or so every day. All Maxwell's friends were quietly deserting him.

The following month, Smith New Court, his brokers, gave renewed—but secret—warnings to institutional shareholders. Then the Swiss Bank Corporation (SBC) discovered that he had still not sent the collateral for the £60 million ($96 million) loan to buy First Tokyo. Maxwell, knowing full well that he had already liquidated the collateral, lied by saying there had been "a terrible mistake" because two fund managers at his private company, Headington Investments, had accidentally sold some of the assets. How long would the Swiss hang on?

Three days after the Swiss Bank protest came BBC's *Panorama,* the program Maxwell had been dreading and which he had foolishly publicized by attacking on the eve of its transmission in a *Sunday Mirror* editorial. Under a headline THE JACKALS OF THE BBC, he then mixed his metaphors by referring to the BBC's senior figures as "the three monkeys of broadcasting."[2] In various contacts with Maxwell prior to the screening, it was obvious that his major concern was what the TV team planned to say about the pension funds. Once again, guilt had gotten the better of sense, but *Panorama*—like the concerned pensioners and their legal advisers—had not managed to uncover any evidence of major illegality.

In fear of what might be said, Maxwell fled to New York to await his fate. Although the program, entitled "The Max Factor," did not mention the pension funds, there were still shocks for Maxwell. The show was split into three sections—looking at influences on the MCC share price, the setting up of offshore trusts in Gibraltar, and the fiddling of *Daily Mirror* competitions. In the MCC section, reporter Nisha Pillai argued that false claims about selling businesses, the first "put option," and Goldman Sachs's large share stake had "distorted the market in MCC shares." The real significance of these points was twofold; presenting them together showed a pattern of disturbing events and presenting them at all showed a new spirit of defiance to the king of the writs.

The Gibraltar section was interesting but not sensational. Maxwell had evidently used the tax haven to register a company called the Inter-European Trust which, in turn, controlled a majority interest in his private company, Headington Investments, which, in turn, owned the Robert Maxwell Group which, in turn, was the owner of Maxwell's 51 percent of the Mirror Group. This showed the impenetrability of his financial arrangements and, the BBC reporter suggested, was hardly the kind of transparency we might expect in a public company.

However, it was the third section, in which *Panorama* revealed Maxwell's involvement in the *Mirror*'s Spot-the-Ball contest, that caught Maxwell off balance. This revealed, as I explained in earlier chapters, how Maxwell ensured that no reader could win the £1 million ($1.6 million) top prize. For the average viewer and the wider audience this simple example of trickery was understandable in the way his share-support operation was not.

At *Panorama*'s celebratory dinner after the screening, Maxwell's reaction was anticipated correctly. Having had relayed to him the allegations in the program, he immediately announced that four writs would be issued in the morning for libel and malicious falsehood. The Mirror Group's senior executives, legal advisers, and the *Mirror* editor were kept at the London office until the early hours of the morning relaying transcripts of the program, monitoring press reaction, and listening to his bombast. Although relieved to find his pension-fund plunder remained a secret and that analysts would realize there was nothing new in the program, he knew the result would be a share price fall.

On the day of the screening, both MCC and MGN slipped; the day after, MGN fell to a new low of 89 pence ($1.40), 36 pence (57 cents) below the issue price, while MCC fell 10 pence (16 cents) to 167.5 pence ($2.68). For a man who had all his shares in hock, this was a disastrous situation, and it got worse as the financial press used *Panorama* as the peg for analyses of MCC's debts. No one could make the sums add up. It appeared to every City journalist that Maxwell's debts exceeded his assets by a huge margin.[3] *The Sunday Times* headlined its full-page article CAP'N BOB AT BAY and its respected City commentator Ivan Fallon argued that the program's effect was far more damaging for its "careful piling of fact upon fact." He also noted the fact that it came two weeks after a long and critical *Wall Street Journal* report headlined BLOATED EMPIRE: MEDIA MOGUL MAXWELL REVELED IN GROWTH, NOW MUST SCALE BACK. By now the truth was far worse than the *Journal,* Fallon, *Panorama,* anyone, me included, could conceive.

Maxwell was beginning to lose battles even within his own organization. In an attempt to cut losses in his private empire he made an attempt to sell *The European* to the Mirror Group, but the independent directors thought this was an offer they could refuse.[4] In fact, the role of the independent directors at MGN—Sir Robert Clark and Alan Clements—was cramping Maxwell's style. At the June 1991 board meeting, a month after the company's public stock issue, the directors asked to see future financial reports two days before board meetings.

It had originally been agreed that decisions could be made by a committee of two directors, one of whom would be Maxwell or his deputy, Ian. Then at the September meeting the directors forced a rule change so that no dealings with Maxwell interests could occur without the majority approval of independent directors. Sir Robert requested that the finance director explain the balance sheet at each meeting and he also asked for all investors with over a million shares to be named at each board meeting with details of changes in their holdings. At this point Maxwell decided he would simply ignore the board.

At the beginning of October Maxwell turned up at the Metropole Hotel in Brighton for his traditional day at the Labour Party conference surrounded by *Daily Mirror* journalists and Mirror Group executives. Before lunch with Labour leader Neil Kinnock, the *Mirror*'s political editor, Alastair Campbell, said Maxwell acted "very oddly." He added, "Just before Neil and Glenys arrived, he took me out on the balcony of the penthouse dining room. He told me, 'The whole world's against me. People are out to destroy me.'"

Though Maxwell often complained loudly of conspiracies and vendettas, it was rare for him to speak so frankly. Maxwell had become aware that the MGN board was about to confront him over missing money; he had assured them that about £38 million ($60.8 million) of operating cash was "in gilts earning interest." The failure to return this money by a given date was endangering the company's cash flow position. The directors were also concerned about a renegotiation of the lease for the Mirror Group's building. Disputes over these matters had broken out between on one side Ernie Burrington, the managing director, and Lawrence Guest, the finance director, and on the other, Michael Stoney, a chartered accountant brought in by Maxwell as "commercial director" during the stock issue.

After lunch, Maxwell's managing director arrived for the private talk he had requested, and Maxwell again chose to confer on the balcony. Burrington told him that his financial director was "very worried" about £47 million ($75.2 million) from MGN's treasury that Maxwell had "out on loan."

Maxwell replied mysteriously, "We should all be pulling together. Are you trying to blow us out of the water?" He then made a vague promise about the money being returned within days but suddenly snapped, "External finance is not your business, nor your financial director's. Your job is to run the operational side. How money is invested, the corporate finance, is not your concern."

Burrington said there was a fundamental difference between them over the definition of duty in a public company as opposed to a private one. "You've got it wrong," Maxwell said.

Privately the directors had sought an independent legal view, and Burrington informed him that they were planning to hold a meeting of the independent directors.

"I forbid you to hold it," Maxwell screamed.

As far as Burrington was concerned, this was to be the final showdown. He said that since their definitions of his role differed, "Isn't it time we talk about my going?"

Maxwell's mood changed in a second. "I thought we were friends," he said. It was agreed the managing director would sort out his pension details ready for departure.

Back in London, Guest, the finance director, and Stoney, the accountant brought in by Maxwell, were locked into a similar dispute. On 3 October, Guest sent Stoney a memo: "When our roles were defined, it was an integral part of the arrangement, to use the Chairman's words, that we would live in each other's pockets. I hope I've kept you abreast of financial matters, but I don't think you've done the same." He added: "As you know, I have been increasingly concerned with regard to the lack of information on short-term deposits made to American banks and Bishopsgate Investment Management. This of itself is causing far too much pressure on creditors."

Two weeks had passed in which there was no sign of the missing £47 million returning, before Guest faced Maxwell. Guest is a quiet, reserved man who was one of the few survivors at senior level from the Reed era. He did not enjoy confrontation, but he was now so troubled by the missing millions he lost all reticence. In front of Burrington, Stoney, and the sympathetic Scottish managing director, Vic Horwood, he questioned Maxwell about the missing money. Inevitably Maxwell stalled, but Guest, realizing the consequences for himself and the board of a public company if there had been wrongdoing, made notes about the meeting.

"I am now convinced that MGN resources have been used to support other parts of the group. But I have no proof," he wrote. "I think I have frightened the Chairman, but my main concern must be to get the money back. I think I am in a situation that nothing more will flow out although I don't have the machinery to stop it."

So concerned was Guest that, placing his job on the line, on 21 October he warned other board members about his worries and ordered an internal investigation. Burrington, the managing director, then met Kevin Maxwell to discuss Guest's concerns and was surprised by the vehemence of Kevin's attack: "What is your man up to? He's no good on corporate finance."

Burrington countered that Guest had a good record with Reed before MGN.

"He's making difficulties," Kevin said. "What's he trying to do— damage the company? Blow us out of the water?"

Burrington realized it was the same phrase Kevin's father had used in Brighton three weeks before.

Later Kevin met Guest with Burrington and adopted a different tone: "My father is one of the biggest gilts players in the world. There's nothing unusual in all this. The money will come back. There's nothing to worry about."

It was a measure of Maxwell's complete contempt for the board, his arrogance, and his desperation, that on that same day, 21 October, he robbed the Mirror Group of £50 million ($80 million). His modus operandi offers a fascinating insight into the amazing speed with which this man could move massive sums around the world. He had already negotiated a revolving credit facility with Bankers Trust of America; though he gave his own special meaning to the word *revolving*. Using this facility he authorized, on his own single signature, a £50 million ($80 million) loan to be used, he said, for "general corporate purposes." This loan was placed into a Mirror

Group account with Shearson Lehman bank in New York. Shearson converted it to dollars and transferred it to the account of Maxwell Newspapers, Inc.—owners of the New York *Daily New*—at another bank, Chase Manhattan. So in two moves the money had left the public company and arrived in his "private side."

Next, of the $80 million, $55 million was transferred back to bankers Trust in London. All this was achieved in one day. Then Robert Maxwell Group, his private company, required his public company, MGN, to pay the interest on the debt. Two weeks later a payment of £43,904 ($70,200) was paid by MGN's NatWest account to Bankers Trust's Midland account on behalf of the Robert Maxwell Group.[5] He now owed Mirror Group £97 million ($155.2 million).

This was the kind of maneuver that made him paranoid about Guest, and he told his sons to be vigilant. After a routine board meeting, Ian Maxwell called Burrington: "Your finance director handed Alan Clements [an independent director] a package. It obviously contained information he wants him to know."

"Is that improper?" Burrington replied.

"Is he for us or against us?" Ian asked, using one of the current Maxwell phrases.

Guest had innocently handed Clements an envelope containing a copy of the stock-issue offer document, but as Burrington remarked, "The sense of guilt was there."

The other argument between the board and Maxwell was over a plan to increase the Mirror Group's lease for its Holborn building. Only six months before, during the stock issue, it was resolved that MGN would pay £7 million ($11.2 million) a year for three years. Maxwell decided that the agreement should be extended for four more years, a precondition to his being able, through his private company, to raise an £80 million ($128 million) loan on the property. Several directors, including Burrington, were opposed to this plan.

Every other newspaper group had moved out of the City to take advantage of cheaper premises, and this would commit the group to a lease for seven years. "We did not need eighty million pounds [$128 million]," Burrington said. "I opposed it and advised the other directors against it. It did not make sense for MGN. I was forbidden by Maxwell to hold a meeting with the independent directors on the proposal or to obtain independent advice."

Maxwell needed board approval though and found a simple way of circumventing these newly turbulent directors. On 24 October, he phoned from America to summon a board meeting at short notice, requiring Stoney, his commercial director, to chair it since he knew Burrington, his managing director, had left the building for an important lunch appointment. The minimum number required to make the meeting quorum turned up. Two directors, including Guest, registered objections by phone. Maxwell compromised, reducing the annual rent for the last four years to £6.15 million ($9.84 million), and drove through the proposition. The next day Robert Maxwell Estates borrowed £80 million ($128 million) by mortgaging the Mirror Building. He had gotten his way again.

He was, however, fed up with the inquisitive Guest by now and decided to strip him of his power. He appointed Stoney as managing director (finance). "His appointment effectively cut Guest, MGN's finance director, out of running MGN's money," Burrington said. Stoney, the man brought in from Maxwell's private companies, now had total control of the public company's treasury.

Guest refused to give in. As a senior banking source was later to say: "Guest was determined to slug it out. He saw it as his duty. He said he would see it through even if he ended up in a one-bedroom flat."[6]

In late October, Guest confronted Maxwell again about the missing £47 million ($75.2 million), saying he was unable to sleep due to the worry.

Maxwell, adopting his paternal role, replied, "Don't worry. You are losing sleep and that's not right. You will receive everything. Don't worry."

After this meeting they agreed to meet on 1 November with Burrington—a meeting that never took place because Maxwell flew out of London the day before.

Though there was deep concern about this missing company money, none of the directors had an inkling that Maxwell had also raided the MGN pension fund of more than three times that amount.

Pensioners were shocked by a twelve-day delay in paying their pensions in October. But the trustees remained in ignorance of the theft.

War at MGN with the finance director was matched by war at MCC with the finance director. Basil Brookes, having found that £240 million ($384 million) had vanished from MCC's treasury, quit on 31 October.[7] He said that MCC's independent directors had pressed Maxwell "on a number of occasions" to return the missing money. Each time, Maxwell said the money was "safe" and would be returned. But there was little any of them could do beyond protest, because of Maxwell's supreme authority to transfer money at will and do deals for MCC without any other directors having to countersign the documents. Maxwell had been granted that power some ten years before by his board and, by law, was therefore within his rights. However, Brookes said directors were pressing him to give up this power. "We [the board] were aware the money was missing and were vigorously trying to get it returned."

On the same day Harry McQuillen, president of Macmillan in New York and an MCC main board director, resigned after less than three months in the job. Maxwell's statement said it was by "amicable arrangement" because McQuillen was going to a top post, as president of K-111, headed by William Reilly, former president of Macmillan. But McQuillen had been seen as a key figure in the American business and his departure "confounded City analysts."[8] I was also told that McQuillen was "a lion of a man" who refused to rubber-stamp Maxwell demands, an indication that there had been disputes.

These pressures at MGN and MCC were minor compared to the concern emanating from Goldman Sachs throughout October. Maxwell was told it was necessary for him to repay loans or the bank would begin selling the collateral. American partners were dismayed at the level of dealings on his behalf, and Eric Sheinberg could no longer hold the line for his old friend. It was not now a case of neutrality by withdrawing but of actively selling their holdings. Goldman also banned Maxwell from indulging in more foreign-exchange transactions since it was still owed $29 million for two forward dollar-sterling contracts executed earlier in the year.[9]

When told the penalty for failing to repay loans might be selling the stock, Maxwell gambled on the fact that Goldman would suffer if they did so. He knew that they knew that selling MCC stock would have a potentially catastrophic effect, leading to a total sell-out by other investors and so wreck the publicly held company. In so doing Goldman would lose millions. It was like a showdown between gunfighters: who would blink first? Goldman started to sell, just enough, they imagined, to teach Maxwell a lesson. They thought he would have to cooperate by paying up for his loans, seemingly unaware that his pockets were empty.

The money Maxwell could scrape together was not going to Goldman but was being used even at this time to slow down the slide in the MCC share price. In early October, a London stockbrokers, Townsley & Co., grew suspicious of a purchase of 2.6 million MCC shares in the name of a nominee company, Edgeport. The oddity was that the payment of just under £4 million ($6.4 million) was made with a cheque from London & Bishopsgate International Investment, Inc., an American twin of Maxwell's London & Bishopgate International Investment Management.

Townsley had become concerned that a Maxwell company was buying MCC shares and questioned the man negotiating the deal, one Sheldon Aboff. It transpired that Aboff, a New York–based lawyer, was a vice president of Macmillan, a director of Maxwell Newspapers—owners of the New York *Daily News*—a director of LBII, and chief executive of Thomas Cook America, 50 percent owned by the Robert Maxwell Group.[10] He had been a friend of Maxwell's going back some thirty years.

Aboff told Townsley he was acting in this transaction as a client of London & Bishopsgate International Investment, Inc., which had lent him the money to buy MCC shares on his own behalf. He must have been a valued client of the firm of which he was a director since, in late October, he bought four million more MCC shares through two other London brokers, using different nominee accounts on both occasions. In total the deals were worth about £10 million ($16 million).[11]

Elsewhere, other banks were getting nervous. A Companies House document shows that Headington Investments paid £5 million ($8 million) into the Channel Islands account of Henry Ansbacher through Headington Holdings in late October. It was said to be security for an unexplained payment to a syndicate organized by First National Bank of Chicago in America. Another £5 million ($8 million) was deposited by the Robert Maxwell Group.[12] Citibank entered into contract with Macmillan to take charge of a number of shares as collateral because of Maxwell's failure to settle a foreign-exchange debt earlier in the month.[13] And the Swiss Bank (SBC) was also pushing for its money. Officials were upset that the promised collateral had not arrived and the bank demanded an explanation. "We were fobbed off for weeks by them saying the takeover wasn't completed," an SBC source said.[14] They were not going to wait any longer.

To avoid the calls Maxwell flew off to New York, and to more problems. The *Daily News* sales were limping along at about 720,000 a day, and that was very bad news indeed because of Maxwell's decision to offer advertisers a refund, or provide free space by 31 December, if the paper failed to sell at least 800,000. It might cost as much as $3 million in refunds. To a man of Maxwell's background that did not seem to be an insurmountable problem. Why did the distribution department not simply lie? Don Nizen, vice president in charge of circulation, said, "Maxwell asked me to be creative with the numbers sold. I refused." Another *News* executive said Maxwell was "furious" when they refused to bend the figures.

That fury would be nothing in comparison with the incandescent rage he was about to exhibit within a few days. On Friday 18 October, a journalist called me to ask if I thought a former colleague, *Daily Mirror* foreign editor Nick Davies, might be a spy. I laughed. It was not a joke, he said, because he had seen overwhelming and detailed documentary evidence. This would conclusively link Davies and Maxwell in gunrunning and spying activities involving the Israeli secret service, Mossad. There was about to be an "explosion" when the story reached newspapers after a certain book was secretly smuggled into bookshops across Britain at the weekend.

Inexplicably, said my contact, *The Sunday Times* had turned down the chance to serialize the book, which was very strange since one of its major allegations was that Davies and Maxwell had helped Mossad track down and kidnap an Israeli nuclear technician, Mordechai Vanunu, the whistle-blower who had been the source of a series of sensational revelations about Israel's nuclear capability to *The Sunday Times* in 1986. It was dynamite, so why was *The Sunday Times* holding back?

If any journalist were to publish verbatim the contents of an average week's telephone calls of story tips it would make for fascinating, if highly libelous, reading. I suspected this colorful conversation would prove to be yet another nonstarter. To begin with, I did not believe for a minute that Nick Davies was a Mossad spy, nor did I really believe Maxwell to be one. However, my informant added an intriguing punchline: The tell-all book was to be published by Faber & Faber. In the publishing world this would be regarded as among one of the more sober, unsensational houses, so why had *The Sunday Times* rejected the book?

Since I was working at the time as a consultant at *The Sunday Times*, it was easy for me to check with the editor, Andrew Neil, and I soon realized that I was not the butt of some practical joke. Far from surprising him when I blurted out my story, he calmly said that not only did he know about it but a reporter, Peter Hounam, could show me the relevant chapter in the book. He was glad I had found out about it from a different source because he had agreed with Faber to maintain confidentiality. Now he could have a second opinion, as long as I honored the secrecy agreement, too.

Before I had finished reading chapter 22 of Seymour Hersh's *Samson Option: Israel, America and the Bomb* that night, I realized why Neil had decided not to serialize it and why Hounam had advised against it. Though both of them were eager to throw more light on the Vanunu case, and all three of us were, as journalists, keen to publish a world exclusive revelation about a figure such as Maxwell, this story was untouchable. From what was written, I could not see a shred of evidence linking Maxwell to Mossad. There also seemed to be little evidence against Davies.

Hounam, who had been involved in talks about the book for weeks, was adamant that the references to the Vanunu case were incorrect. True or not, we all realized the book's publication was bound to provoke a huge story, and we were in the unique position, having agreed to respect confidentiality, of waiting for the storm to break elsewhere. In our last conversation that weekend—as Faber began to deliver twenty thousand copies of *The Samson Option* to bookshops—Neil and I judged that Maxwell would make a fortune in libel damages.

It did not take long for the story to break, emerging under the safety of Parliamentary privilege, in Tuesday's *London Evening Standard* and in every national the next day. Although the major allegations were against Davies, it was Maxwell's name that featured in front-page headlines: BOOK LINKS MAXWELL TO MOSSAD, said the *Daily Telegraph*; MP ALLEGES MAXWELL TIES WITH ISRAELI INTEL-LIGENCE, said the *Independent*; and MAXWELL MAN IN ARMS STORM, screamed the *Daily Mail,* neatly dubbing the affair Mirror-gate, the tag that everyone was to adopt thereafter.

This story was to assume a huge importance, far exceeding its merits, in the coming weeks and was to prey on Maxwell's mind more than any of us might have imagined. Not, I would argue, out of guilt but out of a sense of impotence, intense sadness that, for once, he could not stop bad publicity, especially at this time of his greatest vulnerability. He was guilty of so many things, but not this charge, not this time. When he was up to no good, Maxwell knew in-stinctively how to react to criticism, lying with a gusto that unnerved his accusers. Now that he really was innocent, his denials seemed unconvincing, even to him.

To understand Mirrorgate, we need to consider just what Hersh was alleging, how it came to public attention, and the anti-Maxwell temper among Britain's press that gave it such significance. Hersh is the Pulizter Prize–winning American journalist who broke the story of the My Lai massacre in South Vietnam in 1969, a pedigree that means he commands attention when he writes and a large factor in Faber's decision to publish him. Only one chapter of the *Samson Option,* which purports to chronicle Israel's secret nuclear weapons program, is relevant to Maxwell and Davies, and it rested almost entirely on the claims of an Israeli called Ari Ben Manashe, who said he was a former Mossad agent and arms dealer.

According to Ben Manashe, in 1983 he and Davies together set up a company called Ora Ltd. from Davies's London home through which they sold arms on behalf of Israel to Iran and other countries. In 1987, for instance, Ora negotiated the sale of four thousand TOW antitank missiles to Iran in contravention of a UN arms embargo.

The Israeli produced telexes and letters addressed to Davies from American arms dealers. Over a period of ten years, he claimed, Davies traded in arms and was "a longstanding and highly paid Israeli intelligence asset." Furthermore, Hersh, relying on Ben Manashe's testimony, claimed Maxwell maintained a "close relationship" with Mossad. The most damaging claim of all was that both Davies and Maxwell had been responsible for betraying to Mossad the whereabouts in London of Mordechai Vanunu, thereby starting the chain of events that led to Vanunu's kidnapping by Mossad and his return to stand trial in Israel for treason.

Vanunu's capture was a particularly sensitive matter for *The Sunday Times* because he was lured away from London days before the paper published photographs and details of Israel's hitherto secret nuclear weapons facility at Dimona. *The Sunday Times*'s publication of the Vanunu scoop in October 1986 was partially marred by the fact that Maxwell's *Sunday Mirror* printed a none-too-subtle "spoiler" the week before, which introduced Vanunu to the British public as a con man who was retailing false stories about Israel's nuclear secrets. It included a picture of Vanunu, then hiding out at a Covent Garden hotel known only to two *Sunday Times* reporters. Within hours of his picture appearing in the *Sunday Mirror* he vanished.

Much later it emerged that Vanunu was lured to Rome by a female Mossad agent, drugged and smuggled out of Italy to Israel, where he was tried and sentenced to eighteen years. He has spent the years since in solitary confinement. I think we might reasonably assume from this that the *Sunday Mirror*'s "story" of Vanunu being a con man was an example of shoddy journalism, but does it prove Maxwell a spy?

Neil and Hounam have long been troubled by the *Sunday Mirror*'s unsavory part in this affair and were both intrigued when Hersh contacted Hounam to tell of his Maxwell-Davies "evidence." Were they at last about to discover the truth of how Mossad discovered Vanunu's whereabouts in London? If so, the serialization of the book was a must, but with Maxwell's litigious history it would need extremely detailed verification.

Hounam subsequently met Hersh and Ben Manashe when Fabers flew them to London, and he spent a couple of hours with them in three meetings in the space of twenty-four hours. *The Sunday Times* reporter, Peter Hounam, whose detailed knowledge on the Vanunu affair is second to none, became convinced that Ben Manashe was unreliable. Apart from his manner and approach, which Hounam considered too excitable for a Mossad agent, he caught the man out on a number of details.

According to Ben Manashe, who claimed to have once been an intelligence adviser to Israeli premier Yitshak Shamir and a secret service chief who "ran" Davies as an agent, he received a call from Davies in 1986. He said that Davies tipped him off that a Colombian called Oscar Guerrero was trying to market Vanunu's story in London. Ben Manashe said he immediately ordered Davies to arrange for the story to be trashed in the *Sunday Mirror* as a disinformation exercise. Ben Manashe also claimed to have met Maxwell in his ninth-floor office, a session that Hersh records: "Maxwell made it clear...that he understood what was to be done about the Vanunu story. 'I know what has to happen,' Maxwell told Ben Manashe. 'I have already spoken to your bosses.'"[15]

That was an authentic-sounding Maxwellian quote all right, but not conclusive proof of a meeting. Unraveling such a story might be difficult for many but not for Peter Hounam; apart from the many inaccuracies *The Sunday Times* reporter detected, he caught Ben Manashe out in one significant lie. How had the *Sunday Mirror* obtained a picture of Vanunu? Ben Manashe said it had been specially flown from Israel and handed to Davies; in fact, Hounam had taken the picture himself and, when Guerrero was still acting on behalf of Vanunu, he had given a copy of it to Guerrero.

There were other reasons for Peter Hounam to suspect the authenticity of Ben Manshe's story, and he is not the kind of man to rein in his views. He told Hersh he had been hoaxed, told Faber the same and, naturally, recommended to Neil that he should not serialize the book. Hounam was not alone in his view. *Newsweek* concluded that far from being a major figure in Israeli intelligence, Ben Manashe was only a translator, while America's ABC Television put him through a lie detector test that he failed spectacularly.

When I read *The Samson Option* chapter I noted that Hersh did not rely entirely on Ben Manashe's testimony in relation to Davies's alleged arms-sales activities. Davies's former wife, actress Janet Fielding, had supported the claims. Could there be more to the story?

Surely not, but only Davies would know. As a friend, should I not tip him off about the book? I worried over the weekend about what to do since to contact Davies would breach the confidentiality agreement. I discovered that Davies was in Harare, Zimbabwe, covering the Commonwealth conference for the *Daily Mirror,* and my hand was on the phone several times—though I held back from making a call.

Other newspapers, particularly the *Daily Mail,* were by now alerted to the existence of *The Samson Option* and its potentially explosive material, but no paper was going to publish the allegations knowing of Maxwell's predilection for using the libel laws. The publishers, or someone working on their behalf, came up with a different, and legally safe, route to publicize the book: an MP could table a motion in the Commons and remain immune from prosecution under Parliamentary privilege. By chance, two MPs were separately briefed on the book's central allegations; one, George Galloway, had long kept an eye on Maxwell while the other, Rupert Allason, is an expert on spies, writing about them under his pen name, Nigel West.

Newspapers were therefore able to report at last on Mirrorgate and to delve deeper into the allegations.

I immediately called Davies in his Harare hotel room, where he was already besieged by the men and women who hours before had been his journalistic drinking buddies. "What's it all about?" I asked. "You don't have to go on the record if you don't want to." He requested that our conversation should be "for background" and said, as I expected, that it was nonsense and he would sue. He revealed that he and Maxwell had known for months about the book because Hersh had approached him. He had said to him then that the allegations were untrue. Though flustered, Davies sounded chirpy and positive. Had he spoken to Maxwell?

"Not yet," he said. "But I know the Old Man is beside himself."

Davies, an avid watcher of the stock market, was also calculating the possible effects of the scandal on the declining MCC share price.

"Nick," I said, "tell me honestly, do you know Ben Manashe?"

"Yes, like I know any contact. You know how you do. But I haven't spoken to him in ages. He used to ring me all the time."

"Did you set up a company with him?"

"No. Never. Totally untrue."

"But you knew him well, enough [for him] to stay with you."

"Not really. I let him use my address for mail, but that was a long time ago. Roy, do you really think I'm a gunrunner?"

"Not for a second, Nick. Nor do I think you're a Mossad spy, of all things."

Davies and I had often conspired to circumvent some of Maxwell's more ludicrous pro-Israeli demands, on one occasion amending a story to provide it with more balance. Of course, a sophisticated Mossad spy would be untroubled by a minor massage of a *Daily Mirror* story, but my conversations with Davies on that occasion and subsequently left me in little doubt that he was not an enthusiast for Israel's policies in the occupied territories. Nor, in fairness, was he spy material, though every paper was about to have fun with his office nickname of "Sneaky."

I continued: "What about your ex-wife? Why should she lie to Hersh?"

"I don't know," Davies said.

"Was it a bad breakup?"

"Not really."

"Is her story a lie?"

"Absolutely," Davies said. "No truth in it at all."

I had approached the conversation as if Davies were entirely innocent of the claims. I did not ask him about being in league with Maxwell since I viewed this as beyond probability, having in mind the lengths to which Maxwell went in trying to get me to fire Davies back in March 1990, hardly the act of a spy sharing a dark secret with another spy. Surely if Maxwell had been involved with Davies in such activities he would have known that he was vulnerable to attack from Davies once he had forced him outside the organization. As far as I was concerned, the claim of collusion between them was manifestly untrue.

Maxwell's response to the book, a predictable reflex after years of use, was to call on his writ-servers. "Writs for libel are being issued against the book's publishers, Faber & Faber, and an injunction is being sought to stop its further distribution," a Maxwell spokesman said. Maxwell, in New York, ordered the *Daily Mirror* into action, calling on Joe Haines to thunder against the two MPs in a vintage piece of vitriol. Under the front-page headline DISHONORABLE MEN

AND DIRTY TRICKS the article claimed the men had "as much honor as a pair of jackals scavenging in a rubbish heap" for telling lies about Davies and making "similarly absurd allegations" against Maxwell. Unsurprisingly, both MPs considered the attack libelous and sued. Davies was happy to speak on the record to his own paper and made a detailed rebuttal of the Hersh book claims. He had never met Vanunu; he had never sold arms; he had not sent telexes relating to arms sales from his home.

Janet Fielding is a thirty-four-year-old Australian who had once starred in BBC Television's *Dr. Who*. She was now working as an administrator for an organization called Women in Film. On that first day, Fielding issued an interesting written statement. She had married Davies in 1982 and, after leaving him in June 1985, she said she had returned to the marital home to collect some belongings when she came across letters addressed to Davies from two Ohio arms companies. She and a friend who had driven her then made a quick dash to a library photocopy machine, and she kept copies of these supposedly incriminating letters locked away for the next six years. The letters came from Custom Camo of Smithville, Ohio, and Armtec International, of Columbus, Ohio. Needless to say, journalists from various papers, including a representative from the *Daily Mirror*, were quickly dispatched to track down these firms.

Meanwhile, Davies also dealt with Fielding's letters, having been sent copies by fax. "This is a total set-up," he was quoted in the *Mirror* as saying. "The letter dated May 31, 1985, alleges that I was in Smithville and spent some days there. I have never been to Ohio in my life and I was not in the United States in 1985." It was a denial so unequivocal that it could not be doubted.

The following day the *Mirror*, warming to its theme of the whole affair being a smear, proclaimed a "world exclusive" with a huge headline: FORGERY. Their man in Ohio, Stewart Dickson, reported that one of the letters copied by Fielding had been shown to a partner in Armtec International, who said its signature was not his. He had met a man called Nick Davies, but this was not the man whose picture Dickson had shown him. The article went on to say that news of the forgery had been broken to Davies as he prepared to fly home, via South Africa, from the Commonwealth conference. "I am delighted," he was quoted as replying. "This confirms everything I have been saying." And he repeated his denial that he had ever been to Ohio.

Maxwell also spoke in a radio interview: "I support Mr. Davies in his denial simply because, when the matter came up some two years or so ago, the American government made some inquiries of us and in the end they took no action against Mr. Davies. From that I read and accept that he is innocent of whatever the allegations are." Maxwell was referring to an investigation by the U.S. authorities into Ben Manashe, who had named Davies at that time. He also denied claims of his own Mossad links.

Perhaps, among the Fleet Street community, the most risible "evidence" of Davis not having been in America at the crucial time was the *Mirror*'s publication of copies of Davies's expenses claims for the relevant May 1985 period, including restaurant bills. "They showed he had *NOT* left Britain," said the report.

The *Mirror* had also discovered stories with Davies's byline during that month. Moreover, Davies's passport number in a telex purportedly appointing Davies as an arms trader, was said to be incorrect. Taken together, all this seemed to be irrefutable proof of Davies's innocence. I know I found it convincing, but the journalist who had tipped me off in the first place called again. "You're not being objective," he said. "There is much more to come yet. Hersh isn't a fool."

After twenty-eight years in journalism it still surprises me how the collected "facts" on an individual one knows, once presented in the form of a tabloid profile, either lend the person a spurious glamour or create deep-seated suspicion. So it was in Davies's case. What could be more suspect than the son of a "rich" Midlands property owner who went to an "expensive" private, Catholic school and into the army, Royal Warwickshires, before a period in the Trucial Oman Scouts where he learned, nudge nudge, "fluent Arabic." Then came what was called "high living," polo-playing days "with Prince Charles," two marriages, and an "antique-filled" and "impressive" Georgian house. We were told of mysterious "inherited wealth," of his (marginally inflated) £50,000 ($80,000) salary, of supposed success with women, of his closeness to Maxwell on flights around the world, of his own assignments to virtually every Arab country, even covering the Israeli raids on Lebanese camps in the early eighties.

A romantic picture emerged of a man who might just be everyone's idea of a secret agent with a double-bluff cover in his "Sneaky" nickname. All of this might have passed away and been forgotten if the story had concerned only Davies, but the real quarry for other newspapers was Maxwell, and there would be no rest for reporters until some hole could be found in the denials.

Of all the groups pursuing Maxwell none was more assiduous than Associated Newspapers. Both the *Daily Mail* and its sister *Mail on Sunday* had dared to run Maxwell stories as we have seen—about pensions worries, failure to pay bills, the Guinness link—that others had ignored. It was therefore not surprising that the *Daily Mail* should scoop the rest of Fleet Street by publishing on Friday 25 October, the picture that proved Davies a liar.

Under the headline MIRRORGATE: MYSTERY OF THE OHIO PHOTO-GRAPH was a smiling Davies and a woman identified as the wife of arms dealer Clarence Ben Kaufman holding glasses of iced tea. It had been taken in Smithville, Ohio, in April or May 1985, when Davies visited the couple after being introduced through Ben Manashe. *The Sun* crowed with a front-page headline: YOU LIAR: MAXWELL'S MAN IS FINALLY UNMASKED...

Suddenly Davies's memory returned, and an embarrassed *Mirror,* keeping the story off the front page, quoted him as recalling that he had in fact met Kaufman "while on holiday" visiting the Amish people in Pennsylvania and Ohio. He told the *Mirror:* "Ari [Ben Manashe] had suggested that while in the Amish area I should visit some friends of his, which I did. I spent several hours with them and I remember going for a walk with Kaufman and he shot a few rabbits."

The writs were flying in every direction now, to and from Maxwell and company, to and from Hersh and company. But the Davies lie effectively ended any chance of the story going away. One paper commented: "The whole business is so confusing that it makes a John le Carré plot seem as simple as a child's book."[16] More of the *Mirror's* defense unraveled: Davies had two more passports, and one did have the disputed number.

Mr. William Johnson, the man who told the *Mirror* he had never met the Nick Davies whose picture he had been shown, hours later said just the opposite to a *Financial Times* reporter. The following day the *Daily Mail,* chirruping with glee over catching the *Mirror* out, reported that an internal inquiry was to be held.

On Sunday the *News of the World* said one "vital ingredient" had been missing—but now, here it was—"the love angle." The paper revealed the romance between Davies and Andrea Martin and quoted an unidentified "Maxwell man": "I don't think Bob ever doubted Andrea's integrity. But on principle. and quite understandably, he didn't like the idea of his confidential secretary sleeping with one of his executives."

The Sunday Times, when it finally got its hands back on its own story, suggested that the *Mirror,* obliged to save face, would leave Davies hanging in the wind. Over the next couple of days, by arrangement with Davies, I spoke to him on the phone several times. I asked why he had lied. He never gave me a satisfactory answer, claiming he had been confused and hinting that his own paper had not dealt intelligently with him once the story broke. In his confusion he claimed to have misunderstood the question about visiting Ohio. He admitted knowing Ben Manashe well enough to dine with occasionally, but maintained that the arms-dealing claims were false.

"What do you think will happen?" Davies asked.

I replied: "They'll get rid of you, Nick, you know they will."

Richard Stott, the editor, and Davies had made no secret of their mutual antipathy over twenty years of working together, but Davies was also unpopular with many—though not all—senior executives, envious of his relationship with Maxwell, though they would have been unaware of how close Davies had come to being fired.

I cannot understand why Davies lied, since he could have openly admitted meeting arms dealers and knowing Ben Manashe very well without there being any proof of being an arms dealer himself.

After a rapid hearing in the office, and with Maxwell still out of the country, Davies was fired. The *Mirror* reported the fact on page 1 and wrote a full-page editorial inside to explain why Davies was being dismissed by the paper and why, at the same time, he was still being defended by the paper. There was a great deal of sense among the hyperbole in the *Mirror's* argument, for there seemed, in spite of the falsehood, to be no justification for the claims against Davies and even less for the claims against Maxwell.

To describe Maxwell as a spy for Israel was the equivalent of naming Margaret Thatcher as a spy for Britain. He was an avowed Zionist, a hawkish believer in the Jewish settlements on the West Bank, and a forthright public speaker on behalf of the Israeli state. Of course, if he had "betrayed" Vanunu, that would have been a wicked act, though not from Maxwell's point of view. While the *Sunday Mirror* spoiler remains a scandalous and unforgiveable blot, with journalists accepting the word of an unknown source without the slightest attempt to double check, there is no proof that this act caused Vanunu's disappearance from London; nor did the passing on of documents to the Israeli embassy. It is much more likely that the relentless Mossad had been trailing Vanunu for a long time after his defection from Israel.

Yet more credence to the unlikelihood of Maxwell being linked to any intelligence service is provided by Peter Jay, his former chief of staff and one-time British ambassador to America. Before taking his job with Maxwell, he took "soundings" within the Foreign Office. He said, "I was quite clear in my mind if any part of the British government service connected with international affairs would have thought there was some reason of propriety, prudence or loyalty, as a former ambassador, I would have got the appropriate signal not to take the employment...I did not." Jay added, I would argue conclusively: "I find it inconceivable that Mossad, with its awesome reputation for efficiency and ruthlessness, would want to have anything to do with this crazy guy, who never took guidance from anybody."[17]

On exactly the same ground, Max Hastings, editor of the *Daily Telegraph,* and one-time television profiler of Maxwell, agreed. The suggestion of his being a Mossad agent "seems absurd on the grounds that his uncertain grip on reality would render him of negligible value to any secret service but it would be hard to imagine Maxwell passing up a Mossad invitation to lunch."[18]

Maxwell could not escape the consequences. It is a fine irony that one of the world's greatest liars was now suffering from a lie. For some weeks I had been keeping a daily, sometimes hourly, eye on Maxwell's MCC and MGN share prices. In light trading, both had drifted downward for weeks, but once Mirrorgate broke, they accelerated, with MGN losing 6 pence (9.6 cents) and MCC 7 pence (11.2 cents) on the first day, finishing at 80 pence ($1.28) and 149 pence ($2.38) respectively. There would be no recovery. As each day passed the slide continued. After spending millions to buy up his own shares and borrowing millions more by mortgaging them, he had no way of boosting the price.

The response to this growing encirclement of Maxwellia by reality was a display of acute paranoia. Like a character in a thirties film-noir thriller, he became convinced "they," whoever "they" were, were out to get him. It was obvious what to do. He had seen the films. It was time to call in a private eye. Not just anyone, of course, but the best.

Maxwell consulted one of world's top private investigators, Jules Kroll, head of Kroll Associates, in a New York hotel in late October. According to one of the participants in this bizarre two-hour meeting, Maxwell appeared "convinced that there were people out to get him, to destroy his life and business in any way they could. He named businessmen and political enemies."[19] At the end of this odd meeting, Maxwell evidently agreed to compile a memo listing the strange events that had led him to this conclusion. Kroll was not officially hired. It might have been better therapy if he had chosen to write down all the legitimate reasons why people should have been out to get him.

Five days after the storm broke over the Hersh book, on Saturday 26 October, Maxwell flew out of New York. His *Daily News* secretary, Carolyn Hinsey, had witnessed many bad days with him but this, the last time she would see him, was "my worst day with RM... he was in the worst mood I have ever seen, very angry."[20]

16

Cap'n Bob's Last Voyage

B Y the end of October the pressure on Maxwell was intolerable. The global giant faced destitution and, when his deceit was revealed, detention. Only he knew how bad the situation was; only he understood the consequences of his acts. As Maxwellia crumbled around him so reality intruded at last. Among the shafts of truth that penetrated were a realization that the show could not go on...and that he was alone. There was nobody in whom he could confide, not his wife, who he thought expected him to solve all problems, nor his sons. He had grown closer to them in these past couple of years and let them share a little of his world, but the man of so many paradoxes could not but realize in these days alone in his lonely tower the awful truth: intimacy with him had sullied the boys he had so wanted to be different from him. He had groomed them to be unlike him, to be polite, to be honest, to be legitimate. Now what would happen?

When drunk Maxwell could be cantankerous. At his last session with his barber, at the end of October, he had been drinking but he was maudlin. George Wheeler, the seventy-five-year-old former Savoy Hotel barber who had dyed Maxwell's hair and eyebrows every two weeks for the past twenty-five years, had seen the man in many moods, but this was a departure. George said, "He stopped me, looked me straight in the eyes, and said, "You know, Mr. Wheeler, you are my oldest friend.' I replied, 'Mr. Maxwell, I am your *only* friend.' He said, 'I think you're right.'"[1]

Maxwell could just about afford a haircut but not much else, and when the authorities caught up with him he might not be provided with the facilities to dye his hair. He had nothing left to pawn. He had just raised an £80 million ($128 million) loan on his London properties, £10 million ($16 million) short of his original ambition, but that was now far too little for his needs. Hundreds of millions were required, and there was no hope on the horizon, not an earthly chance of finding enough. Both the MCC and MGN share prices were in freefall, with MGN hitting new lows every day and MCC, more dangerously, reaching the point at which all the banks holding his stock as collateral would be demanding more shares. Goldman Sachs was pulling the plug.

Little people whom he would normally squash without a thought were challenging him. The Lilliputians were hauling Gulliver to the ground. It was over. He had called in every favor, rallying business acquaintances of years' standing to help him. It was no good now. He must be found out. The auditors would have to look at the books of MCC, of MGN and, of course, at the pension funds. He had held them off, but he could not hope to do so much longer.

His immediate problems were the Swiss Bank Corporation; Goldman; and Shearson Lehman Brothers, the American bank. On 30 October, his private company Adviser (188) suddenly told the Swiss that instead of delivering shares—which it no longer had anyway—it would repay the loan in cash, in full, on 5 November. However, there were no funds available. He was also told in advance of Goldman's plans to sell shares due to his failure to repay a $60 million loan. In New York, he had pledged 1.9 million Berlitz shares to Shearson Lehman, almost 10 percent of the company, as collateral for yet another loan worth about £25 million ($40 million). They, too, threatened to sell unless he paid up. He also faced a critical meeting with MGN's finance director on 1 November. Maxwell, given to colds, often at critical periods, decided to get away, to give himself time to think, perhaps, time to stand back and review the mess from afar. It was a decision made swiftly, and it caught everyone by surprise.

In the late afternoon of 30 October, he told Bob Cole, his long-suffering aide, that he was off for a couple of days. "He bade me an extremely fond and emotional farewell," Cole said. "He took me in his arms and kissed me." He had kissed Cole perfunctorily twice before, but this embrace was warm and with it came a little speech: "You've done a superb job dealing with the press over this Hersh business. All the editors were saying precisely that at lunch today." Maxwell could not resist a patronizing dig. "You're well on your way to being a good press officer. But you will never be good for me. You still try to help the press. I want someone who will hinder the press." Cole, used to Maxwell's eccentricities, took no notice of this behavior for six days.

Later that evening, Maxwell called his yacht in Gibraltar from his tenth-floor apartment to announce that he would be arriving the next day, which threw Captain Gus Rankin's careful plans into reverse. The skipper of the *Lady Ghislaine* was preparing to sail it across the Atlantic, to Bermuda, in readiness for the usual Maxwellian Caribbean Christmas. Rankin told Maxwell the boat was not ready to receive visitors, but Maxwell said it did not matter since he was not bringing any staff or guests aboard. He was suffering from a cold that he could not shake off, he said, and hoped relaxation in the sunshine would cure him. It was unusual for Maxwell to be alone. If he did not take his Spanish butler, the slyly amusing Joseph Caetano Pereira, then it would be a secretary, such as his program manager, Charlotte Thornton. "I cannot remember a time when I did not go to the boat with him," Joseph said.[2]

Maxwell's last journey began at 6:30 A.M. on Thursday 31 October, when the Maxwell-owned Aerospatiale helicopter carried him off Maxwell House for a twenty-minute journey to Luton, where he boarded the Maxwell-owned Gulfstream 4 jet. This toy was his favorite. One night, when editor, my phone rang and his voice boomed over heavy static: "Where am I?"

"I don't know, Bob. Israel? Russia—"

"I'm above you."

I remember foolishly looking up at the ceiling as I contemplated the airborne Maxwell.

"What do you think of the phone system?"

"Remarkable. Isn't technology a wonderful thing?"

"I left Montreal this morning, I was in New York this afternoon. Now I'm going to Hungary. Not bad for a pensioner, eh?"

I was told later that he had called several people to boast of his marvelous new in-flight phone in his G4, as he liked everyone to refer to his plane.

There was too much luggage when Maxwell traveled to fit into his helicopter so it had to be driven separately to the airport in his Rolls by John Featley, whose engaging personality had amused Maxwell so much he had lasted three years as chauffeur, longer than many a predecessor. According to Featley, who spoke to him before leaving the building that day, "I said to the guv'nor that the share prices were going down the tubes, what was occurring? He just chuckled and started talking about football." Featley said he seemed carefree. "I thought, Here we go again, the boss is going to pull another giant white rabbit out of the hat at the eleventh hour."[3]

Maxwell arrived in Gibraltar at 10:40 A.M. where he was met by Rankin and Charlie Rodriguez, a local shipping agent, and was driven by limousine to the gleaming *Lady Ghislaine*. Rankin told David Wyatt, an employee at a quayside ship's chandlers, that Maxwell was going to spend a few days with the boat and its eleven crewmembers en route to Madeira, where his plane would meet him. Gus Rankin, a six-foot-two-inch man of two hundred-some pounds and known for his bluntness, had a good relationship with Maxwell. The forty-five-year-old experienced skipper was an Englishman by birth, having been raised in Essex, but had adopted United States citizenship fourteen years before, settling with his wife, Pamela, in the backwoods of Arkansas. He was the kind of man who could cope with a sudden change of direction.

The yacht sailed southwest for Madeira, a six-hundred-mile journey taking the rest of Thursday and all of Friday, with Maxwell telling the crew he would fly home from the island on the weekend. He spent the time aboard dealing with the half dozen briefcases full of documents he had brought with him, made a number of phone calls, and appeared in a good mood—to the point of congratulating members of the crew on the upkeep of the yacht, the service, and the standard of food, despite the fact that his usual gastronomic favorites were not available.

Given the nature and content of the phone calls and faxes he was receiving, this was a truly amazing public-relations performance. A fax arrived informing him that Shearson Lehman had taken possession of the Berlitz shares, and he was also told that Goldman had carried out its threat; the day before it had sold 2.2 million MCC shares. The market could not fail to notice that the great buyer was now a seller.

But Goldman still had 24.2 million MCC shares left, 3.71 percent of the company. If they were planning to dump them, then they would have to do so gradually or the price might reach zero before they had finished selling the stock. It might just do that anyway since brokers across the City had long ago been urging those very few clients with stock to sell. Maxwell would also have been informed that MCC was about to be officially removed from the top one hundred companies in the stock market, which would lead to a desertion by the index-linked funds, almost the only big holders of shares.

More frightening still was that day's news. Kevin had been visited in his office by lawyers acting for the Swiss Bank Corporation who officially informed him that they had approached the police about the failure to pay the loan. In-house lawyer Neil Stocks, advised by the top-flight solicitors Allen & Overy, had been told by a senior officer they met to compile a file on the case and present it to City of London police. Kevin was left under no illusion that the Swiss Bank Corporation would pursue the complaint unless settlement was reached. That agreement to pay on 5 November would have to be honored.

On Saturday morning, about 8:30 A.M. (for ease of reference, all times are Greenwich Mean Time), the yacht docked at Funchal, Madeira. Maxwell went ashore at 11 A.M. with Mark Atkins, second mate and a former policeman. He went shopping, bought newspapers, and seemed particularly keen on looking for a history book of the island, which he couldn't find. Taking a taxi, he and Atkins visited a local landmark, Reid's Hotel. Maxwell spent about ten minutes inside alone before rejoining Atkins in the car. They then went for a beer in one of the town's bars.

Returning to the yacht, he told the skipper he wanted to visit a nearby small uninhabited island, La Desertas, where they spent two hours. He took a swim and watched a colony of seals cavorting in the warm waters. The yacht returned to Funchal at 7 P.M. and Maxwell dined alone on board in the evening before going ashore for a drink at a local bar with Atkins. While there, he noticed Ta-Madeira casino and sent Atkins to inquire whether he could get in. He returned to the *Lady Ghislaine* for his passport and $3,000 from the safe. Maxwell spent twenty-five minutes alone in the casino. Manager Jean-Paul Vendeoil said Maxwell went to the second floor where roulette and blackjack was being played but did not say how lucky his customer was.[4] Then he rejoined his crewmember in the bar. On returning to the yacht, he told the skipper before going to bed that he intended to leave the following day.

The crew, most of whom had not long been with the boat, were scurrying around the next day, Sunday, to prepare the yacht for her transatlantic trip. Suddenly Maxwell said he had changed his mind about leaving. To those locals who saw him that morning, he appeared to be relaxed as he sat reading aboard the yacht, soaking up the weak sunshine. He was polite but firm—"Roy, remember, I am always firm but fair"—in refusing to answer questions from local journalists who turned up on quayside.

In the afternoon there are opposing views about his demeanor. Gus Rankin, the yacht's captain, said he was in a "very, very good mood," but a Funchal shipping agent thought "he was not very happy, he wasn't talking too much. He didn't look cheerful."[5] Then Maxwell asked the captain if there was anywhere en route across the Atlantic where he could be dropped off. When told that was not possible, he said he had decided to stay aboard for a few more days and they agreed to set sail from Funchal, 250 miles south to the Canary Islands.

Before leaving, Maxwell made the strangest of requests. He asked for his personal jet to fly to London to collect his two sons, Kevin and Ian, an instruction that was relayed to Captain David Whiteman, the pilot. Ten minutes later he rescinded the order, and his sons knew nothing about it. A whim had passed...but not quite. Early in the afternoon, he asked the yacht to make ready to leave port and demanded that his plane fly to Tenerife, because he said he would be returning to London the following day. He also asked for the plane to rendezvous with the yacht before flying on. Rankin later explained that Maxwell had seemed irritable that morning although the flypast by the plane seemed "to humor him." He told investigators: "He seemed in very good spirits watching the aircraft circle the boat."[6]

They left Funchal at 3:30 P.M. for the all-day journey. That night Ian rang him to remind him about his commitment to speak at the Anglo-Israeli Association dinner on the following evening. "That was important to him and he had been very keen to do it," Ian said.

But Maxwell replied: "I'm really not too well, and I'm not sure I'm going to be up to it."[7]

Ian knew the routine; as so often in the past, he would be expected to step in. Maxwell said he would speak to him again the following morning, Monday the 4th, and he did. Though Maxwell was still hours from port, Ian said, "He was still planning to fly back although still complaining he didn't feel well enough."[8] In the end it was obvious that Maxwell was not going to return, and on phone and fax father and son began writing the speech together.

In the course of the afternoon Maxwell also spoke on a couple of occasions to Samuel Pisar, a Paris-based international lawyer who had been influential in Maxwell's contacts with Gorbachev and other Eastern European leaders and with the Israeli government. Pisar, the youngest survivor of Auschwitz, had been one of Maxwell's closest confidants in recent years. Certainly they shared a commitment to Zionism, and Pisar was also close to Betty Maxwell for the same reason. He offered Maxwell a number of ideas for the speech. They spoke of plans for the immediate future. Evidently Maxwell was about to be nominated by the Scientific Institute of France to receive the *Légion d'Honneur*, the nation's highest award. He was also to be made Man of the Year by the Jewish Scientific and Cultural Institute at the Plaza Hotel in New York later that month.

At lunchtime Maxwell called MGN's managing director, Ernie Burrington, then enjoying a meal in the Mirror Group executive dining room, known as the Rotunda. As he was called to the phone in the corner, Burrington had in mind the series of confrontational meetings of the past month and his agreement to leave. He was expecting a tough inquisition. Instead Maxwell was politeness itself, considerate, almost apologetic: "I'm sorry to disturb you during your lunch. I just wanted to know if there was anything I should know." Burrington did not want to speak about business and, not wishing to enter into confidential matters in a public area, he assured Maxwell that all was quiet. Guest's internal investigation was continuing but had yet to turn up the fact that £50 million ($80 million) more was missing from MGN, let alone the pension-fund misappropriation. Maxwell let Burrington understand that he would be returning the next day "when I will deal with everything." Burrington was baffled by the tone of the call.

At 4 P.M., the yacht reached Porto Dorsona Pasquatra in Tenerife, and Maxwell was still undecided about his plans. He told Rankin that he might return to London that day but maybe the next. He wanted another swim, and the yacht moored in an area off shore for him to take his dip. Maxwell was not regarded as a strong swimmer and never stayed too long in the water nor strayed too far from the boat, but his former first mate, Nigel Hodson, told me, "He couldn't sink. He floated so well that he didn't need to make a stroke." After his swim he relaxed and the yacht returned to port. Maxwell said he would dine ashore and said, once more, that he would go home the next day.

He stepped ashore at about 8:15 P.M., to be driven alone by taxi to the restaurant of the five-star Hotel Mencey, in Santa Cruz, Tenerife. He was shown to table one and asked the hotel's head waiter, Sergio Rodriguez, for his recommendation, taking his advice, starting with a salad and then enjoying a light meal of hake with clams in a mushroom-and-parsley sauce, washed down with three beers.

According to *The Sunday Times* Insight team he then removed a cigar from his jacket and lit it.[9] I never saw him smoke in my fourteen months with him, and he banned smoking in his presence, or even in his ninth-floor offices. His son, Ian, smoked without his father's knowledge and went to extraordinary lengths to conceal the fact. Though Maxwell obeyed few rules—pretending to stick to diets at public lunches while gorging himself on "snacks" or meals in private—it was very rare indeed for him to smoke even cigars.

He did not court attention, in spite of wearing one of his trademark baseball caps. He appeared to be absorbed, in an introspective mood. Waiters noted he was short of breath and seemed frustrated at not being able to make a call on the walkie-talkie he had brought with him. He complimented a waiter on the food—"very good"—and paid the bill of 3,000 pesetas (about $25) with cash, adding a 20 percent tip. As he left he forgot to pick up his jacket, which was retrieved by waiter Rodriguez, and he walked briskly to a taxi waiting to take him to the yacht less than a mile away. By 10 P.M. he was back on board.

Back in London the Anglo-Israeli Association dinner was going ahead at the Grosvenor House hotel without him. Typically, organizers had only been told one hour before that their guest of honor could not be there due to illness. I once delivered a phone message to Greville Janner MP on Maxwell's behalf about his missing a Jewish charity function only a short time before it was due to start. Janner indicated that this was par for the course. Maxwell's speech, delivered by Ian, "reflected Mr. Maxwell's statesmanlike self-image."[10] Strongly pro-Israeli, it stated that there should be no giving up of land for peace. "It was...typical Bob, full of fight and vigor, kicking the hell out of Syria," Ian said.[11]

On arriving back at the yacht, Maxwell collected some phone messages and instructed the captain to put to sea. "Mr. Maxwell wanted to cruise all night out at sea and we decided to head in the direction of Gran Canaria." He said he thought the trip would make it easier for him to sleep. As the *Lady Ghislaine* cruised down the eastern coast of Gran Canaria, Maxwell made and received a number of calls and was faxed the front page of next day's *Daily Mirror* as normal. He spoke to Richard Stott, *Mirror* editor, who said the next day, "He seemed okay. He was not depressed, he was very angry about the allegations in Seymour Hersh's book."[12] He also spoke to Sam Pisar after having retired to his stateroom. A little later he went to the pantry to complain about the exhaust fumes from the engine, and the two stewardesses tried to clear the air with a fan. At 10:15

P.M., Liza Kordalski, one of the two stewardesses, went to see if Maxwell required anything further. As she left through the main stateroom door Maxwell asked her to lock it and leave through the bathroom, which leads to the study and through the dining area to midships.

At 11:15 P.M. Maxwell answered a satellite call from Ian, having said that he would accept calls only from him or Kevin. Ian said, "He was in a good mood."

He wanted to know how his speech had gone down. Ian referred to the next day being "a big day" with "big meetings." Their conversation ended with Ian saying,

"See you tomorrow then."

"You bet."

Five minutes later there was a call from Rabbi Feivish Vogel in Moscow. He was very persuasive with Rankin, and Maxwell agreed to take the call. He wanted to talk about his campaign to secure the release of the Lubavitch Jewish archives from Moscow. "I found him to be as robust and as helpful and positive in his last call as in all our other calls," said the rabbi.[13]

As watches changed on the bridge in the night, one of the crew, Graham Leonard, saw Maxwell looking over the stern rail toward the lights of Gran Canaria at around 4:10 A.M.. The weather was calm and there was only a light easterly wind. The pair exchanged greetings and Maxwell said, "It's hot." Leonard dealt with the complaint by switching on the air conditioning. But at 4:45 A.M. Maxwell rang the bridge and asked for the fans to be switched off. This was the last command of Robert Maxwell, who was never seen alive again.

Duty inspections of the vessel continued during the night and the *Lady Ghislaine*'s voyage ended with her mooring off Los Christianos in the south of Tenerife at 9:30 A.M. in the morning, all aboard unaware that her most important passenger was missing. An hour later a caller from the New York office of Rothschild's was told Maxwell had not yet risen and was asleep.

At 11 A.M., however, a call came from John Bender, senior vice president of Maxwell Macmillan in America, who said his call was urgent. Gus Rankin, the skipper, said, "Shall I put it through to the stateroom?"

Bender told me: "I said yes, and after a couple of minutes he came back and said, 'He'll have to get back to you.'"

Bender, who says he cannot remember why he was calling, was unaware for some time that his call had triggered the search. Once Maxwell did not answer his phone the crew went looking for him. There was an initial quick search in which it was discovered that all doors to Maxwell's stateroom were locked. Stewardess Liza Kordalski remembered leaving the key in the lock on Maxwell's instructions and that the yacht's captain opened it with his passkey. He found the nightshirt Kordalski had seen Maxwell wearing earlier abandoned on the floor. The key was never found, the assumption being that before going out on deck Maxwell himself had locked all entrances to the stateroom. All the crew then made three more thorough searches and after a swimmer seen a short distance away turned out not to be Maxwell, the alarm was raised.

Rankin lifted the plastic cover on the bridge, pressed the red button underneath, and dialed a three-digit code to send a "priority 3" mayday call through the Inmarsat satellite network. This initial attempt to raise the alarm failed as his mayday call found no response, but he was able to contact the local port agents to relay a message to Tenerife radio station. Another call was made to Brian Hill, his immediate superior based at the Farnborough airstrip, who told him to contact Maxwell's son, Ian. The Publisher's disappearance was also reported to the rescue coordination center at Stavanger, Norway, and confirmed by telex. This was part of the official procedure because the yacht was located in Atlantic Ocean East Zone, whose maritime rescue coordination center is controlled from Norway, which in turn alerted the marine safety center in Madrid.

Rankin also followed procedure by going ashore to report to the Los Christianos harbormaster. At 12:25 P.M. the mayday call was relayed to all ships. At 1:08 P.M. the first rescue helicopter reached the scene. Two others followed, accompanied by a Fokker Friendship light plane. Back in London, at Maxwell House, Ian was talking in his office to an executive from *The European* when Kevin burst in at about noon. After asking the other person to leave, Kevin blurted out the news: "Dad seems to have fallen off the boat. He's fallen into the sea."[14] Kevin had twice failed to get through to his father, which surprised him, since Maxwell rarely refused Kevin's calls, and on his third call Rankin admitted: "We can't find him. He's not on the boat." Ian then called Rankin to receive the same news and to be told that an air-sea search was underway, tracking over the course the boat had taken. "Once we realized he had been overboard for a couple of hours, it was pretty clear he was dead," said Ian. "We didn't immediately abandon hope, but we had to make the worst assumption."[15]

The brothers decided to tell their mother the news as soon as possible and then called their elder brother, Philip, in France. Within an hour Betty had organized the private jet to pick up her and Philip to fly them to Tenerife. The search continued. But Kevin and Ian were worried by news from the stock market where MCC shares, which had opened at 139 pence ($2.22), were now plunging. MGN's price was falling too.

Could the City know the truth? Ship-to-shore and satellite communications are hardly secure, and Rankin confirmed that searchers had been told that they were looking not for an ordinary mortal but for Robert Maxwell. It was possible that someone had overheard and so the City knew Maxwell was missing.

On reflection, it is just as possible that the City did not know at all but had gotten wind of Goldman's notification to the stock exchange of its 31 October share sale. The note had reached Maxwell House at 4:15 P.M., but Bob Cole was under instructions from Kevin Maxwell not to release it until exactly eleven in the morning. Cole thinks it "too much of a coincidence" that Bender's call occurred at exactly the same minute he was told to release the Goldman sale to the stock exchange. But coincidence remains the only rational explanation.

Anyway, it meant that the City might have heard of the Goldman sale before Kevin decided to ask Smith New Court to arrange for the suspension of both MCC and MGN shares. That occurred at 2:58 P.M.; MCC had reached 121 pence, its lowest point for eight years, and MGN had hit 77.5 pence, a new low. Ten minutes later the world was told that Maxwell was missing.

It is a measure of Maxwell's fame, his zest for self-publicity and extraordinary personality combining to make him Britain's best-known businessman, that for weeks afterward people would, as in the Kennedy assassination of 1963, talk of where they were and what they were doing the moment they heard he had vanished. For some of us, of course, there was work to be done. After my enforced six months of Maxwell-induced leisure, I had accepted a short-term contract as a consultant editor at *Today* and *The Sunday Times*. But on that fateful Tuesday I was in no mood for work after being uncomfortably prodded during an afternoon hospital checkup. I was thinking of going home from Westminister Hospital but instead returned to the office.

As I entered the *Today* newsroom at about 3:30 P.M. people ran at me and began shouting. "Maxwell's missing...his plane's gone down...Martin [the editor] wants you urgently...isn't it amazing...you can have all the space in the world...the shares have been suspended...you can have my terminal..."

If atmospheres are ever charged with electricity then this was one of those occasions. A newsroom during a big story has a loud hum, and this was louder than usual. The excitement and adrenaline seized every department. The editor, Martin Dunn, appeared from his office: "Roy, thank God! You're here! Just write."

As details trickled in over the wires, we soon learned that neither his plane nor his boat had gone down. He had. I sat down at a keyboard and went numb. Maxwell, the man who had haunted me for twenty-three months, had probably drowned. For the only time I can recall in my years as a journalist I froze. That stock of anecdotes I knew so well and had told so often deserted me. I sat staring at the blank screen, nodding as a succession of people told me the latest news from the agencies or pushed pictures in front of me from the files to check whether this one was Kevin or that one was Ghislaine.

I answered a score of questions as that residue of mythology about Maxwell, even among journalists, bubbled to the surface...Was Betty Jewish?...Wasn't that Board of Trade report overturned in court?...How well did he know Gorbachev?...So, was he working for Mossad after all?

Still my fingers had not touched the keys. My memory had gone in the confusion and I called my wife, fortunately working at home, and asked her to fax to me the synopsis I had prepared that would grow into this book. I handed it to an executive to choose a headline and started to write.

After a couple of hundred words I realized that if this were all a mistake, if Maxwell were alive somewhere, then simply by writing it

I was likely to face court action from him once again. This was in the front of my mind when someone shouted: "They've found a body in the water!" I jumped from my chair and punched the air, quietly subsiding in embarrassment as I realized I was celebrating a man's death. I wrote on without another word.

It was 5:50 P.M. when Maxwell's body was spotted floating, naked, lying on his back, eyes open to the skies. José Francisco Perdoma, a Spanish air-sea rescue diver, went into the water to help manipulate the 294-pound bulk into the special basket lowered from the helicopter above. But the basket was too small, and the six men were forced to use a large nylon harness instead. "It was...floating face up, not face down, which is normal," said the frogman. At 6:15 P.M., the naked corpse of Maxwell was winched aboard a helicopter and flown to Gando airfield in Las Palmas, Gran Canaria.

In the initial confusion, as always in these sorts of situations, there was a suggestion that a fishing boat had found the body. It was also inaccurately said to have been found in a different area. In such a way, innocently, because people are too excited or inexperienced, myths are born. A third false report would suggest that the *Lady Ghislaine* had docked at Los Christianos at 7 A.M., not 9:30 A.M.. These would all contribute to journalists making much out of nothing. At Gando, the body was initially identified by Rankin, and soon after by the newly arrived Betty and Philip.

"He's a colossus lying here," Betty said, "as he had been in life."

Colossus was to become a favored epitaph. The body was removed to a morgue on the outskirts of Las Palmas for pathologists to carry out an autopsy.

If there can be a honeymoon in death then Maxwell was to enjoy one. In his own paper he was "The man who saved the *Daily Mirror*" and a "giant with vision" who "plowed enormous sums into the latest newspaper technology." This made it sound as though Maxwell had invested his own rather than the *Mirror*'s money. The last sentence of that day's editorial was poignant: "We shall miss him." Joe Haines, in his signed obituary, wrote: "His death removes a colossus from the scene...love him or hate him his like will never be seen again." Columnist Anne Robinson observed, not without a hint of irony: "He enriched many lives. Mine was one of them."

Outside the *Mirror*, the obituaries were a little less adulatory, a little more cynical, but the tone was generally respectful. The Department of Trade inspectors' criticism of 1971 "would have broken a lesser man" said *The Times*, suggesting a sort of heroism for withstanding the truth. The *Guardian* editorial concluded unconvincingly that "everyone who knew him will have learned something worth remembering."

My own memoir, which made it clear that he was difficult to work for but stopped short of condemnation, concluded: "It is a relationship I will never forget, and I regret the manner of his passing."

Max Hastings, editor of the *Daily Telegraph*, wrote a perceptive piece that captured Maxwell better than almost anyone on that first day, but its criticism was nevertheless cloaked in terms of admiration: "The nation's headlines will be much poorer for his passing, and the length of his journey from the place and circumstances of his birth demands respect from all of us who have had to travel much less far, to rise much less high." This seemed to suggest that the ends justified the means.

Only one newspaper broke ranks, and this was days later, to remind us that an old man's death should not blind us to that old man's evil. He was "a liar, a cheat and bully", said the *Independent on Sunday* leading article. "His untruthfulness was not a matter of occasional slips. It was an instinct, a habit, and above all, a weapon." It debunked his claim to have suffered from the Establishment; it scorned those who aided him; it ridiculed his claim to greatness; it accused him of gross misuse of the libel laws.

I cherished this piece from the moment I read it, commending it to everyone I met. In a few hundred words this newspaper was asking us all to cast off our reticence, to tell it like it was, to tell the truth. The *Independent on Sunday* did not then know of the missing pension funds, the share-support operation, the plunder of his public companies. The paper was basing its view on Maxwell's public record as it stood then, five days after his death. It was not, as I have heard some suggest, a case of prophesy. Maxwell deserved those words on the strength of his career even without the grand larceny that was to be exposed weeks later.

The obituaries were accompanied by tributes from the great and the good and, of course, his sons. Ian said: "It is very sad for me and my brother. For my mother and our five brothers and sisters. For all those who work for us throughout the world, and there are 15 to 20,000. For all the shareholders of our company." He added: "It's particularly sad for Mirror Group which has lost its publisher and its chairman and its savior." Kevin said: "My father was a maverick...he touched the lives of millions of people."

Prime minister John Major described him as "a great character" who had given "valuable insights" into the Soviet Union during the attempted coup against Gorbachev. His predecessor, Margaret Thatcher, declared, "Mr. Maxwell kept me informed about what was happening in Eastern European countries and what their leaders were thinking." Ex-premier Ted Heath called him a "charismatic figure" while Labour leader Neil Kinnock, choosing his words carefully, referred to him as "a unique figure who attracted controversy, envy, and loyalty in great measure throughout his rumbustious life."

More flowed in from abroad. President Gorbachev said he was "deeply grieved" but gave no hint of Maxwell's alleged powerbroking role by referring only to his "very significant contribution to cooperation...in such an important sphere as publishing and mass media." Two of Israel's most prominent politicians issued lengthy statements. "It is impossible to compare him with anybody. He is above comparison," said Shimon Peres, leader of the Labour Party and a former prime minister. The then premier, Yitzhak Shamir, said Maxwell "was a passionate friend of Israel" who "offered to put his wide contacts on the international arena at Israel's service." Politicians in France, Germany, Hungary, and America also had words of praise, though New York's mayor David Dinkins was guarded: "He has done a lot for our city." Britain's former U.S. ambassador, Peter Jay, paid a most handsome homage: "I think he had more physical and moral courage than anyone I ever met."

Along with the tributes came definite views about how he had *not* died. "Suicide is absolutely out of the question," Betty said. Captain Rankin told the *Mirror* he was mystified as to how Maxwell might have fallen and added that he was "enjoying the boat more on this trip than he had ever done."

"He wasn't the sort of man to shoot himself, take an overdose, or throw himself off a boat," offered his friend, Sir Michael Richardson. The biographer Maxwell had maligned, Tom Bower, said, "I can't believe he committed suicide, because he was a fighter." MGN editorial director Charles Wilson said with some justification: "He had too much of an arrogance of his own abilities to conceive of such a thing." He added wisely that his death was "a complete mystery, one that may never be solved." And no comment was more apposite than that of James Whitaker, the *Mirror*'s royal correspondent, who said: "It's funny isn't it? He was a mystery at the beginning and surrounded by mystery at the end." It was left to the irreverent *Sun* to ask the question on everybody's mind in a front-page headline: DID HE FALL... DID HE JUMP?

Most financial journalists, having a clear understanding of the kind of peril he faced over his debts, leaned toward suicide. The *Financial Times*, by coincidence, had spent weeks looking at the empire. Their journalist, former Kleinwort analyst Bronwen Maddox, had put together a complex diagram illustrating in greater detail than anyone had ever managed before the various private companies and their relationships to each other. On the morning of 5 November, after canceling a couple of previous interviews, Kevin had finally agreed to see Maddox. The appointment was for 9 A.M., but following in his father's footsteps, he kept her waiting in the ninth-floor corridor until 9:45 A.M.

When they did meet, Maddox said, it "turned into farce." If she wanted to understand the company she would need a map, he said with a condescension also borrowed from his father, and she smiled as he produced a simplistic and crude legend with three boxes representing MCC, MGN, and the private side. So Maddox drew out from her briefcase her own version of the empire, with forty-six boxes linked like a railway network showing the various forms of ownership. "He went really quiet," she said. Then Kevin began to quibble over various minor points, such as the ownership of a soccer team.

They moved on to talk about the debt, and Maddox mentioned a figure of £750 million to $1 billion ($1.2 to 1.6 billion). "I can accept that," said Kevin, whose initial confidence had vanished. After Maddox left his office, they both knew the kind of story she would publish, its likely reception in the financial community, and its probable effect on the MCC share price. That was one reason for his three phone calls to his father on the boat.

Outside the financial community, where Maxwell's City problems were only half understood, there was more support for the idea that he had suffered a heart attack while standing at the guardrail and the seizure had caused him to topple over the side. Quite sensible people believed this for weeks, though most of the yachting fraternity were skeptical that he had fallen over by accident. "It would be about as hard as falling off a cross-Channel ferry," said Nick Baker of Camper & Nicholson, the international yacht agency that chartered the boat. The railings of the 430-ton, 180-foot *Lady Ghislaine* were waist to chest high. Sarah Norbury of *Boat International* magazine agreed: "Having studied the boat I am extremely surprised that he should have gone missing from it. The safety standards are of the highest level." Nothing was conclusive, and this was only the beginning of a tiresome but typical round of a newspaper game called anything-your-expert-can-say-mine-can-say-different. Maxwell was dead but Maxwellia continued to exist. So Mike Insull, two years a skipper on the *Lady Ghislaine*, said he thought Maxwell could have toppled over because of his size in relation to the height of the railings.

I interviewed two former crewmembers aboard a yacht in drydock at Portsmouth with railings approximately the height of those on *Lady Ghislaine*. We tried to fall over. It appeared unlikely that Maxwell could have done so, even with his bulk, and top-heaviness, which made his center of gravity different from ours. But the *Mirror* loyally came up with a farfetched story headlined NEW PLUNGE DRAMA ON MAXWELL YACHT about a "burly sailor," none other than rugby-playing Yorkshireman Mark Atkins, who had "nearly toppled" off the boat. It would be mild by comparison with what followed.

Two days after the death, virtually everyone agreed that Maxwell had died of a heart attack because the investigating magistrate on Gran Canaria, Luis Gutierrez San Juan, issued a statement after the first postmortem saying: "The provisional result given by forensic authority points to a natural death before Maxwell hit the water." There was little water in the lungs, he said, so "it does not seem there was death by drowning." The three-hour "initial" postmortem was carried out by three pathologists, and each of the three was induced to talk on different days to different reporters and to say different things, none of them in fairness in the slightest bit indiscreet or misleading.

But even the blanket of quotes, once garnered and fed into the febrile mind of the reporting rumor factory, could be teased into mysteries. Dr. Louisa Garcia Cohen warned early on about placing "too much importance" on marks on the face. The amateur Sherlocks nodded. Dr. Maria José Meilan Ramos said: "There is always the possibility of a substance in the body that wasn't found." Aha, the poison possibility. The senior of the three, Dr. Carlos Lopez de Lamela, director of the Las Palmas Institute of Forensic Medicine, complained that his mortuary was not well enough equipped for certain crucial tests. So, Watson, there was room for error.

The headlines came thick and fast over the weeks in spite of de Lamela stating categorically that "nothing in principle supports the theory of a violent death," backed by the investigating judge Isabel Oliva, who asked everyone to wait for the official postmortem report. Innumerable officials, onlookers, and experts were quoted or encouraged to leak tidbits of information. Wild speculation, fueled by rumor and the completely artificial creation of nonexistent "errors" or "gaps," turned it into a Kennedyesque affair.

We would hear of murder by assassin, of a mysterious boat that shadowed the *Lady Ghislaine*, of poison to induce a heart attack, of frogmen boarding by stealth—a previously untried feat on a smooth-sided yacht moving at fifteen knots.

Then conspiracy theorists got their fix with the *Guardian*, of all papers, offering an apparently sober full-page article of fallacious analysis in which the writer tried to argue that the body in the sea might not have been Robert Maxwell's after all. I read this piece, summarized on the front page under the headline REVELATIONS DEEPEN MYSTERY OVER ROBERT MAXWELL'S DEATH with incredulity. By suggesting there were inconsistencies and discrepancies, most of which were the result of the normal errors that can be found in the reporting in the first hours of any major news event and which had been dealt with days before, the *Guardian* actually claimed that the corpse had not been properly identified "other than [by] the word of his family."

Apart from the fact that this was untrue because Captain Rankin had positively identified the body earlier, it was tantamount to calling his wife and eldest son liars and parties to a bizarre conspiracy. On reflection, I am sure senior executives on the paper with a reputation for exposing some of the more sensational aspects of tabloid reporting regretted this contribution. Betty reacted angrily the next day and the press wondered at its own activities for a moment, summed up brilliantly in one *Daily Mail* headline MAX-WELL ADRIFT ON A SEA OF RUMORS and elsewhere called an "irresponsible rush to judgment." It did not stem the tide, and the nonsense continued, blinding us to proper clues, on hindsight, that did merit attention. Four days after the death, one excellent example was presented as "the mystery of the doors" with references to Agatha Christie.[16] The writer asked why the two doors to Maxwell's state-room were shut when Maxwell was known never to close doors. This was overlooked but if the sleuths had followed it up perhaps the important fact that the doors were also locked would have emerged sooner.

Journalists were certainly right about one mystery, the speed with which the Maxwell family managed to persuade the Spanish authorities to release the body for burial. Given that the initial postmortem had been inconclusive, providing only a provisional finding about how he died and no clue about what had led up to the death, it was strange that they allowed the body to be flown out of their jurisdiction within four days. The only holdup appeared to be that his coffin was too big for the plane and a larger one had to be found.

The family's haste to reach Israel stemmed, we were told, from the Jewish tradition of quick burials. It meant that the British insurers facing a £20 million ($32 million) payout, had to move fast, sending off Dr. Iain West, of Guy's Hospital, to Tel Aviv to carry out a second postmortem with all the disadvantages of organs having been disturbed and, in some cases, removed. The body had been partially embalmed as well, in readiness for the funeral. West worked with three Israeli pathologists, and they were videotaped as they went about their grisly task. It would be months before West presented his final report.

The next day, on Sunday 10 November, the body of the man born

Abraham Lajbi Hoch was buried in the city that figured in one of the erroneous proverbs I often heard him utter: "Jerusalem wasn't built in a day." Had he not also said some five years before: "I was born a Jew and I shall die a Jew." As Betty put it: "Now the circle closes. He has returned to his roots."

Perhaps a senior Israeli Treasury official captured best Maxwell's late enthusiasm for the country by describing him as "a missing rich uncle who suddenly turned up on our doorstep."[17] Now he would be on their doorstep forever, on the Mount of Olives, in the eternal company of the rich, the powerful, and the prophetic (Zechariah is believed to be buried at the foot of the mount).

Funerals in Jerusalem, even one such as this attended by the mightiest in the state and by dignitaries from around the world, are austere. The body is consigned to the ground in a white shroud rather than a coffin. In the ceremony before, Maxwell's son, Philip, his voice often weak with emotion, said of his father: "He climbed one hundred mountains and moved one thousand more."

Among the listening mourners were six of the children—Christine, the missing seventh, was pregnant and could not fly; planeloads of friends from Britain, including Smith New Court chairman Sir Michael Richardson, Gerald Kaufman, Labour's shadow foreign secretary, and Samuel Pisar, who had helped to organize the funeral, and several members of the Israeli cabinet.

Israel's President, Chaim Herzog, who fought in the British army in the war, was effusive in describing the dead tycoon "a colossus . . . a figure of almost mythological stature. We in Israel have been deeply moved by his feeling for this land and our cause; the feeling that led him to profound concern and commitment, expressed in significant involvement in many facets of our struggle for economic independence, for the absorption of the Russian immigrants, for the security of the country, and for the achievement of peace." That reference to security gave the Mirrorgate conspiracists a smile of undeserved satisfaction.

Ehud Olmert, the Israeli health minister, recalled Maxwell saying of his own career: "Not so bad for a Jewish boy from the *shtetl*." Said Olment: "Indeed, Bob Maxwell, not so bad at all."

Next day's *Daily Mirror* editorial picked up the same theme under the headline THE LAST TYCOON, saying: "Nobody has come from less and achieved more."

Lots of people wanted to know why this man who had always exhibited such pride in being British should choose to be buried in Israel rather than some Oxford churchyard. Why did he have a quasi-state funeral? Was it money or the Mossad connection? One writer thought it reflected "the loyalty of an instinctive Zionist who never lived in the Jewish state but became its biggest single foreign investor and was a useful and well-connected friend."[18]

I would dispute the investment claim, but the rest makes sense. The instinctive Zionism was a memory of his mother's political passion; he did help to bring out to Israel a group of children from Chernobyl so that they could get better treatment; he did, as I have said, act as a go-between for Shamir with Gorbachev. As far as the Jewish state was concerned, he had helped them. But we cannot afford to look at this compartment alone. We must not forget that he also made a lot of money in an illicit fashion in Israel, selling his take in Scitex for a vast profit. Those shares were not his to sell—they belonged to the pension funds—and yet, once sold, the money went to one of his private companies. He paid for his heroic status in Israel by robbing pensioners in Britain.

After the funeral, the detective-thriller writers returned to their work, with more crazy theories based on fantasy—even sexual fantasy, though there was little to merit it—and imagination. The two female stewardesses suffered early on from unsympathetic questioning. Susanne Kjaer, a Dane, said: "It is being suggested me and Liza were Mr. Maxwell's lovers. We were not. We only served coffee, cleaned up, and made his bed."[19]

No luck, so on to the next bit of nonsense. His last taxi ride was "mysterious" because the cab stopped twice. Where did he go? Whom did he see? Answer: the taxi never stopped twice. There was no mystery. Another paper suggested a "strange" package had arrived for him in Funchal before he set off on his last voyage. It appeared to have been some routine documents from London. The *Daily Mirror* tried to inject sinister motives into the fact that Ghislaine "shredded documents" aboard the yacht soon after his death. It led nowhere. One of the funniest stemmed from Dr. Lamela, revealing that Maxwell had a partially digested banana in his stomach; of course, he had fallen overboard after slipping on a banana peel.

Finally, on 13 December, 1991, the Spanish pathologists released their medical report. His death was from natural causes, they concluded, and Judge Isabel Oliva said he "probably" died by accident and recommended the case be closed since she could find no evidence of a crime. Dr. West was near to completing his report to the insurers, with a different conclusion from that of his Spanish colleagues, and the investigator for the loss adjusters was still interviewing so his report was far from finished. It would be two months before their reports were made public.

As the wild theories continued, I recalled a remark Maxwell had made to Nicholas Tomalin of *The Sunday Times* back in 1973, after one of the Department of Trade reports had savaged him: "If things were half as bad as some people persist in believing I'd have retired with a bottle of Scotch and a pistol a long time ago."

When Maxwell set off on his journey things were a hundred times worse than people could ever have imagined. Suicide was not such a farfetched idea once Maxwell's darkest secret was shared by the world.

17

"He Said He Would Leave Us Nothing"

Robert Maxwell had taken his life because he could not face up to the public ignominy of being revealed as a cheat and a thief. He realized that his powers as a bluffer were unlikely to keep him out of jail because he understood just how close his empire was to crumbling. For months he had juggled with money, but he had run out of collateral to raise loans and run out of banks to borrow from. Maxwell knew the game was up, as his sons were to discover in the course of the next thirty days.

Maxwell's death in the ocean left his sons to flail helplessly in his sea of debt. Their first strokes, however, were swift and apparently effortless. Kevin, the younger, cool, clever one, assumed the chairmanship of Maxwell Communications Corporation while Ian, the awfully nice chap with a winning smile, stepped up as chairman of the Mirror Group.

Within minutes of the suspension of share dealing, before Maxwell's body was found, Kevin held a meeting in his office with his father's confidant, Eric Sheinberg of Goldman Sachs. It is not known what was said but some kind of agreement was obviously reached about a halt on share sales. Goldman did circumvent the London suspension by selling two million MGN shares in New York that day, but it appears to have been their only trade. It must have been nerve-racking for Goldman, still holding more than twenty-four million MCC and forty million MGN shares.

So Kevin's first deal was, in his eyes, successful, and his father would have been proud of him. But I knew, as did hundreds of others in the financial world, he was swimming against the tide.

Like most other commentators at the time I did not know exactly what Maxwell had done, but I was more convinced than ever that we were about to find out. For weeks I had kept a close eye on the relentless decline of the MCC share price, noting the low level of trading and waiting for that inevitable moment when the fall would trigger the banks' call for more collateral. That would be the signal for "meltdown," the complete collapse of the Maxwell empire. No one had watched it as keenly as Maxwell who, as the spider at the center of the web, had been the only person who knew the hopelessness of his position. How could Kevin, let alone Ian, hope to reverse the irreversible?

There was an early diversion from the financial dramas when Seymour Hersh and his publishers, Faber & Faber, decided to take advantage of the death to kick more life back into their Mossad spy scandal. Hersh chose the afternoon of Maxwell's disappearance to announce that he was about to produce new evidence of *Mirror* arms-dealing skulduggery. There would be a video giving incontrovertible proof of not only Nick Davies but yet another *Mirror* reporter carrying out arms-deal negotiations in a Geneva hotel. The new gunrunning reporter was supposed to be Frank Thorne, a man I have known well for twenty years. While I was predisposed not to believe the allegations, this was the most preposterous and laughable of them all.

I called Thorne to commiserate and to offer support, not even to question him, since I knew it was a pack of lies. So did the rest of Fleet Street, and the usual rivalry among British papers gave way to unanimity. *The Sunday Times* and the *Sunday Express,* along with the *Daily Mirror,* exposed the new Hersh "story" as a hoax perpetrated by a well-known con man, a fact that the author himself was forced to admit days later.

For an investigative reporter of Hersh's reputation, it was a lamentable lapse and hardly added credence to his original disputed story, the more so because the *Mirror* had tried to warn Faber in advance that they were the victims of a hoax. And that, unbelievably, was the last we heard of the Mirrorgate saga. I shall be surprised if any of the writs ever lead to conclusive court action.

Back in the real world, Kevin tackled his first major headache, the threat of police action from the Swiss Bank Corporation (SBC) because of the outstanding loan to Adviser (188), the Maxwell company. SBC were told that the original collateral, the portfolio of shares, had been sold and that the money had been paid to the Robert Maxwell Group and to one of the Bishopsgate companies. Adviser (188) told them it would all be sorted out but, right now, it could not meet the loan and was therefore withdrawing its offer to repay. What they could offer instead were forty million MGN shares. It did not impress the Swiss, who said the repayment offer was irrevocable. The Serious Fraud Office, the special Scotland Yard unit set up to look into financial crime, was informed. Kevin had not found a quick-fix solution.

In public, during their first couple of days at the helm, the bereaved brothers presented an impressive front of calm in the face of crisis. In a different style from their father but drawing on his public-relations skills, they coolly denied there was any need for a sell-off, agreed with the banks to launch a steering committee to organize repayments of debts, even completed the sale of MCC's 55.6 percent stake in the American-based Berlitz lanugage school to Fukutake of Japan for a healthy $265 million. Kevin was no stranger to London's financial district and had supporters, among them a director at merchant bankers Henry Ansbacher who said, "He has put to bed more deals than most in the City. He is already respected in his own right for his abilities."[1]

Kevin gave an upbeat view of MCC to the many inquirers: "The financial problems are more in the eye of the beholder than they are real... there is no pressure... We can cope." Over at MGN, Ian wrote a long article for the *Daily Mirror* headlined MY PLEDGE TO YOU, promising that the paper would go on as before. Once stock-market trading restarted, MCC shares plunged from 121 pence ($1.93) to 74 pence ($1.18) while MGN took off from 77.5 pence ($1.24) to 106 pence ($1.69).These movements had been anticipated because MCC was perceived as too indebted to offer a return, while MGN was viewed as worthwhile. Kevin was surprised by the MCC dive, which did slow once it was confirmed that the banks were prepared to give them a breathing space.

The banks were plainly embarrassed by the quantity and size of the loans, having discovered only that week each other's various commitments to Maxwell and realizing that many loans appeared to be unsecured. There was truth in the *Financial Times*'s comment that "the sound of the banks closing ranks was clearly audible."[2] It was in their interest to keep the companies trading if possible though the share prices of MCC and MGN would be crucial.

Every decision was fraught with impending disasters. Should, for instance, MCC pay its interim dividend? If it did not, the share price would fall and the family would get no money from its share holdings, so there would be no relief of the private debt. If it decided to pay, it would need still more loans because there was no money.

The financial press, freed from Maxwellian legal threats and sure of MCC's impending implosion, raised the "black hole theory." Briefly, one wit explained, this amounted to a single sentence: What was owed, to whom and how often? The fear of Maxwell having pledged the same collateral twice, maybe more times over, began to concern banks as they discussed details of their loans with each other. I conjured up fantasies of bankers swapping information and suddenly exclaiming: "But we've got the same ten percent!"

There were odd signs of discontent at certain banks. The American Citibank, for instance, which already had twenty-five million MCC shares, equal to almost 4 percent of the company, took possession of a further two million as "a warning shot" when a loan was not repaid. But Kevin announced that MCC was to sell off Macmillan Computer Publishing to Paramount for $157.5 million, so there was some money coming in. He announced, sensibly, that the battery of Maxwell secretaries was going, along with the cars, jets, and the yacht. In public, at least, he was making the right moves.

Then the *Independent on Sunday* revelation on 17 November about the Serious Fraud Office investigating the Swiss Bank Corporation's complaint over its unpaid £60 million ($96 million) loan changed everything. Repeating what was to become his mantra, Kevin said, "There is no pressure on anyone and we are now going to sit down and view the business."[3] No pressure? MCC dropped to 60 pence (96 cents) while MGN fell to 117 pence ($1.87); the banks were asking awkward questions, and the Fraud office was about to raid Maxwell House. *Mirror* editor Richard Stott advised Ian that to ignore the story would be a public-relations error, so the paper carried the fact of the SFO inquiry tucked away under the City prices, which struck me as a clue to a changing wind at the *Mirror*.

The announcement of the Serious Fraud Office investigation was the first crack, and the City realized it too. An analyst said: "Whenever you get this sort of fraud inquiry all bets are off."[4] The investors were off, too, and MCC's price fell by 14 pence (22 cents) to 46 pence (73 cents). Ian Watson, a Maxwell aide, said: "It's like Dubrovnik here—we're being bombed from every side." But you would not have known it from the impassive Kevin. In an article aptly headed THE BOYS ON THE BURNING DECK," Kevin told *The Sunday Times* that the Swiss Bank situation "was the greatest surprise since Bob died," adding that "the timing could not be worse."[5] It was strange that he should have expressed surprise. Had he forgotten his meeting with SBC's lawyers on 1 November, and the attempts to delay repayment on 5 November, and his offer of MGN shares?

So fifteen days after Maxwell's death, the core of his empire had lost two-thirds of its value, diving from about £900 million ($1.4 billion) to £300 million ($480 million). For two weeks the banks had been patient with Kevin, but the speed of the collapse suggested that they could not go on being helpful out of a sense of propriety. Then again, what were they to do? They had outstanding loans to the private companies dependent on the MCC share price. If they tried to sell their shares they could not hope to regain anything like their outstanding loans. So they could not do anything that might cause the share price to fall any faster. On the other hand there might come a point at which getting something was better than nothing at all. How long would it, could it, last?

The young Maxwells were about to discover that their name was against them; their father had left them, as he always promised, nothing. Nothing but debts, drama, public humiliation and, possibly, worse. MCC fell by another 10 pence (16 cents) to 36 pence (57 cents) while MGN rose 12 pence (19 cents) to 126 pence ($2), the highest-ever, on unfounded rumors that Australian media magnate Kerry Packer was to bid for the group. At this point it looked as though the sale of MGN might relieve the pressure a little. Since the family held 51 percent, it might be able to cash in and pay off some loans.

I found myself writing for the daily newspaper *Today* about the unfolding drama of the Maxwell empire and kept in touch with as many insiders as I could. The phone calls would have made fascinating listening. One morning I would hear, confidentially of course, that everything was just fine. By the early evening the same speaker would say, "It's hell. He can't hold the line anymore." And so it went on for several days, with Kevin pinning his hopes on the banks agreeing to a moratorium. What the Maxwells needed was time; what the banks needed was an orderly agreement to ensure repayment of massive loans. They grew more anxious as the extent of their folly leaked to the public.

There were more than forty banks with outstanding loans totaling about $1.4 billion, some of which were unsecured, while others were underwritten with weakening MCC or volatile MGN shares. The list was mind-boggling, with banks from Britain, France, the United States, Switzerland, Japan, and a host of smaller countries. Some of the "exposures" as banks refer to such loans, showed why there was alarm: NatWest was thought to have £200 million ($320 million) outstanding; Lloyds £170 million ($272 million); Barclays £150 million ($240 million); Midland £140 million ($224 million); Swiss Bank Corporation had £56 million ($89.6 million) apart from its £60 million ($96 million) First Tokyo loan; a syndicate headed by Crédit Lyonnais, which included Crédit Agricole and Societé Generale of France and Japan's Long Term Credit Bank, was still owed £150 million ($240 million) for the 1988 Macmillan purchase. Goldman Sachs and Lehman Brothers were both owed millions. The scale of bank debt, in effect to one man, was without precedent.

With the MCC share price at such a low level after the announcement of a fraud inquiry, newspapers started to predict collapse.
MAXWELL EMPIRE FACING DISINTEGRATION, said one headline,
while another referred to the fact that receivers were on standby.
Kevin, trying to narrow the drama by talking only about MCC as if
the great weight of private debt were unrelated, said MCC would sell
whatever was necessary. "There are no sacred cows," he said, though
there appeared to be no cows at all. He told the *Wall Street Journal*
that MCC could meet its October 1992 $750 million loan repayment
already. Kevin sounded as if he had swallowed a looped tape: "There
is no pressure on MCC from its bankers, so why get panicked?"

Smith New Court chairman Sir Michael Richardson joined in the
charade: "There is no real pressure at MCC and no pressure at all at
the *Mirror*."[6]

Real pressure was coming. "It emerged yesterday," said the
Guardian, "that several creditors may have been promised the same
assets as security for loans."[7] At last the whisper had been published,
and it came on the eve of the banks' meeting, chaired by NatWest
director John Melbourn, which agreed to a four-week suspension,
freezing repayments on loans totaling £850 million ($1.36 billion).
The banks even lent £5 million ($8 million) to the private companies
to allow them to continue trading. Pictures after the meeting showed
the smiling brothers, who were said to have impressed their bankers.
MCC's share price rose by 11 pence (17 cents) to 55 pence (88 cents),
its first major move upward since Maxwell's death three weeks
before, but *Independent* columnist Clare Dobie wrote presciently:
"Don't be fooled by the rally in MCC shares... The shares will
collapse again."

Questions were being asked about the "optimistic" valuations of
assets presented to the bankers' meeting when Kevin stunned the
banks and the City by postponing MCC's interim results. Once more
borrowing a favorite phrase of his father's he said, "It would be
appropriate in current circumstances" to delay the report. MCC
dived 10 pence (16 cents) to 45 pence (72 cents).

"This is all rather odd," said one commentator. "The picture
becomes gloomier by the hour."[8] Lex of the *Financial Times* witheringly referred to its abruptness as being "almost an act of homage"
to Maxwell.[9]

The MCC share price dropped to 36 pence (57 cents) at the end of the week, and those banks with shares as collateral were now holding virtually worthless stock. But worse was about to come. The Sunday papers on 1 December were rightly doubtful about whether the brothers could hold on. One thought they might have to give up virtually the entire business empire and quoted a Rothschild's source who said: "It's like untangling a ball of string. Nobody appears to have any knowledge of how it was tangled up except Robert Maxwell." That evening, at last, the reason for its entanglements was revealed.

A meeting was called at night in Maxwell House attended by Kevin and Ian, Peter Laister, and Alan Clements, independent directors respectively of MCC and MGN, and various bankers. They were addressed by Richard Stone of Coopers & Lybrand Deloitte, whose fifteen-member accountancy team had uncovered the truth about Maxwell's theft of millions from the pension funds. The funds and the companies, said Stone, had been milked of funds on a substantial scale.

Ian McIntosh, of Samuel Montagu merchant bank, arranger of ring-fencing for the MGN stock issue, sat with his head in his hands saying, "This is awful." Clements and Laister were open-mouthed. Stone, in somber mood, said initial inquiries showed that they could not account for at least £300 million ($480 million) in pension funds. Furthermore, MCC had lent £275 million ($440 million) to Headington Investments and the Robert Maxwell Group. MGN had lent £97 million ($155 million) for the supposed investment in gilts through London & Bishopsgate International Investment Management.

Ian was said to be "incoherent," devastated. Kevin remained calm.

While the Monday-morning papers speculated about the chances of a sale of the American companies, or likely bidders for the Mirror Group and assorted buyers for other little bits of the empire, the empire was about to implode. The sons knew the game was up. Share dealings were suspended, with MCC having fallen to 35 pence (56 cents), its lowest ever; and MGN remained at its 125 pence ($2) flotation price. There is little doubt it would have plunged once the pension-fund news was made public. The suspension was supposed to await "clarification of the financial position of the Maxwell family companies." The *Financial Times*'s Lex rightly thought this "an undeniably ugly turn of events."

There was bafflement among most commentators until the next day when the truth finally emerged, albeit only a sanitized version. Kevin and Ian resigned as chairmen and members of the MCC and MGN boards, along with the ubiquitous Michael Stoney, because of "a conflict of interests," namely their involvement in the private companies that were at the center of a massive plunder of various company pension funds, most notably that of the Mirror Group.

Stone's report on the finances to bankers a couple of days later left them visibly shaken. The headline on page 2 of his report was not the sort to encourage tabloid readers to rush out and buy a paper: INTER-COMPANY INDEBTEDNESS FAR HIGHER THAN EXPECTED ON NOVEMBER 25. Millions of people would understand soon enough that the facts contained under that heading would put the final seal on the Maxwell Myth. The accountants had discovered that Maxwell's private companies owed at least £602 million ($963.2 million) to the public companies, MCC and MGN, and detailed just how much each company owed.

It was a bit like a magistrates' court charge sheet. "On such and such a day you, Robert Maxwell, did remove £29 million ($46.4 million) from MCC and place it within your private investment company Bishopsgate Investment Management and subsequently you did then transfer it to your private family company, Headington Holdings." After that the money vanished. As did many other tranches of money on a circuitous route to banks to raise loans or used to fund his share-support operation. The report also pointed out that collateral might be pledged twice and much of it would be disputed because pension funds were likely to try to reclaim it as stolen property.

The report went on to explain the risk to the banks. Those with security in the form of shares—nine banks and one syndicate—were facing losses on their total loans of £655 million ($1 billion) because of the fall in the value of the shares, which in the case of MCC would probably be worthless. There were a further eight banks and three syndicates with only partial security on loans totaling £478 million ($764 million). A third group of banks had no security for £45 million ($72 million) in loans.[10]

The enormity of the theft was almost too great for people to visualize: £526 million ($841.6 million) had been taken. The brothers had tried to stave off the end by mentioning a "white knight" who was supposed to be prepared to inject £200 million ($320 million) into the private companies. Bankers sniffed. For Ian and Kevin it was not a case of merely walking away. They were revealed as pension-fund trustees, as directors of the key companies Maxwell had used to siphon away money, and some money was said to have been removed *after* Maxwell's death. How could that be explained? We learned that the total Maxwellian debt stood at about £2.7 billion ($4.3 billion). At a press conference, Kevin said without apparent emotion, "Clearly we did not know everything, clearly he had a style of business run on a need-to-know basis."

The pension revelations totally altered the tone of the Maxwell coverage. The Swiss Bank saga was too complex for most people to follow, but everybody could understand the theft of pensions. The dam of good manners burst and a reservoir of resentment flowed as journalists inside and outside the Mirror Group felt free at last to tell the world the truth.

Before anyone had seemingly had a chance to grasp what had happened, the paper that Robert Maxwell was alleged to have saved turned on him. MILLIONS MISSING FROM *MIRROR*, said the huge front-page headline and inside, across two pages, it announced the departure of Ian—the man who had given readers a pledge of loyalty only a month before—under the headline: HE HAD TO GO BECAUSE HIS NAME IS MAXWELL.

Over the coming days and weeks the paper not only disowned Maxwell, but ridiculed him in the most artless and tasteless display of impotent rage. It was to be expected that the rival *Sun* would take this opportunity to heap abuse on the man who had so often scorned it. But its full-page editorial was the most savage and contemptuous anyone could recall, concluding: "Maxwell's resting place is close by the Garden of Gethsemane where Judas Iscariot betrayed Christ for thirty pieces of silver. He should feel at home there."

As thousands of people began to contemplate their fate, facing the worry of losing their income at a time of their lives when there was no way to earn more, it was difficult even for *Mirror* journalists to disagree with that view.

Ernie Burrington, the new MGN chairman, could not conceal his dismay, referring to the pensions plunder as the "increasingly desperate acts of a desperate man." The *Mirror*'s editor, Richard Stott, said, "We have been heavily mugged." At a journalists' union meeting columnist Paul Foot dared to say what everyone was thinking: "We are just delighted he is dead." The *Daily Mail* editorial said: "Was there ever such a bloated humbug." The *Daily Telegraph* headline reveled in the freedom to say at last, "Yes, he was a crook."

One month after Maxwell's death the appalling legacy from his corrupt empire became headline news around the world, attracting massive coverage. Over the weeks it became obvious that his desperate acts of plunder had touched countless thousands of people, hundreds of companies, scores of institutions, and his family, which he had lauded as "my greatest success," especially those members of it closest to him. Having clasped his two youngest boys to his bosom, invited them into Maxwellia, he had left them to bear the brunt of society's outrage.

As the administrators moved in, gradually placing more and more of the 430 Maxwell-related companies under their control, the revelatory drips became a torrent. Kevin's speedy sale of Berlitz the day after his father's death could not go ahead because the relevant shares were "missing," presumed drowned. In the end it was discovered that Maxwell had used virtually all the 56 percent Berlitz stock owned by MCC to raise private loans with five banks—Swiss Volksbank, Shearson Lehman, Crédit Suisse, Advest, and Morgan Stanley. He had removed the shares from MCC to place them under his private control and then put these up as collateral for loans. To him, it was just a switch of pockets again. More banks revealed their holdings, giving a clue to the widening spread of Maxwell's search for funds. A syndicate of foreign banks—including French-owned Paribas's Swiss and Luxembourg operations, the Luxembourg government-owned savings bank and United Overseas Bank of Geneva—informed the London Stock Exchange they had interest in 20 percent of MCC shares pledged as security on a £100 million ($160 million) loan. Then NatWest, so long a Maxwell backer, revealed it owned 30 percent of MGN, a third of the company stock issued only months before. It was a graphic example of the way the staff at the Mirror Group would not be able to control ownership in the future.

In early December there was said to be a total of £770 million ($1.23 billion) missing, including £350 million ($560 million) from Mirror pension funds and £79 million ($126 million) from other Maxwell company pension funds. With ever-larger figures for his thefts emerging almost every day, financial commentators struggled to find adjectives to describe the dimension of his robbery. *The Sunday Times*'s Ivan Fallon explained it best by stating simply, "In the twenty-five years I have been writing about the City I have never come across anything even approaching the Maxwell story." But people were already asking how it had come to pass.

Why had the City institutions not taken to heart those three reports of the inquiry by the Board of Trade twenty years before? One of the inspectors, Sir Ronald Leach, now eighty-four and living in Jersey, issued an I-told-you-so statement it was impossible to fault for its brevity and sincerity. "I said he wasn't a suitable person to be in charge of a public company. It was his capacity to regard the world as his own, which we thought was extremely dangerous." Exactly. All those years before they had identified the existence of Maxwellia, where things were because he said they were. The banks had had their chance to choose to do business with Maxwell or not, but what of the employees who had no choice?

There were tears among staff at the New York *Daily News* and *The European* when the papers were placed into receivership. Elsewhere in the far-flung empire, echoes of the scandal reverberated. The *Kenya Times* went into receivership; the *Irish Tatler* was forced to close; in Bulgaria, trades unionists occupied a hotel and business school that they alleged Maxwell had bought for less than a fifth of its value from the former Communist government; two Swiss banks announced profit slumps because of outstanding loans; Gruner & Jahr, partners in the Berlin paper company, accused Kevin of failing to pay back £2.1 million ($3.36 million) "borrowed" from their joint venture. Wherever Maxwell had alighted and helped himself to another morsel there were problems.

By coincidence, it was also the end of the line for a statesman Maxwell had courted for years. One day there was an interesting juxtaposition of stories, with the latest episode in the decline and fall of Robert Maxwell on the same page as the departure from the world stage of his supposed friend President Gorbachev. "As the Soviet Union crumbled around him, the once all-powerful President conceded, 'I have done all that I can.'"[11]

It was open season now on Maxwell, and, apart from the indelicate reporting of the *Daily Mirror*, its sister *Sunday Mirror* outdid it by several degrees in publishing the sordid tale of a twenty-one-year-old secretary who claimed Maxwell had seduced her, while the *News of the World* ran a farfetched story about a woman who claimed she had overheard Maxwell plotting to vanish by staging his own death. One week we were expected to believe that Maxwell spied for the Soviet Union, according to the KGB, and the next that he spied for Britain, according to a different KGB man.[12] I think this was about as believable as the Mossad allegations.

In the *Mail on Sunday* was a story lots of people thought was fantasy, but I knew better. Author Wendy Leigh—biographer of Arnold Schwarzenegger—told of a seven-year romance with Maxwell that had begun when she went to interview him for a book in September 1976. Although this tale was universally disparaged, Wendy had told me, and others, about it years before. Apart from the fact that I know her to be a truth-teller, every quote from Maxwell in her four-page saga read as if it had tripped from Maxwell's lips. She could not have made up the form and content of his speech so perfectly without having been in his company for long periods. What's more, and surely for the cynics this is a clinching factor, she asked for no payment for telling her story. "I just wanted to show there was a romantic side to him that no one else was telling," she told me. Having reread her article once more, I think the relationship fits perfectly within the compartmentalized, secretive world we know he lived.

At first Kevin and Ian Maxwell graciously agreed to help trace every penny of the missing millions. Soon they decided to say nothing at all as the Serious Fraud Office launched itself into five separate inquiries, almost all of which required the boys to provide information. After the Swiss Bank investigation, there were formal inquiries into the pension-fund frauds, the transfers of money out of MGN, the share-support operation, and the removal of money from MCC.

Would Kevin help? He decided to fight in the High Court for the right to remain silent, not wishing to incriminate himself, in a series of hearings that overlapped with another polite request he and his brother ignored—an "invitation" from the Parliamentary Select Committee on Social Security which, by coincidence, had been sitting to consider pension law. Once the scandal broke, the committee altered its terms of reference to include the Maxwell affair.

The administrators asked the court to freeze Kevin's assets and to remove his and Ian's passports while inquiries continued. It was thought Kevin might be planning to sell his £1 million ($1.6 million) London home. But the judge did allow Kevin £1,500 ($2,400) a week for living expenses.[13] Kevin was being assailed on all sides; he was sued for £450 million ($720 million) by the liquidators of Bishopsgate Investment Management, and it was revealed that his signature was on papers moving pensioners' assets from the investment fund to a private company.[14]

Within a couple of weeks it was shown that both Kevin and Ian had signed documents authorizing the transfer of millions to the private companies.[15] In such circumstances Kevin was perhaps fortunate to obtain his passport for a trip to New York during a late-night High Court sitting. There was an amusing incident before the hearing when Mr. Justice Harman found reporters and photographers outside his house while leaving for court. He lost his temper and was pictured aiming a kick at a taxi driver under the mistaken impression he was a journalist.

On his Concorde trip to America, Kevin was confronted by *Daily Mirror* reporter Harry Arnold, who coaxed him into talking. It was an old-fashioned scoop that did not get its due. "I have to be honest," Kevin said. "The debts are so enormous that when everything is sorted out there will be nothing left." He also described reports of his father as a villain and a crook as "fair comment."

Kevin went on: "The whole involvement of the pension funds and the worries of the pensioners themselves is something which is extremely saddening. I am desperately sorry for them."

Arnold asked, knowing now what had happened, if Kevin had changed his mind about how his father had died.

"Suicide? Not the remotest possibility. For my father to commit suicide is as likely as for me to abscond from Britain because of the pressures. It's ludicrous." He added, "He left me this mess and I have to sort it out."

Later, in New York, where *Newsweek* was carrying the headline about his father THE CROOK OF THE CENTURY, Kevin was said to look "eerily composed" when addressing journalists outside the *Daily News* building. In that talk he said, "Some of the events are so shocking I wouldn't believe them in a novel."[16]

Kevin's bout of talkativeness did not persuade him to speak to the administrators even though the High Court ordered him to do so. Advised by George Carman, arguably Britain's most high profile attorney, he appealed. Before that hearing he and Ian were compelled by subpoena to appear in front of the Commons Select Committee and, since it was televised, in front of the British people. If two people staying silent can be said to be compulsive viewing then this was, mainly for Carman's star performance. Kevin and Ian, flanked by their lawyers, George Carman and John Jarvis, refused to answer questions. Their two counsel set out the reasons for the silence, claiming that though no charges had been lodged against the boys they were anticipating them soon. Therefore, they should be granted their constitutional right to silence. The committee retired and thought otherwise.

We were treated to Frank Field MP, the chairman, putting test questions to each brother, who mumbled in turn: "I will answer through my counsel." Carman replied in the first instance: "It is plain and clear and respectful but unambiguous that Kevin is not going to answer any questions."

Afterward Field said he thought the boys were likely to be held in contempt of Parliament. Newspapers greeted the affair differently. According to one, their silence "mocks the law,"[17] but most, like *The Times,* thought it "theatrical . . . a stage-managed climb on to a rolling bandwagon" or "mistaken."[18]

Most commentators defended the right of the brothers not to speak, and the committee eventually put forward a compromise by sending the boys written questions, which were not answered.

However, the Appeal Court decided Kevin could not remain silent, arguing that Britain's Insolvency Act specifically removed the privilege, so he was finally forced to undergo an intense interrogation by Robson Rhodes, the liquidators of Bishopsgate Investment Management, in a closed court over a number of days in early February. That was not all he had to reveal. A number of journalists had been asking how Kevin could afford to pay his enormous legal bills, and the liquidators, who were supposed to prevent any drain on the resources of Maxwell's estate, demanded to know. Kevin agreed to reveal the source of his legal funding to Robson Rhodes as long as it remained secret, though it eventually leaked out.

Back at MCC, administration had run anything but smoothly. The board angered the banks by seeking U.S. bankruptcy protection, so placing a British company under American law. It was, said one banker, "a complete bugger's muddle," as everyone tried to come to grips with how the company was to be sold off to raise cash. The banks' mood was not helped when Price Waterhouse, the accountants appointed in place of Coopers & Lybrand, gave their initial report. Alan Wheatley, the team leader, suggested that £763 million ($1.2 billion) had been improperly removed from shareholders' funds and another £240 million ($384 million) had gone due to property write-downs. So MCC's tangible assets had slumped from £1.1 billion ($1.76 billion) to just £100 million ($160 million).

The debt was so large, said one commentator, it "must qualify for the *Guinness Book of Records*."[19] A banker at the meeting said, "I didn't think I could be shocked any more. But Wheatley's presentation left us open-mouthed. I just cannot come to terms with what Maxwell was up to." With masterly understatement, Brian Pearse, Midland Bank chief executive, said the collapse of the Maxwell empire is "possibly the worst thing that ever happened to the banks." Peter Laister, briefly MCC chairman, said it was "a horror story the like of which I've never seen."

Eventually there was agreement between the U.S. and British administrators on a joint plan of action, and Laister, feeling there was no role for him, quit the company. Before going, the MCC chairman made one telling point: "Perhaps the most awful thing about all this is that the pressure we [the board] were putting on the Maxwells so forcibly last summer to pay off debt to MCC may have tipped them over the edge into plundering the pension funds."[20]

However, Maxwell had long been weakening the hold of the trustees and pulling the wool over the eyes of interested parties, including the professionals paid to ensure everything was aboveboard, as the Commons Committee heard in hearings throughout December and January.

It was a piece of serendipity that the members of the Parliamentary Select Committee on Social Security were concerning themselves with pensions at just the moment the scandal broke and were able to provide a platform, with the added joy of privilege, for a public airing of pensioners' complaints. Better still, the committee had the power to summon all those the pensioners were complaining about, such as the regulators and advisers. All except, of course, Maxwell himself.

What emerged in weeks of hearings was a sad story, each chapter of which showed a new maneuver by Maxwell to frustrate inquiries from people with genuine concerns about their pensions. He had bamboozled them by quoting back at them a host of professional advisers—accountants, actuaries, auditors, and lawyers—who, he said, could see nothing wrong. So why should you, mister, be so worried? As Mike Gallemore, *Sporting Life* editor, and an honest man I have known for some twenty-five years, put it, he had become a pension-fund trustee because of "concern that Robert Maxwell might do what everybody said he might do, and that was pinch the pension fund." But he added, echoing the multitude, it was hard to challenge Maxwell without the evidence. And Maxwell prevented anyone from getting hold of any evidence.

Less than three weeks before Maxwell's death, the Mirror pensioners' lawyer, Giles Orton, received a letter from Nicholson Graham & Jones, attorneys for the pension fund, stating that they considered "the arrangements for making and monitoring its investments perfectly satisfactory."[21] It also said: "Bishopsgate Investment Management applies investment criteria which are designed to benefit the pension fund beneficiaries.[22] However, the attorneys later explained that their reply was specific to the questions they had been asked, based on the assumption that they had been told the truth by Maxwell. When auditors wanted to examine the accounts, Maxwell "requested" that they hold off, and for eight crucial months Coopers & Lybrand Deloitte agreed because they thought it reasonable to do so at the time.[23] After Maxwell's death, as we have seen, it took them just two days to discover what he had been up to.

Captain Peter Jackson, who became a Mirror pension-fund trustee for two years from 1987, after Maxwell acquired British Airways' helicopter division, told the committee Maxwell doctored minutes of trustees' meetings, called them at short notice, and then kept members waiting for hours before conducting business in five or six minutes. He also told how Maxwell had persuaded the trustees to accept the Bishopsgate company as investment fund manager; they received a letter from the fund's attorneys in August 1987 saying that the requirements of the new Financial Services Act, under which Maxwell would have to obtain authorization to conduct investment business from a self-regulatory organization, were time-consuming and expensive. So, urged the letter, Bishopsgate Investment Management, having already been authorized by the Investment Management Regulatory Organization (IMRO), was the best choice to do the job.

Several trustees, such as Gallemore and Brian Chapman, the Mirror fund's general manager, said Maxwell used the IMRO seal of approval as a weapon to defeat any inquirers. Then the committee heard from IMRO, which revealed that its authorization for Maxwell's two Bishopsgate firms did not go through "easily"; there had been "unease" but, said IMRO chief executive, John Morgan: "Maxwell had been endorsed by his successful commercial development, which had been aided and abetted by leading banks."[24] Others, of course, would claim it was the endorsement of IMRO that influenced their decision to deal with Maxwell. And so went the cycle of special privilege into which the so-called outsider had managed to insert himself with such success.

The Investment Management Regulatory Organization even visited Bishopsgate fund managers in June, when stock-lending was well under way, and found nothing irregular.[25] Sadly, we learned that concerned staff at Bishopsgate thought IMRO would discover Maxwell's activities, while IMRO thought the staff should have spoken up. The catalogue of "near misses" grew over the course of the Commons hearings. Accountants Coopers & Lybrand Deloitte said that some of their officials found serious control weaknesses and deficiencies at Bishopsgate Investment Management as early as

February 1991. Stock-lending activities were not documented, and there was no record of the fees these activities were to have generated. But they still saw no need to qualify accounts, nor did they feel they needed to inform regulators or pension-fund trustees.

While the stories were being told, thousands of pensioners started to suffer, and the wide-ranging scale of Maxwell's theft came to light. Although the Mirror fund gained most of the publicity, the smaller funds began to go to the wall first. Pensioners of Floform, a motor trade components offshoot of Maxwell's Hollis Engineering Group, were told there were no assets to pay the December checks.[26] Having sold the company in 1989, Maxwell had retained the firm's pension-fund management, and retired workers in the rest of the Hollis Group began to worry about their pensions. In late January, it was announced that four funds covering four thousand people in the AGB market-research companies were to be closed down. Later, it was announced that £40 million ($64 million) was missing from the fund.[27]

Administrators also decided the giant MCC pension plan covering five thousand workers had to be terminated. Finally, the Mirror Group decided to close its old pension fund in favor of a new scheme, a move greeted by the Association of Mirror Pensioners as a positive step. *Mirror* staff followed up by launching a publicity campaign to embarrass the banks holding £217 million ($347 million) of pension-fund assets, used by Maxwell as security for loans, to return them.

Through a bulletin to members a committee announced they were drawing up a "hit list" of banks holding pension-fund stock.[28] One of the first to respond, NatWest, said it would "probably" repay £20 million ($32 million) as long as MGN was sold at a price equal to its 125 pence-a-share ($2) float value. Most thought the strings unfair. An employee of British International Helicopters, Joe West, was in no doubt that the money should come back from NatWest since the holding had metaphorically "fallen off the back of a lorry."[29]

A video turned up in January with Maxwell warning, in 1988, of the perils of private pensions and extolling the virtues of his company funds.[30] Its message—stay safe, stay with Bob—rested once more on the notion of Maxwell's impeccable character. It was a reminder of Maxwell's duplicity for individuals such as Brian Moss, all thirty years of his working life to date spent with Maxwell. Moss, head of Maxwell Fleet & Facilities, loyal to his boss throughout the 1970s Pergamon debacle, suddenly realized he had nothing to show for his efforts: "I've lost everything I've worked for. Not for one moment did I think he'd take pension money. It was diabolical."

Harry Barrett, managing director of a business communications division, said, "I was going to retire in two years. I reckon he's had half a million of mine."[31]

Terry Pattinson, industrial editor of the *Daily Mirror,* declared: "I must have lost £50,000 ($80,000)... It is quite a shock to realize I have been putting money into a holed bucket going over Niagara Falls."

At least these three were working. The fear for those already retired, in spite of well-meant promises, could not be soothed. John Chaplin, a former *Mirror* colleague of mine years ago, told of his worry once when his £260-a-month ($416) pension check arrived late in November. Would it one day fail to arrive at all?[32]

Even in such a crisis there was some wit; Mirror pensioner Pamela Duveen wrote to the *Independent,* "You remark that the Maxwell family has, for too long, had its cake and eaten it. Sadly, it appears they have eaten mine as well."[33]

Then, in early March 1992, almost four months to the day after Maxwell's death, a major blow came for thousands of people. It was announced that the Mirror Group was suspending pension payments for eighty-five hundred members of the Maxwell Communication Works Pension Scheme from the end of June. There was simply no longer enough money in the Mirror funds to pay those people temporarily brought under its umbrella, but who did not work directly for the paper. MGN agreed, however, to support another twenty-five hundred members who were present or former company employees.

So life was due to change, apparently irreparably, for the staff of eighty-eight disparate printing and publishing companies that Maxwell had gobbled up. There was even a suggestion by Ken Trench, chairman of the Maxwell Private Pensioners' Association, that Maxwell had taken over companies with overfunded pension schemes with the object of removing surpluses. After analyzing reports from various members, he was convinced he could see such a trend emerging.[34] Maxwell was also able, of course, to use the "pensions holiday" provision in every case to avoid making any employer contributions.

The human cost of the Maxwell pension blight was brought home in an interview with Ernest Oborne, ex-Mirror Building manager, who was due to be deprived of his £600-a-month ($960) check. Worry at losing his income had caused him to lose weight, his wife was "absolutely destroyed," they had canceled their annual vacation, cut their shopping list, and were "preparing for penury."[35]

Mr. Oborne's plight was highlighted on March 9, the day the Commons Committee on Social Security released its pensions report. It castigated almost everyone involved in the Maxwell scandal. Chairman Frank Field said:

> If the regulators had acted with a proper degree of suspicion, if the directors had carried out their duties fully, if professional advisers' common sense had been commensurate to their fees, if insiders had been brave enough to resign and talk, if newspaper editors had been prepared to stand up to Maxwell's bile and legal attacks, if brokers and merchant bankers had cared about their tasks as much as they did about their fees, if parliament had not been so beguiled by its own rhetoric about the special status of trust law, the Maxwell pension funds would have been secure.

There are a lot of "ifs" in that piece of hindsight, and I would argue with some of them. Quite how one was expected to fight the law, for instance, remains unclear. However, there was obvious merit in the Committee's comment that during their inquiry into the role of highly paid actuaries, accountants, and lawyers they sometimes felt they were witnessing a bizarre game of pass-the-pensions-parcel.

"Pontius Pilate would have blushed at the spectacle of so many witnesses washing their hands in public...of their responsibilities," said the report. Its major recommendation was to sweep away medieval trust laws. On the subject of the deprived Maxwell pensioners, it stopped short of demanding that the government fund compensation, but it did call on the incoming government to stress to the banks that they had a moral, if not legal, duty to return pension-fund assets. It also called on investment bankers, such as Goldman Sachs, whose "questionable and dubious" transactions in support of

Maxwell had led him to raid funds, to make a "substantial" contribution. Goldman said later it would be rejecting the call.

The last word on this subject undoubtedly belongs to a Scottish manager of one of Maxwell's former companies who said, "Throughout the length and breadth of the land, in this agonizingly protracted affair, there are people going to bed at night wondering if they will wake up to any future at all. We feel like digging him up and hanging him."[36]

18

End of the Empire

In life Maxwell made many people miserable. In death, as we have seen, the misery was to worsen for thousands of people, even those who had left his companies years before. But what of the companies themselves, especially the newspapers, that he left behind? Here, too, the story is one of conflict and confusion. Most remain in a state of limbo as I write.

First and foremost there was the Mirror Group. He considered these papers his pride and joy. Those of us who have worked for one of them for any length of time always considered it to be *our* pride and joy. The newspapers are greater than any owner. Within a couple of days of Maxwell's death the question of what might happen to the Mirror papers became one of the most talked-about topics. I maintained the closest interest in the paper I had "lost," as the drama of Maxwell's duplicity unfolded throughout November. With Ian Maxwell initially in the chair it looked as though life might be quite pleasant for everyone connected with the Mirror.

Almost the only executive decision Ian made was the perfectly decent one of banning phone-sex advertisements from all MGN titles.

These ads were disliked by the staff, especially the women. When I was editor, one of the office's best organizers, Christine Garbutt, who had taken a great personal risk to expose the sordid activities inside one of the phone-sex companies, persuaded almost everyone to sign a petition protesting at the *Mirror* publishing the ads. I was proud to place my name at the top and naïvely thought Maxwell would agree.

"They're worth a million quid," he said, shaking his head as if to suggest I lacked commercial sense. I argued that women were offended—which was already tacitly agreed since the ads were confined to the sports pages—and we were being accused of hypocrisy for exposing shady companies involved in the contemptible trade while taking their money. It was attracting bad publicity also because *The Sun* had banned them. "They're harmless fun—I've listened to them," he said, finally adding, "I'll look at it." We both knew he would not. So full marks to Ian for refusing to follow in his father's footsteps.

On the financial front, there was general agreement that the Group was profitable, but there was also unease once everyone realized the shares had been pledged to banks. Since the Maxwell family's 51 percent stake was in the hands of banks to support loans that could not be repaid, it was obvious that anyone theoretically could buy a major, or even controlling, stake in the Group. This led to the second concern, that the papers might lose their distinctive Labour-supporting political tone. I was not alone in arguing in various TV and radio interviews that for anyone to buy MGN and change its political allegiance would be commercial suicide. As the only major popular newspaper supporting Labour, even Conservatives believed democracy was better served by having the *Daily Mirror* maintain its public identity. However, in what way could the senior executives and staff who shared this view stop someone from acquiring control of the Group? There was no mechanism in a free market to prevent it.

The rosy glow of "freedom" soon passed once the pension plunder emerged and Ian stepped down as chairman at the insistence of almost all the board. Only two directors requested him to stay on. Then the *Daily Mirror* found itself making the headlines as the paper's editor, Richard Stott, decided to solve within a couple of days of each other both the problem of being identified with Maxwell and the problem of the Group's ownership. Overnight he transformed the savior into Satan, and soon after announced to the staff and to the world that he was leading a management buyout of MGN.

Mirror readers awoke on 4 December to discover that Robert Maxwell, who had been acclaimed "a Trojan of a man"—as the heading over several readers' laudatory letters had put it—was now the most evil villain imaginable. The scurrilous opportunist Maxwell would have appreciated his *Mirror* image going from one extreme to the other in a month. I might have accepted the *Mirror*'s overnight conversion to anti-Maxwellism a little better had the editor taken the trouble to explain to the readership the reason for his own conversion. It was all too sudden and too complete a change of mind for me to feel entirely sure that it was not a marketing gimmick.

I was not alone. "There is something deeply vulgar about the way this rudderless newspaper now deals with its own, as well as its ex-owner's shame," wrote the *Guardian*'s respected senior political columnist Ian Aitken.[1] However, I shared that sense of shame, and unless someone had also been sullied by working closely for Maxwell he could not have known how joyous it must have been to suddenly experience the exhilaration of release from the compromise. Having discovered the awful truth, it was not surprising that the paper got a lot off its chest in a cathartic exercise.

Amid the frankly awful—the fake picture of Maxwell with the white hair he would have had if it had not been regularly dyed—there were genuine revelations, such as that of the struggle against Maxwell in the last two weeks of October 1991 by finance director Lawrence Guest. The paper also revealed that Maxwell had wire-tapped Guest and managing director Ernie Burrington. Later came stories that he had bugged Basil Brookes, MCC's finance director; Susan Aldridge, finance vice president of Maxwell Macmillan, Inc.; Jean-Pierre Anselmini, MCC deputy chairman; and even his own son, Kevin, in the office next door.

Better still, the *Mirror* was able to name the culprit, Maxwell's security chief, John Pole, a former chief superintendent with Scotland Yard's Serious Crimes Squad. The paper revealed that Pole had given himself away in a conversation with Les Williams, former Maxwell chauffeur, now employed in MGN's circulation department. Pole told him: "If only Lawrie Guest knew I had really been looking after him." Williams asked what Pole meant. A flustered Pole replied, "Nothing, nothing." But Pole's demeanor raised Williams's suspicions, and a quick check in Guest's office revealed a phone tap.

Pole was fired.

There was not going to be a clear run for Stott's so-called management buyout. In December, Pearson, publishers of the *Financial Times,* considered buying the group, as did Lonrho, owners of *The Observer.* The "black hole" of the depleted pension fund scared them off, but other potential buyers took their place. Even Arthur Scargill, miners' union president, thought about making a bid. It was impossible, though, for any buyer to be certain just what they might be purchasing. At the end of the year MGN improved its position by selling its 25 percent stake in the Canadian newsprint supplier, Quebecor, back to that company for about £55 million ($88 million).[2] However, the £350 million ($560 million) pension-fund deficit and the £97 million ($155 million) theft from the company itself meant that buyers would have to take care. The Mirror Group was forced to secure new loans from the banks to continue trading.

In mid-January 1992, the former head of British Rail, Sir Peter Parker, agreed to head the management purchase of MGN, which was backed by a venture capital group, Electra. Then four other serious contenders suddenly emerged. Tony O'Reilly, chairman and chief executive of Heinz and owner of the Irish Independent Group, confirmed his interest; Conrad Black, proprietor of the Telegraph Group, expressed "informal interest"; D.C. Thomson, owners of the *Sunday Post* in Scotland and the *Beano* comic, announced that it might put together a consortium; and the *Guardian* said it was involved in a consortium led by Hambros Bank.

All of this interest from potential buyers proved academic because, at the end of January, the administrators of the Maxwell-controlled 51 percent—the accounting firm Arthur Andersen—withdrew the Mirror Group from sale. Andersen said it "saw no reason to sell the shares rapidly and they are currently not being offered for sale." This remained the case at the time of writing. Meanwhile, the current Mirror board went on the attack to try to regain some stolen cash by suing the Maxwell boys over the missing $97 million ($155 million) and suing Goldman Sachs and Lehman Brothers for £80 million ($128 million).

Anyone who knew anything about newspapers, including me, realized that one paper would close following a decent interval after Maxwell's death. *The European* was losing money and I imagined it would be buried a month or so after its founder. Ian Maxwell signed an editorial pledging its continuance, but it was written for him and he was left with little choice but to put his name to it when it was placed in front of him. The paper's future was in doubt throughout November, but the December crisis convinced almost everyone that Maxwell's grandiose dream was over. The 6 December issue—the eighty-third—was expected to be the last once the administrators moved in, even by Ian and the editor John Bryant, who declared, "It is clear that most of the Maxwell subsidiaries are bust and that means that, unless someone buys *The European,* it will close.[3] Loyal staff said there were plenty of "potential buyers," but I hardly gave this much credence. I thought they might be looking at the technology rather than the paper.

The following week the majority of the 145 staff showed their commitment to the paper and, in the slim hope of saving their jobs, agreed to produce the next edition without pay. The issue contained a short interview with Ian Maxwell, who defended his father for having "created huge businesses" and so given employment to thousands. He also described some attacks on his father as "despicable and scurrilous," adding that some of the claims about massive fraud were "without foundation and unnecessarily hurtful." He added, "Robert Maxwell was my father and I love him. I will always continue to do that and to cherish the very good memories I have of him."

The week ended with unemployment for *The European* staff when the administrator dismissed them. Bryant told them they should leave "not with bitterness and despair but with pride in what they have done—producing an award-winning paper despite the vagaries of the Maxwell management." He added: "I don't want Maxwell to make them lose more from beyond the grave."[4]

Some angrily marched into the neighboring Mirror Building to demand new jobs, waving their MGN-titled contract letters, a dispute likely to end in court sometime in the future. But Bryant's ever-optimistic deputy, Charles Garside, never lost hope. He told me that week: "I think I've found someone."

Days later, Bryant became deputy editor of *The Times,* his former job, and Garside continued his fight to find a new owner for *The European* over Christmas. In the first week of January he astounded Fleet Street by locating two fresh newspaper entrepreneurs, Frederick and David Barclay. The fifty-eight-year-old identical twins, owners of ships and hotels, agreed to pay about £6 million ($9.6 million) for the paper and quite properly rewarded Garside with the editorship. The Barclays, it transpired, were contented readers of *The European* from their homes in Monte Carlo, were impressed by the staff's response to the crisis, had the money, and decided to buy the paper. In the first week Garside said, "It's so refreshing to work for people who don't want their pictures in the paper." *The European* has been produced every week since, retaining some of its former staff.

If Maxwell had kept just a couple of his promises to the New York *Daily News* it might have helped. He did not spend the time he had promised in the city and, even if he had, I would contend, after my experience with him, that it might have been worse for the paper. He lacked the two major qualities required—concentration and managerial skills—to sort out an ailing paper in an alien environment. What would have been invaluable would have been the investment he had pledged and fewer of those top-of-the-head decisions, such as suddenly raising the cover price and agreeing to rebates for advertisers if circulation did not reach 800,000. In fact, *News* sales limped along at about 720,000 most weekdays until the day of Maxwell's death. That single edition beat the 800,000 target, but it was not an act he could repeat, nor would it save the *News* from the rebate agreement.

Maxwell's failings were largely hidden from the vast majority of the workforce. It was the top echelon of management who soon realized they had an absentee landlord whose occasional visits were about collecting rent rather than improving the roof. "The Maxwell commitment to the *Daily News* was more personal than corporate, more an ego trip than an investment," said John Morton, a Washington media analyst.

Nevertheless, in the eyes of many *News* staffers, Miracle Max had offered hope, and there was still a lot of goodwill toward the name Maxwell when Kevin flew in for a twenty-four-hour visit three days after his father's death. With the building's flags at half mast, he met the unions and made all the right sounds, telling them of his "continuing commitment." He said, "There's no sword of Damocles hanging over the *Daily News*."[5] This was a reference to the March 1992 deadline by which time Maxwell had stipulated the paper must reach profitability or be closed.

He even replicated his father by posing for photographers in a baseball cap holding up the *News* in front of the same 42nd Street newsstand where his dad had stood on the day he had bought the paper eight months before. He sold a few copies to passersby, just as his father had done. But somehow the role did not fit the shy boy. The visit was well received. Newspaper Guild president Barry Lipton said it was a positive sign that Kevin "met with us even before the funeral took place."

During the next month *News* workers revived the spirit of their pre-Maxwell strike period, determined that the show would go on in spite of continuing losses and sales resistance. Kevin made a second visit to New York two weeks later and said, "The warmth of my reception from the printers in Brooklyn was astonishing. What is amazing is the impact Bob had on that paper in a very, very brief period. And that type of loyalty in this situation is sustaining."[6] What was amazing was what was about to happen when news broke of his father's pension thefts. The *News* was back in the news and back in the mire. As one staffer commented, "We're so numbed by all that has happened in the last year, our attitude is, 'What else can go wrong?'"[7]

Unlike the *Daily Mirror,* the *News* did not report the collapse with big headlines on the day it broke, placing a short piece at the bottom of page 4 quoting Kevin as saying there "should be no impact" on the *News*. The sober *New York Times* was less certain: "The future of the *Daily News* is now in the hands of bankers who might sell it or conceivably even close it."[8] To avoid the London administrators selling it off quickly behind their backs, the paper filed for protection under United States bankruptcy laws on 5 December after Kevin had taken part in a board meeting by phone from London. James Willse, the editor, told staff the Chapter Eleven move was to protect us from "the landslide over there."

The documents filed with the court showed just how bad the situation was, with the paper desperately in need of short-term investment. It listed its assets at $37.4 million and liabilities at $53.3 million. James Hoge, the former publisher, said the paper suffered losses of $60 million in the first three months of 1991. But John Campi, the *News* spokesman, tried to suggest there was a bright future, claiming the 1991 operating loss would be around $35 million. The cost of funding retirements to reduce the workforce from twenty-seven hundred to nineteen hundred had been met by the Tribune cash. Kevin told staff the paper had cash and was not for sale, but the Maxwell family was thought to have used up $60 million plus $25 million more.[9]

After persuading a London judge in the early hours of the morning of 9 December to return his passport, Kevin flew by Concorde to New York—paid for by an unidentified donor—to help organize a rescue package for the *News*. He told senior journalists the Maxwell story was "huge" and they should treat it accordingly. It was important for the *News* to retain its integrity, he said. They had done their best already. The paper's headline as he had flown in was CAPTAIN CROOK and the article referred to Maxwell as "possibly the greatest flim-flam artist of them all," adding that the capitalist villains such as junk-bond kings Michael Milken and Ivan Boesky, and even Filipino president Marcos were "rank amateurs in the theft department compared with Maxwell."

Kevin seemed immune to this language when saying the paper had "an excellent chance of a stable future" while facing television cameras at a press conference with Mayor David Dinkins. In the evening he shared a meal with his father's friend, Bob Pirie, Rothschild's president. Next day the *News* took him at his word about retaining its integrity by headlining his visit NO ECONOMIZING FOR KEVIN describing its publisher as "going first class in the Big Apple."

It is difficult when studying the public statements of Kevin not to be struck by his father's influence. Kevin was, perhaps unconsciously, mimicking his dad. There was that mixture of absurd arrogance and overoptimism when he knew better than most that the *News* had little chance of a stable future. There *was* pressure. Everything was *not* going to be all right just because he said so. In fact everything was far from all right even for him, as the staff began to realize. Maxwell had promised to establish a pension fund for three hundred senior management from part of the $60 million given to the *News* by its previous owner, the Tribune Group, for that purpose. He had not done so. He also vowed to give $8 million to Brooklyn's Polytechnic University and donate hundreds of thousands to encourage racial harmony. These donations were never made.

Then on 12 December came the news that advertisers would have to be reimbursed $4.3 million because the *News* had failed to hit the promised circulation targets. It must therefore give free space before 31 December or the cash, in a period when the paper was projecting it would lose $1.8 million. While Kevin and the *News* executives met to discuss the crisis—deciding to renegotiate leases and attempt to cut expenses to $500,000 a week—pupils from a junior high school sang Christmas carols in the lobby.

Later Kevin admitted on television that the *News* needed a miracle in the form of $150 million to ensure its long-term survival. The paper was sorely in need of new printing presses, the very ones promised by Maxwell all those months before when he was the city's hero. At an impromptu press conference, Kevin also said that he had no immediate plans to resign as publisher. "What I have promised is that if I become a liability I would be the one to step down. I have a duty to the administrator."

Confidence among staff sagged when the New York district attorney's office launched an investigation into whether Maxwell had broken the law by failing to set up the management pension fund. One union said it had looked at the current $77 million pension fund and found it intact, but a legal official said, "We are monitoring the situation because we realize there is the potential that the *News* funds were mismanaged or looted. Our investigation focus on the integrity of the assets."

The unions had run out of patience and were worried that the crisis was not getting full-time attention from Kevin so, on 18 December, they urged him to quit. Ted Kheel, adviser to the unions, said: "The unions are not passing judgment on him, they have affection for his father and are impressed by his sincerity, but there is concern that he will not be available to spend time to lead the troubled company. You can't run an important publication with absentee management."[10]

Kevin finally went at the end of December, soon after the resignation from the board of Sheldon Aboff, his father's long-time associate, whose assets had been frozen by the London High Court because of his part in buying MCC shares just before Maxwell's death. It had been Aboff's letter demanding Kevin's presence in New York that had persuaded the court to return Kevin's passport for his second trip to the States. On his third trip he had to give an undertaking to the court that he would not speak to Aboff.

At the end of the year Mort Zuckerman, the real-estate developer with whom Maxwell was rumored to have talked on his last visit to New York two weeks before he died, emerged as a possible buyer. He said, "We have had talks with various people at the *News* and left them in no doubt that we are a serious contender for the paper."[11] Zuckerman, publisher of *US News and World Report* magazine, is reputed to have a $375 million personal fortune and had been interested in the *News* before Maxwell. But nothing came of it.

In February, the Canadian tycoon Conrad Black—owner of the *Daily Telegraph* and Australia's Fairfax group—expressed an interest, as did Peter Kalikow, owner of the rival *New York Post*. Meanwhile, the *News* show did go on, with the paper winning court approval in mid-February for a $10 million credit line. It had survived the short reign of Maxwell, but its future still remains in doubt, with Conrad Black the most likely buyer at the time of writing.

Macmillan began to shrink. A string of asset sales occurred in what were identified as nonstrategic businesses. There was only one big sale—Macmillan computer publishing, which included Que, the best-selling computer-book imprint—which went to Paramount for $157.5 million.

Smaller sales were more common, and Macmillan was reluctant in most cases to reveal sale prices. Conglomerates were quick to scoop up firms that fitted neatly into their major businesses. McGraw-Hill, for instance, took over a small Indiana-based publisher serving the construction industry to integrate into its Prentice-Hall division. The same division took over Macmillan's behavioral-science assets and Macmillan's college foreign-language lists. Macmillan's college textbooks in Spanish and French went to Simon & Schuster, a Paramount subsidiary, and the Cassell's English-Spanish dictionaries were sold to the Oxford University Press. Columbia University Press bought the women's-studies titles.

But Maxwell had made one jewel of a Macmillan asset impossible to realize—Berlitz. MCC's agreement to sell its 55.6 percent holding in the Berlitz language schools to Japan's Fukutake for $256 million was bogged down because five banks claimed ownership of the shares that Maxwell had pledged as collateral for loans. In April 1992, the argument over whether the banks had the right to sell the shares ended up in London's High Court. A judge decided to refuse Macmillan's plea to prevent the stock sales because the banks might stand to lose more than Macmillan if they were forced to hold on to the shares.

Another American victim was the new horse-racing newspaper, the *Racing Times,* which closed on 8 February after losing an estimated $16 million in ten months. Its assets were sold off to the rival *Daily Racing Form,* but had to be investigated by the New York State Attorney General's Office for possible anticompetition implications.

Elsewhere in the world, the Maxwell empire withered away. In Israel, the second-largest daily newspaper, *Maa'riv,* was sold to Yaacov Nimrodi, an arms dealer.

In Germany, the Berliner Verlag publishing house was sold to Maxwell's joint-venture partner, the giant German publishing group Bertelsmann.

In Hungary, Maxwell's newspaper printing works was sold to a Swiss company, Jurg Marquard, which also bought Maxwell's holding in the daily paper *Magyar Hirlap.* A group of Swiss and Italian investors began negotiations to buy Maxwell's Hungarian evening paper, *Esti Hirlap,* in company with the state-owned publishing house.

It was the same story in Britain. Macdonald, the publisher, was bought for $30 million by American publishers Little, Brown. One of Macdonald's offshoots, a popular children's book character called Noddy, which had been overseen for years by Sylvia Rosen, Maxwell's sister, was bought by the BBC. Mrs. Rosen found herself as just another Maxwell victim—losing her pension.

Most of Maxwell's privately owned market-research firm, AGB Research, was sold off to the Addison Consultancy for $23.6 million.

Several of the Maxwell Communications magazine divisions, in which Maxwell had shown little interest, soon attracted buyers. Maxwell Consumer Publishing & Communications, producers of titles such as British Airways' in-flight magazine and the Metropolitan Police paper *The Job,* was bought by its management, led by Terry Humphreys, whom I witnessed impressively withstanding a Maxwellian assault during our Disney comic dispute. Twenty-five magazines, such as *Architect's Journal, Media Week,* and various fishing titles, went for £20 million ($32 million). By the middle of March half of MCC's 430 subsidiaries had been sold or were in the process of being sold.

While the companies were going so was "The Complete Contents of the Chairman's Apartment at Maxwell House," as the Sotheby's catalogue put it. If anything, the tenth-floor penthouse looked grander in the pictures than in real life. There was the sofa in which I had so often sunk back in despair at his latest mad idea; here the study desk at which I had read my departure document. Over his bed, that picture my wife had bought for him. But I craved nothing of the so-called fine antiques, and I was not alone. Prices were on the low side and bidding was sluggish at the St. Valentine's Day auction, but everything—from the bed to baseball caps—went, raising £472,500 ($756,000) in total.

"It all helps the creditors," said someone who was not a Maxwell pensioner. A month later the contents of Maxwell's Headington Hill Hall wine cellars went under the hammer as well, raising £93,000 ($148,800). Michael Broadbent, Christie's master of wine, described one of the finer wines, Chateau Figeac, as "sweet, rounded, and rich—a little like Mr. Maxwell, on the last two counts, I would say."

The other possessions were much harder to sell. Betty's raspberry-colored Rolls-Royce was bought for about £40,000 ($64,000) by a Cheltenham boutique owner. But there was less interest in his own Rolls. The two jets and the helicopter were considered salable, but the yacht had no takers in Palma, Majorca, where it was moored for months, and so set sail in mid-February, with Captain Rankin at the helm, hoping to catch the eye of a passing tycoon in a new mooring at Antibes, on the French Riviera.

Receivers also began trying to sell the lease of the Oxford mansion of Headington Hill Hall in January, along with several other valuable sites owned by various of the private companies. The twenty-nine-room mansion had been Betty's home for years, and the end of her reign there spelled the end of jobs for her private staff. There was a mystery about the ownership of two chateaux in southwest France; would Betty Maxwell get the chance to live out her days in the peace of Montagnac-sur-Lède?

All the journalists who saw Betty in Tenerife and in Israel spoke of her dignity. She spoke of the journalists' lack of it. For a month she remained silent, and then suddenly, angry over The *Guardian*'s suggestion that it was not Maxwell's body that had been fished from the sea and identified by her, she gave one interview to express her outrage. Her loyalty to her husband remained intact: "I have lost the best friend I ever had and ever will have."[12]

But I detected that her earlier certainty about whether he had committed suicide was waning. She said what I expected to hear at first, then trailed off into speculation: "I can't see him doing it...he was a tremendous fighter...something bizarre must have happened in his mind for him to do that. I can't see it."

In the following days, as her sons faced inquiries by the Serious Fraud Office, she became less sure. Her friend Samuel Pisar said, "Betty is asking herself what she and her sons have done to deserve such humiliation. Why has this happened to them? She is in an emotional turmoil. Why has he done this to her sons?"

By the time Pisar arranged for her to talk to an American magazine this mixture of anger and bewilderment came bubbling to the surface. She also spoke more frankly, and critically, about her husband than ever before, daring to suggest that some of what had been said and written about the man to whom she was married for forty-eight years just might have been true. Between the lines you can hear her inner dialogue: "I know I must defend him, but was he, after all, guilty of deceiving me too?

"I knew he had enormous intelligence but he must have been even more clever if he fooled so many people for so long." Then she qualified it: "If some of the things that appeared to have happened in the last months of his life actually happened, they can only have been the acts of a desperate man."[13] She clung to the belief that his death was an accident, but "with hindsight you go from one end of the spectrum of speculation to another."

Some of her complaints showed that she had still not come to terms with the enormity of her husband's activities. To express surprise at her Mirror Group pension being stopped seemed a bit rich, especially since the trustees were applying a rule that Maxwell had insisted on: relatives of a fund member are not entitled to payments if the member has committed a fraudulent or negligent act. I can imagine his sanctimonious smile as he demanded its inclusion in the rules.

Maxwell had also convinced his wife that people were out to get him. Soon after his death she said, "There were so many people who hated him. He had many threats. Many people would be delighted to bump him off."[14]

Betty was right about people hating him, most of them with some justice, but there was no evidence of genuine threats to his life. She cannot understand why there was a sustained attack on Maxwell over decades except by blaming an English lack of appreciation for "success."

That brings us to the question of whether Betty knew much or anything about his business dealings. Those who argue that she must have, assert that with her intelligence she could not have remained in ignorance. I have little doubt that the combination of Maxwell's penchant for secrecy and Betty's total lack of interest in business meant that she did not know the least detail of his activities. She viewed her husband as a romantic figure, a great survivor, a child of the Holocaust, a hero who ran at guns, a rough peasant who improved himself against the odds, a young businessman who had nothing to start with yet provided her with luxury, a misunderstood politician, and, finally, a misunderstood genius. To undermine this image, to suggest that it was all built on sand, is to deny any point to her relationship. Though his crimes are exposed, she loyally excuses them as an unfortunate act of desperation by a man who was not getting a fair crack of the whip. There is, however, one intrusion that threatens this fantasy, one question that will nag away forever: How could he have done this to the children?

In late March it emerged that Betty had provided "at the drop of a hat" £900,000 ($1.44 million) to fund Kevin and Ian's legal costs. Quite how she squared this with her claim in *Vanity Fair* that she was "in great financial difficulty" is unclear. Her personal finances, it seems, are another of those Maxwellian mysteries.

More understandable was Betty's anger in January when the French magazine *Paris Match* published pictures of Maxwell's corpse taken from the video of the postmortem carried out by Dr. Iain West in Israel the day before burial in Tel Aviv. There was a ridiculous claim that the pictures "proved" he had been beaten, possibly murdered. They did no such thing. Dr. West, head of forensic medicine at Guy's Hospital in London, said the article contained "considerable inaccuracies" because it was the previous forensic work that had caused the facial wounds. Betty took court action and on 17 January a Paris judge ordered the magazine to withdraw its issue, ruling it had gone "beyond the limits of freedom of speech." It was, of course, too late because the weekly had been distributed across the world by then. She was awarded £10,300 ($16,480) damages.

On 3 February, Lloyds insurers announced that they were not prepared to pay up on Maxwell's £20 million ($32 million) life-insurance policy, stating that, in their opinion, there was no liability. They had been heavily influenced by the reports they had commissioned from the loss adjusters, Rich Wheeler & Co., and Dr. West, who is recognized as one of Britain's foremost pathologists. Maxwell would have liked to know he had the top man on the job.

Taken together, these reports make a powerful case for Maxwell having committed suicide. On 2 February, more than fifteen weeks after his death, these reports emerged in public when *The Sun* obtained copies, detailed extracts of which also appeared in *The London Times*. In a sixteen-page report, dated 15 January, Roger Rich, Rich Wheeler's investigator, concluded that evidence suggesting Maxwell had taken his own life was "more compelling than any other cause." It took account of the pressures Maxwell was under, details of his final days, and the postmortem examinations. It was therefore the only investigation to stand back and consider all the various facts as a whole.

Cynics might argue that the report made the conclusion the

insurance companies wanted to hear since suicide would preclude a payout. Apart from the doubts this would cast on the professional integrity of Rich Wheeler, which seem wide of the mark, I would argue strongly that suicide remains by far the most plausible explanation. At the time of his death and in the month afterward I thought it was probably an accident but always said in public my verdict was open. Once the sheer scale of his villainy and the inevitability of its discovery was revealed I was convinced of suicide.

Asked in a radio interview in early December what I thought, I replied, "I think Mr. Maxwell took his own life while the balance of his mind was briefly undisturbed." This was not the joke everyone took it to be. We cannot think of Maxwell as having had a complete grasp of reality for the last year in Maxwellia. It must be blindingly obvious that to have stolen the assets of pension funds and raised huge loans without any possibility of repaying them were not the actions of a rational man. He had to be found out at some stage, and in the lucid moments that intruded into his mania, he knew that moment was moving closer. I do not believe he set out for the boat absolutely certain of committing suicide, though it is significant that in the day or so prior to going he was unusually pleasant to people around him. And, of course, he went alone.

It is inconsistent with all that we have seen of Maxwell to believe he planned anything more than an hour or so ahead. However, I think suicide was on his mind as a possibility. The telephone calls and the faxes he received on the *Lady Ghislaine* in those final five days confirmed that his slim hopes of surviving a little longer were over.

I hear those voices: he was a fighter; he had overcome seemingly impossible odds in the past. The objections are familiar enough, and it is true that his remarkable recovery after the 1971 Department of Trade inspectors' reports showed him to be thick-skinned.

Surely though, everyone can see that the pension-fund theft is of an entirely different order from his Pergamon activities. He got away without being charged in 1971, but he could not hope to escape criminal charges for removing the pension-fund assets, quite apart from charges he might face for the thefts from two public companies and the fraud he perpetrated on the Swiss Bank Corporation. Then there was the public ignominy, the crowing of all those he most despised, the threat of jail. He had every motive for suicide on that November day.

The loss adjuster's report points to specific, strange factors about those days. There was the odd idea of having his plane pick up his sons, which was transformed into a sort of would-be royal flypast over his yacht. There was the locking of his stateroom door. He was on his own boat at sea and if he was only stepping outside for a breath of fresh air, or because he felt sick, he would not have locked the door behind him. In fact, he was never known to lock his door when aboard. The fact that he had asked the stewardess to leave the key behind is convincing proof of his preconceived plan to lock the door and thereby prevent any crewmember from entering his stateroom and discovering that he was missing. He was taking no chances of being found alive in the ocean.

A third factor alluded to by the loss adjuster, but which seems less convincing, concerns Maxwell's supposedly "complimentary and almost amicable" attitude toward the crew. As far as I can discover, Maxwell was generally well disposed to his yacht crew throughout his five years of ownership. Nigel Hodson, first mate on the *Lady Ghislaine* for eighteen months until December 1990, told me, "We often heard him bellow at people on the phone, but he was always nice to us. Every time he came aboard we noticed how happy he seemed on the yacht."

Hodson left the boat days before its famous accident in the Virgin Islands when it ran aground and knew the skipper responsible, Steve Taylor, well. "Far from sacking him, Mr. Maxwell wanted him to stay," he said. "It was Steve's decision to go."

Another former crewmember of eight months' standing, second engineer Roy Whiteford, agreed that Maxwell was always courteous. Captain Gus Rankin, regarded as being a little taciturn himself, seemed to enjoy an easy relationship with his employer. However, since "niceness" can be a matter of degree, it is possible that he was even nicer on this last voyage. One strange sign not mentioned by the loss adjuster is that of Maxwell smoking a cigar which, if true, might suggest his long-term health was no longer important to him.

Turning to the separate pathology report by Dr. West, there is still more evidence pointing to suicide. Dr. West could not detect a clearly defined cause of death but thought drowning most likely, and all other explanations unlikely. He thought a heart attack would have caused Maxwell to fall down, not roll over the rail. It was therefore a case of Maxwell having fallen over accidentally or on purpose. But it was his next explanation for an injury that had received hardly any attention that, to my mind, proved conclusive.

On 12 January, the *Mail on Sunday* had published an exclusive front-page story about Maxwell having had torn muscles on his left shoulder and lower back. This was consistent with a man of Maxwell's weight grabbing at the yacht rail and therefore, said the paper, it indicated an accident. Maxwell had fallen over and grabbed at the rail to save himself. He had been unable to hold on and fell into the sea. Dr. West was known to hold this theory, said the article.

Well, almost. In his report Dr. West agreed that the injuries suggested Maxwell had held on, but voluntarily. He said: "The tearing and bleeding into the muscles on the back of the left shoulder and into the muscles by the spine resulted from sudden physical stress to the muscles, causing them to stretch and tear." This was indeed consistent with Maxwell hanging on to the guardrail with his left hand, with all his weight being carried by that hand.

In other words, he might have climbed over the rail and gradually lowered himself into the water, holding on at the end by one hand. Dr. West commented: "One sees this pattern of injury on occasions in individuals who kill themselves as a result of falling from high buildings. Whilst some will jump or let themselves topple over a balcony or out of a window, others will actually ease themselves over the edge and hold on for a time with one or both hands before letting go."

Surely, if he had fallen over, apart from the unlikelihood of gripping the rail, he would have screamed for help. There were two crew on the bridge throughout the night who heard nothing.

The circumstantial, pathological, and financial evidence suggests suicide, and I am in no doubt about it. In a life of mystery, it is perhaps not surprising that Robert Maxwell should want it to end in mystery. After what he did we should not grant him this wish. The twentieth century's greatest confidence man—bully, braggart, liar, cheat, thief—drowned himself because he knew he was about to be found out at last.

Epilogue

And Maxwell still has his defenders. Even after the pension fraud was revealed, people spoke up for him. John Junor, a columnist working on beyond pensionable age and therefore untroubled by a lack of money, wrote: "Despite all his wrongdoing...I even have to admit a sneaking admiration for the heroic grandeur of his larceny." Though realizing this would "not make me popular with Mirror pensioners," he thought them unlikely to lose out in the end.

Junor enjoys his maverick status, but I was disappointed with the usually sensible Dominic Lawson, *Spectator* editor and *Financial Times* columnist, who seemed careless even of the pensioners' problems when extolling the virtues of the job-creating Maxwell. It was their own fault for getting mixed up with him, he suggested, illustrating his considerable lack of understanding about both the nature of capitalist newspaper ownership and the consequent hierarchical form of management it spawns. The Mirror pensioners and staff did not ask for Maxwell; he bought them and there was no defense against him.

I have heard lots of people suggest that if Maxwell took the banks for a ride then all well and good. "Of course," they add lamely, "it is sad about the pensioners." The corollary of this argument is that he was a buccaneer, the favorite euphemism, whose theft of millions was an uncharacteristic lapse forced on him by unfortunate circumstances in the final months of his life. This is the favored argument of the faithful cronies who cannot bring themselves to realize the truth about the man they lauded for so long.

The question most people ask—and I have a lot more to ask—center on why he got away with it for so long. Why didn't the authorities stop him? Why did the banks lend him so much? Why did all those high-caliber professional firms work for him? The answers are money and British secrecy.

First, the money. Banks make money by loaning money, so the greater the loan, the greater the profit. Stockbrokers make money by trading in shares, so the more shares they trade in, the more they make. Merchant bankers and accountants (and lawyers) make money by earning fees from clients, so the bigger the client, the bigger the fee. None of these institutions are asked to consider the morality of the people and companies they lend money to or work for. Their raison d'être is to make money, and Maxwell was a sure-fire way to earn a fortune. As long as they observe certain rules of conduct in their self-regulated world, then all is considered fair and within the law.

Second, the British tradition of secrecy. This takes two forms. There is the secrecy Maxwell legally employed by concealing the ultimate ownership of his companies, including his major holdings in both MCC and the Mirror Group, in Liechtenstein and Gibraltar. There is also the cozy secrecy of the financial establishment, which provides a guarantee of opaqueness under the guise of what is always referred to as "client confidentiality." He took the fullest possible advantage of Britain's lax and secretive commercial laws to prevent anyone from seeing into Maxwellia.

Employing a combination of money and secrecy, he was able to present himself, in spite of his image and his past, as a respectable businessman. Up to a point. Are we to believe that those 1971 Department of Trade reports are little bits of window dressing that nobody need ever worry about? If two inspectors produce lengthy and detailed reports that lead them to the inescapable conclusion that a man is unfit to run a public company, then is this to be written off as history?

Scores of the world's mightiest banks loaned him money in the full knowledge of his unfitness. Perhaps they were misled by the apparent confidence placed in him by National Westminster, which had been Pergamon's clearing bank and therefore should well have known his track record. NatWest was responsible for his return from the backwoods in 1980. You can imagine the reasoning. While he was unfit in the seventies, that was then and this is now. He pays up, doesn't he, and that's all that counts. If one bank is happy to lend then others are emboldened to do the same.

Even so, there are questions. Was there no one at a senior level in any bank who did not wonder for one moment about why every Maxwell company and holding ended up in Liechtenstein? Did no one ponder on reports about his intercompany deals? Did no one raise an eyebrow over the annual reports that suggested all was far from well at Maxwell House? Did no one have his ear close enough to the ground to realize that there were virtually no institutional investors prepared to risk holding stock in MCC? Did no one think to stop and ask: Are we doing the right thing?

Next are the merchant banks who not only advised him, but paid court, and in so doing lent him the respectability of their names— Henry Ansbacher, Samuel Montagu, and most curious of all, NM Rothschild, which knew all about him when acting for Leasco during the Pergamon debacle. Did they mislay their records of that affair? Did they choose to forget? Or did they, against all the odds, sincerely believe Maxwell had changed?

So, too, the auditors. Many of the leading accountancy firms would have nothing to do with Maxwell. Yet Coopers & Lybrand Deloitte acted for him even though, as auditors for Pergamon after Maxwell had been ousted, they knew of his past accounting malpractices. Why then did they consider acting for him at MCC? Is a fat fee alone enough justification to work for a man they knew had been capable of twisting figures? Or did they, too, think he had turned over a new leaf?

Then there were his stockbrokers, Smith New Court. So confident were this firm in their views of Maxwell being a bad bet that they issued secret advice to a tight circle of investors telling them to shed Maxwell Communications stock. What can we make of hypocritical behavior like that? How can they justify taking his money and whispering behind his back? And what are investors who were not told the truth to think of them?

And we must not forget Goldman Sachs. All my polite requests for them to explain their role were met with obfuscation and prevarication. In my last conversation, a sweet-voiced French spokeswoman said, "Someone is dealing with your inquiries. Don't worry, we will be in touch." Perhaps their silence says it all. How can they explain the extraordinary size and numbers of deals they did on Maxwell's behalf?

If these institutions were misguided, then we might, in such circumstances, have expected the British "authorities" to have stepped in. The Stock Exchange and the Department of Trade and Industry have no excuses since both were informed well in advance of Maxwell's death of strange happenings at Maxwell Communications; in fact, in advance of the Mirror Group's issue of stock to the public.

In early December 1990 one private investor wrote to the London Stock Exchange to complain about the nature of Maxwell's August 1990 put option. Later that same month a second private investor, John C. Robertson, wrote a detailed three-page letter to the Stock Exchange's director of quotations setting out his worries over the same put option. After his letter was acknowledged and said to be "receiving attention," he followed it up by sending a second letter "to express additional concerns over events in August and September which may have led to the creation of a false market in [Maxwell Communications] shares."

The stock exchange's reply, dated 21 January, stated that his questions would be answered after "an investigation." Robertson, who had lost money, wrote two more letters and then sent a file to the Department of Trade's investigations division. He was informed that his complaints would be considered "in detail." Eventually, after six months, Robertson wrote directly to Peter Lilley, the government minister in charge of the Department of Trade, who replied on 17 October that his complaint was "under consideration by my officials."

What was going on over those months? The correspondence between Robertson and the stock exchange and the Department of Trade illustrates that months *before* Maxwell had taken large quantities of pension-fund money, months *before* he had robbed Maxwell Communications and Mirror Group, months *before* he had taken out fresh bank loans, these "authorities" had *prima facie* evidence of possible misfeasance in Maxwell's empire.

How long did they need? What steps did they take? Why was nothing done? In a self-regulated environment these were the only hope everyone—investors, employees, and pensioners—had of ensuring that all was aboveboard.

We might therefore ask whether self-regulation in this arcane world is worth anything at all. Is it not time, considering the roll call of other spectacular corporate collapses in Britain in the past two years, for an American-style Securities and Exchange Commission? I hear the reply. Maxwell was one of a kind, an unprecedented nightmare, nothing could have stopped him, no laws, no regulation. We will not see his like again, so there's no need to be hasty. This rogue-elephant thesis is a convenient way for the London Stock Exchange and the British government to deny any failing.

The five current Scotland Yard investigations will not discover why the authorities failed to act, because their job is only to consider whether to bring charges against people or companies. If they do discover lapses by the authorities they are not empowered to do anything about them. What is required therefore is a judicial inquiry to discover just why Maxwell was allowed to get away with robbery while the authorities were supposed to be investigating. Nothing less is due the thousands who have suffered, and will suffer, because of Maxwell.

There is, in conclusion, one pressing human drama that the British government must deal with as soon as possible. There were many sensible changes spelled out in the report by the Parliamentary Select Committee on Social Security to improve the safety of pension funds in the future. But that report did not answer the immediate problem: the legitimate cry of instantaneous support for the victims of Maxwell's theft.

All of the pensioners have an irrefutable case for government compensation. Moreover, the banks have a moral duty to return pension-fund assets. I declare an interest as the husband of a Mirror pension-fund member and a friend of hundreds of others. It is unconscionable that a single person should suffer a penny loss in retirement because one man was given the freedom to steal his or her savings.

Notes

CHAPTER 1

1. Tom Bower, *Maxwell: The Outsider* (Mandarin, London, 1991), p. 316.
2. Robert Edwards, *Goodbye Fleet Street* (Jonathan Cape, London, 1988), p. 245.
3. Ibid., p. 246.

CHAPTER 2

1. Judi Bevan, *Sunday Telegraph*, 14 April 1991.
2. Bower, p. 19.
3. Joe Haines, *Maxwell* (Macdonald, London, 1988), pp. 51–2.
4. Interview with Graham Lord, *Sunday Express,* 1968.
5. *Playboy,* October 1991.
6. Haines, p. 50.
7. Ibid., p. 61.
8. Peter Thompson and Anthony Delano, *Maxwell: A Portrait of Power* (Corgi, London, 1991), p. 49.
9. *The Sunday Times,* 24 August 1969.
10. Haines, p. 93.
11. *Evening Standard,* 7 November 1991.
12. Haines, p. 105.
13. *Playboy,* October 1991.
14. Haines, p. 108.
15. Ibid., p. 114.

CHAPTER 3

1. Haines, p. 138.
2. Thompson and Delano, p. 90.
3. Bower, p. 162.
4. Haines, p. 181.
5. *Financial Times,* 9 July 1964.

360

6. Bower, p. 161, and *The Times,* 6 December 1991.
7. Letter to *Daily Telegraph,* 10 November 1991.
8. Haines, p. 297.
9. Bower, p. 184.
10. Ibid., p. 262.
11. Haines, p. 310.
12. *Playboy,* October 1991.
13. Haines, p. 329.
14. *Playboy,* October 1991.
15. Haines, p. 203.
16. Bower, p. 334.
17. *The Times,* 15 November 1991.
18. *The Sunday Times* magazine, 29 September 1991.
19. Haines, p. 438.
20. Ibid., p. 447.
21. Ibid., p. 448.
22. *Columbus Citizen Journal,* 1 September 1967.

CHAPTER 4

1. *The Sunday Times,* 21 September 1975.
2. Brian Barr and Ron McKay, *The Story of the Scottish Daily News* (Canongate, Edinburgh, 1976), p. 120.
3. *Accountancy,* September 1973.
4. Bower, p. 318.
5. Haines, p. 318.
6. Barr and McKay, p. 16, 45.
7. *Financial Times,* 6 August 1990.
8. Haines, p. 386.
9. Bower, p. 358.
10. Haines, p. 388.
11. Bower, p. 373.
12. John Pilger, *Heroes* (Jonathan Cape, London, 1986), p. 516.
13. Haines, p. 417.
14. Ibid., p. vii.
15. Edwards, op. cit., p. 229.
16. Pilger, op. cit., p. 521.
17. Ibid., p. 527, and Haines, p. 402.
18. *The Times,* 25 June 1985.
19. *The Sunday Correspondent,* 29 October 1989.
20. Edwards, op. cit., p. 242.
21. Ibid., p. 236.
22. *Guardian* and *The Daily Telegraph,* 7 February 1992.
23. Michael Williams, *New Society,* 20 September 1984.
24. Haines, p. 415.
25. *The Times,* 12 June 1991.
26. Judi Bevan, *Sunday Telegraph,* 14 April 1991.
27. *Vanity Fair,* June 1991.
28. *Vanity Fair,* March 1992.
29. *Daily Telegraph,* 4 November 1986.

30. *Malice in Wonderland* (Macdonald, London, 1986).
31. Bower, p. 109.
32. Haines, p. 2.
33. *IPI Report,* International Press Institute, January 1992.
34. *Daily Telegraph,* 19 May 1987.
35. Haines, p. 23.
36. Ibid., p. 23.
37. *Wall Street Journal* and *Los Angeles Times,* 19 May 1987.
38. *Financial Times,* 27 May 1987.
39. Haines, p. 24.
40. *Financial Times,* 23 May 1987.
41. *Daily Telegraph,* 22 August 1987.

CHAPTER 5

1. *The Sunday Times,* 24 July 1988.
2. *Today,* 22 July 1988.
3. Delaware Supreme Court. Court of Chancery Opinion, 3-5-89, p. 25.
4. Ibid., pp. 9–10, 15, 21.
5. Ibid., p. 22.
6. Ibid., p. 26.
7. Ibid., pp. 31–2.
8. Ibid., p. 39.
9. Ibid., p. 42.
10. Ibid., p. 49.
11. Ibid., p. 50.
12. *Guardian,* 1 July 1989.
13. *Today,* 4 January 1989.

CHAPTER 7

1. *Wall Street Journal,* 13 October 1987.
2. *The Observer,* 15 December 1991.

CHAPTER 8

1. Hugh Cudlipp, *Walking On Water* (Bodley Head, London, 1976).
2. Haines, p. 36.
3. *Financial Times,* 6 August 1990.
4. Haines, pp. 34–35.
5. *Independent on Sunday,* 8 December 1991.
6. *The Sunday Times* magazine, 29 September 1991.
7. *The Observer* magazine, 24 June 1990.
8. Author interview with Andy McSmith.

CHAPTER 9

1. *The Observer* magazine, 24 June 1990.
2. *Guardian,* 5 March 1990.

CHAPTER 10

1. Geoffrey Goodman, *Guardian,* 6 December 1991.
2. Bronwen Maddox, *Financial Times,* 10 January 1992.
3. *UK Press Gazette,* 16 December 1991.
4. *The Times,* 29 November 1990.
5. Roger Cowe, *Guardian,* 29 November 1990.

CHAPTER 11

1. *Mail on Sunday,* 13 January 1991.

CHAPTER 12

1. Mary Brasier, *Guardian,* 14 January 1991.
2. *Financial Times,* 21 February 1991.
3. *Independent on Sunday,* 17 March 1991.
4. *Vanity Fair,* March 1992.
5. Ibid.
6. *The Sunday Times,* 31 March 1991.
7. *New York,* 10 March 1992.
8. *Vanity Fair,* June 1991.

CHAPTER 13

1. Hugo Young, *Guardian,* 5 March 1990.
2. *The Sunday Times,* 13 January 1991.
3. *The Times,* 8 March 1991.
4. *The Sunday Times,* 10 March 1991.
5. Margareta Pagano, *Independent on Sunday,* 24 February 1991.
6. *The Sunday Times,* 14 April 1991.
7. *Independent on Sunday,* 10 November 1991.
8. *Vanity Fair,* June 1991.
9. *Financial Times,* 30 March 1991.
10. *Guardian,* 25 April 1991.
11. *London Evening Standard,* 14 January 1992.
12. *Sunday Telegraph,* 18 December 1991.
13. Jeff Randall, *The Sunday Times,* 31 March 1991.
14. *The Observer,* 15 December 1991.
15. *Financial Times,* 22 January 1992.
16. *Financial Times,* 18 April 1991.
17. Ian Griffiths, *Independent,* 18 April 1991.
18. Alex Brummer, *Guardian,* 18 April 1991.
19. *Financial Times,* 18 April 1991.
20. Andrew Davidson, *The Sunday Times,* 14 April 1991.
21. *UK Press Gazette,* 22 April 1991.
22. *UK Press Gazette,* 3 June 1991.
23. *Mail on Sunday,* 3 March 1991, 17 March 1991, 19 May 1991, and 9 June 1991.
24. *Wall Street Journal,* 12 December 1991.

25. *Independent on Sunday*, 8 December 1991.
26. *Financial Times*, 30 January 1992.
27. *Independent*, 6 December 1991.

CHAPTER 14

1. *Financial Times*, 18 December 1991.
2. *The Sunday Times*, 8 December 1991; *The Times*, 9 December 1991.
3. *The Times*, 10 December 1991.
4. *Guardian*, 12 December 1991.
5. *Financial Times*, 13 December 1991.
6. Ibid.
7. *The Times*, 10 December 1991.
8. *Financial Times*, 10 December 1991.
9. *Guardian*, 7 December 1991.
10. *London Evening Standard*, 13 December 1991.
11. *Independent*, 7 December 1991.
12. *Vanity Fair*, March 1992.
13. *The Observer*, 23 February 1992.
14. Jason Nisse, *Independent*, 16 July 1991.
15. *London Evening Standard*, 16 July 1991.
16. *Financial Times*, 17 July 1991.
17. *London Evening Standard*, 16 July 1991.
18. *Sunday Telegraph*, 8 December 1991.
19. *London Evening Standard*, 14 January 1992.
20. *Independent on Sunday*, 29 November 1991.
21. *Daily Mail*, 29 December 1991.
22. *Independent on Sunday*, 22 December 1991.
23. *Guardian*, 16 January 1992.

CHAPTER 15

1. *Daily Mail*, 29 December 1991.
2. *Sunday Mirror*, 22 September 1991.
3. *Independent*, 24 September 1991; *Observer*, 29 September 1991.
4. *Guardian*, 25 September 1991.
5. *Daily Telegraph*, 17 February 1992.
6. *Sunday Telegraph*, 18 December 1991.
7. *Independent*, 9 December 1991.
8. *Daily Telegraph*, 31 October 1991.
9. *Financial Times*, 18 December 1991.
10. *Financial Times*, 17 December 1991.
11. *Daily Mail*, 19 December 1991.
12. *The Times*, 20 November 1991.
13. *Guardian*, 11 December 1991.
14. *The Sunday Times*, 24 November 1991.
15. Seymour Hersh, *The Samson Option: Israel, America and The Bomb*, (Faber & Faber, London, 1991), p. 312.
16. *Today*, 25 October 1991.

17. *Vanity Fair,* March 1992.
18. *Daily Telegraph,* 6 November 1991.
19. *Vanity Fair,* March 1992.
20. *New York,* 10 March 1992.

CHAPTER 16

1. *Daily Mirror,* 10 December 1991.
2. *The Sunday Times,* 10 November 1991.
3. Bill Frost, *The Times,* 11 December 1991.
4. *Daily Mail,* 7 November 1991.
5. *The Sunday Times,* 10 November 1991.
6. *The Times,* 21 January 1992.
7. *The Sunday Times,* 10 November 1991.
8. Ibid.
9. Ibid.
10. *Guardian,* 6 November 1991.
11. *The Sunday Times,* 10 November 1991.
12. *Independent,* 6 November 1991.
13. *Daily Telegraph,* 6 November 1991.
14. *The Sunday Times,* 10 November 1991.
15. Ibid.
16. Geoffrey Levy, *Daily Mail,* 19 November 1991.
17. *Guardian,* 6 November 1991.
18. *Guardian,* 7 November 1991.
19. *Today,* 14 November 1991.

CHAPTER 17

1. *The Observer,* 10 November 1991.
2. *Financial Times,* 11 November 1991.
3. *Daily Telegraph,* 18 November 1991.
4. *Today,* 18 November 1991.
5. *The Sunday Times,* 24 November 1991.
6. *Daily Mail,* 21 November 1991.
7. *Guardian,* 23 November 1991.
8. Alex Brummer, *Guardian,* 28 November 1991.
9. *Financial Times,* 28 November 1991.
10. *Financial Times,* 12 December 1991.
11. *Daily Express,* 13 November 1991.
12. *The Sunday Times,* 8 December 1991, 15 December 1991.
13. *Sunday Telegraph,* 15 December 1991.
14. *Guardian,* 7 December 1991.
15. *Financial Times,* 13 January 1992, 18 January 1992.
16. *Independent,* 11 December 1991.
17. *Today,* 14 January 1992.
18. *Financial Times,* 14 January 1992.
19. *The Sunday Times,* 22 December 1991.
20. Independent on Sunday, 29 December 1991.

21. *Independent,* 18 December 1991.
22. *The Observer,* 16 February 1992.
23. *Daily Telegraph,* 12 February 1992.
24. *Daily Telegraph,* 11 February 1992.
25. *Independent on Sunday,* 26 January 1992.
26. *Independent on Sunday,* 12 January 1992.
27. *Financial Times,* 3 March 1992.
28. *Mirror Staff Sentinel,* 5 March 1992.
29. *The Times,* 2 March 1992.
30. *The Observer,* 26 January 1992.
31. *The Times,* 31 January 1992.
32. *Daily Mail,* 14 December 1991.
33. *Independent,* 17 January 1992.
34. *Guardian,* 9 March 1992.
35. *The Times,* 10 March 1992.
36. *Guardian,* 9 March 1992.

CHAPTER 18

1. *Guardian,* 11 December 1991.
 2. *The Observer,* 29 December 1991.
 3. *The Times,* 6 December 1991.
 4. *Daily Telegraph,* 13 December 1991.
 5. *The Observer,* 10 December 1991.
 6. Ivan Fallon, *The Sunday Times,* 24 November 1991.
 7. *The Times,* 5 December 1991.
 8. *New York Times,* 4 December 1991.
 9. *Guardian,* 9 December 1991.
10. *Guardian,* 18 December 1991.
11. *The Sunday Times,* 29 December 1991.
12. *Daily Express,* 3 December 1991.
13. *Vanity Fair,* March 1992.
14. *The Sunday Times,* 10 November 1991.

Index

Aboff, Sheldon, 277, 345
Acquisitions, 66;
  aftermath of Maxwell's
  death and, 346–47;
  American printworks,
  63; British Printing Corporation (BPC), 40–42;
  Butterworth's, 26–27;
  early postwar, 24–25;
  EPPAC, 25; French, 70;
  Harcourt Brace Jovano-
  vich (attempted), 70–75;
  Hollis Bros., 66; *Kenya
  Times*, 69–70; Liechtens-
  tein trusts and, 136–38;
  Macmillan, 81–90; 1983,
  42; 1988, 85–86;
  Quebecor and Donohue,
  166, 168; *Scottish Daily
  News*, 50–51; soccer
  clubs, 130, 153–54;
  Springer, 25; TV sta-
  tions, 70; unsuccessful
  attempts, 42, 49, 51, 62,
  70–75, 80, 88, 105,
  136–37, 153–54
Adam, Prince Hans II, 244
Adass, Bill, 175–78
Adjani, R., 176–77
Advest, 324
Adviser (188), 259–60, 316
AE engineering group, 66
AGB Research, 85–86,
  266, 332, 346–47
Age, The, 88
Agence Centrale de
  France, 70
Airplane, Maxwell's, 162,
  296–97

Aldridge, Susan, 338
Alexanders Laing &
  Cruickshank, 79, 150
Allason, Rupert, 283
Allen & Overy, 295
Angol-Israeli Association,
  297, 299
Anselmini, Jean-Pierre, 80,
  251–52, 338
Arap Moi, Daniel, 69–70
Arnold, Harry, 327–28
Arthur Andersen, 339
Association of Mirror Pen-
  sioners, 173, 256, 332
Atkins, Mark, 295–96, 308

Baddeley, Jean, 5, 128, 138
Baistow, Tom, 33–34
Baker, Nick, 308
Baker, Richard, 215,
  250–51
Bales, Keith, 185
Bankers Trust of America,
  273
Banker Trust, 274
Banking community;
  confidence in Maxwell
  of, 11, 28, 66, 83–84, 86,
  91, 145, 172, 236; death
  of Maxwell and, 302,
  317–23; ease of transactions with, 273–74;
  Maxwell's resignation as
  MCC chairman and,
  239; Mirror Group
  Newspapers (MIG) stock
  and, 204–5; pension
  fund scandal and, 332,
  334–35; pig-on-pork

loans, 89; responsibility
  of, 356–59; rules of,
  146–47; self-regulation
  and, 359; shares as col-
  lateral and, 89, 147–49,
  240, 278, 322, 324,
  331–32, 346; share-sup-
  port operations and,
  277–78; total amount of
  loans, 319
Banks, John, 115
Bannenberg, Jon, 2
Barclay, David, 341
Barclay, Frederick, 341
Barclays Bank, 131, 169,
  172, 319
Barclays de Zoete Wedd
  (BZW), 169–72
Barrett, Harry, 333
Barrett, Neil, 241
Basham, Brian, 114, 116
Bass, Robert, 82
BBC *Panorama* exposé,
  104–5, 265, 269–70
Beaver, Bob, 154
Bell & Howell, 80, 82
Bender, John, 300–302
Ben Manashe, Ari, 280–84
Benton, Tim, 190
Berliner Verlag, 105,
  155–56, 240–45, 346
Berliner Zeitung, 155
Berlitz language schools,
  82, 91, 295, 316, 324,
  346–47
Berlusconi, Silvio, 85
Bernstein, Carl, 64
Bertelsmann group, 155,
  346

Besley, Verdun, 21
Biographies of Maxwell.
   See Bower, Tom;
   Haines, Joe
Birt, John, 64
Bishopsgate Investment
   Management (BIM), 174,
   255–59, 331
Bishopsgate Investment
   Trust, 42, 148, 172, 239
Black, Conrad, 339, 345
Blake, John, 88
Blakenham, Viscount, 212
Bogdanovich, Peter, 7
Bond, Alan, 105, 131, 169
Boram, Tony, 173–75, 256
Bowen, Mike, 126
Bower, Tom, 15–17, 25, 27,
   31, 33, 40, 53, 65, 80–81,
   91, 225
Bradford football club fire,
   59
Bramall, Lord, 210
Branson, Richard, 184
Breslin, Jimmy, 222
Briston, Richard, 50–51
British Book Center, 29–30
British International Heli-
   copters, 332
British Printing and Com-
   munications Corp.
   (BPCC; later Maxwell
   Communications Corp.),
   40–42, 54, 71, 131;
   Liechtenstein trusts and,
   62, 72–74; losses at, 62;
   Mirror Group's printing
   transferred to, 63. See
   also Maxwell Communi-
   cations Corporation
Broadbent, Michael,
   347–48
Brookes, Basil, 251–52,
   264, 276, 338
Brumback, Charles T.,
   218, 220
Bryant, John, 340–41
Budapest, 18–19
Bulgaria, 105, 132–33, 325
Bunn, Robert, 259
Burrington, Ernie, 3, 157,
   201, 210–11, 234, 271–75,
   297–98, 324, 338
Bush, George, 224
Business practices;

compartmentalization,
   26, 93–94, 119, 135–38,
   252; daily routine,
   94–99; dawn raids, 41;
   early postwar, 23–31;
   economic climate and,
   81; foreign-exchange
   transactions, 248–49,
   276; intercompany dealings, 63, 66, 34–36, 72,
   87–90, 101, 130–31
   138–39, 166, 168–69,
   207, 228–30, 258,
   269–71, 307; meetings,
   98; need for personal
   control in, 138, 323; robbing of own companies,
   273–76; self-destructive
   tendencies and, 99, 128,
   160, 184; selling off of
   assets, 101; shares as collateral, 89, 147–49, 240,
   278, 322, 324, 331–32,
   346; share-support operations, 147–48, 172, 181,
   215, 239, 251, 177–78;
   stock-lending, 258–61,
   263–66; telephone calls
   and, 96–98, 102, 177–78,
   190, 213, 293–94; under-
   handed style of, 16–17,
   26, 28–29, 31, 42, 88,
   267–68, 338–39; unions
   and, 39, 41
Business Week, 225–26
Butterworth's, 26–27
Butterworth-Springer, 27

Caborn, Dick, 107
Calcutt, David, 199
Callaghan, James, 64
Callan, Paul, 1, 8
Campbell, Alastair, 107–8,
   161, 188–92, 271
Campbell, Duncan, 228
Campi, John, 343
Carlisle, Tony, 236
Carman, George, 328
Carpenter, Les, 55
Carr family, 49
Carthew-Yorstoun, Brig.
   Gary, 20
Caxton, 33
Celebrity, Maxwell's,
   143–44

Central Television, 42
Chaplin, John, 333
Chapman, Brian, 331
Charitable donations, an-
   nounced but unmade, 9,
   64–65, 89, 128
Chase Manhattan, 274
Children, Maxwell's,
   43–47. See also specific
   individuals
Churchill, Winston, 15
Citibank, 278, 317
City, the, 28, 33, 145–47,
   166. See also Banking
   community
City Takeover Panel, 35
Clarke, Sir Robert, 242, 271
Class reaction to Maxwell,
   27, 38
Clements, Alan, 242, 271,
   274, 321
Cohen, Louisa Garcia, 309
Cole, Bob, 244, 293, 302,
   304
Collier's encyclopedias, 81
Color pictures, 63
Commonwealth athletic
   games, 64–65
Companies Act, 264
Companies House, 277
Compartmentalization, 26,
   93–94, 119, 135–38, 252
Complete Publicity Serv-
   ices, 247
Connor, Terry, 249
Conservative Party (Great
   Britain), 37, 56–57,
   187–92, 196
Coopers & Lybrand De-
   loitte, 321, 329–31, 357
Council of Christians and
   Jews, 46–47
Crédit Agricole, 319
Crédit Lyonnais, 83–84,
   319
Crédit Suisse, 261, 324
Cudlipp, Hugh, 125
Cunningham, Jack, 162,
   199

Daily Herald, 49
Daily Mail, 150, 173–74,
   280, 283, 287–88
Daily Mirror, 1–9; after-
   math of Maxwell's death

and, 317, 336–40; age of journalists at, 99–100; anti-Maxwellism of, 91–92, 338; circulation, 133, 159; competition with *The Sun*, 7–8, 49–50, 56, 97, 100–105, 123, 133, 148; cuts at, 62–63; Disney comics and, 185–86, 204, 212; firing of Greenslade, 231–33, 243–46; Greenslade made editor of, 2–5, 8–9, 92; Greenslade interview on, 195–96, 203–6, 231, 233, 243–44; influence of, 55–56; journalists' union and, 163–64; Labour Party and, 199–200; as main interest of Maxwell, 99; Mandela tribute and, 107–9; Maxwell's death and, 310–11; Maxwell's interference with, 58–61, 90, 99–101, 122–23, 125–27, 130, 139–41, 150–53, 157, 159, 178–79, 181–85, 188–92, 208–12, 227–34; Mirrorgate and, 280, 284–88, 316; Mirror Woman, 183; news-desk, 97; obituary in, 14; pension fund scandal and, 323, 327–28; price increase, 158–60; print unions and, 62–63; promotional advertising, 157, 183–84, 196–99; regime at, 56–61; as role model for New York *Daily News*, 217; self-promotion and, 58–60, 80, 122–23, 128–30; Spot-the-Ball contest, 269–70; Thatcher's resignation and, 187–92, 194–95; TV listings section, 212–15, 232–33; vitamin pill promotion, 227–29, 232; weekly supplement, 139–40; World Cup promotion (1990), 126–28
Daily News. See New York *Daily News*

Davidson, Andrew, 235
Davies, Nick, 209; Martin and, 118–22, 288; Mirrorgate accusations and, 278–88, 315
Dawn raids, 41
D. C. Thomson, 339
Death, Maxwell's, 13–14, 300–313; burial, 310–12; mystery surrounding, 309–10, 312–13, 348–54; obituaries and tributes, 14–15, 304–6, 311–12
Debt; coverup of, 130–31, 143–45; robbing of own companies to cover, 273–75; selling assets to cover, 131–32, 147–49, 168–69, 236–37, 242–43, 248, 271; size of, 307–8
De Lamela, Carlos Lopez, 309, 312
Delano, Tony, 31, 81, 235
De La Rue, 168–69
Department of Trade investigation, 35–36, 80, 351, 356
Der Telegraph, 23
Dewe Rogerson, 236
Diamond, John, 133, 181–82, 193, 199–202, 211–13, 233, 244
Dickson, Stewart, 285
Dinkins, David, 219, 224, 306, 343
Disasters, as publicity coups, 59
Disney comics, 185–86, 212
Dobie, Clare, 320
Donohue, 131, 166, 168, 242
Donoughue, Lord, 257, 261–62
Drinking habits, Maxwell's, 142, 189, 291–92
Duffy, Eugene, 180
Dun & Bradstreet, 85–86
Dunn, Martin, 303
Duveen, Pamela, 333

Eastern Europe, 39–40, 72–73, 150, 155–56, 169, 297, 306
East Germany, 155–56
Eastoe, Roger, 115, 142, 184, 186, 212

Edgeport, 277
Editors, Maxwell's control of, 57–61, 93, 102–3, 125–26, 129–30, 151–53, 157–59, 182–85, 188–91, 194–95, 199–202, 208–11, 230–31, 233–34, 244
Edwards, Bob, 7, 57, 60
Electra, 339
Elsevier, 236
Encyclopedias, 33, 176–77
Ephron, Nora, 64
Ethiopia, 59
European, The, 39, 110–18, 240, 266, 325; aftermath of Maxwell's death and, 340–41; launching of, 112–16; Maxwell's interference with, 113–15; origin of idea for, 110–12; promotional advertising for, 115–16
European Periodicals, Publicity and Advertising Corporation (EPPAC), 25
Evans, Edward "Ned," 82–85
Evening News, 69
Extel, 62, 137

Faber & Faber, 279–81, 284, 315–16
Fallon, Ivan, 270, 325
Featley, John, 294
Ferguson, Jack, 165
Fictional characters, Maxwell compared to, 78–79
Field, Frank, 328, 334
Fielding, Janet, 282, 284–85
Financial analysts, 28, 145, 148, 166, 241, 263, 320, 322
Financial Services Act, 264, 331
Financial Times, 145, 168, 225, 307, 339
First Tokyo, 259–61, 269
Fisher, Edmund, 42
Floform, 332
Foot, Michael, 55, 57
Foot, Paul, 182, 324
Forbes, Malcolm, 144
Foreign exchange transactions, 248–49, 276. *See also* Liechtenstein trusts

France, 63, 70, 105
Freedman, Ellis, 239
Frommelt, Egmond, 244
Fukutake, 316, 346
Fuller, Albert, 250, 252
Funeral, Maxwell's, 311

Gallemore, Mike, 264, 330–31
Gallimard, 105
Galloway, George, 283
Garbutt, Christine, 337
Garside, Charles, 341
General Cinema, 75
George Newnes, 33
Germany, 21–23; Berliner Verlag and, 105, 155–56, 240–45, 346; Springer and, 25–27, 29, 31
Gibraltar, 269
Gilbert, Brian, 250
Globe, The, 105
Gold Greenlees Trott (GGT), 197
Goldman Sachs, 91, 197, 249, 292, 319; pension fund scandal and, 334–35; put option and, 147–50, 181, 215, 268, 358; responsibility of, 357–58; shares in Maxwell's companies held by, 239–40, 268, 276–77, 295, 302, 315
Goodman, Geoffrey, 58–59
Gorbachev, Mikhail, 87, 105, 128–29, 179–79, 208–10, 297, 306, 312, 326
Gorbachev, Raisa 86–87
Graham, Ted, 70
Grant, Baron, 79
Great Britain; history of popular newspapers in, 56; Maxwell's arrival in, 19–20; tradition of secrecy in, 356
Greenslade, Noreen, 1–2, 4–5, 86–87, 105–7
Greenslade, Roy; accused of mismanagement, 245–46; becomes editor of Daily Mirror, 2–5, 8–9, 92; circulation under, 133; firing of, 231–35, 243–46; first

meeting with Maxwell, 5–7; legal actions against, 246–47, 265; Maxwell's death and, 303–4; Maxwell's treatment of, 93, 102–3, 129–30, 151–53, 157–59, 182–85, 188–90, 194–95, 199–206, 211–15, 227–34, 243–46; resignation considered by, 101, 104; UK Press Gazette interview, 195–96, 203–6, 231, 233, 243–44
Griffin, Charles, 92, 209
Grosvenor Group, 66
Gruner & Jahr, 155, 325
Guardian, 244, 309, 320, 338
Guerrero, Oscar, 282
Guest, Lawrence, 271–75, 298, 338–39
Guinness case, 141, 152–53
Gulf War, 152, 175–78, 204, 210, 227, 229–30
Gump's, 90
Gutstein, Ludwig, 137
Gyorke, Jozsef, 150–51

Hagerty, Bill, 126, 204, 210, 232
Haines, Joe; biography of Maxwell by, 15–18, 20, 22, 30–31, 34–35, 45, 51, 53, 80–81, ; initial reaction to Maxwell, 55–57; Malice in Wonderland, 67; Mirrorgate and, 284, 287; obituary by, 304; relationship with Maxwell, 62, 86–87, 99, 116, 132, 141, 154, 161, 179, 182, 199; resignation of, 133–34
Hambro, Sir Charles, 26–27, 29, 32
Harcourt Brace Jovanovich, 70–75, 137
Harman, Justice, 327
Harris, Harry, 126
Hastings, Max, 289, 305
Hattersley, Roy, 55
Havers, Lord, 98
Head, Robert, 129
Headington Hill Hall, 33, 43, 143, 347–48

Headington Holdings, 278
Headington Investments, 258, 264, 269, 277, 321
Health problems, 32
Hearst, William Randolph, 58
Heartburn (Ephron), 64
Heath, Edward, 156
Heathfield, Peter, 58
Helicopter, Maxwell's, 162–63
Hely-Hutchinson, Tim, 42
Henry, Georgina, 244
Henry, Wendy, 5
Henry Ansbacher, 32, 277–78, 316, 357
Herbertson, Iain, 181
Herrington, John, 75
Hersh, Seymour, 279–81, 290, 299, 315–16
Herzog, Chaim, 311
Heseltine, Michael, 186–89
Hightower, Dennis, 186
Hill, Brian, 301
Hinsey, Carolyn, 224, 290
Hoch, Abraham Lajbi, 16. See also Maxwell, Ian Robert
Hoch, Chanca, 16–17
Hodson, Nigel, 144, 298, 352
Hoge, James, 218, 220, 223, 343
Holborn building, 235–36, 241–42
Hollis Bros. & Educational Supply Association, 66
Hollis Engineering Group, 332
Holloran, John, 250
Honecker, Erich, 156
Horwood, Vic, 138, 273
Hotopf, Max, 173–74
Hounam, Peter, 279–83
House of Commons, 37–39
Howell, Grover, 223
Hudgell, Ken, 174
Hunter-Gault, Charlene, 225

Independent, The, 180
Independent on Sunday, 168, 305, 318
Inheritance, Maxwell's, 47
Insull, Mike, 308
Inter-European Trust, 269

International Learning Systems Corporation (ILSC), 33, 35
International Publishing Corporation, 49
Investment Management Regulatory Organization (IMRO), 331
Irish Tatler, 325
Israel, 68, 76, 89, 213, 297, 306, 346; Maxwell's burial in, 310–12; editorial on, 178–79; Mirrorgate and, 278–90, 299, 315–16; purchasing of soccer clubs in, 130

Jackson, Jesse, 108–9, 219
Jackson, Capt. Peter, 214–15, 331
James Capel, 144
Janner, Greville, 299
Jarratt, Alex, 54
Jarvis, John, 328
Jay, John, 167
Jay, Peter, 64–66, 76, 86, 289, 306
Jenkins, Clive, 162, 164
Jenkinson, John, 102–5
Jerusalem Post, 88
Jewish Chronicle, 67–68
John Waddington, 42, 62, 136–37
Journalists; Maxwell's relationship with, 167–68
Journalists' union, 163–64
Jovanovich, Peter, 75
Jovanovich, William, 71–75
Judaism, 16–17, 67–68, 133, 224, 289, 310–12 Soviet, 179–80
Junor, John, 355
Jurg Marquard, 346

Kalikow, Peter, 221, 345
Katherine Gibbs Secretarial Schools, 90
Kaufman, Clarence Ben, 287
Kaufman, Gerald, 311
Keays, Sara, 60–61
Keenan, Tony, 140
Keicher, Walter, 136–37
Keicher, Werner, 137

Kennedy, Jack, 221
Kenny, John, 248
Kenya Television Network, 70
Kenya Times, 69–70, 325
Keyes, Bill, 41
Kheel, Ted, 344–45
Killing of the Unicorn, The (Bogdanovich), 7
King, Lord, 106, 114
Kinnock, Glenys, 161–62
Kinnock, Neil, 55, 67, 161, 230–31, 271, 306
Kjaer, Susanne, 312
Kleinwort Benson, 73
Kohlberg Kravis Roberts (KKR), 83–85, 90
Kordalski, Liza, 300–301, 312
Koven, Ronald, 111–12
Kroll Associates, 73, 290

Labor issues, 39, 41, 52, 163, 245–46; New York *Daily News* and, 216–21, 225; pension funds and, 256–57; purchase of Mirror Group Newspapers (MGN) and, 55, 57
Labour Party (Great Britain), 37–39, 49, 54–56, 160–61, 188, 199–200, 271, 337
Lady Ghislaine, 70, 220–21, 347–48, 352, 293–302, 308
Laister, Peter, 264, 321, 329
Lamont, Norman, 191–92
Lancaster, Terry, 59
Lange, Maxwell & Springer (LMS), 26, 29
Last Exit to Brooklyn (Selby), 38
Lawson, Dominic, 355
Leach, Sir Ronald, 325
Leasco Data Processing Company, 34–37, 34
Legal issues: bad debts and, 247–48; Greenslade and, 246–47, 265; libel suits, 48–49, 67; Guinness case and, 152–53; Macmillan bid and, 85; Mirrorgate and, 284,

287; Spot-the-Ball exposure and, 105; writ ploy, 30, 48, 80–81
Lehman Brothers, 261, 319
Leicester Square, 79
Leigh, Wendy, 326
Lennox, Ken, 175–76, 192
Leonard, Graham, 300
Lever, Lawrence, 247–48
Lex, 145, 241, 263, 320, 322
Libel suits, 48–49, 67
Liddell, Helen, 132
Liechtenstein trusts, 62, 72–74, 86, 135–38, 153, 172, 239, 356–57
Lifestyle, Maxwell's, 142–43
Lilley, Peter, 358
Lind, Harold, 61
Lindsay, Bob, 155–56
Linklater, Magnus, 68
Lipton, Barry, 342
Lithuania, 208–9
Lloyds, 319
Lloyd Webber, Andrew, 90–91
Lobl, Arnos, 24
London & Bishopsgate Holdings (LBH), 262
London & Bishopsgate International Investment, Inc., 277
London & Bishopsgate International Investment Management (LBIIM), 256–57, 259, 261–62, 321
London Daily News, 68–69, 75, 113–14
London Stock Exchange, 358
Long, Gerry, 110, 112
Long Term Credit Bank, 319
Lonrho organization, 51, 75, 339
Lopatin, John, 268
Low-Bell, 24
Ludvik, Jan, 16. *See* Maxwell, Ian Robert
Lung surgery, 32
Lynas, Steve, 150, 177
Lynk, Roy, 163

Maa'riv, 229–30, 346
McAlary, Mike, 225

MacArthur, Brian, 230, 233
McDonald (publisher), 42, 67, 346
McDonald, George, 219, 220, 224–25
McGraw-Hill, 82, 345
McIntosh, Ian, 204, 234, 321
MacKenzie, Kelvin, 4, 7–8, 100
MacKichan, Robin, 112–15, 117
McLaughlin, Peter, 221
Macmillan, 81–90, 169, 262, 278, 300–301; aftermath of Maxwell's death and, 345–46; Bass Group's attempt to takeover, 82; breaking up of, 90; Maxwell's acquisition of, 82–87; resignations at, 276
Macmillan, Harold, 37
Macmillan Computer Publishing, 317
MacNeil-Lehrer Report, The, 225
McQuillen, Harry, 276
McSmith, Andy, 155, 167, 213
Maddox, Bronwen, 307
Magyar Hirlap, 91, 346
Mail on Sunday, 326
Maislish, David, 143, 247–48
Major, John, 189, 191–92, 306
Malice in Wonderland, 67
Mandela, Nelson, 100, 107–9
Martin, Andrea, 118–19, 121, 288
Matthews, Bruce, 8
Maxwell, Anne, 43
Maxwell, Betty (née Meynard), 20–22, 43, 46–47, 68, 86-87, 160–63, 193, 297; Maxwell's death and, 302, 304, 306–7, 310, 348–50
Maxwell, Christine, 43, 311
Maxwell, Ghislaine, 43–44, 117
Maxwell, Ian Robert

(Robert): ambition of, 70, 76–77, 79; background of, 14–23; celebrity of, 143–44, 221–24, 302; childhood influences, 16–17; daily life of, 94–98; eating and drinking habits, 5–7, 142–43, , 189, 291–92, 298–99; effect of presence of, 134–35; family of, 13, 16–17, 22, 193–94, 291, 298; first newspaper job, 23; invention of past by, 15, 17–19, 68; Judaism and, 16–17, 67–68, 133, 179–80, 224, 289, 310–12; lying and manipulation of truth by, 9–12, 18, 33, 52, 128, 144–45, 156, 161, 170–72, 202 226, 243–46; maxims of, 57; names and nicknames of, 16, 20–21, 24, 37, 59; personal characteristics of, 2–3, 5, 7, 9, 21–23, 38, 41, 42, 53, 94–99, 102–3, 160; physical appearance of, 3; playing reporter, 140–41; psychological portrait of, 13; public image of, 58; role-playing by, 171; self-destructive tendencies, 99, 128, 160, 184; self-image of, 12, 48, 53; self-promotion of, 58–60, 80, 122–23, 128–30; use of people by, 50–51; world view of, 10–12
Maxwell, Ian, 44–45, 70, 110, 112, 155, 193, 242, 251–52, 271, 274; aftermath of Maxwell's death and, 314–28; birthday tributes to father, 45; as chairman of MGN, 314–15, 322–23, 336–37; *The European* and, 116–17, 340; events leading up to Maxwell's death and, 296; fired by father, 44–45; Maxwell's death and, 301–2, 305–6; Maxwell's influ-

ence on, 298; pension fund scandal and, 321–23, 326–29; personal characteristics of, 45
Maxwell, Isabel, 43, 193, 202
Maxwell, Karine, 43
Maxwell, Kevin, 44–46, 117, 155, 193–94, 237–38, 251, 260, 262, 273, 295; aftermath of Maxwell's death and, 301, 306, 314–29; as chairman of MCC, 314, 322; events leading up to Maxwell's death and, 296, 307–8; influence of Maxwell on, 343–44; legal funding of, 329, 350; New York *Daily News* and, 342–45; office of, 96; pension fund scandal and, 321–23, 326–29
Maxwell, Michael, 43
Maxwell, Pandora (née Warnford-Davis), 45–46
Maxwell, Philip, 43, 302, 304, 311
Maxwell, Robert. *See* Maxwell, Ian Robert
Maxwell: The Outsider (Bower), 15–17, 25, 27, 31, 33, 40, 53, 65, 80–81, 91, 225
Maxwell Communications Corp. (MCC; formerly British Printing and Communications Corp.), 45; aftermath of Maxwell's death and, 347; board of directors of, 249–51, 276; BZW report on, 169–72; creditrating of, 215; daily cash management at, 249–52; debt of, 114, 122, 130–31, 144–45, 226, 248–49, 252, 262; finance director, 276; Goldman Sachs shares in, 268, 276–77, 295, 302; intercompany dealing, 147–50, 166, 168–69; Kevin as chairman of, 314–15, 322; Macmillan deal and, 84,

87–88; Maxwell's death and, 302, 317; Maxwell's robbing of, 276; Mirror-gate and, 283, 289–90; put option and, 147–50, 181, 215, 268; share price, 131, 147–48, 168, 180, 181, 215, 239–40, 248, 263, 268, 270, 283, 289–90, 292, 302, 315, 317–21; share-support operations and, 147–48, 172, 181, 215, 239, 251, 177–78; shares as collateral for loans and, 89, 292; Walker as chairman of, 237–39, 262–63
Maxwell Fleet & Facilities, 333
Maxwell Foundation, 135–37, 172, 239–40
Maxwell Graphics, 101
Maxwell (Haines), 15–18, 20, 22, 30–31, 34–35, 45, 51, 53, 80–81,
Maxwell House, 2, 94, 347
Maxwell Newspapers, Inc., 274
Maxwell Private Pensioners' Association, 333
Meetings, 98
Melbourn, John, 320
Mellor, Philip, 97–98, 190
Melmotte, 78–79
Merdle, 78–79
Merrill Lynch, 150
Micawber, 78–79
Michie legal publishers, 81
Microforms International Marketing Corporation (MIMC), 37
Midland Bank, 319, 329
Military service, 20–22
Millar, Peter, 116
Mineworkers, 100–101, 163
Mirror Colour Institute, 138–39
Mirrorgate, 278–90, 299, 315–16
Mirror Group Newspapers (MIG), 3, 5, 39, 41, 90; board of directors of, 166–68, 271–75, 298; bought by Maxwell, 51–56; circulation losses, 61; color pictures and,

63; compartmentalization within, 138–39; control of editors at, 57–61; debt of, 271–76; finance director, 271–75; Goldman Sachs shares in, 268, 276–77, 295, 302; Holborn building and, 235–36, 241–42; Ian as chairman of, 314–15, 322, 336–37; intercompany dealing, 90, 138–39, 166, 168–69; interference of Maxwell with, 138–41; Labour Party and, 54–56, 337; Maxwell's death and, 302, 317; Mirrorgate and, 289–90; pension fund scandal and, 173–75, 253–58, 275–76, 322–27, 330–34, 349; phone-sex advertisements and, 336–37; proposed management buyout of, 337–39; robbing by Maxwell of, 273–75; share price, 266, 268, 270, 292, 302, 317; stock issue, 226, 234–36, 240–46, 249, 259; strategy conference, 156–58; Tuesday lunches, 141–42, 165–66; unions and, 55, 57, 163–64; value of, 56; wiretapping at, 338–39
Mirror Group Pensions Trust (MGPT), 255
Mirror Woman, 183
Mitchell, Lance Corp., 20
Mogg, Reg, 250–51
Molloy, Mike, 3, 58
Molloy, Sandy, 5–6
Morgan, Jean, 195–96
Morgan, John, 331
Morgan, Grenfell, 153
Morgan, Stanley, 324
Morton, John, 342
Moscow News, 128–29
Moss, Brian, 237, 332–33
Mossad, Mirrorgate and, 278–79, 299, 315–16
MTV, 169
Mueller, Rudi, 246–47
Murdoch, Rupert, 6, 49, 51, 122, 203, 214; Max-

well's rivalry with, 60–61, 75–76, 100, 114, 138, 198, 214, 216. *See also Sun, The*

National AIDS Trust, 89
National Enquirer Group, 88
National Westminster bank (NatWest), 54, 274, 319–20, 324, 332, 356–57
Neeman, Yaacov, 94–96
Neil, Andrew, 206–7, 279–81
Newsagents, price increases and, 159–60
News International, 6
News of the World, 49, 326
Newspapers: attempted acquisitions, 49–50, 88; history of popular British, 56; jargon, 140, 194; partisan politics and, 53–54; privacy laws and, 199–200; twenty-four-hour concept, 69
New Statesman, 33–34
New York *Daily News*, 39, 105, 167, 207, 216–26, 265, 325, 328; advertisers and, 223–24, 341, 344; aftermath of Maxwell's death and, 341–45; circulation, 278; history of, 217–18; journalists at, 222–23; MGN stock offering and, 242; price increase and, 224; reaction to Maxwell's purchase of, 221–25; strike at, 216–21
New York Post, 216, 218
New York Times, 225
Nicholson Graham & Jones, 330
Nimrodi, Yaacov, 346
Nisse, Jason, 180–81
Nizen, Don, 278
Norbury, Sarah, 308
Not The Private Eye, 67

Obituaries and tributes, 14–15, 304–6, 311–12
Oborne, Ernest, 334–35
Observer, The, 51, 204–6

Odhams Press, 42
Office, Maxwell's, 94–98
Official Airline Guides, 85,
    91, 262
Okill, Philip, 33
Oliva, Isabel, 309, 313
Olmert, Ehud, 311
Operation Blackcock, 21
Ora Ltd., 280
O'Reilly, Tony, 339
Orton, Giles, 256, 330
Outnabs, 29
Oxford football club, 42
Oyez, 66
Ozal, Turgut, 133

Packer, Kerry, 319
Panini, 85–86, 185
Panorama exposé, 104–5,
    265, 269–70
Paribas, 324
Paris Match, 350
Parker, Sir Peter, 339
Parker-Jervis, 204–5
Parkinson, Cecil, 60
Parkinson, Michael, 133
Parnes, Anthony, 152–53
Pattinson, Terry, 333
Pavlov, Valentin, 209–10
Pearl, Alex, 19
Pearse, Brian, 329
Pearson, 339
Pension funds, plundering
    of, 40, 173–75, 253–58,
    262, 264, 275–76,
    321–26; companies af-
    fected by, 332; discovery
    of, 321; government re-
    sponsibility and, 359;
    inquiry into, 326–29,
    334; Kevin's and Ian's
    role in, 323, 327; Max-
    well's death and, 351;
    mechanics of, 330–32;
    MGN and, 173–75,
    253–58, 275–76, 322–27,
    330–34, 349; pensioners'
    reactions to, 332–35;
    press reaction to,
    323–28; repercussions of,
    325
Perdoma, José Francisco,
    304
Pereira, Joseph Caetano,
    293
Peres, Shimon, 306

Pergamon Holding Foun-
    dation, 137, 153. *See also*
    Liechtenstein trusts
Pergamon Holdings (U.S.)
    Inc., 173
Pergamon Press, 28, 31–37,
    39–40, 54, 66, 356–57;
    Leasco and, 34–37; offer
    to sell, 202; profits
    claimed, 34–36; sale of,
    236–37; strike at, 162,
    164; World Leaders se-
    ries, 39–40
Perpich, Rudy, 128
Phillips & Drew, 83
Phone-sex advertisements,
    336–37
Pig on pork loans, 89
Pilger, John, 58–59
Pillai, Nisha, 269
Pirie, Robert, 71, 80, 222,
    343
Pisar, Samuel, 297, 299,
    311, 348
Poland, 59, 132
Pole, John, 92, 121, 338
Political career, 37–39, 46
Political parties: news-
    papers and, 49, 53–54.
    See also Conservative
    Party; Labour Party
Pollard, Eve, 142, 195
Poole, Henry, 79, 88
Pradelle, Geoffre de la,
    239
Press, the: criticism of
    Maxwell by, 48–49, 67;
    Mirrorgate and, 278–82,
    284–90, 315, 316; obitu-
    aries and tributes, 14–15,
    304–6, 311–12; partisan
    politics and, 53–54; pen-
    sion fund scandal and,
    323–28
Price, Quintin, 144–45
Price Waterhouse, 329
Print unions, 41, 49,
    62–63, 163
Privacy laws, 199–200
Private Eye, 61, 67, 91,
    136, 161
Project Whale, 71
Promises, unkept, 9,
    64–65, 89, 128, 163–64
Proops, Marje, 167, 182
Publicity stunts, 58–60,

64, 80, 107, 115, 122–23,
    128–30, 143–44, 163
New York *Daily News*
    and, 220–24
Public Relations and Infor-
    mation Services Control
    (PRISC), 23
Public relations staff,
    154–55
Put option, 147–50, 181,
    215, 268, 358

Quebecor, 131, 166, 168,
    242, 339
Que computer publishing,
    81
Quinton, Sir John, 170

Racing Times, 346
Ramos, Maria José Meilan,
    309
Ramphal, Sonny, 107–8
Randall, Jeff, 167
Rankin, Capt. Gus,
    293–94, 296–98,
    300–302, 306, 304,
    347–48, 352
Really Useful Group, 90
Rechsteiner, Werner, 137,
    239–40
Reed International, 42,
    52–56
Reilly, William, 82–85
Rich, Roger, 350
Richardson, Melissa, 139,
    150
Richardson, Sir Michael,
    139, 150, 249, 307, 311,
    320
Rich Wheeler & Co., 350
Rippon, Lord, 98
Robert Maxwell Estates,
    266, 275
Robert Maxwell Group,
    239, 258, 269, 274,
    277–78, 321
Robertson, John C., 358
Robinson, Anne, 182, 304
Robson Rhodes, 329
Rodriguez, Charlie, 294
Rodriguez, Sergio, 298–99
Ronson, Gerald, 141, 152–53
Rosen, Sylvia, 346–47
Rothermere, Lord, 69
Rothschild, Sir Evelyn de,
    213

Rothschild, NM (bank), 71, 80, 139, 213, 321, 357
Rowland, Tiny, 51, 75
Ryder, Mike, 123

Sadleir, John, 79
Samson Option: Israel, America and the Bomb (Hersh), 279–81, 290, 299, 315–16
Samuel Montagu, 83, 204, 234, 242, 256, 321, 357
Sanders, Terry, 115–16
San Juan, Luis Gutierrez, 308
Saudi Arabia, 175–77
Saunders, Ernest, 152–53
Scargill, Arthur, 58, 100–101, 339
Scheinberg, Eric, 276
Schlomovitch, Irving, 67
Schlomovitch, Yaacov, 16
Schmidt, Helmut, 111–12
Scholtz, Arno, 23, 25
Schwarzkopf, Norman, 227, 229
Science publishing, 25–28, 31–32, 40. *See also* Pergamon Press
Scitex, 89, 112, 263
Scottish Daily News, 50–51
Sea World, 71, 75
Secrecy, British tradition of, 356
Selby, Hubert, 38
Sense of humor, 97
Serious Fraud Office, 318, 326
Servex, 239
Shamir, Yitzhak, 94–96, 179, 282, 306, 312
Share-support operations, 147–48, 172, 181, 215, 239, 251, 277–78
Shearson Lehman Brothers, 274, 292, 295, 324
Sheinberg, Eric, 239–40, 268, 315
Sherrard, Michael, 141
Shields, Brian, 116
Simon, Harland, 248
Simpkin Marshall, 28–31, 48–49, 37
Skadden Arps, 74

Smilgis, Martha, 225
Smith, Liz, 222
Smith New Court, 139, 150, 242, 245, 249, 268, 320, 357
Smoking, 32
Snoddy, Ray, 168, 243
Soccer teams, 130, 153–54
Socialism, 37, 39, 72–73
Societé General of France, 319
Society of Graphical and Allied Trades (Sogat), 49
Solidarity, 59
Soviet Union, 31–32, 40, 73, 86–87, 89, 105, 128–29, 208–9. *See also* Gorbachev, Mikhail
Speculation, 40
Spending habits, 105–7
Sporting Life, 62, 194
Sportsweek, 68
Spot-the-Ball contest, 101–5, 269–70
Springer, Ferdinand, 25–27, 29, 31
Staff: public relations, 154–55; treatment of, 94–96, 100, 102, 124–25, 129, 155, 181. *See also* Editors
Steinberg, Saul, 34–37, 72
Stock-lending, 258–61, 263–66
Stocks. *See specific companies*
Stocks, Neil, 295
Stone, Richard, 321
Stoney, Michael, 271–73, 275, 322
Stothert & Pitt, 66
Stott, Richard, 80, 234, 288, 299, 324, 337–39
Stratten, Dorothy, 7
Student Games, 64
Sturgess, Brian, 130–31, 169, 172
Sun, The, 3–5, 7–8, 49, 101–5, 159, 214, 323; *Daily Mirror's* competition with, 7–8, 49–50, 56, 97, 100–105, 123, 133, 148
Sunday Citizen, 49
Sunday Correspondent, The, 117

Sunday Mirror, 281–82, 326
Sunday People, 3
Sunday Times, The, 3, 49, 51, 206–7, 325; Mirrorgate and, 278–79, 281–82, 288, 315
Swico Foundation, 137, 239–40
Swiss Bank Corporation (SBC), 259–61, 269, 278, 292, 295, 316, 318–19, 351
Swiss Volksbank, 324

Taylor, Steve, 352
Telephone calls, 96–98, 102, 177–78, 190, 213, 293–94
Tennant, Colin, 207
Terrington, Derek, 83, 131, 246–47
Teva Pharmaceuticals, 89
Thatcher, Margaret, 39, 105, 133, 306; resignation of, 187–92, 194–95
Thomas Cook America, 277
Thomas Cook Travel, 86
Thompson, David, 55, 57, 178
Thompson, Jeremy, 70
Thompson, Peter, 31, 81
Thomson Organization, 51
Thorne, Frank, 315–16
Thornton, Charlotte, 210, 293
Thornton, Clive, 54
Times, The, 51
Today, 75, 319
Tomalin, Nicholas, 313
Tottenham Hotspur soccer team, 153–54
Townsley & Co., 277
Tractenberg, Larry, 256–57, 259
Trench, Ken, 333
Tribune Company, 216–20, 222
Turner, Steve, 163–64

UBS Phillips & Drew, 131, 246–47
UK Press Gazette, 203–6, 210, 231, 233, 243–46
Ulanova, Galina, 99
Underwood, John, 199

Unions; journalists',
163–64; miners', 100–1;
print, 41, 49, 62–63, 163.
See also Labor issues
United Overseas Bank of
Geneva, 324
Ustinov, Peter, 116–17

Vanunu, Mordechai,
278–79, 281–82
Vendeoil, Jean-Paul, 296
Vitachieve pills, 227–29,
232
Vogel, Rabbi Feivish, 300

Walker, Ian, 193, 195
Walker, Peter, 237–39, 249,
262–63
Walker, Rob, 104, 197–98
Wallersteiner, Kurt, 30
Waterhouse, Keith, 59, 201

Watson, Ian, 112–16, 220,
318
Webb, Nick, 42, 63
West, Dr. Iain, 350, 353
West, Joe, 313, 332
West, Nigel, 283
Wheatley, Alan, 329
Wheeler, George, 292
Whitaker, James, 307
Whiteman, Capt. David,
296
Whitlock, Maj. John,
26–27
Whittam-Smith, Andreas,
168
Whitteford, Roy, 352
Whitty, Larry, 162
Williams, Les, 338
Williams, Lord, 242
Willse, James, 222, 226,
343

Wilson, Charles, 194, 220,
227, 233, 307
Wilson, Harold, 55–56
Wolfenden, Paul, 116
Wood, Don, 174
World Cup promotion
(1990), 126–28
World Leaders series,
39–40
World War II, 17–22
Wright, Nigel, 108
Wyatt, David, 294

Yakosa, 239–40
Young, Hugo, 156
Young and Rubicam,
115–16

Zhivkov, Todor, 132
Zionism, 289, 312
Zuckerman, Mort, 216, 345